P9-DUZ-749

Military Transition to
Civilian Success

The Complete Guide for Veterans and Their Families

*Mary T. Hay, Lani H. Rorrer, James R. Rivera,
Ron and Caryl Krannich, Ph.Ds – National Association
of Veteran-Owned Businesses, Inc. (NAVOBI)*

IMPACT PUBLICATIONS
Manassas Park, Virginia

ISBN: 1-57023-255-5

Library of Congress: 2005935001

Publisher: For information on Impact Publications, including current and forthcoming publications, authors, press kits, online bookstore, and submission requirements, visit the left navigation bar on the front page of our main company website: www.impactpublications.com.

Publicity/Rights: For information on publicity, author interviews, and subsidiary rights, contact the Media Relations Department: Tel. 703-361-7300, Fax 703-335-9486, or em ail: query@impactpublications.com.

Sales/Distribution: All bookstore sales are handled through Impact's trade distributor: National Book Network, 15200 NBN Way, Blue Ridge Summit, PA 17214, Tel. 1-800-462-6420. All special sales and distribution inquiries should be directed to the publisher: Sales Department, IMPACT PUBLICATIONS, 9104 Manassas Drive, Suite N, Manassas Park, VA 20111-5211, Tel. 703-361-7300, Fax 703-335-9486, or email: query@impactpublications.com.

The Authors: The authors are principals in the National Association of Veteran-Owned Businesses, Inc. (NAVOBI), a nonprofit organization dedicated to assisting veterans and their families with jobs, education, self-employment, and benefits. For more information on NAVOBI, see pages 465-466 as well as visit www.navobi.org.

Military transition to
civilian success

Contents

Part I
Understanding the Path Ahead

Part II
Develop Powerful Career Transition Skills

Part III
Make Smart Decisions the Rest of Your Life

Preface

WELCOME TO THE CIVILIAN world where life is less structured and where your career future is often unpredictable. While you were in the armed forces, the military took primary ownership of your work and your life and stressed the importance of leadership, character, and responsibility – values that will serve you well in the future.

In the civilian world you are free to become whatever you want to be. But with freedom come many new choices and challenges. Accordingly, you face numerous decisions that can take you and your family down many different paths. Where you will be – work, community, family – 10 years from now is anyone's guess. But one thing is certain for now – you have the power within you to change your life! You can shape that path in many different ways by making smart choices **now**. That's our mission in writing this book – to help you make good transition decisions to fulfill your dreams of civilian success.

This book grew out of a collective vision we have of you and the military. As authors and friends of the armed forces, we have served the military in many ways, as service and family members, contractors, veterans, advisors, and helping hands. Indeed, we know all too well that many members of our military are not well prepared for the challenges facing them in the highly competitive civilian world. The role of the armed forces in the global war on terrorism and in military operations in Afghanistan and Iraq has heightened our concerns about the assistance service members receive when they re-enter civilian life.

In 2004 and 2005, over 300,000 men and women were discharged or released from active military service. While they are eligible for many benefits and services, a significant number of service members do not take

advantage of them. In fact, service members often do not realize that many benefits become available to them once they have separated and become veterans. Furthermore, to become eligible for certain benefits, service members must take specific actions while on active duty. If you are still in the military, be sure to take advantage of the career transition services available to you by writing a first-class resume, practicing interviewing skills, attending job fairs, and using the Internet to explore job opportunities. This book will help you with these and many other critical job search tasks that are central to making a successful transition to the civilian work world.

Military Transition to Civilian Success is our initial effort at bringing together some of the best strategies and techniques for making a career change. As the founding members of the National Association of Veteran-Owned Businesses, Inc. (NAVOBI), our mission is to continue providing you with the very best transition services. Thus, NAVOBI embraces a hybrid of techniques, methodologies, and technologies, which offers interactive programs that let participants work through independently and at their own pace. For more information on NAVOBI, please see pages 465-466 as well as visit our website: www.navobi.org.

We dedicate this book to the thousands of men and women in our armed forces who put their lives on the line every day in operations around the world. Our vision is to help you turn your military experience into civilian success both as a transitioning service member and a veteran.

Over the years, we have worked with thousands of service members. But one thing stands out more than anything else – you are talented men and women who deserve the very best. Your transition to the civilian world should be one of the most exciting periods in your lives. Most important of all, you should find jobs and launch careers that build on your positive attitudes, strengths, and values. With this book and our vision, we wish you the very best as you navigate your way to a new and joyful life!

Military Transition
to Civilian Success

1

Discover a New Life You Really Love

WELCOME TO THE REST of your life! Thanks for your dedicated service and sacrifice to your country. It's time to pack up and go. Best of luck in the future. Here's an award, some forms to complete, a transition book, and some advice on how to make it in the civilian world. Since you're a loyal, enthusiastic, disciplined, take-charge, self-starter with lots of military presence and perseverance, it shouldn't take too long before you'll be up and running as a civilian. We hope you land a great job, make lots of money, and become successful in whatever you do. Keep in touch!

Exit Into the Unknown

That's what it all comes down to in the end – firm handshakes, awards, some paperwork, a few parties, many goodbyes, several encouraging words, and a graceful exit from your immediate military family into the unknown civilian world. It's a new transition time which may or may not work out according to plan. For many veterans and their families, this will be a great adventure filled with mixed emotions.

For most transitioning military personnel, this exit is not quite retirement, since most still have several years of work life ahead of them. If all goes well, you'll have many exciting years ahead as you turn your military experience into civilian successes.

Each year over 300,000 service members share a similar experience – they leave the military for a new and yet uncharted life in the civilian

world. Nearly 90 percent seek new jobs and careers. A large percentage will leave their new job within the first 12 months for a variety of personal and professional reasons, but the most important reason for leaving relates to how well prepared they were in making the transition to their first job out.

More Transition Issues

Landing a civilian job is only one, albeit the most important, aspect of your transition. As you leave the military, you must deal with a host of additional issues affecting your family and finances, from relocation and housing to schools, wardrobe, communication, and benefits, which are no longer covered by the military. Indeed, you may be surprised by so many new out-of-pocket expenses that come with being a civilian. After a while, you may reflect on your military pay and benefits – it wasn't really as low as you thought. Indeed, many officers quickly discover they earned more in the military than in their first post-military job! The big bucks may come

> *You may be surprised by so many new out-of-pocket expenses that come with being a civilian.*

sometime down the road, after you've had a chance to figure out what you want to do and establish a new track record of bottom-line performance with civilian employers. In the meantime, it's best to have realistic expectations, get motivated, and keep focused on this next important stage of your life.

Attitude and Motivation

Attitude is everything in keeping motivated and focused. You'll soon develop an attitude about this new life you are about to shape for you and your family. This attitude will be important to developing and sustaining your motivation in the weeks and months ahead.

It's best to keep your attitude focused and positive. While you will in time get through this transition, you want to do it right from the very start. That means making smart decisions about where you want to go next with your new civilian life.

Plan for the Big Transition

This is time for serious long-term planning – at least 12 months before discharge you should start planning your transition. If you procrastinate

and put transition decisions off until the last few weeks, you may be in for a shock when you hit the streets as a civilian. You may quickly find you had unrealistic expectations about how long it would take to find a job and just how much you are worth in the salaried civilian work world. Indeed, few people can afford to spend three to six months looking for a job after leaving the military. If you are married, your spouse may be very anxiety-ridden about the unknown – possible unemployment and limited income – and may pressure you into taking the first job that comes along, even though you know it's not right for you. If you plan properly by attending job fairs, networking, and contacting employers while on active duty, you may have a great new job lined up the very day you leave the service.

If you are a veteran who has been out of the service for some time, chances are you are still in transition. You may have gone through one or two, possibly more, jobs since you left the service. By now you've really tested the waters and know what you don't like or want to do any longer. In the following pages, we'll help you discover what you really want to do, which is to find a job you both do well and enjoy doing, as well as pursue a lifestyle that gives you great joy and happiness.

So let's put on your planning hat and deal with this whole issue of military-to-civilian transition in the most positive and proactive manner possible. That's the goal of this book – to prepare you for a very successful military-to-civilian transition in which both you and your family are center stage. You deserve to live a life you love.

The Pursuit of Civilian Money

The old adage, which is also a title of a book – *Do What You Love, the Money Will Follow* – is very appropriate given the underlying philosophy and approach of this book. We all need money, the more the better. Money helps us keep score of where we are vis-a-vis others as well as frees us of money-related worries. When you have lots of money, you have the power to do things you want to do, from buying bigger and more expensive toys (house, car, boat, computer, art, entertainment centers) to helping others (family members, church, charities), gambling (casinos, property, businesses), travel, and entertainment.

But the pure pursuit of money can lead you down a very unhappy and unhealthy road – you never quite have enough since you're consistently pursuing it to the detriment of other more important values, and consequently, you may experience high levels of stress. You may end up in a job you hate just because you like the salary and benefits. Indeed, we know many lawyers, doctors, and other highly paid professionals who

suffer this unhappy money fate. They would love to do something else, but they make excellent money and have too many big toys to support. This is a form of "job lock" that also can lead to strokes and heart attacks.

We also know many highly paid professionals who gave it all up to pursue their dreams. After several years of making lots of money in a corporate rat race, one day they finally had the courage to stop themselves and ask: *"Is there more to life than this?"* They answered *"Yes,"* quit their jobs, and changed careers. Their incomes eventually rebounded as they pursued their new love.

We live in the world's biggest debtor society, which also is largely responsible for fueling the world's economy. As your friendly credit card company and auto loan officer will readily testify, we're addicted shoppers who buy a lot of depreciating "stuff" we like but can't really afford. Many people get lucky when selling their one appreciating asset – their house.

We recognize the importance of money, and we encourage you to put your financial house in order. If you're spending more than you earn and have ongoing credit card debt you're unable to pay off in full each month, you need to develop some new money management habits. Go on a spending diet for a few months. The only thing you will probably lose is paying interest to the loan sharks. Put limits on your shopping, cut up most of your credit cards, and see a financial planner who can tell you the truth about where you are headed financially and who can help you plan accordingly.

Do What You Love

Most people want to be happy in what they do. Indeed, they want to enjoy themselves and their family. We've also learned over the years that the happiest and most productive people love what they do both on and off their jobs. They fall into jobs that are perfect "fits" given their particular mix of interests, skills, abilities, and values. Rather than focus on themselves, they pursue a **passion** that contributes to the goals of others. They love what they do because they do things that matter a great deal to themselves and others. They are employer- and organization-centered rather than self-centered. They ask not what they can get from the job – more money, a new title, and a bigger office – but what they can contribute to the company that makes a difference in the lives of others. They become valued and successful employees, because they contributed value to the organization and everyone around them.

Anyone can find a job, but only a few people find a job they really love. You should be one of those few. In the following pages we outline a seven-step job search approach that is designed to help you find a job

you both do well and enjoy doing. If you follow this advice, we're confident that you will find a job you love. As you turn that job into a new career, the money will eventually follow.

But don't short-change yourself by turning down a great job just because you think it's beneath your salary expectations. When you do something you love, you'll be rewarded with more than just money. You'll get up in the morning and return home in the evening with enthusiasm, energy, and a positive outlook on life. Your attitude will be contagious among those around you. You'll be-come the person you want to be. While you may not be financially rich, you will live a very rich and ful-filling life centered around values that really count for you and your family.

> *Anyone can find a job, but only a few people find a job they really love.*

But Do You Know What You Want to Do?

Do you know what you really want to do once you leave the military? If you hope to make big money so you can buy lots of "stuff," what kind of job do you plan to pursue and with what psychological costs? Or perhaps you want certain lifestyle and happiness goals – family, travel, leisure, education, and personal development – that don't center around the constant passion for work and money. Maybe you need a flexible job that allows you to pursue what you and your family really want to do in life. Are you prepared for what comes next?

What Comes Next

The following pages are designed to help you make a positive transition to the civilian work world. Whether you are currently in the service preparing to leave within the next year or two or a veteran several years removed from separation, this book should help you organize the most important aspect of any transition – finding a job you both do well and enjoy doing. With the right job, many other transition issues will eventually resolve themselves.

This is also a family-friendly book. Whatever you do, make sure you involve your spouse in all phases of your job search. In fact, you may discover your spouse will be your most important resource for making a successful military-to-civilian transition. Spouses provide important perspectives and keep the process grounded in reality. In fact, if you have a working spouse or one who wants to work, you may want to conduct a job search together by carefully following each of the following chapters.

You'll find this process will go much easier, and it will be much more enjoyable, if you work together at each stage of your transition.

The book is divided into three major sections and 19 separate chapters. Part I, *Understanding the Path Ahead*, provides an overview of the transition process in reference to today's job market as well as projected changes in the economy. The goals here are to better understand today's employment realities and develop an effective strategy for maximizing your potential in the years ahead. This section describes, explains, predicts, and prescribes actions necessary for organizing an effective transition. It covers everything from 40 myths/realities and seven steps to job search success to 20 principles for job search success and best job options, useful websites, and military job fairs.

Part II, *Develop Powerful Career Transition Skills*, addresses each step in the job search process. It shows how you can best identify your transferable abilities and skills, formulate an objective, write resumes and letters, research the job market, network, interview, and negotiate salary and benefits. Followed carefully, this section will equip you with the necessary knowledge and skills to find a job you really love.

Part III, *Make Smart Decisions the Rest of Your Life*, addresses major issues of concern to thousands of veterans: keeping a job, advancing a career, relocating to the right community, and starting a business.

Taken together, these chapters present a comprehensive approach to making a successful transition to the civilian world.

Achieve Results

Our goals in writing this book are concrete, specific, and oriented toward action and results. You should acquire certain transition skills relating to finding jobs, launching careers, relocating, and managing finances. Upon completing this book you should be able to:

- Understand the changing nature of jobs and careers in the decade ahead and how they relate to your future.

- Identify desirable jobs and careers you may wish to pursue.

- Assess your goals in relation to your values and the demands of the job market.

- Identify your present interests and skills as well as the skills you can best transfer to other jobs and careers.

- Communicate your goals, skills, and qualifications to employers.

- Conduct targeted research on alternative jobs, careers, organizations, and communities.

- Write different types of resumes and job search letters.

- Prospect and network for job information, advice, referrals, and job leads.

- Conduct informational and job interviews.

- Negotiate salaries and the terms of employment.

- Advance your career.

- Relocate to other communities.

- Start your own business.

- Implement your plan of action.

We're All in Transition

We're all in transition, from the day we are born to the day we die. In fact, you've made important transitions before – left home for school; joined the military; moved from one assignment to another; been promoted and acquired new positions; got married and raised a family; became divorced; experienced a serious accident or illness or deaths in the family; and moved from renter to homeowner and debtor. Try as we may to control our destiny, life is often tough, unpredictable, and serendipitous.

We all have hopes and dreams, highs and lows, successes and failures, joys and fears as we travel through the many seasons in life. While you and your family have probably sacrificed a great deal during your years in the military, you've also made some great friends, traveled to interesting places, acquired some wonderful stories, achieved many personal and professional successes, and lived a unique lifestyle courtesy of your government and fellow taxpayers. Now, all that is about to change as you head toward a relatively unstructured civilian world where you are responsible for your own employment and financial fate. Life will never be the same again, but it may be as good as or better than before. You

may get a little help along the way, which includes this book, but you are basically on your own in a sea of millions of employers and jobs.

You Can Make It Happen

In the end, our goal is to help you take the necessary actions that will have a positive impact on your future. While most of this book focuses on understanding concepts, following processes, and developing effective job search strategies, the real rewards of this book come when you put these concepts, processes, and strategies into practice by implementing a realistic plan of action. We address this pivotal issue of **implementation** at the end of Chapter 3.

In the meantime, we wish you well as you deal with many important military-to-civilian transition issues. While you will inevitably encounter some rejections and disappointments, don't let them get you down and derail you from achieving your ultimate goals. They will quickly pass, especially when you achieve successes. Keep in mind that you are not alone. Rejections and disappointments are part of any transition process. With the right attitude and a great deal of drive and persistence, you will succeed in achieving your dreams. Only **you** can make it happen by working hard at shaping your future according to the advice found in this book.

Part I

Understanding Your Path Ahead

2

Welcome to the Challenging Civilian World

W HEN WAS THE LAST TIME you wrote a resume, completed an application, called an employer for a job interview, asked friends for job leads, surveyed the classified ads, posted your resume online, dressed for an interview, attended a job interview, or negotiated salary, benefits, and terms of employment? Chances are you have never had to do these things, because the military was your first employer, or it has been many years since you've engaged in these job search activities. Welcome to the civilian job search world where finding a job is both an art and science!

You're New Again

Whatever your past civilian employment history, you're new again to the civilian job market. If you did conduct a job search before entering the military, you'll quickly discover that looking for a job today is very different than before. Indeed, more and more employers are now using the Internet to recruit candidates, conducting multiple interviews, and subjecting candidates to different kinds of interviews, such as behavioral and situational interviews. Today you need to produce both a paper and electronic resume that is likely to be scanned into employment databases. The whole structure of compensation and how you negotiate salary and benefits also has changed in recent years.

Since you are relatively new to the civilian job market, you need to acquire a set of job search skills that will help you find the best employers

11

as well as to clearly communicate your qualifications to those employers. That's our task in preparing you for today's job market.

Face an Uncertain Future

Most transitioning military face an uncertain future. Perhaps you have big dreams or at least some vision of your future. What, for example, will your life be like in another 6, 12, or 24 months? Will you be in a job you enjoy doing, or will you be anxious to find another more rewarding job? Will you and your family settle into a nice community where you have good schools, neighbors, and opportunities for leisure and cultural activities, or end up in a less than desirable community?

The best way to minimize uncertainty is to develop a realistic transition plan. Central to that plan is a set of job search skills that will enable you to quickly find the perfect job for you. While your transition involves many issues (family, relocation, finances), we believe a job is the most important consideration. With the right job, you have the freedom to choose where to live, what to do with your life, and manage your finances. A good job will help minimize uncertainty and maximize your skills and experience.

40 Myths and Realities

What do you know about the civilian job market? What type of jobs does it have for transitioning military personnel? Where do you start your search? How will you approach it? What role will your spouse play in this transition? What do you do when you get there? Whom do you talk to? What do you say? How well will you adjust to a civilian job?

The abstract notion of a "job market" generates several images of structures, processes, decision points, and outcomes. In one sense the job market appears to be well structured for dispensing job information and assistance. After all, you will find various elements that supposedly make up the **structure** of the job market: online employment sites with job listings and resume databases; classified ads in newspapers listing job vacancies; personnel offices with vacancy announcements; employment agencies and electronic databases linking candidates to job openings; and a variety of "helpers" known as career counselors, coaches, employment specialists, and executive recruiters, who make a living by serving as gatekeepers to the "job market."

At the same time, we know various **processes** are key to making this job market function for individual job seekers: self-assessment, career objectives, research, applications, resume and letter writing, networking,

interviewing, negotiating, and hiring. You need to become very familiar with each process as well as integrate each into a coherent job search.

Understanding the job market is like the blind person exploring an elephant: you may recognize a trunk, a leg, and a tail, but you're not sure what it is as a whole. As we will see shortly, the job market is anything but organized, centralized, and coherent. It is more an abstraction, or convenient shorthand way of talking about finding jobs, than a set of well defined and related structures. Your job will be to organize much of the chaos that characterizes the reality of the job market by developing a well organized job search focused on your career objective.

Most people have an image of how the job market works as well as how they should relate to it. This image is based upon a combination of facts, stereotypes, and myths learned from experience and from the advice of well-meaning individuals. It's an unfortunate image when it guides people into unproductive job search channels by advising them to spend most of their time responding to vacancy announcements and waiting to hear from employers. In so doing, it reconfirms the often-heard lament of the unsuccessful job searcher – *"What more can I do? There are no jobs out there for me."*

Let's examine 40 myths about jobs, careers, and the job search before you proceed to organize yourself for today's and tomorrow's employment realities. These myths illustrate important points, or basic principles, for organizing and implementing your job search. Taken together, they provide a quick overview of the many realities and challenges facing transitioning military in the process of finding a civilian job:

MYTH 1: **Finding a civilian job shouldn't take very long since I have a great deal of experience that can be trans- ferred to many civilian jobs.**

REALITY: It shouldn't take long if you're just looking for **any** job in a community that has many job opportunities. Indeed, anyone can find a job. But finding a job you **do well** and **enjoy doing**, even under the best of circumstances, will take some time. In fact, the average time for making a job change within the civilian job market is between three and six months. Are you prepared financially and psychologically for a lengthy job search? While you can substantially shorten your job search time by following the many principles outlined in this book, nonetheless, be prepared to invest a great deal of time in your job search. It may be anything but quick and easy.

MYTH 2: **I should be able to significantly increase my income once I find a civilian job.**

REALITY: That may be true in the long run. However, in the short run, many transitioning military personnel, especially officers, are surprised to discover their new civilian take-home pay is often less than their active-duty pay! Given their new civilian cost of living, which does not include many benefits received while on active duty, their new incomes are often less than what they expected.

MYTH 3: **Employers are eager to hire ex-military personnel.**

REALITY: It depends on the employer. Government contractors working for the Department of Defense and related security agencies are most eager to hire ex-military personnel with security clearances because of the military nature of their operations. Many of them regularly attend military job fairs in order to recruit transitioning military and veterans (see Chapters 7 and 13). In fact, these employers represent part of the "revolving door" between government and the private sector. Other civilian employers may be reluctant to hire ex-military personnel, because they are aware that such career changers are likely to quit their first post-military job within 12 months as they try to figure out what they really want to do. Some employers are more willing to hire a veteran who is changing civilian jobs than hire one who is first leaving the military. Remember, in the eyes of many employers, you are not just a service member or a veteran – you are a **career changer**. You need to be prepared to overcome any objections to hiring a career changer. Junior military officers especially appeal to civilian employers in search of individuals with leadership and management qualities.

MYTH 4: **As a mid-level manager in the military, I should be able to land a mid-level management position in corporate, nonprofit, or government organizations.**

REALITY: Don't bet on it. Mid-level management positions in the military are not necessarily equivalent to mid-level management positions in other sectors. Organizational cultures and structures can be very different. Co rporations look for relevant experience in their particular operations. While you

perceived as someone with mid-level management potential, you will have to prove yourself before being given such management responsibilities. You first need to learn operational details, management styles, and organizational structures before you can settle in to learn how to become an effective mid-level manager in such an organization. Nonprofit organizations pose many challenges for individuals used to working in organizational settings with well-defined roles and clear, structured lines of command and control. Indeed, many nonprofits are organizational nightmares that can challenge your notions of good management practices!

MYTH 5: **I expect my spouse will support me as I look for a job, just as she/he was supportive of my military career.**

REALITY: A military-to-civilian transition can be a time of great stress in families. Your decision to leave the military has consequences unlike any other decision you have made while in the military. Spouses tend to be very concerned about a career change that could have a significant impact on their family and themselves. This change is not the same as just another reassignment courtesy of the military. Lacking the usual safety nets that come with periodic moves to new bases, many spouses are especially worried about family finances, housing, schools, and starting a new life outside the military. Many also feel they should have a larger say in what comes next in your personal and professional life. After all, you and the military may have made most relocation decisions in the past. Your spouse may believe it is now her/his turn. Some also will want to start or re-start their own careers. Since your spouse may feel you are over-confident or have unrealistic expectations of your ability to quickly find a suitable job, and few are prepared for a three-to six-month period of unemployment (see Myth 1), she or he may pressure you into taking the first job that becomes available rather than wait for a job that best fits your particular interests, skills, and goals. Whatever you do, be sure to involve your spouse in this transition process from the very **beginning**. Make this a family transition by planning everything together, starting with attending base-sponsored transition seminars with your spouse.

MYTH 6: **I expect to find a job with an organization that will offer me long-term career advancement.**

REALITY: Jobs and careers in the civilian world tend to be very fluid and unpredictable. The old days when you could expect to work for one company most of your life have all but vanished. Most people entering today's job market can expect to undergo three to five career changes and hold more than 15 different jobs. Long-term loyalty to a single employer is not expected, since many people change jobs and employers within a few years. Whatever job you land with an employer today, for instance, will most likely not be the same job nor with the same employer three to five years from now. Chances are you will move on to another employer once you have a clearer idea of opportunities in the civilian world. You'll once again go through a job search process involving research, networking, resume and letter writing, interviewing, and negotiating salary. Indeed, you will most likely use and reuse the job search skills outlined in this book several times in the years ahead as you undergo several job and career changes.

MYTH 7: **I'm not sure when and where to start my transition.**

REALITY: That may be true, but only if you are not aware of your surroundings and the many support systems in place to assist people in your situation. If you are still on active duty, your base offers several transition services which both you and your spouse should take advantage of at least six months before separation. These include seminars and one-on-one counseling concerning retirement benefits, financial planning, and finding a job. Counselors will even help you craft a transition resume. Be sure to visit your transition office for information on the various services. If you are a veteran, you'll find several transition services available to you through veterans' organizations and federal, state, and local governments. A few military-friendly career transition companies, such as www.corporategray.com, also sponsor military job fairs, especially in the Washington, DC, San Diego, and Norfolk areas, as well as offer online career assistance. Additional career services are available through community colleges and private companies on both free and fee-paid bases. We'll review several of these services,

including the relative advantages and disadvantages of each, in Chapter 6.

MYTH 8: **I'll probably only work for a few years before retiring on a pension.**

REALITY: Chances are you will be in the civilian workforce for many years to come, and many employers will not offer a pension plan. Traditional retirement is all but disappearing for large segments of the population. Indeed, today's baby boomers are postponing retirement for several reasons: high cost of living, lack of or inadequate retirement pensions, pursuing new dreams, enjoying their work, and desiring to keep active in the workforce. As you approach the traditional retirement ages of 60 to 65, you may discover that there are many things you want to do, and that you now have the financial freedom to pursue new careers you've dreamed about for years. This may be a time when you will continue in a job you love doing, or actually change careers, start a business, and/or invest in new ventures. In other words, don't plan on retirement. Keep dreaming. Plan to do something exciting with your life when you turn 50, 60, 70, or 80.

MYTH 9: **Nearly 85 percent of Americans are unhappy with their jobs. They would change jobs if only they felt they could.**

REALITY: This is one of those phony statistics thrown out by so-called career specialists who want to make themselves and their services highly visible. Unfortunately, such assertions get quoted by others as employment "facts" and evidence of a job "crisis." The truth, based upon numerous annual studies of worker attitudes, is that over 80 percent of workers are relatively happy with their jobs. Less than 15 percent report they may be interested in making a job change. Half of that number indicate they are unhappy with their current jobs. The statistical distribution of these supposedly happy/unhappy workers has been very consistent over the past three decades. However, the number of dissatisfied workers began to increase significantly in 2005. This was probably due in part to the dramatic increases in oil prices coupled with several other bad news economic events that eroded the generally positive disposition of the American worker.

MYTH 10: **We are now in a revolutionary period where we are witnessing the end of jobs.**

REALITY: Let's not get carried away with another trendy concept based on a skewed, anecdotal view of the job market. Jobs are here to stay and in a very big way. However, careers are clearly disappearing for many people. Careers, not jobs, may become obsolete. While traditional manufacturing jobs have been transformed in terms of skills required, jobs are still the basic means by which work gets organized and accomplished. Employers still fill **positions** which consist of various assigned duties and responsibilities that define particular jobs. Certain jobs in certain industries, especially those using nontraditional organizational forms, have become less well defined and thus do not conform to the traditional concept of an assigned job. But such changes are no reason for thinking that jobs are ending. What is ending is the notion of a career. Individuals entering the job market today expect to have many different jobs throughout their worklife. These jobs may or may not constitute a well-defined career.

MYTH 11: **My employment future and income look uncertain because many jobs, both manufacturing and service, are being offshored to cheap labor markets abroad.**

REALITY: While many such jobs are being offshored, this trend has existed for several decades. Indeed, within the United States, millions of jobs have moved from expensive labor markets in high-cost metropolitan areas to cheaper labor markets (from New York and Michigan to Alabama and South Dakota) within the country during the past 50 years. Known as "outsourcing," this is not a new nor alarming phenomenon. Outsourcing or offshoring of jobs tends to cut production costs and thus make businesses more efficient and competitive in the long run. While some people will lose their jobs to outsourcing, many others will be hired to manage the growth of such companies. Since many jobs require face-to-face relationships, outsourcing only affects certain types of jobs, which are estimated to be no more than 15 percent of all jobs. Your best guard against long-term job loss and declining income is **education and training**.

MYTH 12: **Anyone can find a job; all I need to know is how to find a job.**

REALITY: This classic "form versus substance" myth is often associated with popular career planning exhortations that stress the importance of having positive attitudes and self-esteem, setting goals, dressing for success, and using interpersonal strategies for finding jobs. While such approaches may work well in an industrial society with low unemployment, they constitute myths in a post-industrial, high-tech society which requires employees to demonstrate both **intelligence and concrete work skills** as well as a **willingness to relocate** to new communities offering greater job opportunities. For example, many of today's unemployed are highly skilled in the old technology of the industrial society, but they live and own homes in communities that offer few rewarding job and career opportunities. These people lack the necessary **skills and mobility** required for getting jobs in high-tech, growth communities. Knowing job search skills alone will not help these people. Indeed, such advice and knowledge will most likely frustrate such highly motivated and immobile individuals who possess skills of the old technology.

MYTH 13: **The best way to find a job is to respond to classified ads, use employment agencies, and submit applications to personnel offices.**

REALITY: Except for certain types of organizations, such as government, these formal application procedures are not the most effective ways of finding jobs. Such approaches assume the presence of an organized, coherent, and centralized job market – but no such thing exists. The job market is highly decentralized, fragmented, and chaotic. Classified ads, employment agencies, and personnel offices tend to list low-paying yet highly competitive jobs or high-paying, highly skilled positions that are hard to fill. Most jobs are neither listed nor advertised; they are most likely discovered through word-of-mouth contacts. Your most fruitful strategy will be to conduct research and informational interviews on what is called the "hidden job market." (See discussion in Chapter 14.)

MYTH 14: **Few jobs are available for me in today's job market.**

REALITY: This may be true if you lack marketable skills and insist on applying for jobs listed in newspapers, employment agencies, personnel offices, or online (the Internet). Competition in the advertised job market usually is high, especially for jobs requiring few skills. Numerous jobs with little competition are available on the hidden job market. Jobs requiring advanced technical skills often go begging. Little competition may occur during periods of high unemployment, because many people quit job hunting after a few disappointing weeks of concentrating job search efforts on working the advertised job market.

MYTH 15: **I know how to find a job, but there are no opportunities for me.**

REALITY: Most people don't know the best way to find a job, or they lack marketable job skills. They continue to use ineffective job search methods, such as only responding to classified ads with resumes and cover letters. Opportunities are readily available for individuals who understand the structure and operation of the job market, have appropriate work-content skills, and use job search methods designed for the hidden job market. They must learn to develop an effective networking and informational interviewing campaign for uncovering promising job leads. And they must persist in prospecting for new job leads as well as learn to handle rejections. In fact, many job seekers are their own worst enemy and thus they turn this myth into a self-fulling prophecy. They make numerous mistakes that can be easily corrected given some basic information on effective job search strategies. This issue is addressed at length in Ron and Caryl Krannich's *No One Will Hire Me! Avoid 15 Mistakes and Win the Job* (Impact Publications, 2004).

MYTH 16: **I'm over-qualified in the eyes of many employers. They don't want to hire over-qualified individuals.**

REALITY: Yes, if you're seeking a $40,000 a year job but you have experience and qualifications for an $80,000 a year job! Why would you even want to consider such a job? Who wants to hire someone who is over-qualified and thus likely

to leave for greener pastures once they get their wake-up call that they are underemployed and under-compensated? This is the classic self-fulfilling prophecy of many career changers who don't know how to best communicate their qualifications to prospective employers. Being over-qualified for a job raises a big red flag in the eyes of the employer. You're never over-qualified if you seek jobs for your level of skills and experience. Employers who view you as over-qualified are the wrong employers to whom to apply. They do you a favor by **not** giving you a job. Thank them for being so discriminating. They serve as your wake-up call. You need to get a better sense of where you fit into the job market. Stop under-selling yourself and thus contributing to this over-qualification myth. You need some job market smarts before you approach any more employers.

MYTH 17: **Employers are in the driver's seat; they have the upper hand with applicants.**

REALITY: Most often no one is in the driver's seat, since both the employer and the job seeker have a problem to solve. Not knowing what they want, many employers make poor hiring decisions. They frequently let applicants define their hiring needs. If you can define employers' needs as your skills, you might end up in the driver's seat!

MYTH 18: **Employers hire the best qualified candidates. Without a great deal of experience and qualifications, I don't have a chance.**

REALITY: Employers hire people for all kinds of reasons. Most rank experience and qualifications third or fourth in their pecking order of hiring criteria. Employers seldom hire the best qualified candidate, because "qualifications" are difficult to define and measure. Employers normally seek people with the following characteristics: competent, intelligent, honest, enthusiastic, and likable. "Likability" tends to be an overall concern of employers – will you "fit in" and get along well with your superiors, co-workers, and clients? Employers want **value** for their money. Therefore, you must communicate to employers that you are the right person. You must overcome employers' objections to any lack of experience or qualifications. But **never** volunteer your weaknesses. The

best qualified person is the one who knows how to get the job – convinces employers that he or she is the **most** desirable for the job.

MYTH 19: **It is best to go into a growing field where jobs are plentiful.**

REALITY: Be careful in following the masses to the "in" fields. First, many so-called growth fields can quickly become no-growth fields, such as aerospace engineering, nuclear energy, law, and defense contracting. Second, by the time you acquire the necessary skills, you may experience the "disappearing job" phenomenon: too many people did the same thing you did and thus glutted the job market. Third, since many people leave no-growth fields, new opportunities may arise for you. Fourth, if you go after a growth field, you will try to fit into a job rather than find a job fit for you. If you know what you do well and enjoy doing, and what additional training you may need, you should look for a job or career conducive to your particular mix of skills, interests, and motivations. In the long run you will be much happier and more productive finding a job fit for you. If you find a job you really love, you will be better compensated emotionally than if you only focused on finding a job that pays a high salary.

MYTH 20: **People over 40 have difficulty finding a good job; employers prefer hiring younger and less expensive workers.**

REALITY: Yes, if they apply for youth jobs. Age should be an insignificant barrier to employment if you conduct a well organized job search and are prepared to handle this potential negative with employers. Age should be a positive and must be communicated as such. After all, employers want experience, maturity, and stability. People over 40 generally possess these qualities. As the population ages and birth rates decline, older individuals should have a much easier time changing jobs and careers.

MYTH 21: **It's best to use an employment firm to find a job.**

REALITY: It depends on the firm and the nature of employment you are seeking. Employment firms that specialize in your skill

area may be well worth contacting. For example, many law firms use employment firms to hire paralegals rather than directly recruit such personnel themselves. Many employers now use temporary employment firms to recruit both temporary and full-time employees at several different levels, from clerical to professional. Indeed, many temporary employment firms have temp-to-perm programs that link qualified candidates to employers who are looking for full-time employees. But make sure you are working with a legitimate employment firm. Such firms get paid by employers or they collect placement fees from applicants only **after** the applicant has accepted a position. Beware of firms that want up-front fees for promised job placement assistance.

MYTH 22: **I must be aggressive in order to find a job.**

REALITY: Aggressive people tend to be offensive and obnoxious. They also make pests of themselves. Try being purposeful, persistent, and pleasant in all job search activities. Such behavior is well received by potential employers who view such candidates as individuals who want to work for them.

MYTH 23: **Hiring a professional to help me find a job is a waste of time and money.**

REALITY: It depends on the professional, the job one is going after, and the personality of the job seeker. Hiring a career professional to help you with your job search can save you a great deal of time and wasted effort. A career professional should serve as a coach in helping you through a job search process. While some people can conduct a job search on their own, most people can benefit from the structure, motivation, discipline, and direction provided by such a professional. If you're interested in contacting a career professional, visit the following websites, which are linked to associations of career professionals: www.nbcc.org, www.ncda.org, www.certifiedcareercoaches.com, and www.careernetwork.com.

MYTH 24: **I should not change jobs and careers more than once or twice. Job-changers are discriminated against in hiring.**

REALITY: While this may have been generally true 30 years ago, it is no longer true today. America is a skills-based society: individuals market their skills to organizations in exchange for money, position, and other on-the-job rewards. Furthermore, since most organizations are small businesses with limited advancement opportunities, careers quickly plateau in such companies. For many employees interested in career advancement, the only way up is to get out and into another organization. Therefore, the best way to advance careers in a society of small businesses is to periodically change jobs. Job-changing is okay as long as such changes demonstrate career advancement and one isn't changing jobs every few months. Most individuals entering the job market today will undergo several career and job changes regardless of their initial desire for a one-job, one-career life plan.

MYTH 25: **People get ahead by working hard and putting in long hours.**

REALITY: Success patterns differ. Many people who are honest, work hard, and put in long hours also get fired, have ulcers, and die young. Some people get ahead even though they are dishonest and lazy. Others simply have good luck or a helpful mentor or patron. Moderation in both work and play will probably get you just as far as the extremes. Your best approach to getting ahead is to get up each day and do the very best work you can to contribute to your employer's goals. Keep focused on the work at hand. Demonstrate that you are a trusted, predictable, and valued employee. There are other ways, as outlined near the end of this chapter, to become successful in addition to hard work and long hours.

MYTH 26: **I should not try to use "connections" to get a job. I should apply through the front door like everyone else. If I'm the best qualified, I'll get the job.**

REALITY: While you may wish to stand in line for tickets, bank deposits, and loans – because you have no clout – standing in line for a job is not the best approach. Every employer has a front door as well as a back door. Try using the back door if you can. It works in many cases. Later we detail how you can develop your contacts, use connections, and enter **both** the front and back doors.

MYTH 27: **I need to get more education and training to qualify for today's jobs.**

REALITY: You may or may not need more education and training, depending on your present skill levels and the needs of employers. Most employers want to recruit individuals who are intelligent, communicate well, take initiative, and are trainable. Since they train their employees to respond to the needs of their organization, they want people who can quickly learn new skills. You first need to know what skills you already possess and whether they appear appropriate for the types of jobs you are seeking. Also, be sure to communicate to employers that you enjoy learning and are trainable.

MYTH 28: **Once I apply for a job, it's best to wait to hear from an employer.**

REALITY: Waiting is not a good job search strategy. If you want action from employers, you must first take action. The key to getting a job interview and offer is follow up, follow up, follow up. You do this by making follow-up telephone calls as well as writing follow-up and thank you letters.

MYTH 29: **I don't need a resume. I can get a job based solely on my network contacts.**

REALITY: While networking is one of the most effective methods for finding employment, it does not erase the need for a resume. The resume is your calling card; it provides a prospective employer with a snapshot of your background and skills. Employers often want to first see you on paper (resume) **before** meeting you in person (interview). Whether you like it or not, chances are you'll need a resume very early in your job search, especially when a contact asks you to "Send me a copy of your resume."

MYTH 30: **A good resume is the key to getting a job.**

REALITY: While resumes play an important role in the job search process, they are often overrated. The purpose of a resume is to communicate your qualifications to employers who, in turn, invite you to job interviews. The key to getting a job is the job interview. No job interview, no job offer.

MYTH 31: **I should include my salary expectations on my resume or in my cover letter.**

REALITY: You should **never** include your salary expectations on your resume or in a cover letter, unless specifically requested to do so. Salary should be the very last thing you discuss with a prospective employer. You do so only **after** you have had a chance to assess the worth of the position and communicate your value to the employer. This usually occurs at the end of your final job interview, just before or after being offered the job. If you prematurely raise the salary issue, you may devalue your worth.

MYTH 32: **My resume should emphasize my work history.**

REALITY: Employers are interested in hiring your future rather than your past. Therefore, your resume should emphasize the skills and abilities you will bring to the job as well as your interests and goals. Let prospective employers know what you are likely to do for them **in the future**. When you present your work history, do so in terms of your major skills and accomplishments. This is especially important for transitioning military, who need to translate their military duties and responsibilities into specific skills and accomplishments readily understood by civilian employers. Avoid military jargon that may not be understood by civilians.

MYTH 33: **It's not necessary to write letters to employers – just send them a resume or complete an application.**

REALITY: You should be prepared to write several types of job search letters – cover, approach, resume, thank you, follow-up, and acceptance. In addition to communicating your level of literacy, these job search letters enable you to express important values sought after by employers – your tactfulness, thoughtfulness, enthusiasm, likability, and follow-up ability. Sending a resume without a cover letter devalues your resume and application.

MYTH 34: **I only need an electronic resume to land a job.**

REALITY: Electronic resumes are increasingly important for job seekers and employers alike. These resumes come in two major forms: e-mail resumes and scannable resumes. More and

more employers request that resumes be sent to them by e-mail. Therefore, you need to create an e-mail version of your resume. Large employers also use the latest resume scanning technology to quickly screen hundreds of resumes. There-fore, it's also in your interest to write a "computer- friendly" resume based on the principles of electronic resumes. These are very different resumes compared to conventional re-sumes. Structured around "keywords" or nouns which stress capabilities, electronic resumes are ideally suited for scan-ners. Keep in mind that electronic resumes are primarily written for electronic scanners and high-tech distribution systems rather than for human beings. But since human beings interview and hire, you should first create a high impact resume that follows the principles of human commu-nication and intelligence.

MYTH 35: **Individuals who post their resumes online to resume databases, such as www.monster.com, www.hotjobs. yahoo.com, and www.careerbuilder.com, are more likely to get high-paying jobs than those who don't.**

REALITY: Don't get carried away in your job search with all the bells, whistles, and hype of the many Internet employment sites that offer resume databases and thousands of job postings. Basically operated for their paying customers – employers – these are largely high-tech classified ad operations that also enable employers to quickly search thousands of online resumes by keywords. There is nothing magical about this search-and-retrieval media. Indeed, there is no evidence that individuals who conduct an online job search find better jobs than those who do not. In fact, the Internet is a big disappointment for many job seekers who spend a dispro-portionate amount of time submitting resumes to databases and applying for jobs online. Recent surveys indicate that fewer than 20 percent of candidates get jobs through their online job search efforts. While this number is increasing, the shift in emphasis for employers is from using commercial employment websites to using their own company websites to recruit candidates. While individuals are well advised to include an Internet component in their job search, especially focusing on employer websites, they also are well advised to spend most of their time engaged in job search activities that have real payoffs, such as networking for information,

advice, and referrals (Chapter 14) and contacting employers by telephone and in person. For job seekers, the real power of the Internet lies in conducting research on jobs, employers, and communities and in communicating by e-mail.

MYTH 36: **The best way to ace the job interview is to practice answers to anticipated interview questions.**

REALITY: The job interview is much more than just providing canned answers to anticipated interview questions. Employers are looking for signs of likability, competence, and intelligence throughout all phases of the interview. Since over 80 percent of what's communicated in the interview is nonverbal, be sure to pay particular attention to your nonverbal behaviors, such as attire, handshake, eye contact, and vocalized pauses. Avoid memorizing answers to questions, since you will most likely appear coached rather than candid. Three of the most important things you should do during the interview are (1) answer questions with tact and confidence, (2) ask intelligent questions, and (3) close the interview properly.

MYTH 37: **Salaries are pre-determined by employers.**

REALITY: Most salaries are negotiable within certain ranges and limits. Before you ever apply or interview for a position, you should know what the salary range is for the type of position you seek. When you finally discuss the salary question – preferably at the end of the final job interview – do so with this range in mind. Assuming you have adequately demonstrated your value to the employer, try to negotiate the highest possible salary within the range.

MYTH 38: **It's best to concentrate on negotiating a gross salary figure rather than focus on benefits and perks.**

REALITY: It depends on the employer and situation. Benefits and perks can translate into a significant amount of compensation. In fact, the U.S. Department of Labor reports that on average 43 percent of total compensation is in the form of benefits. Benefits such as stock options, profit sharing, disability insurance, and child care can add up to a significant amount of compensation. Make sure you look at the total compensation package rather than just the gross salary

figure. For example, a $50,000 base salary with Employer X may actually be worth $80,000 with benefits, whereas a $60,000 base salary with Employer Y may only be worth $70,000 with benefits.

MYTH 39: **It's best to relocate to a booming community.**

REALITY: Similar to the "disappearing job" phenomenon (Myth 19), today's economically booming communities may be tomorrow's busts. It's best to select a community that is conducive to your lifestyle preferences as well as has a diversified economy to weather boom-and-bust economic cycles.

MYTH 40: **It's best to broadcast or "shotgun" my resume to as many employers as possible.**

REALITY: Broadcasting your resume to employers is a game of chance in which you usually waste your time and money. It's always best to target your resume on those employers who have vacancies or who might have openings in the near future. Your single best approach for uncovering job leads will be the process called networking.

You also should be aware of several other realities which will affect your job search or which you might find helpful in developing your plan of action for finding a job or changing your career:

- **You will find less competition for high-level jobs than for middle- and low-level jobs.** If you aim high, yet are realistic, you may be pleasantly surprised with the results.

- **Human resources or personnel offices seldom hire.** They primarily screen candidates for employers who are found in operating units of organizations. Knowing this, you should focus your job search efforts on those who do the actual hiring – the hiring managers.

- **Employment firms and personnel agencies may not help you.** Most work for employers and themselves rather than for applicants. Few have your best interests at heart. Use them only after you have investigated their effectiveness. Avoid firms that require up-front money for vague promises of performance.

- **It is best to narrow or "rifle" your job search on partic-ular organizations and individuals** rather than broaden or "shotgun" it to many alternatives. If you remain focused, you will be better able to accomplish your goals.

- **Most people make satisfying job and career changes.** They should minimize efforts in the advertised job market and concentrate instead on planning and implementing a well organized job search tailored to the realities of the hidden job market.

- **Jobs and careers tend to be fluid and changing.** Knowing this, you should concentrate on acquiring and marketing skills, talents, and abilities which can be transferred from one job to another.

- **Millions of job vacancies are available every day** because new jobs are created, and people resign, retire, get fired, or die.

- **Most people, regardless of their position or status, love to talk about their work and give advice** to both friends and strangers. You can learn the most about job opportunities and alternative careers by talking to such people.

- **Politics are both ubiquitous and dangerous in many organizations.** If you think you are above politics, you may quickly become one of its victims. Unfortunately, you only learn about "local politics" **after** you accept a position and begin getting acquainted with players in the organization.

As you conduct your job search, you will encounter many of these and other myths and realities about how you should relate to the job market. Several people will give you advice. While much of this advice will be useful, a great deal of it will be useless and misleading. You should be skeptical of well-meaning individuals who most likely will reiterate the same job and career myths. You should be particularly leery of those who try to **sell** you their advice. Always remember you are entering a relatively disorganized and chaotic job market where you can find numerous job opportunities. Your task is to organize the chaos around your skills and interests. You must convince prospective employers that they will like you more than other "qualified" candidates!

3

Get Started Right

I F YOU ARE READING THIS BOOK 12 months before separation from your service, you have time to develop and implement a well organized transition plan and test the employment waters. Indeed, this may be the last time in your life that you have so much time to do such critical planning and testing. If you're a veteran who is either looking for a job or considering a job or career change, you need to use your time wisely in making important career and job search decisions.

In this chapter we outline some of the major issues involved in putting together a well organized transition plan. At the very least you need to do six things:

1. Avoid mistakes made by other job seekers.
2. Understand the career development and job search processes.
3. Properly organize and sequence your job search activities.
4. Find time to implement each stage of your job search.
5. Follow key principles of job search success.
6. Commit yourself to effective implementation.

Once you have a clear idea of what it is you need to do to achieve a successful transition, you should be able to focus laser-like on implementing your plan of action.

Looking for a Job

Each year more than 30 million Americans actively conduct a job search. Another 30 million contemplate leaving their jobs for new opportunities elsewhere. While millions of people look for their first full-time job after

31

leaving school, millions of others, including a large percentage who are in their first year of work, decide to quit their jobs because they are unhappy with their work. And millions of others get fired or laid off, re-enter the job market after a lengthy absence, decide to come out of retirement, take a second or third job, seek part-time work as students and homemakers, or transition from a different work world or lifestyle. In addition to over 300,000 individuals who leave the military each year for the civilian world, nearly 2,500 Peace Corps Volunteers re-enter the job market, over two million government workers look for second careers upon retiring from federal, state, and local governments, and more than 600,000 ex-offenders annually seek employment upon release from prisons. All of these individuals have one thing in common – they must conduct a job search that requires communicating their qualifications to strangers on applications, resumes, and letters as well as in job interviews.

It's Hard Ego-Bruising Work

Looking for a job is no fun, especially for the shy and sensitive who are forced to introduce themselves to strangers, ask for assistance, and encounter the inevitable rejections. Indeed, finding a job may be the hardest, most frustrating, and ego-bruising work you ever do. Depending on how you approach the process, it also can be an extremely educational, exciting, and exhilarating experience. If done properly, you'll meet many new and interesting people, learn a great deal about yourself and others, and land a job that is the perfect fit for both you and the employer. You'll enjoy going to work each day where you can use your many gifts and talents. If all goes well, your new job will become an important step in your overall career or worklife.

> *Finding a job may be the hardest, most frustrating, and ego-bruising work you ever do.*

But not everyone approaches the job search in the same manner and implement it with the same degree of success. Some people are immensely talented, very extroverted, and quickly find great jobs. Others are less talented, somewhat introverted, and find job hunting especially challenging and time consuming. These people may have skills and experience, but they don't stand out from the crowd with exceptional backgrounds, and many lack the confidence to move ahead with their job search.

You need to conduct a job search that best showcases your major strengths and talents to prospective employers and brings out the best in you. You need to do this right from the very start.

Lessons Learned

Over the years we have learned numerous job hunting lessons from thousands of job seekers, employers, and career experts. Representing many occupations and walks of life, these individuals reveal a rich collection of job hunting tips that are equally applicable to people with hot and not-so-hot backgrounds. The tips constitute a set of principles for conducting an effective job search. By examining these tips, you should be able to better organize and target your own job search, lessen your anxiety, and go on to land a job that best fits your interests, skills, and abilities. Better still, you should be able to substantially shorten your job search time by following our seasoned advice.

You're Under Scrutiny

Here's the sobering situation you are likely to encounter these days: employers are suspicious of most candidates who come to them as strangers. You're asking them to give you a position, salary, and benefits in exchange for the promise of performance. In the past, they have had bad experiences with candidates who exaggerated their qualifications, lied on their resumes, performed far below expectations, or quit within the first year. Trusting the information provided by the candidate, they eventually felt deceived when they had to deal with the realities of the person's day-to-day performance.

Not surprisingly, employers want better control of the hiring process. They want to more successfully predict an individual's future performance based on an accurate assessment of his or her past accomplishments. As employers increasingly screen candidates through background checks, testing, references, and behavioral and situational interviews, fewer prospective employees can avoid close scrutiny of their backgrounds and claims of performance. Indeed, in today's high-tech, security-conscious, and behavior-oriented society, there is no place to hide! Employers want to know your work history and related patterns of behavior – both positives and negatives – that they will inherit when they hire you.

Mistakes You Should Avoid

Over the years we have worked with numerous people who frequently lamented what they considered to be a fact of job search life – *"No one will hire me!"* After spending weeks looking for a job, they encountered numerous rejections and thus concluded there were few jobs available for people with their qualifications. On closer examination, however, we

found that much of the problem in finding employment related to the individual rather than the job market. Many of these people spent most of their job search time responding to classified ads in newspapers and job postings on the Internet – the least effective ways of finding a job.

Regardless of their stellar or not-so-stellar backgrounds, most of them made several job search mistakes that knocked them out of the competition. These mistakes include:

1. Lack clear goals and a work objective
2. Harbor negative and self-defeating "can't do" attitudes
3. Misunderstand the sequential nature of a job search
4. Engage in several ineffective job search activities
5. Fail to network, or network with the wrong people
6. Provide little evidence of skills, accomplishments, and a productive pattern of behavior
7. Write and distribute awful resumes and letters
8. Include negative or incomplete information on applications
9. Commit several job interview sins, from arriving late to failing to close the interview properly
10. Fail to ask questions, listen, and change interview directions if necessary
11. Lack tactfulness and honesty
12. Conduct an outdated job search
13. Over-rely on technology, especially the Internet
14. Avoid taking risks
15. Unprepared to handle rejections
16. Fail to develop and implement a plan of action
17. Exhibit weak follow-up skills
18. Try to conduct a job search on their own rather than seek professional help at critical steps in their job search
19. Resist changing behaviors and acquiring new habits
20. Fail to keep motivated and focused throughout the job search

Taken together, these mistakes project an unflattering image of the candidate – someone who is not quite up to doing the job. Why hire someone who makes such mistakes? If you add to this list any personal or professional red flags in your background, you may have a powerful set of factors working against your best interests. Indeed, your success in finding a job that's right for you may be limited by your inability to clearly communicate your positive qualifications to strangers – prospective employers who know little or nothing about your qualifications and potential performance beyond initial impressions you communicate.

Finding Jobs and Changing Careers

As you transition from the military, you will join millions of other people who look for jobs and change careers each year. Indeed, between 10 and 15 million people find themselves unemployed each year. Millions of others try to increase their satisfaction within the workplace as well as advance their careers by looking for alternative jobs and careers. If you are like most other Americans, you will make more than 15 job changes and between three and five career changes during your lifetime.

Most people make job or career transitions by accident. They do little other than take advantage of opportunities that may arise unexpectedly. While chance and luck do play important roles in finding employment, we recommend that you **plan** for future job and career changes so that you will experience even greater degrees of chance and luck!

Finding a job or changing a career in a systematic and well-planned manner is hard yet rewarding work. The task should first be based upon a clear understanding of the key ingredients that define jobs and careers. Starting with this understanding, you should next convert key concepts into action steps for implementing your job search.

A **career** is a series of jobs which have common skill, interest, and motivational bases. You may change jobs several times without changing careers. But once you change skills, interests, and motivations, you change careers.

It's not easy to find a job given the present structure of the job market. You will find the job market to be relatively disorganized, although it projects an outward appearance of coherence. If you seek comprehensive, accurate, and timely job information, the job market will frustrate you with its poor communication. While you will find many employment services ready to assist you, such services tend to be fragmented and their performance is often disappointing. Job search methods are controversial and many are ineffective.

No system is organized to give people jobs. At best you will encounter a **decentralized and fragmented system** consisting of job listings in newspapers, trade journals, employment offices, or on the Internet – all designed to link candidates to job openings. Many people will try to sell you questionable job services and information. In the end, most systems organized to help you find a job do not provide you with the information you need in order to land a job that is most related to your skills and interests.

Seven Steps to Job Search Success

Finding a job is both an art and a science; it encompasses a variety of basic facts, principles, and skills which can be learned but which also must be adapted to individual situations. Thus, **learning how to find a job** can be as important to career success as **knowing how to perform a job**. Indeed, job finding skills are often as important to career success as job performance or work-content skills.

Our understanding of how to find jobs and change careers is illustrated on pages 37 and 39. As outlined on page 37, you should involve yourself in a four-step career development process as you prepare to move from one job to another:

1. **Conduct a self-assessment**

 This first step involves assessing your skills, abilities, motiva-tions, interests, values, temperaments, experience, and ac-complishments – the major concern of this book. Your basic strategy is to develop a firm foundation of information on **you** before proceeding to other stages in the career development process. This self-assessment develops the necessary self-awareness upon which you can effectively communicate your qualifications to employers as well as focus and build your career.

2. **Gather career and job information**

 Closely related to the first step, this second step is an exploratory, research phase of your career development. Here you need to formulate goals, gather information about alternative jobs and careers through reading and talking to informed people, and then narrow your alternatives to specific jobs.

3. **Develop job search skills**

 The third step focuses on specific job search skills for landing the job you want. As further outlined on page 8, these job search skills are closely related to one another as a series of **job search steps**. They involve conducting research, writing resumes and letters, prospecting and networking, conducting informational interviews, interviewing for a job, and negotiating salary and terms of employment. Each of these job search skills involves

The Career Development Process

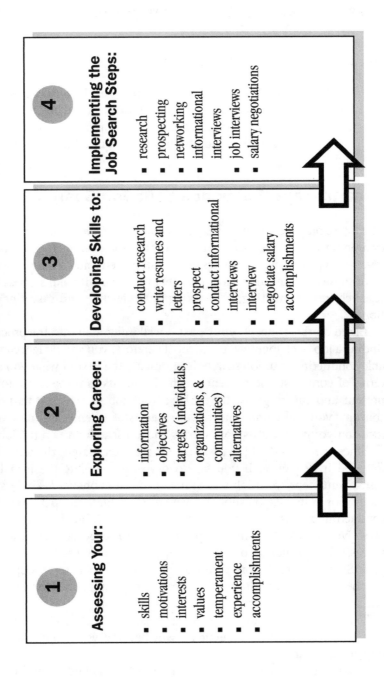

1

Assessing Your:

- skills
- motivations
- interests
- values
- temperament
- experience
- accomplishments

2

Exploring Career:

- information
- objectives
- targets (individuals, organizations, & communities)
- alternatives

3

Developing Skills to:

- conduct research
- write resumes and letters
- prospect
- conduct informational interviews
- interview
- negotiate salary
- accomplishments

4

Implementing the Job Search Steps:

- research
- prospecting
- networking
- informational interviews
- job interviews
- salary negotiations

well-defined strategies and tactics you must learn in order to be effective in the job market.

4. Implement each job search step

The final career development step emphasizes the importance of transforming understanding into **action**. You do this by implementing each job search step which already incorporates the knowledge, skills, and abilities you acquired in Steps 1, 2, and 3.

Organize and Sequence Your Job Search

The figure on page 39 further expands our career development process by examining the key elements in a successful job search. It consists of a seven-step process which relates your past, present, and future. We cover all of these steps in subsequent chapters that deal with skills assessment, research, resume writing, networking, interviewing, and salary negotiations.

Based on this concept, **your past** is well integrated into the process of finding a job or changing your career. Therefore, you should feel comfortable conducting your job search: it represents the best of what you are in terms of your past and present accomplishments as these relate to your present and future goals. If you base your job search on this process concept, you will communicate your **best self** to employers as well as focus on **your strengths** both during the job search and on the job.

Since the individual job search steps are interrelated, they should be followed in sequence. If you fail to properly complete the initial self-assessment steps, your job search may become haphazard, aimless, and costly. For example, you should never write a resume (Step 3) before first conducting an assessment of your skills (Step 1) and identifying your objective (Step 2). Relating Step 1 to Step 2 is especially critical to the successful implementation of all other job search steps. You must complete Steps 1 and 2 **before** continuing on to the other steps. Steps 3 to 6 may be conducted simultaneously because they complement and reinforce one another.

Try to sequence your job search as closely to these steps as possible. The true value of this sequencing will become very apparent as you implement your plan.

You must do much more than just know how to find a job. In the job markets of today and tomorrow, you need to constantly review your work-content skills to make sure they are appropriate for the changing job mar-

Job Search Steps and Stages

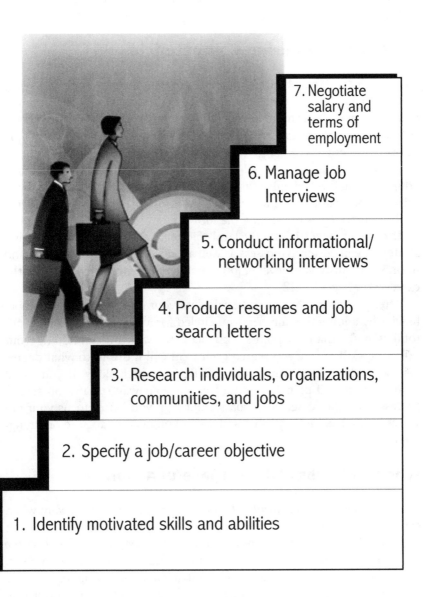

7. Negotiate salary and terms of employment

6. Manage Job Interviews

5. Conduct informational/ networking interviews

4. Produce resumes and job search letters

3. Research individuals, organizations, communities, and jobs

2. Specify a job/career objective

1. Identify motivated skills and abilities

ket. Assuming you have the necessary work-content skills, you should be ready to target your skills on particular jobs and careers that you do well and enjoy doing. You will be able to avoid the trap of trying to fit into jobs that are not conducive to your particular mix of interests, abilities, skills, and motivations.

Test Your Careering Competencies

Knowing **where** the jobs are is important to your job search. But knowing **how to find a job** is even more important. Before you acquire names, addresses, and phone numbers of potential employers, you should possess the necessary job search knowledge and skills for gathering and using job information effectively.

Answers to many of your job-related questions are found by examining your present level of job search knowledge and skills. Successful job seekers, for example, use a great deal of information as well as specific skills and strategies for getting the jobs they want.

Let's begin by testing for the level of job search information, skills, and strategies you currently possess as well as those you need to develop and improve. Identify your level of job search competence by completing the exercise on pages 41-42.

After you finish this exercise, calculate your overall careering competencies by adding the numbers you circled for a composite score. If your total is more than 75 points, you need to work on developing your careering skills. How you scored each item will indicate to what degree you need to work on improving specific job search skills. If your total score is under 50 points, you are well on your way toward job search success. In either case, this book should help you better focus your job search as well as identify job search skills you need to acquire or strengthen.

When In Doubt, Take Purposeful Action

The old adage *"When in doubt, do something"* is especially relevant when expanded to include a thoughtful plan of action related to the job search process: *"When in doubt, engage in a concrete activity related to the sequence of job search steps."* This might include conducting research on communities, companies, positions, and salaries; surveying job vacancy announcements; writing a resume and job search letters; or contacting three employers each day.

But developing a plan and taking action are much easier said than done. If conducted properly, a job search can become an extremely time-

Your Careering Competencies

INSTRUCTIONS: Respond to each statement by circling which number at the right best represents your situation.

SCALE: 1 = strongly agree 4 = disagree
 2 = agree 5 = strongly disagree
 3 = maybe, not certain

1. I know what motivates me to excel at work. 1 2 3 4 5

2. I can identify my strongest abilities and skills. 1 2 3 4 5

3. I have seven major achievements that clarify
 a pattern of interests and abilities that
 are relevant to my job and career. 1 2 3 4 5

4. I know what I both like and dislike in work. 1 2 3 4 5

5. I know what I want to do during the next
 10 years. 1 2 3 4 5

6. I have a well defined career objective that
 focuses my job search on particular
 organizations and employers. 1 2 3 4 5

7. I know what skills I can offer employers in
 different occupations. 1 2 3 4 5

8. I know what skills employers most seek in
 candidates. 1 2 3 4 5

9. I can clearly explain to employers what I do
 well and enjoy doing. 1 2 3 4 5

10. I can specify why employers should hire me. 1 2 3 4 5

11. I can gain the support of family and friends
 for making a job or career change. 1 2 3 4 5

12. I can find 10 to 20 hours a week to
 conduct a part-time job search. 1 2 3 4 5

13. I have the financial ability to sustain a
 three-month job search. 1 2 3 4 5

14. I can conduct library and interview research
on different occupations, employers,
organizations, and communities. 1 2 3 4 5

15. I can write different types of effective
resumes and job search/thank you letters. 1 2 3 4 5

16. I can produce and distribute resumes and
letters to the right people. 1 2 3 4 5

17. I can list my major accomplishments in
action terms. 1 2 3 4 5

18. I can identify and target employers I
want to interview. 1 2 3 4 5

19. I can develop a job referral network. 1 2 3 4 5

20. I can persuade others to join in forming
a job search support group. 1 2 3 4 5

21. I can prospect for job leads. 1 2 3 4 5

22. I can use the telephone to develop prospects
and get referrals and interviews. 1 2 3 4 5

23. I can plan and implement an effective
direct-mail job search campaign. 1 2 3 4 5

24. I can generate at least one job interview
for every 10 job search contacts I make. 1 2 3 4 5

25. I can follow up on job interviews. 1 2 3 4 5

26. I can negotiate a salary 10-20% above
what an employer initially offers. 1 2 3 4 5

27. I can persuade an employer to renegotiate
my salary after six months on the job. 1 2 3 4 5

28. I can create a position for myself
in an organization. 1 2 3 4 5

 TOTAL _____

consuming activity. It inevitably competes with other personal and professional priorities. That's why you need to make some initial decisions as to how and when you will conduct a job search. How much time, for example, are you willing to set aside each day or week to engage in each of the seven job search activities outlined at the beginning of this chapter? After you've spent numerous hours identifying your abilities and skills and formulating an objective, are you willing to commit yourself to 20 hours a week to network for information and advice? If you are unwilling to commit both your time and your attention to each activity within the process, you may remain stuck, and inevitably frustrated, at the initial stages of self-awareness and understanding. Success only comes to those who take action at other stages in the job search process.

Use Time Wisely

If you decide to conduct your own job search with minimum assistance from professionals, your major cost will be your time. Therefore, you must find sufficient time to devote to your job search. Ask yourself this question:

> *"How valuable is my time in relation to finding a
> job or changing my career?"*

Assign a dollar value to your time. For example, is your time worth $3, $5, $10, $25, $50, or $100 an hour? Compare your figure with what you might pay a professional for doing much of the job search work for you. Normal professional fees range from $1,500 to $10,000.

The time you devote to your job search will depend on whether you want to work at it on a full-time or part-time basis. If you are unemployed, by all means make this a full-time endeavor – 40 to 80 hours per week. If you are presently employed, we do not recommend quitting your job in order to look for employment. You will probably need the steady income and health benefits during your transition period. Furthermore, it is easier to find new employment by appearing employed. Unemployed people project a negative image in the eyes of many employers – they appear to **need** a job. **Your goal is to find a job based on your strengths rather than your needs.**

However, if you go back to school for skills retraining, your present employment status may be less relevant to employers. Your major strength is the fact that you have acquired a skill the employer needs. If you quit your job and spend money retraining, you will communicate a certain degree of risk-taking, drive, responsibility, and dedication which

employers readily seek, but seldom find, in candidates today.

Assuming you will be conducting a job search on a part-time basis – 15 to 25 hours per week – you will need to find the necessary time for these job activities. Unfortunately, most people are busy, having programmed every hour to "important" personal and professional activities. Thus, conducting a job search for 15 or more hours a week means that some things will have to go or receive low priority in relation to your job search.

This is easier said than done. The job search often gets low priority. It competes with other important daily routines, such as attending meetings, taking children to games, going shopping, watching favorite TV programs, and using the Internet. Rather than fight with your routines – and create family disharmony and stress – make your job search part of your daily routines by improving your overall management of time.

Certain time management techniques will help you make your job search a high-priority activity in your daily schedule. These practices may actually lower your present stress level and thus enhance your overall effectiveness.

Time management experts estimate that most people waste their time on unimportant matters. Lacking priorities, people spend 80 percent of their time on trivia and 20 percent of their time on the important matters that should get the most attention. If you reverse this emphasis, you could have a great deal of excess time – and probably experience less stress attendant with the common practice of crisis-managing the critical 20 percent.

Before reorganizing your time, you must know how you normally use your time. Therefore, complete the exercise on pages 45-46 to assess your time management behavior. While many of these statements are relevant to individuals in managerial positions, respond to those statements that are most relevant to your employment situation. If you answered "no" to many of these statements, you should consider incorporating a few basic time management principles and practices into your daily schedule.

Don't go to extremes by drastically restructuring your life around the "religion" of time management. If you followed all the advice of time management experts, you would probably alienate your family, friends, and colleagues with your narrow efficiency mentality! A realistic approach is to start monitoring your time use and then gradually re-organize your time according to goals and priorities. This is all you need to do. Forget the elaborate flow charts that are the stuff of expensive time management workshops and consultants. Start by developing a time management log that helps you monitor your present use of time. Keep daily records of how you use your time over a two-week period. Identify who controls your time and the results of your time utilization. Within two weeks,

Your Time Management Inventory

Respond to each statement by circling "yes" or "no," depending on which response best represents your normal pattern of behavior.

1. I have a written set of long, intermediate, and short-range goals for myself (and my family). Yes No

2. I have a clear idea of what I will do today at work and at home. Yes No

3. I have a clear idea of what I want to accomplish at work this coming week and month. Yes No

4. I set priorities and follow through on the most important tasks first. Yes No

5. I judge my success by the results I produce in relation to my goals. Yes No

6. I use a daily, weekly, and monthly calendar for scheduling appointments and setting work targets. Yes No

7. I delegate as much work as possible. Yes No

8. I get my subordinates to organize their time in relation to mine. Yes No

9. I file only those things which are essential to my work. When in doubt, I throw it out. Yes No

10. I throw away junk mail. Yes No

11. My briefcase is uncluttered, including only essential materials; it serves as my office away from the office. Yes No

12. I minimize the number of meetings and concentrate on making decisions rather than discussing aimlessly. Yes No

13. I make frequent use of the telephone and face-to-face encounters rather than written communications. Yes No

14. I make minor decisions quickly. Yes No

15. I concentrate on accomplishing one thing
 at a time. Yes No

16. I handle each piece of paper once and
 only once. Yes No

17. I answer most letters on the letter I receive
 with either a handwritten or typed message. Yes No

18. I set deadlines for myself and others and
 follow through in meeting them. Yes No

19. I reserve time each week to plan. Yes No

20. My desk and work area are well organized
 and clear. Yes No

21. I know how to say "no" and do so. Yes No

22. I first skim books, articles, and other forms
 of written communication for ideas before
 reading further. Yes No

23. I monitor my time use during the day by
 asking myself "How can I best use my
 time at present?" Yes No

24. I deal with the present by getting things
 done that need to be done. Yes No

25. I maintain a time log to monitor the best
 use of my time. Yes No

26. I place a dollar value on my time and
 behave accordingly. Yes No

27. I – not others – control my time. Yes No

28. My briefcase includes items I can work on
 during spare time in waiting rooms, lines,
 and airports. Yes No

29. I keep my door shut when I'm working. Yes No

30. I regularly evaluate to what degree I am
 achieving my stated goals. Yes No

clear patterns will emerge. You may learn that you have an "open door" policy that enables others to control your time, leaving little time to do your own work. Based on this information, you may need to close your door and be more selective about access. You may find from your analysis that you use most time for activities that have few if any important outcomes. If this is the case, then you may need to set goals and prioritize daily activities.

A simple yet effective technique for improving your time management practices is to complete a "to do" list for each day. You can purchase tablets of these forms in many stationery and office supply stores, or you can develop your own "Things To Do Today" list. This list also should prioritize which activities are most important to accomplish each day. Include at the top of your list a particular job search activity or several activi-

Start monitoring your time use and then gradually re-organize your time according to goals and priorities.

ties that should be completed on each day. If you follow this simple time management practice, you will find the necessary time to include your job search in your daily routines. You can give your job search top priority. Better still, you will accomplish more in less time, and with better results.

Plan to Take Action

While we recommend that you plan your job search, we also caution you to avoid the excesses of too much planning. Like time management, planning should not be all-consuming. Planning makes sense because it focuses attention and directs action toward specific goals and targets. It requires you to set goals and develop strategies for achieving the goals. However, too much planning can blind you to unexpected occurrences and opportunities – that wonderful experience called serendipity. Given the highly decentralized and chaotic nature of the job market, you want to do just enough planning so you will be in a position to take advantage of what will inevitably be unexpected occurrences and opportunities arising from your planned job search activities. Therefore, as you plan your job search, be sure you are flexible enough to take advantage of new opportunities.

Based on our previous discussion of the sequence of job search steps, we outline on page 48 a hypothetical plan for conducting an effective job search. This plan incorporates the individual job search activities over a six-month period. If you phase in the first five job search steps during the

Organization of Job Search Activities

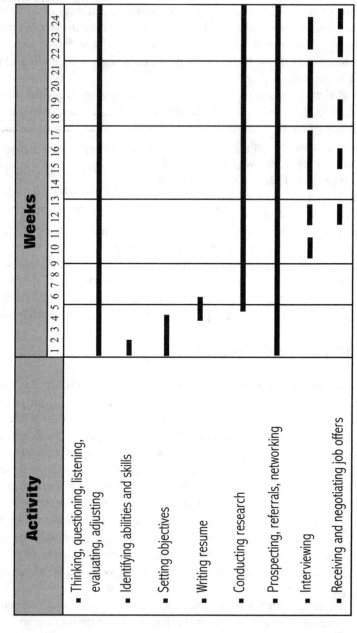

Activity	Weeks
	1 2 3 4 5 6 7 8 9 10 11 12 13 14 15 16 17 18 19 20 21 22 23 24
▪ Thinking, questioning, listening, evaluating, adjusting	
▪ Identifying abilities and skills	
▪ Setting objectives	
▪ Writing resume	
▪ Conducting research	
▪ Prospecting, referrals, networking	
▪ Interviewing	
▪ Receiving and negotiating job offers	

initial three to four weeks and continue the final four steps in subsequent weeks and months, you should begin receiving job offers within two to three months after initiating your job search. Interviews and job offers can come anytime – often unexpectedly – as you conduct your job search. An average time is three months, but it can occur within a week or take as long as five months or more. If you plan, prepare, and persist at the job search, the pay-off will be job interviews and offers.

While three months may seem a long time, especially if you need work immediately, you can shorten your job search time by increasing the frequency of your individual job search activities. If you are job hunting on a full-time basis, you may be able to cut your job search time in half. But don't expect to get a job – especially a job that's right for you – within a week or two. Job hunting requires time and hard work – perhaps the hardest work you will ever do – but if done properly, it pays off with a job that is right for you.

20 Principles for Job Search Success

Success is determined by more than just a good plan getting implemented. We know success is not determined primarily by intelligence, time management, or luck. Based upon experience, theory, research, common sense, and some self-transformation principles, we believe you will achieve job search success by following most of these 20 principles:

1. **You should work hard at finding a job:** Make this a daily endeavor and involve your family. Focus on specifics.

2. **You should not be discouraged by setbacks:** You are playing the odds, so expect disappointments and handle them in stride. You will get many "no's" before finding the one "yes" which is right for you.

3. **You should be patient and persevere:** Expect three to six months of hard work before you connect with the right job.

4. **You should be honest with yourself and others:** Honesty is always the best policy. But don't be naive and stupid by confessing your negatives and shortcomings to others.

5. **You should develop a positive attitude toward yourself:** Nobody wants to employ guilt-ridden people with inferiority complexes. Focus on your positive characteristics.

6. **You should associate with positive and successful people:** Finding a job largely depends on how well you relate to others. Avoid associating with negative and depressing people who complain and have a "you can't do it" attitude. Run with winners who have a positive "can do" outlook on life.

7. **You should set goals:** You should have a clear idea of what you want and where you are going. Without these, you will present a confusing and indecisive image to others. Clear goals direct your job search into productive channels. Setting high goals will help make you work hard to get what you want.

8. **You should plan:** Convert your goals into action steps that are organized as short-, intermediate-, and long-range plans.

9. **You should get organized:** Translate your plans into activities, targets, names, addresses, telephone numbers, and materials. Develop an efficient and effective filing system and use a large calendar to set time targets, record appointments, and compile useful information.

10. **You should be a good communicator:** Take stock of your oral, written, and nonverbal communication skills. How well do you communicate? Since most aspects of your job search involve communicating with others, and communication skills are one of the most sought-after skills, always present yourself well both verbally and nonverbally.

11. **You should be energetic and enthusiastic:** Employers are attracted to positive people. They don't like negative and depressing people who toil at their work. Generate enthusiasm both verbally and nonverbally. Check on your telephone voice with a friend or relative – it may be more unenthusiastic than your face-to-face voice.

12. **You should ask questions:** Your best information comes from asking questions. Learn to develop intelligent questions that are non-aggressive, polite, and interesting to others. But don't ask too many questions and thereby become a bore.

13. **You should be a good listener:** Being a good listener is often more important than being a good questioner or talker. Learn to

improve your face-to-face listening behavior (nonverbal cues) as well as remember and use information gained from others. Make others feel they enjoyed talking with you, i.e., you are one of the few people who actually **listens** to what they say.

14. **You should be civil, which means being polite, courteous, and thoughtful:** Treat gatekeepers, especially receptionists, like human beings. Avoid being aggressive. Try to be polite, courteous, and gracious. Your social graces are being observed. Remember to send thank you letters – a very thoughtful thing to do in a job search. Even if rejected, thank employers for the "opportunity." They may later have additional opportunities, and they will remember you.

15. **You should be tactful:** Watch what you say to others about people. Don't be a gossip, back-stabber, or confessor. Avoid talking ill of others, especially previous employers and colleagues.

16. **You should maintain a professional stance:** Be neat in what you do and wear, and speak with the confidence, authority, and maturity of a professional.

17. **You should demonstrate your intelligence and competence:** Present yourself as someone who gets things done and achieves results – a **producer.** Employers generally seek people who are bright, hard working, responsible, communicate well, have positive personalities, maintain good interpersonal relations, are likable, observe dress and social codes, take initiative, are talented, possess expertise in particular areas, use good judgment, are cooperative, trustworthy, and loyal, generate confidence and credibility, and are conventional. In other words, they like people who score in the "excellent" to "outstanding" categories of a performance evaluation. Above all, they want memorable people who are talented, dependable, and predictable – those they can turn to with confidence for solving problems.

18. **You should not overdo your job search:** Don't engage in overkill and bore everyone with your "job search" stories. Achieve balance in everything you do. Occasionally take a few days off to do nothing related to your job search. Develop a system of incentives and rewards – such as two non-job search days a week, if you accomplish targets A, B, C, and D.

19. **You should be open-minded and keep an eye open for "luck":** Too much planning can blind you to unexpected and fruitful opportunities. You should welcome serendipity. Learn to re-evaluate your goals and strategies. Seize new opportunities if appropriate.

20. **You should evaluate your progress and adjust:** Take two hours once every two weeks and evaluate your accomplishments. If necessary, tinker with your plans and reorganize your activities and priorities. Don't become too routinized and thereby kill creativity and innovation.

These principles should provide you with an initial orientation for starting your job search. As you become more experienced at finding a job, you will develop your own set of operating principles that should work for you.

Take Risks and Handle Rejections

You can approach a job or career change in various ways. Some actions have higher pay-offs than others. Many people waste time by doing nothing, reconstructing the past, worrying about the future, and thinking about what they should have done. This negative approach impedes rather than advances careers.

A second approach is to do what most people do when looking for a job. They examine classified ads, respond to vacancy announcements, put their resume online, and complete applications in personnel offices or online. While this approach is better than doing nothing, it is relatively inefficient as well as ineffective. You compete with many others who are using the same approach. Furthermore, the vacancy announcements do not represent the true number of job vacancies, nor do they offer the best opportunities. As we will see later, you should use this approach to some degree, but it should not preoccupy your time. Responding to vacancy announcements is a game of chance, and the odds are usually against you. It makes you too dependent upon others to give you a job.

The third approach to making a job change requires **taking creative action** on your part. You must become a self-reliant risk-taker. You identify what it is you want to do, what you can do (acquired skills and catalogued accomplishments), and organize yourself accordingly by following the methods outlined in subsequent chapters. You don't need to spend much time with classified ads, employment agencies, personnel offices, and Internet recruitment sites. And you don't need to worry about your

future. You take charge of your future by initiating a job search that pays off with interviews and job offers. Your major investment is **time**. Your major risk is **rejection**.

Job hunting is a highly ego-involved activity. You place your past, abilities, and self-image before strangers who don't know who you are or what you can do. Being rejected or having someone say "no" to you will probably be your greatest job hunting difficulty. We know most people can handle two or three "no's" before they get discouraged. If you approach your job search from a less ego-involved perspective, you can take "no's" in stride; they are a normal aspect of your job search experience. Be prepared to encounter 10, 20, or 50 "no's." Remember, the odds are in your favor. For every 20 "no's" you get, you also should uncover one or two "yeses." The more rejections you get, the more acceptances you also will get. Therefore, you must encounter rejections **before** you get acceptances.

This third approach is the approach of this book. Experience with thousands of clients shows that the most successful job seekers are those who develop a high degree of self-reliance, maintain a positive self-image, and are willing to risk being rejected time after time without becoming discouraged. This approach will work for you if you follow our advice on how to become a self-reliant risk-taker in today's job market. Better yet, use the networking strategies outlined in this book as well as more fully developed in the two books by Ron and Caryl Krannich, *Interview for Success* and *The Savvy Networker*, and you can significantly decrease the number of "no's" you receive on your way to a job that's right for you.

Consider Forming a Support Group

We believe most people can conduct a successful job search on their own by following the step-by-step procedures of this book. We know they work because these methods have been used by thousands of successful job hunters. We also know it's difficult to become a risk-taker, especially in an area where few people have a base of experience and knowledge. Therefore, we recommend sharing the risks with others.

Self-directed methods work well when you join others in forming a job search group or club. The group provides a certain degree of security that is often necessary when launching a new and unknown adventure. In addition, the group can provide important information on job leads. Members will critique your approach and progress. They will provide you with psychological supports as you experience the frustration of rejections and the joys of success. You also will be helping others who will be helping you. Some career counselors estimate that membership in such

groups can cut one's job search time by as much as 50 percent!

You can form your own group by working with your spouse or by finding friends who are interested in looking for a new job. Your friends may know other friends or colleagues who are interested in doing the same. Some of your friends may surprise you by indicating they would like to join your group out of curiosity. If you are over 40 years of age, check to see if there is a chapter of the 40-Plus Club (www.40plus.org/chapters) or Five O'Clock Club (www.fiveoclockclub.com) in your community. These groups are organized as job search clubs.

Your group should meet regularly – once a week. At the meetings discuss your experiences, critique each other's approaches and progress, reward those who have accepted their weekly goals, and share information on what you are learning or what you feel you need to know more about and do more effectively. Include your spouse in this group. You'll quickly discover that you are not alone, rejections will be easier to handle when shared with others, and you're acquire invaluable advice for fine tuning your job search.

Professional Assistance and Honesty

One other aspect of this self-directed book should be clarified. We recommend that you first read this book **before** seeking professional assistance. A professional career counselor, for example, can provide important assistance at certain stages, depending on individual needs. Take, for example, the chapter which focuses on skills identification. While we present the necessary information for you to identify your skills, you may wish to enhance this step of the job search with the assistance of a professional career counselor who has access to more sophisticated testing instruments for meeting your assessment needs.

On the other hand, if you bring to your job search certain health and psychological problems which affect your job performance, you should seek professional help rather than try to solve your problems with this book. This is especially true for those with addiction problems who really need some form of professional therapy before putting into practice the job search steps identified here. If you are in serious financial trouble or a separation or divorce is greatly troubling you, seek professional help. Only after you get yourself together physically and mentally will this book produce its intended results for you. Remember, no employer wants to hire alcohol, drug, mental health, financial, or marital problems. They want productive, job-centered individuals who are capable of handling their personal problems.

You must be honest with yourself before you can be honest with others. The whole philosophy underlying this book is one of personal honesty and integrity in everything you do related to your job search.

Risk Implementation

Understanding without action is a waste of time. And buying a how-to book without implementing it is a waste of money. Many people read how-to books, attend how-to seminars, and do nothing other than read more books, attend more seminars, and engage in more wishful thinking. While these activities become forms of therapy for some individuals, they should lead to positive actions for you.

Throughout this book we stress the importance of understanding the job market and developing appropriate job search strategies for getting the job you want. We make no assumptions nor claim any magic is contained in this book. Rather, we have attempted to assemble useful information to help you organize an effective job search that will best communicate your qualifications to potential employers. Individual chapters examine the present and future job markets as well as outline in how-to terms specific skills for shaping your own future.

The methods outlined in this book have worked for thousands of individuals who paid thousands of dollars to get similar information from highly paid professionals. While you may want to see a professional for assistance at certain steps in your job search, if you are self-motivated, you can do everything outlined in this book on your own and with a minimum expenditure of money. The major cost will be your time and effort. However, if you feel you need professional assistance, by all means seek out the best professionals to help you with your job search.

Get Motivated and Work Hard

Assuming you have a firm understanding of each job search step and how to relate them to your goals, what do you do next? The next steps involve **motivation and hard work**. Just how motivated are you to seek a new job or career and thus change your life? Our experience is that individuals need to be sufficiently **motivated** to make the first move and do it properly. If you go about your job search half-heartedly – you just want to "test the waters" to see what's out there – don't expect to be successful. You must be committed to achieving specific goals. Make the decision to properly develop and implement your job search and be prepared to work hard in achieving your goals.

Find Time

Once you've convinced yourself to take the necessary steps to find a job or change and advance your career, you need to find the **time** to properly implement your job search. This requires setting aside specific blocks of time for identifying your motivated abilities and skills, developing your resume, writing letters, making telephone calls, and conducting the necessary research and networking required for success. This whole process takes time. If you are a busy person, like most people, you simply must make the time. As noted earlier in this chapter about time management practices, you should practice your own versions of time management. Get better organized, give some things up, or cut back on all your activities. If, for example, you can set aside one hour each day to devote to your job search, you will spend seven hours a week or 28 hours a month on your search. However, you should and can find more time than this for these activities.

Time and again we find successful job hunters are the ones who routinize specific job search activities. They make contact after contact, conduct numerous informational interviews, submit many applications and resumes, and keep repeating these activities in spite of encountering rejections. They learn that success is just a few more "no's" and informational interviews away. They face each day with a positive attitude fit for someone desiring to change their life – **I must collect my ten "no's" today because each "no" brings me closer to another "yes"**!

Commit Yourself in Writing

You may find it helpful to commit yourself in writing to achieving job search success. This is a very useful way to get both motivated and directed for action. Start by completing the job search contract on page 57 and keep it near you – in your briefcase, on your desk, or on your computer with a calendar reminder to review it frequently.

In addition, you should complete weekly performance reports. These reports identify what you actually accomplished rather than what your good intentions tell you to do. Make copies of the performance and planning report form on page 58 and use one each week to track your actual progress and to plan your activities for the next week.

If you fail to meet these written commitments, issue yourself a revised and updated contract. But if you do this three or more times, we strongly suggest you stop kidding yourself about your commitment to find a job. Start over again, but this time consult a professional career counselor who can assist you with your job search. A professional may not be cheap, but

if paying for help gets you on the right track and results in the job you want, it's money well spent. Do not be *"penny wise but pound foolish"* with your future. If you must seek professional advice, be sure you are an informed consumer according to our advice on "shopping for a professional" in Chapter 6.

Feel Free to Change Jobs and Careers

Careers and jobs should not be viewed as life sentences. You should feel free to change jobs and careers when you want to or need to. In fact, millions of people make successful career transitions each year. Some are more successful than others in finding the right job. If you plan your career transition according to the methods outlined in this book and focus on your accomplishments, you should be able to successfully land the job you want – one you do well and really enjoy doing.

Treat yourself right. Take the time and effort to sail into today's job market with a plan of action that links your qualifications to the needs of employers. You are first and foremost an individual with knowledge, abilities, and skills that many employers need and want. If you follow the advice of this book, you will put your best foot forward in communicating your qualifications to employers.

Job Search Contract

1. I'm committed to changing my life by changing my job. Today's date is _____.

2. I will manage my time so that I can successfully complete my job search and find a high quality job. I will complete my time management inventory (pages 15-16) and begin changing my time management behavior on _____.

3. I will begin my job search on _____.

4. I will involve _____ with my job search.
 (individual/group)

5. I will spend at least one week conducting library research on different jobs, employers, and organizations. I will begin this research during the week of _____.

6. I will complete my skills identification step by _____.

7. I will complete my objective statement by _____.

8. I will complete my resume by _____.

9. Each week I will:

 ▪ make _____ new job contacts.

 ▪ conduct _____ informational interviews.

 ▪ follow up on _____ referrals.

10. My first job interview will take place during the week of _____.

11. I will begin my new job by _____.

12. I will make a habit of learning one new skill each year.

Signature: _____

Date: _____

Weekly Job Performance and Planning Report

1. The week of: _____.

2. This week I:

 - wrote ____ job search letters.
 - sent ____ resumes and ____ letters to potential employers.
 - completed ____ applications.
 - made ____ job search telephone calls.
 - completed ____ hours of job research.
 - set up ____ appointments for informational interviews.
 - conducted ____ informational interviews.
 - received ____ invitations to a job interview.
 - followed up on ____ contacts and ____ referrals.

3. Next week I will:

 - write ____ job search letters.
 - send ____ resumes and ____ letters to potential employers.
 - complete ____ applications.
 - make ____ job search telephone calls.
 - complete ____ hours of job research.
 - set up ____ appointments for informational interviews.
 - conduct ____ informational interviews.
 - follow up on ____ contacts and ____ referrals.

4. Summary of progress this week in reference to my Job Search
 Contract commitments:

4

Changing Trends, Jobs, Careers, and Employers

WHETHER OR NOT WE REALIZE IT, we all have some image of the future that influences important decisions in our lives. If you are getting ready to leave the military, you've probably imagined or dreamed about what you will be doing in the civilian world over the next few years. If you are a veteran with experience in the civilian work world, you may have some sense of what you don't want to do as well as what you want to do with the rest of your life. After working in one or two civilian jobs, you may still be trying to find a job that best fits your interests, skills, and lifestyle.

We all want to predict the future to some degree. You would not, for example, purchase a new home, relocate to another community, or change jobs unless you first projected what the future might hold for you over the next three, five, or ten years. To help you do this, let's take a look at what the future may bring in the world of work and how you might best deal with this future.

Getting Oriented

What type of job or career most interests you? Will it be related to your military background or take a new direction? Are you just looking for a paycheck, or do you want a job directly related to your interests, skills, goals, and dreams? Do you have many interests and lots of experience which are difficult to narrow down to a specific civilian job? Are you looking in many different directions but without a clue as to what you

want to do? Have you already decided where you want to live but you're not sure about employment opportunities? Is your spouse also planning to look for a job? Do you need to explore job and career alternatives before launching your job search, or do you just want to start hitting the ground running and, in the process, let serendipity run its course in discovering various job alternatives appropriate for you?

A New and Challenging Work World

How well do you understand today's civilian job market and the many trends that could affect your career future? This chapter is designed as a quick primer to today's changing job market and how it may relate to you as a job seeker. It often challenges you to think outside the box when planning your career. Since you come from an organizational culture that values loyalty, team work, and a vertical command and control structure, you'll need to reorient yourself to multiple organizational cultures in the civilian world. In the civilian sector, loyalty is no longer a central value, and horizontal relationships are often more important than vertical authority governed by well defined rules and regulations. While team work and group think are ostensibly central values, so too are individual achievement, creativity, and innovation. Entrepreneurism, which challenges existing practices and results in competitive edges and increased profitability, is especially valued in the civilian world.

Where to Live and Work

Decisions, decisions, decisions. Many become the proverbial chicken or the egg decisions. Which should come first, the job or the community?

Many ex-military decide where they want to live before securing employment in or around their new community. Perhaps you would like to move to a lovely community in Virginia, Florida, Georgia, North Carolina, Colorado, or California. But what about finding employment in this place? Unfortunately, some people make the move before securing a job and then discover there are few jobs available for someone with their interests and skills. After struggling to find a job, they settle for one that's really not right for them, but it does pay the bills. After awhile, they may become unhappy where they live because of the lack of job opportunities. Again, anyone can find a job, but finding one you really do well and enjoy doing is what you should be focusing on in your job search.

We strongly recommend making employment decisions **before** making a relocation decision. Decide where you would like to move, but be sure to explore the local job market and secure a job before making the move.

Where In the World Do You Want to Work?

Will your future job and career relate to your previous work in the military, or are you interested in acquiring new skills and pursuing a new career in the civilian world? Are you primarily looking for a job in government where you will have an application advantage because of Veterans Preferences? What about working in the private sector with a large corporation, medium-size company, or a small business? In fact, 85 percent of all employees work for small businesses.

Perhaps you can work for a firm that has government contracts with the military and intelligence communities. Known as the "Beltway Bandits" in the Washington, DC metropolitan area, these firms hire hundreds of ex-military to work on a variety of military- and intelligence-related contracts.

Have you thought of a job or career that has a social purpose? If so, have you considered working for a nonprofit organization, association, or school? What about becoming a teacher in a public or private school? Perhaps you should contact the "Troops to Teachers" program (www.nc troops.org, Tel. 800- 452-6616) for information on special teaching opportunities for transitioning military.

What about working for yourself as a freelancer, consultant, or businessperson? Are you entrepreneurial enough to start your own business? Perhaps you can buy a business, acquire a franchise, or start a business from scratch. Do you have the right stuff to make it on your own as an entrepreneur? If you're interested in going into business for yourself, check out the relevant resources in Impact's *The Entrepreneurial Veteran Kit* at www.impactpublications.com as well as review the advice and resources in Chapter 19.

Changing Economic and Employment Trends

We're not sure how closely you have followed the ups and downs of the civilian job market over the past decade or two. As you enter this market, you should be aware of several trends that can affect your job search and your long-term employment future. These trends are affected by the larger demographic and technological changes taking place within society.

We see 40 important changes and trends emerging in the areas of job creation, unemployment, youth, elderly, minorities, women, immigrants, part-time employment, service jobs, education and training, unions and labor-management relations, urban-rural shifts, regionalism, small businesses and entrepreneurship, compensation, advancement opportunities, and relocation. Together these changes point to new challenges and

opportunities for job and career changers. You may want to incorporate some of these trends into your future plans, especially if you expect to acquire new skills, pursue a particular career field, or start a business.

TREND 1: A shortage of competent workers, with basic literacy and learning skills, creates serious problems in developing a strong U.S. economy.

Given the double whammy of nearly 30 million functionally illiterate adults – or one-sixth of the potential labor force unable to read, write, or perform simple computations – and the availability of fewer easily trainable young entry-level workers, a large portion of the workforce is destined to remain at the lowest end of the job market despite the fact that two to three million new jobs are created each year. Most of these adults will remain permanently unemployed or underemployed, contributing little to economic growth, while major labor shortages exist. As skill requirements rise rapidly for those who are both entering and advancing within the workforce, the nation's economic development will slow due to the lack of skilled workers. Both public and private sector worker literacy, basic education, and training programs will continue to expand, but their contribution to improving the overall skill levels of the workforce will be minimal. The American economy and workforce increasingly show classic signs of Second and Third World economies – potential economic performance outstrips, and is limited by, the availability of a skilled workforce.

TREND 2: A renewed and strong U.S. manufacturing sector will create few new jobs; face-to-face service industries will be responsible for most job growth in the decade ahead.

Despite popular notions of the "decline" of American manufacturing industries, these industries are following the model of American agriculture – increased productivity accompanied by the increased displacement of workers. American manufacturing industry is becoming one of the strongest economic sectors in terms of production output but the weakest sector in terms of its contribution to job growth and job creation. At the same time, American

manufacturing has already moved in the direction of Peter Drucker's "production sharing system" by exporting or outsourcing the remaining high-cost, labor-intensive aspects of the industries. As large manufacturing companies rebounded in recent years by becoming more productive with smaller and more highly skilled workforces, most new manufacturing jobs will continue to develop among small manufacturing "job shops" employing fewer than 50 workers. Face-to-face service industries, especially those in finance, retail, food, and health care, will continue to expand their workforces in the decade ahead. These industries also will experience major "productivity" and "management" improvements, much of which took place in other industries that "reinvented" themselves in the previous decade, due to (1) major labor shortages, (2) increased competition, (3) greater emphasis on customer service, and (4) the adaptation of new technology to what had become increasingly inefficient, high-cost, labor-intensive service industries, especially in the retail and health care industries.

TREND 3: **Be careful what you wish for when acquiring education and training for today's so-called hot jobs and careers. In the coming decade, expect keen competition both at home and abroad for several white-collar and professional jobs, because of continuing outsourcing of these jobs to cheap and skilled labor markets abroad. Many of the safest jobs will be for blue-collar workers with a high school education.**

The past decade has been a turbulent one for jobs and careers in America. A recurring boom/bust and cowboy/casino economy (described in Ron Krannich's *Change Your Job, Change Your Life*, 9th edition, Impact Publications, 2005) created millions of new jobs as well as witnessed the disappearance of millions of other jobs. Some jobs and their occupants became victims of **structural unemployment** (permanent displacement of old-economy jobs due to technological advances that make industries and skills obsolete, such as slide-rule, VCR, and film camera makers) while others experienced **cyclical unemployment** (temporary business downturns that rebound with improved economic conditions, such as real estate and

automobile manufacturing). And still others have become unemployed due to the **outsourcing and offshoring** of jobs to cheaper labor markets at home and abroad. One result of these changes is what many observers optimistically refer to as the New Economy – an unpredictable high-tech driven economy that is constantly evolving within a rapidly changing global economy.

One of the major implications of today's uncertain New Economy is clearly expressed in a key question millions of individuals ask themselves each year:

> How should I prepare for the future when I don't know what the good jobs will look like in the future? After all, a so-called "hot job" today could well become another victim of structural, cyclical, or outsourced unemployment within the next decade!

This question becomes increasingly important in what was termed a "jobless recovery" in the highly charged political environment of 2003-2004 – economic growth accelerated due to increased productivity, but this growth was not part of the traditional pattern of cyclical unemployment. Jobs that normally would return to the American economy were, instead, outsourced to other countries. According to Goldman Sachs (_Forbes_, April 12, 2004: 98), between 2001 and 2003 nearly 400,000 service jobs and 1 million manufacturing jobs in the U.S. were lost to offshoring. Between 2004 and 2013, another 3.3 million white-collar jobs ($136 billion in wages) are expected to be offshored. Many of these jobs used to be considered hot growth jobs within the U.S. that required various levels of higher education – engineer, radiologist, software designer, and accountant. Many of these jobs can now be easily offshored to Bangalore, Shanghai, Hong Kong, Manila, Singapore, Kuala Lumpur, or Penang.

Offshoring of white-collar jobs, many of which require a college degree, appears to be a new and perhaps permanent pattern of employment change in America. This new phenomenon has developed in response to structural changes in the global economy brought about by the convergence of seven important developments:

1. improved Internet connections
2. increased bandwidth
3. powerful fiber optic cable
4. cheap international telecom prices
5. large pool of well-educated and trained English-speaking workers in several developing countries
6. efficient international transportation links and delivery services
7. enhanced global organization and management systems

White-collar jobs that were once part of cyclical unemployment were increasingly absorbed into a new form of structural unemployment – the geographic shift of jobs to cheaper labor markets. Creation of new jobs to replace what were once attractive value-added jobs supporting the middle- and upper-middle classes in the American economy perplexed many politicians, economists, and employment specialists, who seemed to be at a loss to identify new and better paying jobs that normally replaced the ones lost to outsourcing and offshoring. Instead, many of tomorrow's **safe jobs** are low-wage face-to-face jobs in the food, entertainment, health care, hospitality, transportation, and personal services industries or minimum-wage part-time and temporary jobs. Requiring only a high school education, many of these jobs offer limited benefits and little career advancement.

At the same time, many other safe jobs can be found in the construction, home improvement, and auto repair trades – carpenters, electricians, plumbers, HVAC specialists, masons, and mechanics. Many of these jobs pay very well and do not require four-year degrees. Indeed, carpenters, electricians, plumbers, and masons making $125+ an hour or earning over $100,000 a year are not uncommon these days.

TREND 4: Employment security and income may no longer be tied to higher levels of education.

During the past few decades, individuals have been well advised to get a college education in order to succeed in the increasingly degree-oriented white-collar world of work. In fact, most studies have shown that individuals with a four-

year college degree earn more than those without a college degree. According to the U.S. Department of Labor in 2002, education definitely pays off in terms of employment security and earnings:

Unemployment rate in 2002 (percent)	Education attained	Median earnings in 2001 (dollars)
2.8	Master's degree	$56,600
3.1	Bachelor's degree	$47,000
4.0	Associate degree	$36,400
4.8	Some college, no degree	$34,300
5.3	High school graduate	$29,200
9.2	Some high school, no diploma	$22,400

However, this pattern may be changing because of a global economy that places highly educated and skilled workers from low-wage countries in direct competition with similarly skilled high-wage earners in America. In other words, your education level in the future will most likely give you a distinct employment and economic advantage in safe jobs – face-to-face jobs that are difficult to offshore. Consequently, you are well advised to avoid becoming educated for jobs that are likely to disappear in the future due to global outsourcing and automation.

In the past most structural employment affected industries and blue-collar jobs that did not require college degrees. Until recently, most outsourcing of jobs to Mexico, Guatemala, China, Indonesia, Thailand, and India affected lower-level manufacturing jobs that required limited education and training. Many of these were low-wage jobs in the textile, clothing, footwear, electronics, furniture, and home furnishings industries. However, within the past few years, outsourcing has increasingly affected white-collar jobs that traditionally required a college degree. This is especially true in the service industries and once hot growth field of information technology.

As a result, an old rule of the employment game, which your mother and teachers articulated – _"get a college education and you'll have a safe and secure employment future,"_ may be eroding in the new high-tech and service-oriented global economy. Today many jobs requiring a

college degree are no longer safe and secure jobs. These jobs are becoming increasingly susceptible to productivity gains and offshoring to low-wage countries that have highly educated and skilled English-speaking populations, such as India, China, Malaysia, and the Philippines. For example, a $70,000 a year software developer in the United States can be replaced with a talented $20,000 a year software developer in Bangalore, India. A $50,000 a year Web designer in the United States can be replaced with a $15,000 a year Web designer in the Philippines, Egypt, or the Ukraine. A $40,000 a year technical support job in the United States can be offshored to Romania, Ukraine, Costa Rica, or Cambodia for less than $15,000 a year. Many hot high-tech jobs of the 1990s can now be offshored to other countries at a fraction of the labor costs incurred in the United States.

Given competitive pressures coupled with today's new technologies and global communication systems, many traditional back office functions can be easily offshored. In fact, a 2005 survey of America's 100 largest companies, conducted by Duke University's Fuqua School of Business and Archstone Consulting, found that human resources, accounting, and finance will be three of the most offshored functions by 2008. Major corporations, especially banks, anticipate significant cost savings and growth opportunities by offshoring thousands of their human resources, accounting, and finance jobs. Offshoring of tax accounting and strategic planning functions is expected to soon follow. India is expected to account for 41 percent of all accounting and finance offshoring. Ironically, managing the supply chain of offshored functions should become one of the hot – and safe – jobs in the decade ahead!

Despite political controversies surrounding this phenomenon (calls for protectionism and trade barriers), such outsourcing and job losses are likely to accelerate in the foreseeable future as the global economy develops into a competitive and global job market where many white-collar jobs will go to the lowest bidder.

Many students pursuing a four-year degree today may find themselves studying in occupational fields that are especially susceptible to offshoring. Many of the best jobs in the decade ahead will be for people without a four-year

degree (see Ron and Caryl Krannich, *America's Top 100 Jobs for People Without a Four-Year Degree*, Impact Publications, 2005). These jobs have a safe and secure future that may soon challenge the standard college-to-career "best jobs" assumption of the past few decades. Indeed, many of the best jobs (high paying and secure) in the future do not require a four-year degree. Accordingly, many individuals with four-year degrees are starting to get re-trained for these increasingly desirable jobs that appear safe and secure for building a long-term career.

TREND 5: Many safe jobs a decade ago are no longer safe because of increased downsizing and outsourcing.

Downsizing and outsourcing have been going on in America for years as companies attempt to cut high labor and overhead costs as well as improve productivity and growth through the use of new technology. Indeed, many companies have moved their operations from high-cost urban centers to low-cost towns and rural areas. For example, in 1989, Philadelphia-based Rosenbluth International, once the nation's largest travel management company (acquired by American Express in 2004), moved many of its back office operations to Fargo, North Dakota. It recently decided to offshore its Fargo, North Dakota operations to an even lower-cost labor market in India. As you may already know, some of the largest telemarketing and customer service operations in the United States are centered in military communities such as Norfolk, Virginia and San Diego, California, which disproportionately employ low-wage military spouses. However, many of these jobs are no longer safe jobs since they can be easily offshored to countries with well trained English speakers.

Given the increased capacity of employers to offshore all types of jobs, you may want to carefully consider whether or not your chosen career path is likely to be susceptible to outsourcing at home or abroad. In fact, many of today's safe jobs do not require a college degree and some only require short- or moderate-term training. Most of these jobs require a physical presence in a community. For example, safety and security, health care, transportation, hospitality, delivery, repair services, building construction, and lawn care are relatively safe jobs. Unsafe jobs include any that

can be performed abroad, via the Internet or telephone, and/or use efficient shipping and delivery services – many manufacturing, back office (accounting, insurance, billing, collections), health care (radiology), engineering, software development, and design functions.

TREND 6: **Unemployment remains very cyclical, fluctuating between a low of 4 percent and a high of 8 percent.**

These fluctuations are attributed to a combination of boom-and-bust cycles in the economy as well as the persistence of structural unemployment exacerbated by millions of functionally illiterate adults on the periphery of the economy. In addition, millions of other Americans will be underemployed in low-paying entry-level positions which offer little or no career advancement.

TREND 7: **Government efforts to stimulate employment growth continue to be primarily concentrated at the periphery of the job market.**

Most government programs aimed at generating jobs and resolving unemployment problems will be aimed at the poor and unskilled. These groups also are the least likely to relocate, use job search skills, develop standard work habits, or be trained in skills for tomorrow's job market. Given the mixed results from such programs, the government eventually develops workfare programs as well as contracts out this class of unemployed to government contractors who will provide them with education and training along with work experience.

TREND 8: **While the U.S. regained its competitive international trade position in the latter half of the 1990s, it is in danger of losing its dominant position in the first decade of the 21st century.**

International and domestic issues become closely tied to employment issues. Emphasis shifts to issues of economic growth, unemployment, productivity, population, consumption, and regional conflicts in Eastern Europe, the independent states of the former Soviet Union, the Middle East, Asia, and other Third and Fourth World countries

that threaten the stability of international markets and thus long-term economic and employment growth in the U.S. New regional trading blocs play a central role in redefining the international economy. Economic, trade, and employment issues take center stage in restructuring a highly unstable international arena. More and more jobs in the U.S. are increasingly tied to the vicissitudes of the global economy and the value of the U.S. dollar. The U.S. economy, with its deficit-ridden federal government, is especially vulnerable to high energy costs, currency trading, increased inflation, a recurring bubble economy, and a substantially weakened U.S. dollar due to several domestic and international misadventures.

TREND 9: A series of domestic and international crises – shocks and "unique events" – are likely to emerge in the early 21st century, creating new boom-and-bust cycles contributing to unemployment.

The most likely sources for the international crises will be problems developing among former communist regimes, poor Third and Fourth World nations, and counties with radical Islamic movements: the disintegration of the nation-states in the former Soviet Union and a few former communist regimes in Eastern Europe; energy and precious metals shortages due to a depletion of current stocks and regional military conflicts; the collapse of financial markets due to default on international debts; dislocation of lucrative resource and consumption markets because of continued wars in the Middle East, Africa, and South Asia; and terrorist movements tied to radical Islamists. The most likely domestic crises center on financial markets, real estate, energy, water, weather, and the environment. Crises in the banking, energy, and telecommunications markets once again create major debt, credit, and bankruptcy problems for the U.S. economy. An energy crisis creates a new boom for the economies of Texas, Colorado, and Alaska. A new crisis – water shortages – in the Southwest, further slows employment growth in Southern California and Arizona. Environmental issues, such as acid rain, air and water pollution, and global warming, emerge as important international and domestic crises. Major health issues and potential international pandemics, such as

HIV/AIDS and avian flu, create new crises threatening millions of people worldwide. Earthquakes, hurricanes, and tornados create economic shocks to regional economies as well as affect the overall national economy.

TREND 10: **New jobs will be created at the rate of 1 to 2 million each year, with some boom years resulting in the creation of more than 3 million jobs annually.**

The good news is that employment will increase in most occupations in the decade ahead, with export-oriented industries leading the way toward economic growth. Economic expansion in the service sector, coupled with the low productivity and low cost of labor in many parts of the service sector, contributes over 90 percent of all new jobs. Large-scale manufacturing experiences labor declines while small-scale manufacturing "job shops" contribute most of the minimal job growth in the manufacturing sector. The labor declines will be offset by increases in related service jobs, especially in manufacturing sales and marketing.

TREND 11: **Major shortages of skilled craftspeople will create numerous production, distribution, and service problems in the coming decade.**

During the past two decades the number of apprenticeship programs declined significantly; fewer individuals received training in blue-collar occupations; and interest among the young in blue-collar trades declined markedly. The impact of these changes will continue to be felt in the early 21st century as production and service industries requiring highly skilled craftspeople experience labor shortages; distribution of products and services will be uneven. Despite government efforts to revitalize apprenticeship programs, expect to personally encounter the effects of such labor shortages – long waits for servicing your automobile and for repairing your home and major appliances as well as very expensive charges for such services.

TREND 12: **As the baby boomers move into retirement and as the birth rate continues at a near zero-population growth rate, fewer young people will be available for entry-level positions in the coming decade.**

Businesses will recruit and train more of the hard-core unemployed, unskilled, immigrants, the elderly, and people with disabilities; they will automate; and/or they will contract for cheap offshore labor for everything from accounting, marketing, and computing services to manufacturing jobs. As a result, more stopgap job opportunities will be available for individuals losing their jobs or wishing to change jobs or careers.

TREND 13: Retirement practices continue to be transformed. More job and career choices will be available for the elderly who are either dissatisfied with traditional retirement or who no longer can afford the high costs of retirement.

As the workforce increasingly ages, traditional retirement practices will change. Many people will never retire, preferring instead part-time or self-employment in their later years. Others will retire from one job and then start a new career after age 50. A continuing financial crisis in the Social Security system results in declining Social Security benefits. Fewer Social Security benefits and higher costs of retirement will further transform retirement practices and systems in the decade ahead. Expect to see more elderly working in the McDonald's and 7-Eleven stores of tomorrow alongside many immigrants who now staff these companies.

TREND 14: More minorities – especially those with disproportionately high birth rates, low education and skill levels, and low economic status – will enter the job market.

A large proportion of minorities will occupy the less skilled entry-level, service positions where they will exhibit marked language, class, and cultural differences. Upwardly mobile minorities may find advancement opportunities blocked because of the glut of supervisors, managers, and executives already in many organizations.

TREND 15: Women will continue to enter the labor market, approaching nearly 90 percent female participation in the labor force. More and more women will enter nontraditional occupations, such as engineering,

construction, high-tech, and sports, which have largely been the preserves of men.

The entry of women into the workforce will continue to accelerate in the decade ahead. This will be due less to the changing role of women than to the economic necessity of women to generate family income in order to survive in an expensive consumer-oriented society. Women will account for two-thirds of the growth in all occupations. They will continue to expand into nontraditional jobs, especially production and management positions. Both men and women in a growing number of two-career families will have greater flexibility to change jobs and careers.

TREND 16: **More immigrants will enter the U.S. – both documented and undocumented – to meet labor shortages at all levels.**

Despite major efforts of the Department of Homeland Security (DHS) to stem the flow of illegal immigrants, labor market demands will require more immigrants to occupy low-paying, entry-level service jobs in the decade ahead. The brain drain of highly skilled scientific and technical workers from developing countries to the U.S. will accelerate. A reverse brain drain – highly skilled immigrants in the U.S. returning to their homelands – also accelerates. Unskilled immigrants will move into service positions vacated by upwardly mobile Americans.

TREND 17: **Part-time and temporary employment opportunities will increase.**

With the increase in two-career families, home-based businesses, and the growing number of retirees from traditional jobs, part-time and temporary employment will become a more normal pattern of employment for millions of Americans. More women, who wish to enter the job market but not as full-time employees, will seek new part-time employment opportunities. Temporary employment services will continue to experience a boom in business as more and more companies attempt to lower personnel costs as well as achieve greater personnel flexibility by hiring larger numbers of temporary employees.

TREND 18: Part-time and contingency workers will constitute a recognized and desirable class of workers.

The number of contingency workers – part-time, temporary, or contract workers – will continue to increase in the decade ahead as businesses try to become more competitive by cutting back costly full-time employees, eliminating generous benefits, lowering health care costs, eliminating pensions, and seeking greater flexibility in hiring and firing employees. Given economic uncertainties, high costs of hiring, and advantages of working with employment firms that manage contingency workers, more and more employers will replace full-time employees with contingency workers. Many businesses employing 100 or fewer employees will routinely use contingency workers to staff at least 30 percent of their positions.

TREND 19: White-collar employment will continue to expand in the fast-growing service sector.

Dramatic growth in service jobs will take place in response to new information technology. The classification of workers into blue- and white-collar occupations, as well as into manufacturing and service jobs, will become meaningless in a service economy dominated by white-collar workers.

TREND 20: The need for a smarter workforce, with specific technical skills, will continue to impact on the traditional education system as both businesses and parents demand greater job and career relevance in educational curricula.

Expensive and overly bureaucratized, many traditional four-year colleges and universities will face stable to declining full-time enrollments as well as the flight of quality faculty to more challenging and lucrative jobs outside academia. Declining enrollments will be due to their slow response to the educational and training skill requirements of the high-tech society; increased competition from private training firms, online training technology, and distance learning groups; and the demographics of fewer numbers in the traditional 18-21 year-old student age population. The flight of quality faculty will be replaced by

less qualified and inexpensive part-time faculty. Most community colleges, as well as specialized private vocational-technical institutions, will adapt to the changing demographics and labor market needs and flourish with programs most responsive to community employment needs. More and more emphasis will be placed on providing efficient short-term, intensive skills-training programs, many of which will be delivered as computer-based and Internet-based individualized training, than on providing traditional degree programs. Career planning will become a major emphasis in education programs.

TREND 21: **Union membership will continue to decline as more blue-collar manufacturing jobs disappear and interest in unions wanes among both blue- and white-collar employees.**

Given declining union membership, unions continue to find themselves on the defensive, with little choice other than to agree to management demands for greater worker productivity and fewer benefits, especially the elimination of costly defined-benefit pensions. In the long run, labor-management relations will shift from the traditional adversarial relationship to one of greater cooperation and participation of labor and management in the decision-making process. Profit sharing and employee ownership will become prominent features of labor-management relations. These changes will contribute to the continuing decline, and eventual disappearance, of traditional unions in many industries.

TREND 22: **The population will continue to move into suburban and semi-rural communities as high-tech industries and services move in this direction.**

Large and older central cities will continue to bear disproportionate welfare, tax, and criminal justice burdens due to their declining industrial bases, deteriorating infrastructures, relatively poor and unskilled populations, and high rates of crime. Urban populations will continue to move into suburban and semi-rural communities. Developing their own economic base, these communities will provide employment for the majority of local residents rather than

serve as bedroom communities from which workers commute to the central city. With few exceptions, and despite noble attempts to "revitalize" downtown areas with new office, shopping, and entertainment complexes, most large central cities will continue to decline as their upwardly mobile residential populations move to the suburbs where they are able to find better jobs, housing, and education; enjoy attractive lifestyles; and experience lower crime rates.

TREND 23: The population, as well as wealth and economic activity, will continue to shift into the Northwest, Southwest, and Florida at the expense of the Northeast and North Central regions.

Nearly 60 percent of the U.S. population now resides in the South and West. These areas also are home for the nation's youngest population. Florida, Georgia, Texas, Colorado, Arizona, Nevada, Utah, and Washington will continue to be the growth states for the decade ahead; construction and local government in these states will experience employment increases. Many states in the Northeast and Midwest, and parts of the South, will experience slow growth due to their declining industrial base, excessive welfare burdens, older population, aging infrastructure, and shrinkage of non-cyclical economic sectors – services, retail trade, and public employment. However, some Midwest states (Ohio, Indiana, Illinois, Wisconsin) will experience strong growth due to important linkages developing between their exceptionally well developed higher educational institutions and high-tech industries which depend on such institutions. Many manufacturing industries in the Midwest, especially auto, will continue to expand as they play an increasingly important role in the expanding U.S. export economy.

TREND 24: In the coming decade the Washington, DC area will remain the country's number one economy for transitioning military personnel and the best place to attend military-friendly job fairs.

Given the continuing growth of the federal government, stimulated by the expansion of the military and homeland security issues, as well as a booming high-tech economy, Washington, DC will offer some of the best job opportuni-

ties for ex-military. Most of these jobs will be found in the federal government and with contracting and consulting firms located in Alexandria and along the Dulles corridor in suburban Virginia. Individuals with security clearances will be in high demand. Transitioning military are well advised to attend several job fairs held in the Washington metropolitan area, which are specifically sponsored for transitioning military personnel and sponsored by such groups as the Military Officers Association of America (MOAA – (www.moaa.org/tops) and Corporate Gray (www.corporate gray.com).

TREND 25: The number of small businesses will continue to increase as new opportunities for entrepreneurs arise in response to the high-tech, Internet, and service revolutions and as more individuals find new opportunities to experiment with changing careers.

Over 900,000 new businesses will be started each year during the coming decade. These businesses will generate 90 percent of all new jobs created each year. The number of business failures will increase accordingly, especially during the bust cycles of the boom/bust economy. Increases in self-employment and small businesses will not provide many new opportunities for career advancement. The small promotion hierarchies of these businesses will help accelerate increased job-hopping and career changes. This new entrepreneurship is likely to breed greater innovation, competition, and productivity.

TREND 26: As large companies continue to downsize, most job growth will take place among small companies and millions of new start-up businesses.

Large Fortune 500 companies will further downsize their operations in the decade ahead. Firms with fewer than 500 employees should generate the most new job growth. Some of the best job opportunities will be with growing companies employing fewer than 50 employees. Large Fortune 500 companies, especially those in service industries, will continue to cut jobs as they attempt to survive intense competition from smaller and more innovative companies, many of which pioneered new forms of e-commerce that threaten traditional "bricks and mortar" businesses. Cut-

backs will further lower the morale of remaining employees, who will seek new job and career opportunities; many will start their own businesses in competition with their former employers.

TREND 27: Opportunities for career advancement will be increasingly limited within most organizations.

Organizations will have difficulty providing career advancement for employees due to (1) the growth of small businesses with short advancement hierarchies, (2) the postponement of retirement, (3) the continuing focus on non-hierarchical forms of organization, and (4) the tendency to hire managers from outside the organization. In the future, many of today's managers will have to find non-managerial positions. Job satisfaction will become less oriented toward advancement up the organizational ladder and more toward such organizational benefits and perks as club memberships, sabbaticals, vacations, retraining opportunities, flexible working hours, family services, and health care packages.

TREND 28: Job satisfaction will become a major problem as many organizations will experience difficulty in retaining highly qualified personnel.

Greater competition, fewer promotions, frustrated expectations, greater discontent, and job-hopping will arise in executive ranks due to limited advancement opportunities. As middle-management positions continue to be eliminated as part of overall downsizing efforts, managerial and executive turnover will increase accordingly. The problem will be especially pronounced for many women and minorities who have traditional aspirations to advance to the top but will be blocked by the glut of managers and executives from the baby boom generation who are trying to survive at both the middle and top of their organizations. Many of these frustrated individuals will become entrepreneurs by starting their own businesses in competition with their former employers.

TREND 29: Many employers will resort to unorthodox hiring practices, improved working conditions, and flexible benefit packages to recruit and retain key personnel.

Hiring and retention of a talented workforce become critical issues for most employers, who face an increasingly competitive business arena in the decade ahead. Facing increased competition for skilled workers, employers will use new and more effective ways of finding and keeping personnel: Internet recruitment; job fair weekends; head-hunters and executive search firms; temporary employment services; raids of competitors' personnel; bonuses to current employees for finding needed personnel; entry-level hiring bonuses for new recruits; stock options; attractive profit-sharing packages for long-term commitments; vacation and travel packages; relocation and housing services; flex-time and job-sharing; home-based work; and daycare services.

TREND 30: Job-hopping will increase as more and more in-dividuals learn how to change careers.

As more job and career opportunities become available for the skilled and savvy worker, as pension systems become more portable, as more individuals use the Internet to browse job opportunities, and as job search and relocation techniques become more widely known, more and more individuals will change jobs and careers in the decade ahead. The typical employee will work in one job and organization for two or three years and then move on to a similar job in another organization. Within 12 years this individual may have acquired new interests and skills and thus decide to change to a new career. Similar three- and 12-year cycles of job and career changes will be repeated by the same individual. Job-hopping will become an accepted and necessary way of getting ahead in the job and career markets of tomorrow.

TREND 31: Geographic relocation will accelerate as more and more individuals become drawn to growing com-munities offering attractive job opportunities.

A favorable real estate market provides incentives to pull up stakes in one community to relocate to another. More and more people will move into the Southeast and West in pursuit of better job and career opportunities.

TREND 32: **The hot jobs in the decade ahead – those offering excellent pay, advancement, and security – will be in health care and high-tech service industries.**

These jobs will require substantial amounts of education, training, and retraining. They also will command top salaries and benefits as well as offer attractive advancement opportunities and numerous career options for individuals interested in changing careers.

TREND 33: **Salaries will only incrementally increase in the decade ahead. In many organizations, executive-level compensation will actually decline as well as be more closely tied to productivity indicators.**

Salary increments will more and more be tied to annual performance evaluations which link pay raises to quantifiable performance indicators. More attractive and portable benefit packages will be offered by organizations seeking to recruit and retain highly skilled workers.

TREND 34: **Benefit packages will undergo increased scrutiny as more and more organizations cut back on personnel expenses.**

Traditional high-cost health insurance and pension plans will be reassessed by employers and subject to cutbacks. More and more employers will require employees to make significant contributions to health insurance and retirement plans. While most employers will offer some form of health insurance, fewer employers will provide company-sponsored defined-benefit retirement plans. Workers can expect to contribute at least 20 percent to the cost of health insurance as well as develop their own retirement plans which will include little or no contribution from employers. More and more employers will opt to hire contingency workers whose benefits are handled by contractors.

TREND 35: **Apprenticeship programs will increase in number as the nation attempts to train and retrain a skilled labor pool for high-demand service industries.**

The coming shortage of skilled labor to service everything from air conditioners to automobiles is directly related to the decline of apprenticeship programs and the lack of

interest in pursuing careers in the trades. The government in cooperation with industry will make a major effort to revitalize such programs. Individuals not pursuing higher education degrees will find excellent career opportunities available through such programs.

TREND 36: **More and more skilled and high-tech service jobs will move offshore as U.S. businesses take advantage of both cheap skilled labor and high-speed communications.**

The next decade will be the decade of the global job market for both skilled and unskilled labor. The stereotypical manufacturing sweatshops with cheap and relatively unskilled labor producing garments, footwear, and toys in China, Indonesia, and India will give way to more high-tech sweatshops in these and many other countries. However, the high-tech sweatshops will focus more and more on the service industries and use skilled labor in Third World countries. For example, given inexpensive high-speed communications, many businesses can now export their accounting, design, telemarketing, and data management functions to India, the Philippines, Mexico, and countries in the Caribbean via the Internet, faxes, and special two- and three-day delivery services (DHL, UPS, Federal Express). Skilled cheap labor will pose a new challenge to the U.S. labor market. While it will help relieve some labor shortages, it also will compete directly with high-wage skilled workers in the U.S.

TREND 37: **The fastest growing jobs in the decade ahead will be for people without a four-year degree.**

A disproportionate number of opportunities will be low-wage, dead-end jobs in the service industries, such as janitors, cafeteria workers, home health aides, security guards, and groundskeepers. Most of these will be face-to-face jobs that cannot be automated nor offshored. While individuals with only a high school diploma and basic literacy skills will find many job opportunities, they also will join the growing ranks of the working poor.

TREND 38: Professional and managerial jobs will continue to grow in the decade ahead and represent some of the best career opportunities available.

At the other end of the job spectrum, the number of well-paying professional and managerial jobs, especially for lawyers, engineers, and nurses, is expected to accelerate in the decade ahead. These jobs require a great deal of education, training, and certification beyond a basic four-year degree. Individuals in these jobs should experience long-term job security as well as advance into well-paying positions. However, many of these people also will experience job burnout and seek to explore more personally rewarding career alternatives.

TREND 39: Individuals will need to take increased responsibility for their employment future, upgrade their learning skills, and behave like entrepreneurs.

The loyalty you learned in the military may not transfer well into the civilian work world where individuals must increasingly take care of their own careers. The old days when you were expected to be a loyal employee who could put your long-term employment fate in the hands of a single employer have all been ended in this new era of multiple jobs, downsizing, and outsourcing. The job you have today may very well disappear in the near future. And the employer you work for today most likely will not be the same one you will be with five years from now.

Unless you want to become a recurring victim of economic vicissitudes affecting your employment future, you must become proactive in taking better care of your career future. Since we live in a constantly changing economy and job market, you are well advised to continue acquiring more skills and keeping yourself in the job market on an ongoing basis. This can easily be done given the numerous education and training opportunities available both on and off the job as well as the ability to post your resume online for free with hundreds of different employment sites. Make a habit of learning one new skill each year and conducting an annual career checkup that includes updating your resume and keeping it online for possible new job opportunities.

Indeed, learning and job seeking will become ongoing processes rather than just periodic ones individuals engage in when they lose their jobs or decide to look for greener pastures. When you become more entrepreneurial about your career, you transform yourself from a passive employee who occasionally looks for a new job to an individual who creates a demand for his or her skills and services. Because of your ongoing career promotion activities, jobs and employers start coming to you rather than you seeking out potential employers.

TREND 40: **Fewer people will be obsessed with chasing traditional careers. More and more people want satisfying jobs that enable them to pursue interesting lifestyle goals.**

The concept of a "career" is deeply rooted in the post-World War II era of big corporations. Until the 1990s, many individuals pursued careers, often within a single organizational setting. Given the changing structure of the job market, the decline of traditional career paths, and the increased interest in pursuing satisfying lifestyles, the future will witness the gradual erosion of careers. More and more individuals today and in the decade ahead will be interested in finding specific jobs which may or may not be related to careers.

Be Realistic

While many individuals look toward the future with unquestioned optimism, there are good reasons to be cautious and less than enthusiastic. The decade ahead may be the worst of times for many people.

The best of times are when you are gainfully employed, enjoy your work, and look to your future with optimism. In a turbulent society, people experience both the best and worst of times at the same time. Those who are unprepared for the growing uncertainty and instability of a turbulent society may get hurt.

We lack a healthy sense of reality in facing change. Indeed, the future is seldom what we think it is. Only recently have we begun to take a second look at the high-tech and service revolutions and raised some sobering questions about their impact on work and the workplace. We have not fully explored unanticipated consequences of new structural

changes on individuals and society.

The 40 changes we forecast will create dislocations for individuals, groups, organizations, communities, and regions. These dislocations will require some form of public-private intervention. For example, the question of renewable energy resources has not been adequately dealt with in relation to the high-tech revolution. Many of the key metals for fueling the high-tech economy are located in politically unstable regions of Africa and the former Soviet Union. Such resources must be secured or substitutions found in order for the revolution to proceed according to optimistic predictions. Capital formation, investment, and world markets must also be secure and stable. New management systems must evolve in response to the changes. In other words, these key factors are variables or "if's" – not the constants underlying most predictions of the future. As such, they are unpredictable.

The clearer picture of unanticipated consequences of technological changes is already evident on the changing assembly lines, in the automated offices, and in the electronic cottages of today. While automation often creates more jobs as it displaces workers – usually at higher skill levels – the jobs may be psychologically and financially less rewarding. Supervising robots eight hours a day can be tedious and boring work with few on-the-job rewards. The same is true for the much touted "office of the future." Interacting with a computer terminal eight hours a day is tedious, tiring, and boring work for many people, and job burnout may accelerate.

The electronic cottage has similar unanticipated consequences. Many people may miss the daily interaction with fellow workers – the gossip, the politics, the strokes. Instead of being rewarding, work at home can become drudgery and low-paying work, a 21st century version of the sweatshop.

The optimists often overlook the fact that the nature of work itself provides rewards. Many people intrinsically enjoy the particular job they perform. Furthermore, many rewards are tied to the human dimension of work – the interaction with others. Thus, the high-tech and service society will have to deal with serious management and motivational problems arising from the changing nature of work and the workplace.

Many workers may need to change jobs and careers in order to overcome the boredom and burnout accompanying many of the new jobs or work situations of tomorrow. And even if the high-tech and service society does not emerge in the form outlined by us and other forecasters, the need to change jobs and careers will become necessary given the employment uncertainty of a turbulent society largely shaped by a cyclical boom/bust economy and affected by international events.

5

Best Job and Career Alternatives for Transitioning Military

A S YOU LEAVE THE MILITARY, you want to know what are the best jobs for someone with your background, skills, and experience. Will your military experience directly transfer to many civilian jobs? Where are the jobs, and how do you get one? Most service members ask these questions as they prepare to transition to the civilian work world.

But one other equally important question should precede these traditional questions:

"*What* are the jobs of tomorrow?"

For the nature of jobs is changing rapidly in response to (1) technological innovations, (2) the development and application of new technology to the workplace, and (3) the demand for a greater variety of consumer services. Today's transitioning military personnel and their families need answers to the "what," "where," and "how" of jobs for today, tomorrow, and in the decade ahead.

Many jobs in the decade ahead will look very different from those of yesterday. Indeed, if we project present trends into the future and believe what futurists tell us about emerging new careers, the coming decade will offer unprecedented and exciting opportunities to build and change careers within the civilian work world.

86

As you may already know from your varied military experience, which involved numerous technological changes to your military workplaces, such changes and opportunities have costs. The change in jobs and occupations will be so rapid that skills learned today may become obsolete in another five to ten years. Therefore, knowing what the jobs are becomes a prerequisite to knowing how to prepare for them, find them, and change them in the future.

Beware of Changing Occupational Profiles

A few words of caution are in order on how you should and should not use the information in this chapter. If you wish to identify a growing career field to plan your own career transition, do so only **after** you identify your interests, skills, and abilities – the subjects of Chapters 8, 9 and 10. You need to know if that career field is appropriate for you and vice versa. Furthermore, you need to determine if you have the proper skills or aptitude and interests to acquire

> *If you wish to identify a growing career field to plan your own career, do so only after you identify your interests, skills, and abilities.*

the necessary skills. The next step is to acquire the training before conducting a job search. Only then should you seriously consider pursuing what appears to be a growing field.

At the same time, you should be aware that the statistics and projections on growing industrial and occupational fields may be inaccurate. First, they are based on traditional models and economic studies conducted by the U.S. Department of Labor, Bureau of Labor Statistics. The Bureau conducts "empirical studies" which assume a steady rate of economic growth. Such occupational projections are nothing more than "best guesses" based upon a traditional model which assumes continual, linear growth. This planning model does not deal well with the realities of cyclical changes and unique events that can significantly alter future projections.

Second, during a period of turbulent change, occupational profiles may become quickly outdated. Training requirements change, and thus individuals encounter greater uncertainty in career choices.

Expect Job Growth for Most Occupations

The growth in jobs has been steady during the past three to four decades. From 1955 to 1980, for example, the number of jobs increased from 68.7

to 105.6 million. This represented an average annual increase of about 1.5 million new jobs. During the 1970s the number of jobs increased by over 2 million per year. And between the years 1983 and 1994 the number of jobs increased by 24.6 million, a strong growth rate of 24 percent over an 11-year period or over 2 million new jobs each year. Between 1995 and 1999, jobs grew by over 2 million each year. By the year 2012, employment is expected to increase from 144 million in 2002 to 165 million in 2012, or by 14.8 percent.

Highlighting these patterns of job growth are 16 forecasts, based on U.S. Department of Labor data and projections and other recent analyses, which represent the recent confluence of demographic, economic, and technological changes in society:

1. Growth of the labor force slows.

The growth in the labor force will slow to 165 million by the year 2012 – a 14.6 percent increase from the year 2002. The U.S. population is expected to increase by 24 million over the 2002-12 period, which is slower than in the two previous decades.

2. The labor force will be racially and ethnically more diverse.

The U.S. workforce will be more diverse by 2012. White, non-Hispanic persons will continue to make up a decreasing share of the labor force, falling from 71.3 percent in 2002 to 65.5 percent in 2012. White, non-Hispanics will remain the largest group in the labor force in 2012. Hispanics are projected to account for an increasing share of the labor force by 2012, growing from 12.4 to 14.7 percent. By 2012, Hispanics will constitute a larger proportion of the labor force than will blacks, whose share will grow from 11.4 percent to 12.2 percent. Asians will continue to be the fastest growing of the four labor force groups.

3. Fewer young people will enter the job market.

The youth labor force, aged 16 to 24, is expected to slightly decrease its share of the overall labor force to 15 percent by 2012 or just over 24 million. Businesses depending on this age group for students, recruits, customers, and part-time workers – especially colleges, the armed forces, eating and drinking establishments, and retail stores – must draw from a smaller pool of young people. Competition among young people for entry-level jobs will decline accordingly.

4. The workforce will continue to gray as it becomes older.

The number of workers 55 and older will increase substantially by the year 2012. This group is expected to increase from 14.3 percent to 19.1 percent of the labor force between 2002 and 2012, due to the aging of the baby-boom generation.

5. Women will continue to enter the labor force in growing numbers.

The male labor force is projected to grow by 10 percent from 2002 to 2012, compared with 14.3 percent for women. Men's share of the labor force is expected to decrease from 53.5 to 52.5 percent, while women's share is expected to increase from 46.5 to 47.5 percent. By the year 2012, four out of five women ages 25-54 will be in the labor force.

6. Education requirements for most new jobs will rise.

Most new jobs will require strong basic skills, such as reading, writing, oral communication, and math. Many of these jobs will include important high-tech components, which will require specialized education and training as well as the demonstrated ability to learn and acquire nontraditional education and training to continuously re-tool.

7. The fastest growing occupations will be in executive, managerial, professional, and technical fields – all requiring the highest levels of education and skill.

Three-quarters of the fastest growing occupational groups will be executive, administrative, and managerial; professional specialty; and technicians and related support occupations – occupations that require the highest levels of education and skill. Few opportunities will be available for high school dropouts or those who cannot read or follow directions. A combination of greater emphasis on productivity in the workplace, increased automation, technological advances, innovations, changes in consumer demands, and import substitutions will decrease the need for workers with little formal education and few skills – helpers, laborers, assemblers, machine operators.

8. Employment will continue to increase for most occupations.

As the population continues to grow and become more middle-aged and affluent, demands for more services will increase accordingly. Except in the cases of agriculture, mining, and traditional manufacturing, the past decade has seen a steady to significant job growth in all occupations. Over 21 million jobs will be added to the U.S. economy between the years 2002 and 2012. However, new jobs will be unevenly distributed across major industrial and occupational groups due to the restructuring of the economy and the increased education and training requirements for most jobs. Professional and related occupations will grow the fastest and add more new jobs than any other major occupational group.

9. The greatest growth in jobs will take place in service industries and occupations as the long-term shift from goods-producing to service-providing employment continues in the decade ahead.

Over 90 percent of all new jobs in the 1990s were in the service-producing industries, with services such as legal, business (advertising, accounting, and computer support), and health care leading the way. The number of jobs in the service-producing industries is expected to account for approximately 20.8 million of the 21.6 million new wage and salary jobs generated over the 2002-2012 period.

10. Education and health services will add more jobs than any other industry supersector.

This industry supersector is expected to grow by 31.8 percent during the 2002-2012 period. About one out of every four new jobs created in the U.S. economy will be in either the health care and social assistance or private education services sector.

11. Government employment will increase at different rates for different levels of government as well as for governmental units in different regions of the country.

Between 2002 and 2012, government employment, including public education and hospitals, is expected to increase by 11.8 percent, form 21.5 million to 24 million jobs. Growth in government employment will be fueled by growth in state and local educational services and the shift of responsibilities from the federal

government to the state and local governments. Local government education services is projected to increase 17.5 percent, adding over 1.3 million jobs. State government education services also are projected to grow 17.5 percent, adding 388,000 jobs. Federal government employment, including the Postal Service, is expected to increase by less than 1 percent as the federal government continues to contract out many government jobs to private companies.

12. Employment growth in education at all levels will be incremental.

Private educational services will grow by 28.7 percent and add 759,000 new jobs through 2012. Rising student enrollments at all levels of education will create demand for educational services. Job opportunities should increase for teachers, teacher aides, counselors, and administrative staff.

13. Jobs in manufacturing will continue to decline.

Manufacturing jobs are expected to decline by nearly 1 percent, or 157,000 jobs, in the period 2002-2012. Most of the decline will affect production jobs; professional, technical, and managerial positions in manufacturing will increase. These declines will be due to productivity gains achieved through automation and improved management as well as the closing of less efficient plants. However, employment in plastics and rubber products manufacturing and machinery manufacturing is expected to grow by 138,000 and 120,000 jobs, respectively. Due to an aging population and increasing life expectancies, pharmaceutical and medicine manufacturing is expected to grow by 23.2 percent and add 68,000 jobs through 2012.

14. Employment in agriculture, forestry, fishing, and mining jobs will continue to decline.

Employment in agriculture, forestry, and fishing is expected to decline by 2 percent from 2002 to 2012, due to advancements in technology. The only supersector expected to grow is support activities for agriculture and forestry, which includes farm labor contractors and farm management services. This industry is expected to grow by 18.4 percent and add 17,000 new jobs. Strong growth will take place in agricultural services industries, especially

landscape, horticultural, and farm management services. Much of the self-employment decline in agriculture will be due to the closing of lucrative export markets as the productivity of agriculture abroad improves and new hybrid crops are introduced from genetic engineering breakthroughs to solve many of the world's food problems.

15. **Glamorous new occupations, responding to new technological developments and consumer demands, will offer exciting new opportunities for job seekers who are well educated and skilled in the jobs of tomorrow.**

New occupations, created through a combination of technological innovations and new service demands, will provide excellent career opportunities for those who possess the necessary skills and drive to succeed in the decade ahead. New occupations with such names as bionic-electronic technician, holographic inspector, cryonics technician, aquaculturist, and search engine optimizer will enter our occupational vocabulary during the coming decade.

16. **The hottest career fields for the first decade of the 21st century will be in science, engineering, computer technology, and health services.**

Look for these jobs to be the highest demand and highest paying jobs for the coming decade: biologist, physician, mechanical engineer, chemical engineer, computer scientist, computer engineer, materials engineer, and medical technologist. Demand also will be high for these less well paid jobs: special education teachers, personal and home care aides, home health aides, and physical therapists.

Examine Growing and Declining Occupations

The U.S. Department of Labor divides occupations into 16 broad groups based on the Standard Occupational Classification, the classification system used by all government agencies for collecting occupational data:

- Executive, administrative, and managerial occupations
- Engineers, scientists, and related occupations
- Social science, social service, and related occupations
- Teachers, librarians, and counselors
- Health-related occupations

- Writers, artists, and entertainers
- Technologists and technicians
- Marketing and sales occupations
- Administrative support occupations, including clerical
- Service occupations
- Agricultural and forestry occupations
- Mechanics and repairers
- Construction occupations
- Production occupations
- Transportation and material moving occupations
- Handlers, equipment cleaners, helpers, and laborers

Every two years the department's Bureau of Labor Statistics updates its employment outlook for the coming decade and publishes the results in the November issue of the *Monthly Labor Review* as well as the latest edition of the biannual *Occupational Outlook Handbook*. For the latest statistics and projections relating to several tables presented in this chapter, please visit the Bureau of Labor Statistics website: http://stats. bls.gov. You also can access online the complete text of the popular *Occupational Outlook Handbook*: www.bls.gov/oco.

Assuming a moderate rate of economic growth in the decade ahead – not boom-and-bust cycles – the U.S. Department of Labor projects an average growth rate of nearly 15 percent for all occupations in the coming decade. Technical and service occupations will grow the fastest:

Fastest Growing Occupations, 2002-2012
(Numbers in thousands of jobs)

Occupational Title	Employment 2002	2012	Percent Change	Postsecondary Education or Training
- Medical assistants [3]	365	579	59	Moderate-term on-the-job training
- Network systems and data communications analysts [1]	186	292	57	Bachelor's degree
- Physician assistants [3]	63	94	49	Bachelor's degree
- Social and human service assistants [3]	305	454	49	Moderate-term on-the-job training
- Home health aides [4]	580	859	48	Short-term on-the-job training
- Medical records and health information technicians [3]	147	216	47	Associate degree

■ Physical therapist aides [3]	37	54	46	Short-term on-the-job training
■ Computer software engineers, applications [1]	394	573	46	Bachelor's degree
■ Computer software engineers [1]	281	409	45	Bachelor's degree
■ Physical therapist assistants [2]	50	73	45	Associate degree
■ Fitness trainers and aerobics instructors [3]	183	264	44	Postsecondary vocational award
■ Database administrators [1]	110	159	44	Bachelor's degree
■ Veterinary technologists and technicians [3]	53	76	44	Associate degree
■ Hazardous materials removal workers [2]	38	54	43	Moderate-term on-the-job training
■ Dental hygienists [1]	148	212	43	Associate degree
■ Occupational therapist aides [3]	8	12	43	Short-term on-the-job training
■ Dental assistants [3]	266	379	42	Moderate-term on-the-job training
■ Personal and home care aides [4]	608	854	40	Short-term on-the-job training
■ Self-enrichment education teachers [2]	200	281	40	Work experience in a related occupation
■ Computer systems analysts [1]	468	653	39	Bachelor's degree
■ Occupational therapist assistants [2]	18	26	39	Associate degree
■ Environmental engineers [1]	47	65	38	Bachelor's degree
■ Postsecondary teachers [1]	1,581	1,284	38	Doctoral degree
■ Network and computer systems administrators [1]	251	345	37	Bachelor's degree
■ Environmental science and protection technicians, including health [2]	28	38	37	Associate degree
■ Preschool teachers, except special education [4]	424	577	36	Postsecondary vocational award
■ Computer and information systems managers [1]	284	387	36	Bachelor's or higher degree, plus work experience
■ Physical therapists [1]	137	185	35	Master's degree
■ Occupational therapists [1]	82	110	35	Bachelor's degree
■ Respiratory therapists [2]	86	116	35	Associate degree

[1] Very high average annual earnings ($42,820 and over)
[2] High average annual earnings ($27,500 to $41,780)
[3] Low average annual earnings ($19,710 to $27,380)
[4] Very low average annual earnings (up to $19,600)

Occupations With the Largest Job Growth, 2002-2012
(Numbers in thousands of jobs)

Occupational Title	Employment 2002	2012	Percent Change	Postsecondary Education or Training
■ Registered nurses [1]	2,284	2,908	27	Associate degree
■ Postsecondary teachers [1]	1,581	2,184	38	Doctoral degree
■ Retail salespersons [4]	4,076	4,672	15	Short-term on-the-job training
■ Customer service representatives [3]	1,894	2,354	24	Moderate-term on-the-job training
■ Combined food preparation and service workers, including fast food [3]	1,990	2,444	23	Short-term on-the-job training
■ Cashiers, except gaming [4]	3,432	2,886	13	Short-term on-the-job training
■ Janitors and cleaners, except maids and housekeeping cleaners [4]	2,267	2,681	18	Short-term on-the-job training
■ General and operations managers [1]	2,049	2,425	18	Bachelor's or higher degree + experience
■ Waiters and waitresses [4]	2,097	2,464	18	Short-term on-the-job training
■ Nursing aides, orderlies, and attendants [3]	1,375	1,718	25	Short-term on-the-job training
■ Truck drivers, heavy and tractor-trailer [2]	1,767	2,104	19	Moderate-term on-the-job training
■ Receptionists and information clerks [3]	1,100	1,425	29	Short-term on-the-job training
■ Security guards [4]	995	1,313	32	Short-term on-the-job training
■ Office clerks, general [3]	2,991	3,301	10	Short-term on-the-job training
■ Teacher assistants [4]	1,277	1,571	23	Short-term on-the-job training
■ Sales representative, wholesale and manufacturing, except technical and scientific products [1]	1,459	1,738	19	Moderate-term on-the-job training
■ Home health aides [4]	580	859	48	Short-term on-the-job training
■ Personal and home care aides [4]	608	854	40	Short-term on-the-job training

■ Truck drivers, light or delivery services [3]	1,022	1,259	23	Short-term on-the-job training
■ Landscaping and groundskeeping workers [3]	1,074	1,311	22	Short-term on-the-job training
■ Elementary school teachers, except special education [2]	1,467	1,690	15	Bachelor's degree
■ Medical assistants [3]	365	579	59	Moderate-term on-the-job training
■ Maintenance and repair workers, general [2]	1,266	1,472	16	Moderate-term on-the-job training
■ Accountants and auditors [1]	1,055	1,261	19	Bachelor's degree
■ Computer systems analysts [1]	468	653	39	Bachelor's degree
■ Secondary school teachers, except special and vocational education [1]	988	1,167	18	Bachelor's degree
■ Computer software engineers [1]	394	573	46	Bachelor's degree
■ Management analysis [1]	577	753	30	Bachelor's or higher degree, plus work experience
■ Food preparation workers [4]	850	1,022	20	Short-term on-the-job training
■ First-line supervisors/ manager of retail sales workers [2]	1,798	1,962	9	Work experience in a related occupation

[1] Very high average annual earnings ($42,820 and over)
[2] High average annual earnings ($27,500 to $41,780)
[3] Low average annual earnings ($19,710 to $27,380)
[4] Very low average annual earnings (up to $19,600)

Fastest Growing Industries, 2002-2012
(Numbers in thousands of jobs)

Industry Description	Jobs		Percent Change	Average annual rate of change
	2002	2012		
■ Software publishers	256.0	429.7	173.7	5.3
■ Management, scientific, and technical consulting services	731.8	1,137.4	405.6	4.5
■ Community care facilities for the elderly and residential care facilities	695.3	1,077.6	382.3	4.5
■ Computer systems design and related services	1,162.7	1,797.7	635.0	4.5
■ Employment services	3,248.8	5,012.3	1,763.5	4.4

▪ Individual, family, community, and vocational rehabilitation services	1,238.8	1,866.6	597.3	3.9
▪ Ambulatory health care services except offices of health practitioners	1,443.6	2,113.4	669.8	3.9
▪ Water, sewage, and other systems	48.5	71.0	22.5	3.9
▪ Internet services, data processing, and other information services	528.8	773.1	244.3	3.9
▪ Child day care services	734.2	1,050.3	316.1	3.6

20 Jobs With High Median Earnings and a Significant Number of Job Openings, 2002–2012

Occupation	Average Annual Projected Job Openings, 2002-2012	Median Earnings 2002
▪ Registered nurses	110,119	$48,090
▪ Postsecondary teachers	95,980	$49,090
▪ General and operations managers	76,245	$68,210
▪ Sales representatives, wholesale and manufacturing, except technical and scientific products	66,239	$42,730
▪ Truck drivers, heavy and tractor-trailer	62,517	$33,210
▪ Elementary school teachers, except special education	54,701	$41,780
▪ First-line supervisors or managers of retail sales workers	48,645	$29,700
▪ Secondary school teachers, except special education	45,761	$43,950
▪ General maintenance and repair workers	44,978	$29,370
▪ Executive secretaries and administrative assistants	42,444	$33,410
▪ First-line supervisors or managers of office and administrative support workers	40,909	$38,820
▪ Accountants and auditors	40,465	$47,000
▪ Carpenters	31,917	$34,190
▪ Automotive service technicians and mechanics	41,887	$30,590

■ Police and sheriff's patrol officers	31,290	$42,270
■ Licenses practical and licensed vocational nurses	29,480	$31,440
■ Electricians	28,485	$41,390
■ Management analysts	25,470	$60,340
■ Computer systems analysts	23,735	$62,890
■ Special education teachers	23,297	$43,450

Certain patterns are clearly evident from the U.S. Department of Labor's employment projections for the coming decade:

1. The hot occupational fields are in health care and computers and involve increased technical education and training on an ongoing basis.

2. Education is closely associated with earnings – the higher the education, the higher the average annual earnings.

3. Many of the fastest growing jobs require short- or moderate-term education.

4. Two-year associate degrees in several medical-related fields offer some of the best paying jobs.

5. Nearly 50 percent of the fastest growing jobs that generate relatively high median earnings, such as carpenters, truck drivers, repair workers, and auto mechanics, do not require a four-year degree.

Identify the "Best" Jobs for You

The fastest growing occupational fields are not necessarily the best ones for you. The best job and career for you will depend on your particular mix of skills, interests, and work and lifestyle values. Money, for example, is only one of many determiners of whether or not a job and career are particularly desirable. A job may pay a great deal of money, but it also may be very stressful, insecure, found in an undesirable location, involve long hours, and require extensive travel, including a long commute each day. The "best" job for you will be one you find rewarding in terms of your own criteria and priorities.

If you know what you do well and enjoy doing – information about yourself acquired through various self-assessment tests and exercises – you

will have a better idea which jobs best fit you. Indeed, we strongly recommend conducting a self-assessment in conjunction with the information included on various jobs. We outline how to do this in Chapters 8, 9, and 10 as well as in Ron and Caryl Krannich's *I Want to Do Something Else, But I'm Not Sure What It Is* (Impact Publications, 2005).

Periodically some observers of the labor market attempt to identify what are the best, the worst, the hottest, the most lucrative, or the most promising jobs and careers of the decade. One of the most ambitious attempts to assemble a list of the "best" jobs in America is presented in Les Krantz's *Jobs Rated Almanac* (Barricade Books, 2002). Similar in methodology to *Places Rated Almanac* for identifying the best places to live in America, the latest edition (6th) of this book evaluates and ranks 250 jobs in terms of six primary "job quality" criteria: income, stress, physical demands, environment, outlook, and security. According to this

> The "best" job for you will be one you find rewarding in terms of your own criteria and priorities.

analysis, the 25 highest ranking ("best") jobs by accumulated score of these criteria are:

The Best Jobs in America

Job title	Overall rank
▪ Biologist	1
▪ Actuary	2
▪ Financial planner	3
▪ Computer system analyst	4
▪ Accountant	5
▪ Software engineer	6
▪ Meteorologist	7
▪ Paralegal assistant	8
▪ Statistician	9
▪ Astronomer	10
▪ Mathematician	11
▪ Parole officer	12
▪ Hospital administrator	13
▪ Architectural drafter	14
▪ Physiologist	15
▪ Dietician	16
▪ Website manager	17
▪ Physicist	18
▪ Audiologist	19
▪ Agency director (nonprofit)	20

- Industrial designer 21
- Chemist 22
- Medical laboratory technician 23
- Archeologist 24
- Economist 25

The 20 worst jobs, or those that rank at the very bottom of the list of 250, include the following:

The Worst Jobs in America

Job title	Overall rank
- Fisherman	250
- Roustabout	249
- Lumberjack	248
- Cowboy	247
- Ironworker	246
- Garbage collector	245
- Construction worker (laborer)	244
- Taxi driver	243
- Stevedore	242
- Welder	241
- Roofer	240
- Dancer	239
- Firefighter	238
- Dairy farmer	237
- Seaman	236
- Farmer	235
- Boilermaker	234
- Carpenter	234
- Sheet metal worker	232
- Butcher	231

For the relative rankings of all 250 jobs as well as the ratings of each job on individual criterion, consult the latest edition of the *Jobs Rated Almanac*, which should be available in your local library or bookstore.

One of the most recent examinations of the best jobs in the decade ahead – those offering high pay, fast growth, and the most new jobs – is found in Ferguson's *25 Jobs That Have It All* (Chicago, IL: Ferguson Publishing Co.). This book identifies 25 jobs as the top ones:

- Advertising account executives
- Business managers
- College professors
- Computer network administrators
- Computer systems programmers/analysts
- Database specialists
- Dental hygienists
- Graphic designers
- Health care managers
- Management analysts and consultants
- Medical record technicians
- Occupational therapists
- Paralegals
- Pharmacy technicians
- Physician assistants
- Police officers
- Public relations specialists
- Registered nurses
- Secondary school teachers
- Software designers
- Software engineers
- Special education teachers
- Speech-language pathologists and audiologists
- Technical support specialists
- Writers and editors

Best Jobs for People Re-Entering the Workforce

Since you are in transition, you may want to examine the best jobs for people who are in similar transition situations. Many of these jobs are relatively easy to find and require limited education and training. Many pay well and lead to exciting careers. Outlined in Ron and Caryl Krannich's *America's Top Jobs for People Re-Entering the Workforce: 85 Opportunities for Jump-Starting Your Career* (Impact Publications, 2005), these jobs are found in several attractive occupational fields:

Education Occupations

- Archivists, Curators, and Museum Technicians
- Childcare Workers
- Instructional Coordinators
- Librarians

- Library Technicians
- Teacher Assistants
- Teachers – Adult Literacy and Remedial
- Teachers – Postsecondary
- Teachers – Preschool, Kindergarten, Elementary, Middle, and Secondary
- Teachers – Special Education

Health and Medical Care Jobs

- Dental Assistants
- Dental Hygienists
- Medical Assistants
- Medical Records and Health Information Technicians
- Occupational Therapists
- Occupational Therapist Aides
- Occupational Therapist Assistants
- Personal and Home Care Aides
- Physical Therapists
- Physical Therapist Assistants and Aides
- Physician Assistants
- Registered Nurses
- Respiratory Therapists
- Veterinary Technologists and Technicians

Government, Legal, and Security Occupations

- Correctional Officers
- Court Reporters
- Firefighters
- Paralegals and Legal Assistants
- Police and Detectives
- Postal Service Workers
- Security Guards

Office and Administrative Support Occupations

- Bill and Account Collectors
- Customer Service Representatives
- Financial Clerks
- Information and Record Clerks
- Secretaries and Administrative Assistants

Sales and Related Occupations

- Qualifications and Education
- Earnings Expectations
- Advertising Sales Agents
- Insurance Sales Agents
- Real Estate Brokers and Sales Agents
- Retail Salespersons
- Sales Representatives, Wholesale, and Manufacturing
- Travel Agents

Sports, Entertainment, and Media Jobs

- Actors
- Athletes, Coaches, Umpires, and Related Workers
- Artists and Related Workers
- Broadcasters and Sound Engineering Technicians and Radio Operators
- Designers
- Desktop Publishers
- Gaming Services
- Musicians, Singers, and Related Workers
- Photographers
- Public Relations Specialists
- Recreation and Fitness Workers
- Television, Video, and Motion Picture Camera Operators and Editors

Construction Trades and Related Workers

- Brickmasons, Blockmasons, and Stonemasons
- Carpenters
- Construction and Building Inspectors
- Drywall Installers, Ceiling Tile Installers and Tapers
- Glaziers
- Hazardous Materials Removal Workers
- Insulation Workers
- Painters and Paperhangers
- Pipelayers, Plumbers, Pipefitters, and Steamfitters
- Sheet Metal Workers
- Structural and Reinforcing Iron and Metal Workers

Installation, Maintenance, and Repair Occupations

- Aircraft and Avionics Equipment Mechanics and Service Technicians
- Automotive Service Technicians and Mechanics
- Coin, Vending, and Amusement Machine Servicers
- Heating, Air-Conditioning, and Refrigeration Mechanics and Installers
- Home Appliance Repairers
- Line Installers and Repairers
- Maintenance and Repair Workers
- Small Engine Mechanics

Production Occupations

- Computer-Control Programmers and Operators
- Food-Processing Occupations
- Machinists
- Tool and Dye Makers
- Welding, Soldering, and Brazing Workers

Transportation and Material Moving Occupations

- Bus Drivers
- Cargo and Freight Agents
- Material Moving Occupations
- Taxi Drivers and Chauffeurs
- Truck Drivers

Look for Exciting New Occupations

In the early 1980s the auto and related industries – steel, rubber, glass, aluminum, railroads, and auto dealers – accounted for one-fifth of all employment in the United States. Today that percentage continues to decline as service occupations further dominate America's occupational structure.

New occupations for the decade ahead will center around information, energy, high-tech, health care, and financial industries. They promise to create a new occupational structure and vocabulary relating to computers, the Internet, robotics, biotechnology, lasers, and fiber optics. By 1999, for example, the Internet reportedly was responsible for 1.3 million new jobs within a four-year period that generated more than $300 billion in

business. And as these fields begin to apply new technologies to developing innovations, they in turn will generate other new occupations in the decades ahead. While most new occupations are not major growth fields – because they do not initially generate a large number of new jobs – they will present individuals with fascinating new opportunities to become leaders in pioneering new fields and industries.

Futurists agree that most new occupations in the coming decade will have two dominant characteristics:

- **They will generate fewer new jobs** in comparison to the overall growth of jobs in hundreds of more traditional service fields, such as sales workers, office clerks, truck drivers, and janitors.

- **They require a high level of education and skills** for entry into the fields as well as continuing training and retraining as each field transforms itself into an additional growth field.

If you plan to pursue an emerging occupation, expect to first acquire highly specialized skills, which may require years of higher education and training.

Prepare for the Cheap Flat World

At the same time, you need to be aware of the potential impact of the global economy on your employment future. Stop thinking about what the economy and job market looked like 5, 10, or 20 years ago. That's history driven in large part by the old economies of the Cold War and U.S. dominance in education and business. Today's world is much more complex, and the U.S. is no longer the dominant player in education and business.

India and China, with a combined population of 2.3 billion and rapidly developing, well educated, skilled, and consumer-oriented middle classes, are transforming the way business is done in the U.S. The job you have today may well go to these countries because of the convergence of seven important developments we noted in Trend 3 of Chapter 4:

- improved Internet connections
- increased bandwidth
- powerful fiber optic cable
- cheap international telecom prices
- large pool of well-educated and trained English-speaking workers in several developing countries

- efficient international transportation links and delivery services
- enhanced global organization and management systems

As Thomas L. Friedman persuasively argues in *The World Is Flat: A Brief History of the Twenty-First Century* (Farrar, Straus, and Giroux, 2005), in the rapidly changing global economy there are no American jobs – only jobs that go to the lowest bidder. By implication Friedman's new flat (interconnected and complex) world will generate few well paying jobs. An increasing number of jobs – both low- and high-tech – go to the cheapest and most efficient workers in the world, who are increasingly found in India, China, Vietnam, Cambodia, the Philippines, Indonesia, South Africa, Mexico, Costa Rica, and a host of other Third and Fourth World countries rather than in high-cost Los Angeles, Seattle, Chicago, Detroit, Cincinnati, Washington, DC, Atlanta, or Miami.

> *The best jobs go to those who are constantly learning new skills, adapting to changing markets, and producing goods and services both inexpensively and efficiently.*

If you as an individual want a competitive edge in this new global economy, the most important skill you need to acquire is the **ability to learn**. The best jobs in this global economy disproportionately favor smart workers who are quick on their feet because they are constantly learning new skills, adapting to changing markets, and producing goods and services both inexpensively and efficiently. In such a world, few workers can expect to get rich working for other people who are constantly under pressure to cut production and service costs, which means keeping labor costs low by reducing benefits, better controlling salary and wage increases, and cutting legacy (primarily pensions) costs. The rich are the entrepreneurs, especially small business owners, who understand how to quickly adapt to and best navigate this global economy to their advantage. Individuals rather than large bureaucratic organizations have a distinct advantage in navigating this fast changing global economy. In the flat world, the entrepreneur is king.

Implications of Future Trends for You

Most growth industries and occupations require training and experience. Moving into one of these fields will require knowledge of job qualifications, the nature of the work, and sources of employment. Fortunately, the U.S. Department of Labor publishes several useful sources of

information available in most libraries to help you. These include the *O*NET Dictionary of Occupational Titles*, which identifies over 1,100 job titles. The *Occupational Outlook Handbook* provides an overview of current labor market conditions and projections, as well as discusses nearly 250 occupations that account for 107 million jobs, or 87 percent of the nation's total jobs. It's organized according to several useful informational categories: nature of work; working conditions; employment; training, other qualifications, and achievement; job outlook; earnings; related occupations; and sources of additional information.

During the past eight years, the U.S. Department of Labor overhauled its traditional job classification system, which was based on an analysis of the U.S. job market of the 1960s, 1970s, and 1980s. This system had generated over 13,000 job titles as outlined in the *Dictionary of Occupational Titles* and numerous related publications. Known as the O*NET project (the Occupational Information Network), this new occupational classification system more accurately reflects the structure of today's new job market; it condenses the 13,000+ job titles into over 1,100 job titles. The new system is being gradually introduced into career education to replace the job classification system that has defined most jobs in the U.S. during the past four decades.

Anyone seeking to enter or re-enter the job market or change careers should initially consult the U.S. Department of Labor publications as well as access information on the new O*NET (www.onetcenter.org). The Department of Labor only makes this data available online (www.online. onetcenter.org). A commercial version of this system, published in book form, also is available. You should be able to find it in your local library. If not, the *O*NET Dictionary of Occupational Titles* is available through Impact Publications (www.impactpublications.com).

However, remember that labor market statistics are for industries and occupations **as a whole**. They tell you little about the shift in employment emphasis **within the industry,** and nothing about the outlook of particular jobs for you, **the individual**. For example, employment in agriculture was projected to decline by 14 percent between 1985 and 2000, but the decline consisted of an important shift in employment emphasis within the industry: there would be 500,000 fewer self-employed workers but 150,000 more wage and salary earners in the service end of agriculture. The employment statistics also assume a steady state of economic growth, with consumers having more and more disposable income to stimulate a wide variety of service and trade industries.

Therefore, be careful how you interpret and use this information in making your own job and career decisions. If, for example, you want to

become a college teacher, and the data tells you there will be a 10-percent decline in this occupation during the next 10 years, this does not mean you would not find employment, as well as advance, in this field. It merely means that, on the whole, competition may be keen for these jobs, and that future advancement and mobility in this occupation may not be very good – **on the whole**. At the same time, there may be numerous job opportunities available in a declining occupational field as many individuals abandon the field for more attractive occupations. In fact, you may do much better in this declining occupation than in a growing field depending on your interests, motivations, abilities, job search savvy, and level of competition. And if the decade ahead experiences more boom-and-bust cycles, expect most of these U.S. Department of Labor statistics and projections to be invalid for the economic realities of this decade.

Use this industrial and occupational data to expand your awareness of various job and career options. By no means should you make critical education, training, and occupational choices based upon this information alone. Such choices require additional types of information about you, the individual, based upon an assessment of your interests, skills, and values. If identified and used properly, this information will help clarify exactly which jobs are best for you.

Our cautionary observations on outsourcing of jobs abroad, the changing global economy, and Friedman's flat world should give pause to ex-military who look toward government contractors for possible employment. Many of these contractors have grown considerably since 2003 because of U.S. military and reconstruction involvement in Afghanistan and Iraq. However, the day may soon come when such involvement will substantially decrease and, accordingly, many contractors will downsize as contracts get smaller or disappear altogether. The same is true for contractors involved with homeland security issues. These are volatile issues that may result in major upsizing and downsizing of employment in the coming decade.

As you will quickly discover in the civilian job market, few organizations and jobs are permanent. You have to take charge of your own career future, be keenly aware of your changing surroundings, and make critical job and career moves when necessary. Assume that your next job will not last long and that you will need to look for another job within a few years. In the end, the best job for you will probably be the next job you nail by using the methods outlined in the remainder of this book.

6

Cast a Net for Renewed Career Success

W E ALL NEED FRIENDS when it comes time to look for a job or change careers. In many ways the military has been your family and best friend for several years. Friends represent familiarity and comradery, provide important psychological support, and often give useful information, advice, and referrals. Your friend can be your commander, a transition officer, a buddy, a girl/boy friend, spouse, relative, a former school mate, or teacher who shares important information and advice as well as contacts that lead to a job interview and offer. Your friend also can be a seasoned career professional who provides important structure, motivation, and support for implementing your job search and landing your dream job. Whatever the case, you should consider acquiring and using as many friends as possible in clarifying what you want to do with whom in the future.

Communicating With Friends

Don't be afraid to talk to friends and associates about your interests, goals, and career plans. Cast as broad an information net as you can. Most important of all, start casting that net at least one year before separation from your service and involve your spouse in transition programs and services available on your base. Once you are into your last

90 days, you and your spouse may become too busy with other separation matters to devote much quality time to conduct an effective job search.

Most of your friends and associates will be interested in what you are doing. Some may even confide in you the fact that they, too, would like to be doing what you are doing – exploring new job and career options. In fact, you may end up creating a support group of individuals who want to join together in discovering what else they would like to do with their lives!

Unfortunately, many individuals try to keep their job and career interests a secret from the very people who might be most helpful. Consider sharing the following statement with your friends:

> *I'm in the process of leaving the military. Over the next few months I'm going to explore some new civilian job and career options. If you don't mind, I may want to ask you for some advice.*

This statement should elicit some interesting responses. You'll discover that many of your friends can relate to your career situation. At some point in their lives they probably encountered a similar career situation. Not surprisingly, most of your friends will be happy to give you free advice. Some will provide excellent referrals to other individuals who will offer you useful information, advice, and referrals. This whole process is what we mean by **networking** – building, maintaining, and extending connections to others for the purposes of acquiring useful information, advice, and referrals and for being remembered for future reference.

As you share your story with friends and associates, you will be building an important **support network** for achieving your goals. Best of all, you'll be **minimizing rejections** by talking to the very people who are willing to help you shape your future. As you gather information, advice, and referrals, you'll learn a great deal about yourself, others, the job market, jobs, careers, and employers. You'll get a better sense of what you want to do, because you have a better understanding of job and career realities that relate to your goals, interests, skills, and abilities.

Be careful in how you present your story to friends and associates. At no time should you try to use friends to get ahead. Share your story and ask for advice. Never ask a friend or associate to find you employment. Once you do that, you cross a fine line that could damage your relationships. While most people are happy to give you advice, few people want to be put upon to take responsibility for your employment fate. Those that do will most likely charge you money, which we'll discuss shortly.

On Your Own and With Others

You have two options in planning your future and organizing an effective job search. First, you can follow the principles and advice outlined in this and many other self-directed books. Just read the chapters and then put them into practice by following the step-by-step instructions. The assumption here is that you are a highly motivated self-starter who just needs some how-to advice and direction to do everything on your own. Not a bad assumption, but it's probably only valid for 10 percent of the population who can successfully do everything on their own, from planning to implementation.

The planning or pre-implementation process is probably the easiest for you to do on your own. You can assess your skills, develop an objective, conduct research, and write resumes and letters on your own. But when it comes time to implement your plan of action, which involves networking and contacting many potential employers, you may encounter numerous difficulties doing it on your own. In addition to the problem of rejections, which we noted in Chapter 3, most people have difficulty implementing a career plan, because they lack a structure for implementation. That structure often comes in the form of a career coach, advisor, or support group that can help individuals through the ego-bruising ups and downs of the career planning and job search processes. Without such a structure, you may end up becoming disillusioned as you wander aimlessly in a sea of rejections. Failing to do first things first, you may make many implementation errors commonly associated with ineffective job searches, such as writing your resume first, spending an inordinate amount of time looking for jobs on the Internet, or responding to classified ads, and failing to network and properly follow up. Just because you understand a process does not mean you also are capable of implementing that process.

Second, you may wish to seek professional help to either supplement or replace this book. If you are currently in the military and plan to soon separate or retire, you can take advantage of several free career transition assistance services provided on your base as well as through DoD and the U.S. Department of Labor. For starters, check out DoD's Web portal for relevant transition information: www.dodtransportal.org.

Over the years we have learned some important lessons about human behavior when it comes to conducting a job search. Many people will read parts of this book – perhaps all of it – and do nothing. They may read several other how-to books and again do nothing. Some will even spend money attending motivational, career planning, and job search seminars and again do nothing. Lacking sufficient time or motivation beyond the

moment it takes to read the book or attend the seminar, or failing to follow through, many people eventually seek professional help to organize and implement their job search. Hopefully, they will work with a career professional or career coach who can provide them with assistance in completing each step outlined in this book. Such assistance may not be cheap – indeed it can be an expensive form of motivation – but it does at least result in creating a structure for implementation.

We've also learned that many people who take advantage of free services do not follow through and implement. Being free, these services are often perceived as having little value. It's only when someone has to spend money on a service that they begin taking it seriously. After all, they want to get good value for their money! Remember this when you take advantage of the free transition services on your base. If you don't take them seriously, the next time you'll probably pay good money for the same services.

We recognize the value of professional assistance. Especially with the critical assessment and objective-setting steps (Chapters 8-11), some individuals may need more assistance than our advice and exercises provide. You may, for example, want to take a battery of tests to better understand your interests and values in relation to alternative jobs and careers. And still others, due to a combination of job loss, failed relationships, or depression, may need therapy best provided by a trained psychologist or psychiatrist rather than career testing and information services provided by career counselors. If any of these situations pertain to you, by all means seek professional help.

Beware of Pitfalls in Hiring a Professional

You also should beware of pitfalls in seeking professional advice. While many services are excellent, some services are useless and fraudulent. Remember, career planning and job assistance are big businesses involving millions of dollars each year. Many people enter these businesses without expertise. Professional certification in these areas is extremely weak to nonexistent in some states. Indeed, many so-called "professionals" get into the business because they are unemployed. In other words, they major in their own problem! Others are frauds and hucksters who prey on vulnerable and naive people who feel they need a "specialist" or "expert" to get them a job. These people will take your money in exchange for promises.

You will find various types of services promising to assist you in finding all types of jobs. You should know something about these professional services before you venture beyond this book.

If you are interested in exploring the services of job specialists, begin by looking in the Yellow Pages of your telephone directory under these headings: Management Consultants, Employment, Resumes, Career Planning, and Social Services. You also should check out a few websites of certified career professionals, which we recommend near the end of this chapter. Several career planning and employment services are available, ranging from highly generalized to very specific services. Most services claim they can help you. If you read this book, you will be in a better position to seek out specific services as well as ask the right questions for screening the services. You may even discover you know more about finding a job than many of the so-called professionals!

Seeking Professional Assistance

At least 13 different career planning and employment services are available to assist you with different phases of your job search. Most of these services include some type of career assessment activity, from self-directed exercises to pencil-and-paper tests. Many rely heavily on the two most popular assessment devices – *Myers-Briggs Type Indicator*® and *Strong Interest Inventory*®. (See Chapter 8 for details.)

Each of these services has certain advantages and disadvantages. Approach them with caution. Always remember that career planning is a big and largely unregulated business where you will occasionally encounter hucksters and fraudulent services aimed at taking advantage of individuals who are psychologically vulnerable and naive. Many of these hucksters self-certify themselves, promise to locate jobs that pay more than your last one, and seal the deal by asking for up-front money – $500 to $15,000 – to find you a job. Lacking good shopping sense and engaging in wishful thinking, many job seekers fall for the false promises of these so-called employment experts.

Our advice is very simple: Never sign a contract before you read the fine print, get a second opinion, and talk to former clients about the **results** they achieved through the service. While most of these services are not free, there is no reason to believe that the most expensive services are the best services or that fee-based services are more effective than free services. In fact, you may get the same quality of services from a group that charges $300 versus one that costs $15,000. At the same time, free or cheap services are not necessarily as good as the more expensive services. While you often get what you pay for in this industry, you also may get much less than what you pay for. Again, before using any employment services or hiring an expert, do your research by contacting a few individuals who have used the services. We recommend career

professionals at certain stages of your job search, especially for self-assessment and resume writing.

With these words of caution in mind, let's examine a variety of services available, which you may or may not want to incorporate in your career planning and job search efforts.

1. **DoD's, Labor's, and the VA's military separation and retirement transition resources:**

 Each service has its own set of transition services to assist members and their families with separation and retirement. You can access information on the location of these services nearest you by visiting the Department of Defense's TransPortal:

 www.dodtransportal.org

 This Web portal also includes a wealth of useful transition resources well worth exploring: Individual Transition Assistance Plan, Education and Training, Health and Life Insurance, Reserve Affiliation, and Retiree Information. DoD and the U.S. Department of Labor have developed a job search site for transitioning and former military personnel which is affiliated with America's Job Bank (www.ajb.org):

 http://dod.jobsearch.org

 Transition services, which include mandatory pre-separation briefings (90 to 180 days before separation) as well as free counseling services on jobs, education, relocation, family, personal finances, and retirement, take on different names and program emphases within each service:

 - **Air Force** TAP (Transition Assistance Program). This program is administered by a TAP Staff assigned to the Family Support Centers.

 - **Army** ACAP (Army Career and Alumni Program): www.acap.army.mil. All Army personnel must attend a pre-separation briefing at least 90 days before separation.

- **Coast Guard** Transition services provided by **Work-Life Staffs**, which are found at Integrated Support Commands and the Headquarters Support Command. These programs are operated by Transition/Relocation Managers.

- **Marines** Transition services provided by **Career Resource Management Centers (CRMCs)**, which are staffed by a Career Retention Specialist at the Personal Services Center (previously known as the Family Services Center).

- **Navy** **TAMP (Transition Assistance Management Program)**. This program is operated on bases by the Fleet and Family Support Centers (FFSCs) and in deployment settings by assigned Command Career Counselors.

The U.S. Department of Labor, in conjunction with the Department of Defense and the Department of Veterans Affairs (VA), also sponsors a three- to four-day **Transition Assistance Program (TAP) Workshop** for all separating service members and their spouses. Disabled service members also receive special help through the Disabled Transition Assistance Program, which includes enrollment in the VA's Vocational Rehabilitation Program.

2. Public employment services

Public employment services usually consist of a state agency which provides employment assistance as well as dispenses unemployment compensation benefits. Employment assistance largely consists of job listings and counseling services. However, counseling services often screen individuals for employers who list with the public employment agency. If you are looking for an entry-level job or a job paying $18,000 to $40,000, contact these services. Most employers still do not list with them, especially for positions paying more than $40,000 a year. Although the main purpose of these offices has been to dispense unemployment benefits, don't overlook them because of past stereotypes. The Workforce Development Act has re-energized

such services. Within the past four years, many of these offices have literally "reinvented" themselves for today's new job market as One-Stop Career Centers, computerized job banks, counseling services, training programs, and other innovative organizational and technical approaches. Many of them offer useful employment services, including self-assessment and job search workshops as well as access to job listings on the Internet. Most of these offices are linked to America's Job Bank (www.ajb.dni.us), an electronic job bank that includes over 1 million job listings throughout the U.S. and abroad. This is one of the premier employment websites that offers a wealth of information and resources for job seekers. It's one all job seekers need to become familiar with. America's Job Bank, in turn, is linked to the U.S. Department of Labor's four other useful websites – America's CareerInfoNet (www.acinet.org), America's Service Locator (www.servicelocator.org), Career OneStop (www.careeronestop. org), and Careeer Voyages (www.careervoyages.org). If you are a veteran, you will find many of the jobs listed with state employment offices give veterans preference in hiring. Go see for yourself if your state employment office offers useful services for you.

3. Private employment agencies

Private employment agencies work for money, either from applicants or employers. Approximately 8,000 such agencies operate nation-wide. Many are highly specialized in technical, scientific, and financial fields. The majority of these firms serve the interests of employers, since employers – not applicants – represent repeat business. While employers normally pay the placement fee, many agencies charge applicants 10 to 15 percent of their first year salary. These firms have one major advantage: job leads which you may have difficulty uncovering elsewhere. Especially for highly specialized fields, a good firm can be extremely helpful. The major disadvantages are that they can be costly and the quality of the firms varies. Be careful in how you deal with them. Make sure you understand the fee structure and what they will do for you before you sign anything.

4. Temporary staffing firms

During the past decade temporary staffing firms have come of age as more and more employers turn to them for recruitment assistance. They offer a variety of employment services to both applicants and

employers who are either looking for temporary work and workers or who want to better screen applicants and employers. Many of these firms, such as Manpower (www.manpower.com), Olsten (www.olsten.com), and Kelly Services (www.kellyservices.com), recruit individuals for a wide range of positions and skill levels as well as full-time employment. Some firms, such as Robert Half International (www.rhii.com), specialize in certain types of workers, such as accounting, law, information technology, and computer personnel. If you want to "test the job waters," you may want to contact these firms for information on their services. Employers – not job seekers – pay for these services. While many of these firms are listed in your community Yellow Pages, most have websites. The following websites are especially popular with individuals interested in part-time, temporary, or contract work: www.net-temps.com, www.elance. com, www.ework.com, www.guru.com, and www.talentmarket.mon ster.com.

5. College/university placement offices

College and university placement offices provide in-house career planning services for graduating students. While some give assistance to alumni, don't expect too much help if you have already graduated; you may, instead, need to contact the alumni office which may offer employment services. Many college placement offices are understaffed or provide only rudimentary services, such as maintaining a career planning library, coordinating on-campus interviews for graduating seniors, and conducting workshops on how to write resumes and interview. Others provide a full range of well supported services including testing and one-on-one counseling. Indeed, many community colleges offer such services to members of the community on a walk-in basis. You can use their libraries and computerized career assessment programs, take personality and interest inventories, or attend special workshops or full-semester career planning courses which will take you through each step of the career planning and job search processes. You may want to enroll in such a course since it is likely to provide just enough structure and content to assess your motivated abilities and skills and to assist you in implementing a successful job search plan. Check with your local campus to see what services you might use. Many of the college and university placement offices belong to the National Association of Colleges and Employers, which operates its own employment website: www.jobweb.com. This site includes a wealth of information

on employment for college graduates (see the "Site Map" section: www.jobweb.com/search/sitemap.htm). Its "Career Library" section includes direct links to hundreds of college and university placement offices: www.jobweb.com/Career-Development/collegeres.htm. To find college alumni offices, visit the following websites: www.alumni.net, www.bcharrispub.com, and www.jobweb.com/After_College. Since colleges and universities tend to be very Web-savvy, you can visit hundreds of their career websites to acquire all types of useful free information on conducting an effective job search. One of our favorites is the website operated by the Career Center at the College of William and Mary (www.wm.edu/career). Indeed, searching many of these college and university websites is comparable to having your own personal career counselor – without having to go to college!

6. Private career and job search firms

Private career and job search firms help individuals acquire job search skills and coach them through the process of finding a job. They do not find you a job. In other words, they teach you much of what is outlined in this book. Expect to pay anywhere from $1,500 to $10,000 for this service. If you need a structured environment for conducting your job search, contract with one of these firms for professional assistance. One of the major such firms used to be Bernard Haldane Associates (they ceased operating under that name and became BH Careers International, www.bhcareers.com, in 2004). Many of their pioneering career planning and job search methods are incorporated in this book as well as can be found in five other key job search books: *Haldane's Best Resumes for Professionals, Haldane's Best Cover Letters for Professionals, Haldane's Best Answers to Tough Interview Questions, Haldane's Best Salary Tips for Professionals*, and *Haldane's Best Employment Websites for Professionals* (Impact Publications). Other firms offering similar services include Right Management Associates (www.right.com), R. L. Stevens & Associates (www.interviewing.com), and Lee Hecht Harrison (www.lhh.com/us).

7. Executive search firms and headhunters

Executive search firms work for employers in finding employees to fill critical positions in the $50,000 plus salary range. They also are called "headhunters," "management consultants," and "executive recruiters." These firms play an important role in linking high level technical and managerial talent to organizations. Don't expect to

contract for these services. Executive recruiters work for employers, not applicants. If a friend or relative is in this business or you have relevant skills of interest to these firms, let them know you are available – and ask for their advice. On the other hand, you may want to contact firms that specialize in recruiting individuals with your skill specialty. Several firms, such as the Lucas Group (www.lucasgroup. com), specialize in marketing ex-military personnel, especially JMOs. For a comprehensive listing of these firms, see the latest annual edition of *The Directory of Executive Recruiters* (Kennedy Information, www.kennedyinfo.com or www.impactpublications. com). Several companies, such as www.resumezapper.com, www. blastmyresume.com, and www.resumeblaster.com, offer e-mail resume blasting services that primarily target headhunters. For a fee, which usually ranges from $50 to $200, these firms will blast your resume to 5,000 to 10,000 headhunters. This is a quick, easy, and inexpensive way to reach thousands of headhunters and executive search firms. This resume distribution method also may be a waste of time and money. Approach it with a sense of healthy skepticism.

8. Marketing services

Marketing services represent an interesting combination of job search and executive search activities. They can cost $2,500 or more, and they work with individuals anticipating a starting salary of at least $75,000 but preferably over $100,000. These firms try to minimize the time and risk of applying for jobs. A typical operation begins with a client paying a $150 fee for developing psychological, skills, and interests profiles. If you pass this stage – most anyone with money does – you go on to the next one-on-one stage. At this point, a marketing plan is outlined and a contract signed for specific services. Work for the clients usually involves activities centered on the resume and interviewing. Using word processing software, the firm normally develops a slick "professional" resume and sends it by mail or e-mail, along with a cover letter, to hundreds – maybe thousands – of firms. Clients are then briefed and sent to interview with interested employers. While you can save money and achieve the same results on your own, these firms do have one major advantage: They save you **time** by doing most of the work for you. Again, approach these services with caution and with the knowledge that you can probably do just as well – if not better – on your own by following the step-by-step advice of this and other job search books.

9. Women's centers and special career services

Women's centers and special career services for displaced workers, such as 40-Plus Clubs (www.40plus.org/chapters) and Five O'Clock Clubs (www.fiveoclockclub.com), have been established to respond to the employment needs of special groups. Women's centers are particularly active in sponsoring career planning workshops and job information networks. These centers tend to be geared toward elementary job search activities, because many of their clientele consist of homemakers who are entering or re-entering the work force with little knowledge of the job market. Special career services arise at times for different categories of employees. For example, unemployed aerospace engineers, teachers, veterans, air traffic controllers, and government employees have formed special groups for developing job search skills and sharing job leads.

10. Testing and assessment centers

Testing and assessment centers provide assistance for identifying vocational skills, interests, and objectives. Usually staffed by trained professionals, these centers administer several types of tests and charge from $200 to $900 per person. We summarize most of these tests and inventories in Chapter 8. You may wish to use some of these services if you feel our activities in Chapters 8-10 generate insufficient information on your skills and interests to formulate your job objective. If you use such services, make sure you are given one or both of the two most popular and reliable tests: *Myers-Briggs Type Indicator®* and the *Strong Interest Inventory®*. You should find both tests helpful in better understanding your interests and decision-making styles. However, try our exercises in the following chapters before you hire a psychologist or visit a testing center. If you first complete these exercises, you will be in a better position to know exactly what you need from such centers. In many cases, the career office at your local community college or women's center can administer these tests at minimum cost ($20 to $40). At the same time, many of these tests and assessments are now available online. Check out these popular websites for interesting collections of self-assessment instruments: www.skillsone.com, www.self-directed-search.com, www.careerlab.com, www.personalityonline.com, www.assessment.com, and www.personalitytype.com.

11. Job fairs and career conferences

Job fairs and career conferences are organized by a variety of groups – from schools and government agencies to headhunters, employment agencies, and professional associations – to link applicants to employers. **Job fairs** are often open to the public and involve many employers. **Career conferences** may be closed to the public (invitation only) and involve a single employer. Usually consisting of one- to two-day meetings in a hotel or conference center, employers meet with applicants as a group and on a one-to-one basis. Employers give presentations on their companies, applicants circulate resumes, and employers interview candidates. Many such conferences are organized to attract hard-to-recruit groups, such as engineers, computer programmers, individuals with security clearances, and clerical and service workers, or for special population groups, such as minorities, transitioning military personnel, women, people with disabilities, and even ex-offenders. These are excellent sources for job leads and information on specific employers and jobs – if you are invited to attend or if the meeting is open to the public. Employers pay for this service, although some job fairs and career conferences may charge job seekers a nominal registration fee. See Chapter 7 for tips on how to best prepare for a military transition job fair.

12. Professional associations

Professional associations often provide placement assistance. This usually consists of listing job vacancies in publications, maintaining a resume database, and organizing a job information exchange at annual conferences. Some may even organize job fairs, such as the Military Officers Association of America (www.moaa.org) and the Non Commissioned Officers Association (www.ncoausa.org). Many large associations operate their own online employment sites; members can include their resume in an electronic database and employers can access the database to search for qualified candidates. Annual conferences are good sources for making job contacts in different geographic locations within a particular professional field. But don't expect too much. Talking to people (networking) at professional conferences may yield better results than reading job listings, placing your resume in a database, or interviewing at conference placement centers. For excellent online directories of professional associations, be sure to visit these two sites: www. ipl.org/ref/aon and www.asaenet.org.

13. Professional resume writers

Professional resume writers are increasingly playing an important role in career planning. Each year thousands of job seekers rely on these professionals for assistance in writing their resumes. Many of these professionals also provide useful job search tips on resume distribution, cover letters, and networking as well as include other career planning and job search services, such as assessment, mentoring, and practice interviewing. Charging from $100 to $600 for writing a resume, they work with the whole spectrum of job seekers – entry-level to senior executives making millions of dollars each year. While some are certified career counselors, many of these professionals have their own associations and certification groups that include a large assortment of often unintelligible initials after their names – CAC, CBC, CCM, CEIP, CHRE, CIPC, CPC, CPRW, JCTC, LPC, NBCC, NCC, NCCC, NCRW, and PCC. If you are interested in working with a professional resume writer, visit the following websites for information on this network of career professionals: www.parw.com, www.careerdirectors.com, www.cmi.com, and www.nrwa.com. Examples of their high-end work can be found in Wendy Enelow's and Louise Kursmark's five books: *Best Resumes for $100,000+ Jobs*, *Best Cover Letters for $100,000+ Jobs*, *Best Career Transition Resumes for $100,000+ Jobs*, *Executive Job Search for $100,000 to $1 Million+ Jobs*, and *Expert Resumes for Military-to-Civilian Transition*. In Chapter 12 on resume writing, we recommend several professional resume writers who specialize on military-to-civilian transitions.

Finding Certified Career Professionals

Certified career professionals are experienced in working one-on-one with clients, with special emphasis on career assessment. They have their own professional associations. If you are interested in contacting a certified career professional for assistance, we advise you to first visit these websites for locating a career professional:

- **National Board for Certified Counselors, Inc.** www.nbcc.org

- **National Career Development Association** www.ncda.org

- Certified Career Coaches www.certifiedcareer
 coaches.com

- Career Planning and Adult
 Development Network www.careernetwork.org

You also can find a great deal of professional career assistance through the U.S. Department of Labor's website, which enables users to locate services within their communities:

- America's Service Locator www.servicelocator.org

Working With the Best

Other types of career planning and employment services are growing and specializing in particular occupational fields. You may wish to use these services as a supplement to this book.

Whatever you do, be a smart shopper for career planning and job search services. Proceed with caution, know exactly what you are getting into, and choose the best. Remember, there is no such thing as a free lunch, and you often get less than what you pay for. At the same time, the most expensive services are not necessarily the best. Indeed, the free and inexpensive career planning services offered on military bases and by many community or junior colleges – libraries, computerized career assessment programs, testing, counseling, and workshops – may be all you need. On the other hand, don't be afraid to spend some money on getting the best services. You may quickly discover that this money was well spent when you land a job that pays 20 to 40 percent more than your previous job! Whatever you do, don't be *"pennywise but pound foolish"* by trying to do your job search on the cheap. If you have difficulty writing a first-class resume, by all means contact a resume-writing pro who can put together a dynamite resume that truly represents what you have done, can do, and will do in the future.

After reading this book, you should be able to make intelligent decisions about what, when, where, and with what results you can use professional assistance. Shop around, compare services and costs, ask questions, talk to former clients, and read the fine print before giving an employment expert a job using your hard earned money. Don't try to be the Lone Ranger all of the time. If necessary, contact a career professional at different stages of your job search. A career expect could very well become your best friend in the process of deciding exactly what you want to do in the future!

Useful Job Clubs and Support Groups

The techniques outlined thus far are designed for individuals conducting a self-directed job search. Job clubs and support groups are two important alternatives to these techniques.

Job clubs are designed to provide a group structure and support system to individuals seeking employment. These groups consist of about 12 individuals who are led by a trained counselor and supported with telephones, copying machines, and a resource center.

Formal job clubs, such as the 40-Plus Clubs (www.40plus.org/chapters) and the Five O'Clock Clubs (www.fiveoclockclub.com), organize job search activities for both the advertised and hidden job markets. Job club activities may include:

- Signing commitment agreements to achieve specific job search goals and targets.

- Contacting friends, relatives, and acquaintances for job leads.

- Completing activity forms.

- Using telephones, computers, photocopy machines, postage, and other equipment and supplies.

- Meeting with fellow participants to discuss job search progress.

- Meeting with career counselors or other career specialists.

- Attending job fairs and hiring conferences.

- Telephoning to uncover job leads.

- Using the Internet to research the job market and contact potential employers.

- Researching newspapers, telephone books, and directories.

- Developing research, telephone, interview, and social skills.

- Writing letters and resumes.

- Responding to want ads.

- Completing employment applications.

- Assessing weekly progress and sharing information with fellow group members.

In other words, the job club formalizes many of the prospecting, networking, and informational interviewing activities within a group context and interjects the role of the telephone as the key communication device for developing and expanding networks.

Many job clubs place excessive reliance on using the telephone and Internet for uncovering job leads. Members call prospective employers and ask about job openings. The Yellow Pages and the Internet become the job hunter's best friends. During a two-week period, a job club member might spend most of his or her mornings telephoning for job leads and scheduling interviews. Afternoons are normally devoted to job interviewing.

Many job club methods are designed for individuals who need a job – any job – quickly. Since individuals try to fit into available vacancies, their specific objectives and skills are of secondary concern. Other job club methods are more consistent with the focus and methods outlined in this book, especially those used by 40-Plus Clubs and Five O'Clock Clubs.

In lieu of participating in such clubs, you may want to form your own **support group** that adapts some job club methods around our central concept of finding a job fit for you – one appropriate to your objective and in line with your particular mix of skills, abilities, and interests. Support groups are a useful alternative to job clubs. They have one major advantage to conducting a job search on your own: they may cut your job search time in half because they provide an important structure for achieving goals. Forming or joining one of these groups can help direct as well as enhance your individual job search activities.

Your support group should consist of three or more individuals who are job hunting. Try to schedule regular meetings with specific purposes in mind. While the group may be highly social, especially if it involves close friends, it also should be **task-oriented**. Meet at least once a week and include your spouse. At each meeting, set **performance goals** for the week. For example, your goal can be to make 20 new contacts and conduct five informational interviews. The contacts can be made by telephone, e-mail, letter, or in person. Share your experiences and job information with each other. **Critique** each other's progress, make suggestions for improving the job search, and develop new strategies together. By doing this, you will be gaining valuable information and

feedback which are normally difficult to gain on one's own. This group should provide important psychological support to help you through your job search. After all, job hunting can be a lonely, frustrating, and exasperating experience. By sharing your experiences with others, you will find you are not alone. You will quickly learn that rejections are part of the game. The group will encourage you, and you will feel good about helping others achieve their goals. Try building small incentives into the group, such as the individual who receives the most job interviews for the month will be treated to dinner by other members of the group.

Online Networking Resources

Networking is increasingly taking on new communication forms in today's high-tech world. Job seekers can take advantage of several websites and electronic databases for conducting a job search, from gathering information on the job market to disseminating resumes to employers. The Internet also allows job seekers to network for information, advice, and job leads. If you belong to one of the major Internet service providers, such as America Online, or have direct access to the Internet's World Wide Web, you can use mailing lists, news groups, bulletin boards, blogs, chat groups, message boards, and e-mail to gather job information and make contacts with potential employers. Using e-mail, you can make personal contacts who give you job leads for further networking via computer or through the more traditional networking methods outlined in this chapter.

Several websites will help you develop networking skills as well as put you in contact with important employment-related networks. These sites include a wealth of information on the networking process:

■ WetFeet	www.wetfeet.com/advice/networking.asp
■ Monster.com	http://network.monster.com
■ Quintessential Careers	www.quintcareers.com/networking.html
■ Riley Guide	www.rileyguide.com/netintv.html
■ WinningTheJob	www.winningthejob.com
■ SchmoozeMonger	www.schmoozemonger.com
■ Susan RoAne	www.susanroane.com/free.html
■ Contacts Count	www.contactscount.com

Once you begin the process of developing your networks, you may want to use the following websites to locate long-lost friends, classmates, and others who might be helpful in your networking campaign:

- Anywho www.anywho.com
- Classmates www.classmates.com
- InfoSpace www.infospace.com
- KnowX www.knowx.com
- Reunion (high school) www.reunion.com
- Switchboard www.switchboard.com
- The Ultimate White Pages www.theultimates.com/white
- People Search Lycos www.whowhere.com
- Yahoo! People Search http://people.yahoo.com

Given your military experience, you may wish to locate some of your former military buddies. Be sure to explore these people finders for locating military personnel:

- GI Search.com www.gisearch.com
- Military.com www.military.com
- Military Connections www.militaryconnections.com
- Military USA www.militaryusa.com

If you've lost contact with your former classmates, try these websites for locating alumni groups:

- Alumni.net www.alumni.net
- Curious Cat Alumni
 Connections www.curiouscat.net/alumni

Many women's groups organize networking opportunities among their members for career development purposes. The following organizations are especially relevant to female networkers:

- Advancing Women www.advancingwomen.com
- American Association of
 University Women www.aauw.org
- American Business
 Women's Association www.abwahq.org
- Systers www.www.systers.org
- Business Women's
 Network www.bwni.com

- Federally Employed
 Women www.few.org
- iVillage www.ivillage.com
- Womans-net www.womans-net.com

Business professionals will find these three networking groups of special interest because they sponsor special online and offline networking events:

- Company of Friends http://fastcompany.com/cof
- ExecuNet www.execunet.com
- Technology Executives
 Networking Group www.theteng.org

Many of the large Internet employment sites maintain message boards. Two of the largest message board operations, which offer opportunities to network for information and advice, are found at these websites:

- Monster.com http://network.monster.com/
 board

- Vault.com www.vault.com/community/mb/
 mb_home.jsp

The latest trend or fad in online networking is based upon the "six degrees of separation theory" – everyone is connected to everyone else in the world by only six other people. A somewhat dubious theory, nonetheless, these networks have been responsible for a great deal of news media hype since 2003 on how to expand one's network of connections for personal and professional purposes. Building electronic communities, these networks are designed to put users into contact with thousands of other people for all types of purposes – from dating to making friends to finding a job to recruiting to developing sales forces to closing business deals to discovering an old high school flame.

The ultimate soft approach to cold calling, these electronic networks tend to be of questionable value to job seekers who have actually used them. They especially appeal to passive job seekers who hope to be "discovered" online. After all, these networks formalize what is essentially an informal, personal process that works best in one degree removed face-to-face situations. Nonetheless, these new electronic networks offer some interesting online networking opportunities for those who have the time and dedication to make them work, which means moving from a passive

to an active networking posture. They probably are most effective for those who need to prospect for new business and potential sales contacts, which is the direction many of the more entrepreneurial such networks now take. The following websites are devoted to promoting this type of networking activity:

- LinkedIn www.linkedin.com
- ZeroDegrees www.zerodegrees.com
- Orkut www.orkut.com
- Friendster www.friendster.com
- Ryze Business Networking http://new.ryze.com
- Spoke www.spoke.com
- EntreMate www.entremate.com
- MySpace www.myspace.com

The first website, www.linkedin.com, tends to be used by more job seekers and recruiters than the other networking sites because it includes job listings along with social networking. A few other social networking sites also are including job postings on their sites. If you want to try your luck with this type of online networking in your job search, we recommend starting with LinkedIn. For information on dozens of business and common interest networking sites, visit this blog:

http://socialsoftware.weblogsinc.com/entry/9817137581524458/

The Internet can significantly enhance your job search. It offers new networking possibilities for individuals who are literate in today's digital technology. If you have access to the Internet, we recommend getting your resume into various employment websites. Explore their bulletin boards, chat groups, message boards, resources, and job vacancies. Within just a few minutes of electronic networking, you may pick up important job information, advice, and leads that could turn into a real job. For more information on online networking, see the electronic networking sections of Ron and Caryl Krannich's two books on networking and the Internet: *The Savvy Networker* and *America's Top Internet Job Sites* (Impact Publications).

Disappointing "In the Moment" Networking

Although networking is important for gathering information, advice, and referrals, don't be surprised if many of your networking contacts become disappointments. Indeed, in today's fast-paced world of multiple and

superficial encounters, networking often becomes an "in the moment" phenomenon. This is especially true with online networking, which is of questionable value for many people.

Individuals you encounter as possible networking contacts often only give you a some attention during your initial encounter – in the moment you meet. It could be a five-, 10-, or 15-minute conversation. You depart with the impression that you have formed a friendship, or at least a valuable contact, since the individual may give you his or her business card and indicate to give them a call or e-mail. But try to follow up on this new-found contact. What you thought might become an important contact can quickly fade away as the initial encounter becomes a one-shot *"you have my attention right now but not necessarily in the future"* meeting. In fact, many networking contacts quickly dissipate after the initial encounter. You may follow up your encounter, but chances are he or she either doesn't remember you or is too busy to give you attention, especially when your follow-up requires some work on the part of the contact.

Like many of today's friendships, network contacts can become very superficial encounters that lead nowhere. Consider these to be dead-end encounters – entertaining during the initial meeting but useless thereafter. To make networking work in your favor, you'll need to cast a very large net with the hope of developing some useful networking contacts. In other words, you'll need to work your network harder than ever to get desirable outcomes.

7

Select the Most Effective Job Search Approaches

HOW WILL YOU GO ABOUT finding a job? Are you planning to do this on your own or rely on others to find a job for you? Will you primarily respond to classified ads in the newspaper with a letter and resume or visit companies to fill out applications? Do you plan to knock on doors to introduce yourself to employers? What about using the telephone to call employers, or searching for job vacancies on bulletin boards or on the Internet? Will you look for jobs through a government One-Stop Career Center, employment agencies, placement services, or friends and family? Do you plan to attend a job fair or some other type of career or job event?

Most anyone can find a job, especially in an economy where demand for workers outstrips available supply. You can always wait tables, drive a vehicle, clean buildings, paint, lift boxes, pick up trash, or use a shovel – high turnover jobs for which there is always an ongoing demand. The real questions are (1) what type of work will you find? and (2) how rewarding will the job be in terms of salary, benefits, and job satisfaction?

How you approach your job search will make a big difference in what type of work you will do as well as the next job you may move to in your worklife. If you choose an appropriate job search approach, you should be able to find a job that's right for you.

131

Become a Self-Reliant Job Seeker

While many transitioning military see themselves as self-starters who should be able to quickly land a civilian job, in reality many have difficulty finding a job on their own. After all, finding a job is not something they have a great deal of experience in doing. As we will see in subsequent chapters, finding a job involves specific writing, communication, and interpersonal skills they may not readily possess. In fact, few ex-military have held many, if any, full-time civilian jobs, and many have never conducted a well organized job search on their own. Few know what they want to do, where to start, whom to contact, how to dress, how to best network for job leads, what type of resume is best for their situation, how to write winning resumes and letters, which Internet employment sites yield the best results, how to answer and ask questions, how a behavioral interview differs from a situational interview, how to ask for the job, what follow-up methods work best, and how to negotiate salary and terms of employment. Their networking and salary negotiation skills are especially weak because they are part of a culture that often stresses the importance of not talking to strangers (you must do this in order to effectively network) and not talking to others about their incomes (you must do this in order to effectively negotiate salary and benefits).

> *Many transitioning military accept jobs that are 15 to 25 percent below their true worth.*

As a result, many transitioning military stumble into the job market without much focus, make numerous mistakes, turn to questionable "professionals" who charge them a great deal of money to ostensibly find them a job, and accept jobs that are 15 to 25 percent below their true worth. In the end, they find a job, but they soon (usually within the first year) want to change jobs because they discover they are in the wrong job or that they prematurely accepted a job that was beneath their true worth. This should not happen to you!

The most effective job search methods require you to take responsibility for your employment and your future career. While you will conduct a job search within your support system, you start by acquiring important job search skills for contacting employers, getting interviews and offers, negotiating compensation, and becoming a star employee. These are important **self-management skills** that you will most likely use throughout your life as you go through several job changes. Since individuals first entering the job market today will make several job and career changes, the more self-reliant you become in finding and keeping

a job, the easier it should be for you to change jobs and careers in the years ahead. One of your major goals should be to acquire the necessary job search skills to land a job on your own.

The Best Job Search Methods

As indicated in the questions at the beginning of this chapter, there are many ways to find a job. In fact, every day hundreds of people find jobs using a variety of methods. However, some of these methods are more effective in finding a job than others.

The best methods are ones that lead to good paying jobs with a future – not just any job. Studies consistently show that the most effective job search method (used by 50 to 80 percent of successful candidates) is **networking** – finding job leads through family members, friends, and acquaintances. The job search experiences of transitioning military also confirm this finding – those who quickly enter the job market do so through the assistance of family and friends. Most military personnel and veterans operate within a rich **network of relationships** – from com-

> *The least effective but most popular job search method is responding to classified ads and job postings.*

manders, subordinates, military buddies, and neighbors to government contractors, business people, and members of churches and other community organizations – developed over time as they move from one position and assignment to another. The least effective job search method, which ironically is the most widely used method, is responding to classified ads and job postings. If you want to use your time wisely, focus the largest amount of your time on those methods that appear to have the greatest payoff in terms of job leads and interviews.

Let's examine the most widely used job search methods. Our advice: Don't rely on any one method; use several of these methods throughout your job search.

Respond to Classified Ads

Pick up any newspaper and thumb through the classified ad section in search of a job related to your interests, skills, and experience. Alternatively, surf the Internet for job postings on many employment websites, such as Monster.com or CareerBuilder.com. Chances are you will identify several interesting jobs, but few of them will relate to your skills and experience. Believing that most job vacancies are found in the newspapers

or on the Internet, thousands of job seekers explore classified ads and job postings each day. Engaging in wishful thinking, they often respond with a resume, letter, or phone call. Unfortunately, two things happen at this stage:

1. Many other people also respond to the same ad and thus they face a great deal of competition for a single position.

2. Lacking the required skills and experience, they stretch their qualifications in the hopes that the employer might hire them anyway.

Not surprisingly, employers often receive numerous responses to their ads. They can immediately disregard 80 percent of the responses, because the candidates do not appear qualified for the position. Indeed, many candidates seem to waste their time applying for a position that does not relate to their skills and experience.

In some cases, an ad or posting may not be for an actual job. Some employers place ads in order to collect resumes or sell candidates on self-employment schemes. Don't assume just because an ad appears in the newspaper or on the Internet that it represents a legitimate job vacancy.

Your chances of getting a job by responding to classified ads and Internet postings are not very good – at best a five percent chance of getting a positive or negative response from an employer! However, many job seekers spend most of their job search time on this single, ineffective job search method. They read the classifieds in newspaper and on the Internet, post their resume to online employment sites, respond to a few job listings, and then sit and wait for employers to call them for an interview. When they don't get a response, they conclude there are no jobs available for them at present.

Here's the truth about classified job ads:

1. **They represent no more than 15 percent of available job vacancies.** Some of the remaining 85 percent of job vacancies may be advertised elsewhere (on the Internet, in employment offices, on bulletin boards, with unions), but most of the jobs (50 to 75 percent) are found on the "hidden job market," which primarily operates by word-of-mouth, and are found through networking.

2. **They tend to represent jobs at the two extreme ends of the job market** – low-wage, high-turnover positions and high-wage, highly skilled positions. In other words, they represent

difficult-to-fill positions. Most jobs, which fall between these two extremes, are not well represented in the classifieds.

3. **They create unrealistic expectations – false hopes** that one will actually get the job or that they are basically unqualified for most jobs. If nothing else, such activities keep them busy (they are doing something however ineffective) and thus give them a false sense of actually making progress with their job search.

Our point here is that you should not waste a great deal of time focused on classified ads and job postings. It's an ego-bruising experience to get rejected by many employers. Explore classified ads and online job postings for a few minutes each day, but move on to more productive job search methods.

If you see a job that seems to be a perfect fit, you can increase your odds of getting a job interview by doing the following:

1. **Respond immediately** with a phone call and ask for a job interview.

2. **Follow the application instructions.** How does the employer want you to contact him – by e-mail, fax, or mail your resume or call for a telephone screening interview? What does he or she want you to send him – resume, letter, references, examples of work?

3. **Dissect the ad carefully and then write a cover letter** in which you respond to each requirement with corresponding examples of your qualifications. If you are applying for a position as an electrician, your letter might include the following statements (see example of "T" letter in Chapter 12):

Your Requirements	My Qualifications
■ One year experience	Completed one-year apprenticeship and served two years as an electrician's helper on complex commercial projects.
■ Responsible	Praised by previous employer and co-workers as being a quick starter who takes initiative, is responsible, and gets the job done well and on time.

4. Follow up your application within five days with a phone call, fax, or e-mail. We prefer a phone call. This will be the single most important action you can take to move your application to the top of the pile and get it read and remembered. Ask if the employer has any questions about your application, restate your qualifications and interest in the position, and ask for a job interview. If you don't ask for the job interview, chances are the employer won't contact you for an interview! Your phone call also gives you a chance to be interviewed over the telephone by the employer – the first screening step in the job interview process.

A good resource for handling classified job ads in your job search is Kenton W. Elderkin's classic *How to Get Interviews From Classified Job Ads* (Impact Publications).

Use the Internet

During the past 10 years the Internet has become a very popular resource for both employers and job seekers. In fact, much of today's job market and recruitment/job search activities have moved to the Internet. If you are not using the Internet in your job search, you are not up-to-date in your job search, and you will be missing out on important segments of the job market. In addition, employers may view you as unprepared for today's workplace, which increasingly values technical skills.

> *Approximately 15 percent of job seekers actually find jobs based upon using the Internet.*

Many employers use the Internet to recruit candidates through a variety of general and specialized employment websites as well as through their own company websites. Job seekers use the Internet to find job vacancies, post their resumes to online resume databases, and research jobs, companies, and employers. Approximately 15 percent of job seekers actually find jobs based upon using the Internet. This percentage has steadily increased – from just five percent five years ago.

In many respects, using the Internet is similar to finding a job through classified ads. Indeed, many classified ads appear on employment websites and are called "job postings." Employers who might normally place classified ads for positions in newspapers find it's cheaper and more effective to post their jobs on websites. They also find resume databases useful for identifying candidates who best meet their hiring requirements.

The largest and most popular employment websites provide a wealth of information for job seekers about jobs, employers, and the job search in general: job search tips, featured articles, career experts, career assessment tests, community forums, chat groups, salary calculators, resume and interview advice, relocation information, success stories, newsletters, career events, online job fairs, polls and surveys, contests, online education and training, company ads, and special channels for students, freelancers, military, and other groups. The nine most popular employment websites are:

- www.ajb.org
- www.monster.com
- www.careerbuilder.com
- www.careerjournal.com
- www.directemployers.com
- http://hotjobs.yahoo.com
- www.nationjob.com
- www.careerflex.com
- www.employment911.com

A few websites allow you to search for millions of job postings on many websites simultaneously. Called "aggregators" or "meta-search job sites," some of the major such websites include:

- www.indeed.com
- www.simplyhired.com
- www.grassisgreener.com
- www.jobfactory.com
- www.job-search-engine.com

As you explore the Internet, you should at least visit these major employment websites. Altogether, over 25,000 websites focus on employment. Since there are over 15 million employers in the United States, millions of employer websites include information on employment with specific companies and organizations.

As you will quickly discover, the Internet is a wonderful information and communication tool if used properly. It's an especially frustrating medium for individuals who spend most of their job search time trying to find a job online by responding to job postings and entering their resume into online resume databases.

While the Internet can be extremely useful for job seekers, few of them know how to use this tool properly. Many mistakenly believe that employers actually hire over the Internet! When you are looking for a job, the Internet is best used for:

- Conducting research on jobs, employers, companies, and communities.

- Acquiring useful advice and referrals.

- Communicating with individuals via e-mail.

Your most productive online activities will relate to **research** and **communication**. While you may, depending on your qualifications, want to post your resume on various employment websites and periodically review online job listings, don't spend a great deal of time doing so and then waiting to hear from employers based on such activities. This whole process is similar to working classified employment ads in newspapers – a low probability of getting a response from employers. Move on to other more productive activities, especially visiting **employer websites**, which are more likely to yield useful information, job listings, and applications than the more general and popular employment websites.

> *More and more employers recruit directly from their own websites rather than use general employment websites.*

In fact, since more and more employers recruit directly from their own websites, rather than use general employment websites. You are well advised to explore employer websites for employment information. If, for example, you have a college education, a strong technical background, and are exceptionally talented, companies such as Microsoft (www.microsoft.com/careers) and Boston Consulting Group (www.bcg.com) provide a wealth of information for such job seekers interested in their companies. Even if you don't qualify for employment with these companies, you can learn a great deal about job hunting by visiting those two websites alone.

But your most useful online job search activity relates to **research**. Thousands of websites can yield useful information for enhancing your job search. For example, use the Internet to explore different jobs (www.bls.gov/oco) and employers (www.hoovers.com), community-based employment assistance (www.careeronestop.org), career counselors (www.nbcc.org), networking groups (www.linkedin.com), salary ranges (www.salary.com), best communities (www.findyourspot.com), relocation (www.monstermoving.com), job search tips (www.winningthejob.com), and career advice (www.wetfeet.com). You can even use the Internet to conduct an online assessment (www.careerlab.com), blast your resume to thousands of employers (www.resumeblaster.com), contact recruiters (www.recruitersonline.com), and explore hundreds of professional associations (www.ipl.org/div/aon) and nonprofit organizations (www.guidestar.org) that are linked to thousands of employers.

The Internet also is a terrific way to **communicate** with people, especially with employers. If you don't have an e-mail address or if you want a separate account just for your job search, you can always set up a free e-mail account through one of the major search engines, such as Google (www.mail.google.com), MSN (www.hotmail.com) or Yahoo (www.yahoo.com), or create a dedicated job search e-mail through a major employment website, such as Monster.com or CareerBuilder. com.

For more information on how to wisely use the Internet in your job search, see Ron and Caryl Krannich's *America's Top Internet Job Sites* (Impact Publications), Margaret Dikel's *Job Searching on the Internet* (McGraw-Hill), and Richard Nelson Bolles's *Job Hunting on the Internet* (Ten Speed Press). Much of this advice can be found online by visiting these useful website:

- http://quintcareers.com
- www.rileyguide.com
- www.jobhuntersbible.com

Contact Employers Directly

One of the most effective methods for finding a job is making direct contact with employers. You can do this many different ways:

1. **Use the telephone:** Few people enjoy making cold calls to strangers, especially since doing so results in many rejections. However, job seekers who contact numerous employers by phone do generate job interviews. In fact, this is the fastest way to get job interviews. Make 100 phone calls to inquire about job vacancies and you may be able to generate one or two job interviews. Since this is largely a numbers game, and you are playing the odds, you must be willing to make many phone calls and endure numerous rejections. Most people you call will politely tell you they have no jobs available at present. But persistence will pay off. You will eventually uncover job vacancies for which you qualify. Use the Yellow Pages as your directory for identifying potential employers.

 When making such calls, have a prepared outline of points to cover in front of you from which you (1) quickly introduce yourself, (2) ask about job vacancies, (3) request a job interview, and (4) thank the person for his or her time and consideration. Don't write it out word for word and read it. If you do this, you will sound as if you are reading it. You

want to sound spontaneous. If you receive a rejection, that's okay. In the process, you may acquire some useful information about jobs elsewhere. And you can now move on to call the next potential employer!

2. **Send e-mail:** You should explore the websites of employers. While many of these websites will post employment opportunities, others may not. If they don't, send an e-mail inquiring about such opportunities. However, if you can find a phone number, it's best to make a telephone call rather than wait for an e-mail reply. Many companies automatically delete unsolicited e-mail inquiries. E-mail is no substitute for using the telephone, which is more efficient and effective than e-mail.

3. **Go door to door:** Many job seekers are successful in finding jobs by literally showing up at the doors or work sites of employers and asking about job opportunities. This approach requires a great deal of initiative, entrepreneurship, and a willingness to accept rejections as part of the game. This is the in-your-face version of the cold telephone call. Many businesses, such as large retailers (Wal-Mart, K-Mart, Target, Home Depot), grocery stores, restaurants, and banks, are well organized to handle walk-in job seekers. You may be asked to sit at a computer terminal or "job kiosk" to complete an electronic application, or you will be given a paper application to complete. Others, such as construction firms, often welcome individuals to show up at their job sites for work.

 If you walk into a small business, such as a warehouse, auto repair shop, or construction company, you may be able to meet directly with the owner and ask about job opportunities. Timing is the key to such walk-in approaches – if you happen to arrive at the right time, when a job needs to be filled immediately, you may get lucky and be offered the job. If that happens, be prepared to interview for a job while inquiring about opportunities. If you use this approach, be prepared for many rejections. However, if you persist and visit 100 employers, chances are you will uncover one or two job opportunities for which you qualify. If you visit 500 employers, you may uncover five job opportunities. But you will probably experience a few hundred rejections in the process of uncovering the right job for you.

4. **Hang around busy corners:** Day-laborer sites, both formal and informal, are used a great deal by illegal immigrants and individuals with limited skills and education. While you most likely will never use this job search method, nonetheless, they are employment options for people who need to quickly find employment. Day-laborer sites may be found on a busy street corner or adjacent to a convenience store or vacant lot. Large day-laborer markets of Hispanics (*jornaleros*) are especially prevalent in Southern California, Arizona, Texas, and Florida.

 Employers – usually homeowners or subcontractors who need cheap day laborers – may stop to check who is available for a few hours or a day or two of temporary work. Most work is physical labor – landscaping, roofing, gardening, construction – and wages are usually negotiated on an hourly, daily, or per job basis. In many communities, informal day-laborer sites represent a gray market of undocumented workers (illegal immigrants) and cash wages (no tax or Social Security deductions). Cities in some states, such as California, Washington, Arizona, Illinois, New York, Connecticut, Maryland, Georgia, Florida, and Washington, DC, actually sponsor formal day-laborer sites where employers can come to hire laborers. In California and Arizona, these markets are 95 percent Hispanic.

Register With Employment Agencies and Placement Services

Public employment services operate One-Stop Career Centers (www.careeronestop.org), which post many vacancies listed by employers in their communities. These centers also are linked to America's Job Bank (www.ajb.dni.us), an electronic job bank which includes over 1 million job listings. You may want to visit your local center and acquaint yourself with the many useful free services available to the public. Many employment agencies and placement services look for candidates they can place with their clients. Registering with these agencies and services can result in temporary or permanent jobs. However, beware of any agency or service that wants you to pay them for employment services. The legitimate firms are paid by employers – not by job seekers. Anyone who asks you to pay them money to find you a job should be avoided. You can find legitimate agencies through a One-Stop Career Center (ask their personnel for recommended agencies and services). Two of the best

known temporary labor and staffing firms found in hundreds of communities across the country are LaborFinders (www.laborfinders.com) and Manpower (www.manpower.com). You may want to visit these firms early in your job search, since they may be able to help you quickly find employment with their many clients. Also, check on dozens of other temporary employment firms that may operate in your community. If you are a college graduate, you can use the placement services of the career center or alumni office. If you are a recent graduate, be sure to sign up for on-campus job interviews through the career services center.

Contact Military Associations

Ex-military should take advantage of placement services available through military associations. The two major associations include:

- **Military Officers Association of America (MOAA)** www.moaa.org/tops
- **Non Commissioned Officers Association (NCOA)** www.ncoausa.org

Military academy graduates should contact the alumni officers of their respective service academy:

- **U.S. Air Force Academy** www.usafa.af.mil
- **U.S. Coast Guard Academy** www.cga.edu
- **U.S. Military Academy** www.usma.edu
- **U.S. Naval Academy** www.usna.edu

Several military-related professional and veterans organizations also may provide some employment assistance:

All Services

- **Armed Forces Communications and Electronics Association (AFCEA)** www.afcea.org
- **American Legion** www.legion.org
- **Veterans of Foreign Wars** www.vfw.org
- **Disabled American Veterans** www.dav.org

Air Force

- Air Force Association www.afa.org

Army

- Association of the United
 States Army (AUSA) www.ausa.org
- US Army Warrant Officers
 Association www.usawoa.org

Navy

- Fleet Reserve Association www.fra.org
- Naval Enlisted Reserve
 Association www.nera.org
- Surface Navy Association www.navysna.org
- Tailhook Association www.tailhook.org

Marines

- Marine Corps League www.mcleague.org
- Marine Corps Reserve www.roa.org/military_
 Officers Association section/mariner_news.asp
- Marine Executive Association www.marineea.org

Intel and Special Ops

- Association of Former
 Intelligence Officers www.afio.com
- International Association of
 Counterterrorism and
 Security Personnel www.iacsp.com
- Military Intelligence
 Corps Association www.micorps.org
- National Military
 Intelligence Association www.nmia.org
- Naval Intelligence
 Professionals www.navintpro.org
- Special Forces Association www.sfahq.org
- UDT-SEAL Association www.udtseal.org
- U.S. Army Ranger
 Association www.ranger.org

Visit Military-Friendly Employment Websites

Several websites are designed for transitioning military personnel. Most include a resume database, job listings, employer profiles, articles, and job search advice for ex-military. The major websites include:

- Corporate Gray Online www.greentogray.com
- TAOnline www.taonline.com
- VetJobs.com www.vetjobs.com
- The Destiny Group www.destinygroup.com
- MilitaryCity.com www.militarycity.com
 (Operated by Monster.com)

Other websites focusing on transitioning military personnel include the following:

- Army Times www.armytimes.com
- Bradley-Morris.com www.bradley-morris.com
- Cameron-Brooks www.cameron-brooks.com
- CareerCommandPost.com www.careercommandpost.com
- Civilian Readiness www.civilianreadiness.com
- Clearance Jobs www.clearancejobs.com
- Defense Talent Network www.defensetalent.com
- DOD Transportal www.dodtransportal.org
- eMilitary.org www.emilitary.org
- G.I. Jobs www.gijobs.net
- Helmets to Hardhats www.helmetstohardhats.org
- HireVetsFirst www.hirevetsfirst.gov
- IntelligenceCareers.com www.intelligencecareers.com
- Lucas Group www.lucascareers.com
- Military.com www.military.com
- Military Candidates www.militarycandidates.com
- Military Exits www.militaryexits.com
- Military Headhunter www.militaryheadhunter.com
- MilitaryHire.com www.militaryhire.com
- MilitaryJobHunts.com www.militaryjobhunts.com
- Military Outplacement Post www.midwestmilitary.com
- Military Partners www.militarypartners.com
- MilitaryResumes.com www.militaryresumes.com
- MilitaryStar.com www.militarystars.com
- Military Transition www.militarytransition.com
- Military Transition Times www.militarytransitiontimes.com

- Orion International — www.orioninternational.com
- RecruitMilitary.com — www.recruitmilitary.com
- TekSystems.com — www.teksystems.com
- SmartStart for New Vets — www.smartstartvets.org
- Veterans' Employment and Training Service (DOL) — www.dol.gov/vets
- VeteransWorld.com — www.veteransworld.com
- Vets4Hire — www.vets4hire.com

Attend Job Fairs

Job fairs are great ways for service members and veterans to survey job opportunities, meet employers, network, practice interview skills, learn about salaries and benefits, and possibly get hired on the spot. While you will find many job fairs operating in large cities (check the classified section of your Sunday newspaper for large ads announcing such events), a few organizations sponsor job fairs specifically for transitioning military, including ones specializing in JMOs, military intelligence, and top secret clearances. Check out these websites for the job fair nearest you:

- Corporate Gray — www.corporategray.com
- Military Officers Association of America — www.moaa.org/tops
- Non Commissioned Officers Association — www.ncoausa.org
- Intelligence Careers — www.intelligencecareers.com
- Tech Expo USA — www.techexposusa.com
- MilitaryStars.com — www.militarystars.com

For current listings of upcoming military job fairs, visit these sections of the TAonline and HireVetsFirst websites:

www.taonline.com/careerpages/careerfairs.asp
www.hirevetsfirst.gov/events.asp

The typical job fair is held in a large conference room of a hotel or a public building and takes place over one day – often from 10am to 2pm or 6pm. Many employers have representatives at tables or booths who advertise their company or organization and are looking for candidates who meet their hiring requirements. Job seekers circulate among the various displays (booths and tables) as they try to learn more about the organizations, pick up literature, talk with a representative, and leave a

resume. Job fairs can be very enlightening experiences for job seekers, especially if they find a good selection of employers and if the job fair also includes special job search workshops, such as writing resumes, interviewing for jobs, or using a job fair in your job search. Job fairs for transitioning military are great places to survey employment options, practice job search skills, meet employer representatives, interview for jobs, and possibly land a job.

You should keep the following nine tips in mind when planning to attend a job fair:

1. **Check to see if you qualify for the job fair.** Some job fairs are open to the general public and involve many different types of employers. These general job fairs are sometimes sponsored by a single company that is opening a new business and needs to recruit hundreds of people, such as a large hotel and conference center, sports arena, or an amusement park, Many job fairs specialize in a particular skill or occupational area. For example, some job fairs only focus on high-tech and computer skills. Others may specialize in clerical skills or the construction trades. And still others may be organized for government-related jobs and the intelligence community.

 Most military job fairs are open to all members of the military as well as veterans. A typical such job fair may include 50 to 100 employers and be attended by several hundred individuals who will soon be separating from the service. Many veterans, who are looking to change civilian employers, may also attend these job fairs. Other military job fairs may be restricted to JMOs, officers, noncommissioned officers, and individuals with top secret security clearances. Special career events, such as career conferences sponsored by a single company, may be by invitation only.

2. **Be sure to pre-register for the job fair.** Some job fairs require you to pre-register for the event – not just show up at the door. Others only require registration at the door. One of the registration requirements is to submit a resume which, in turn, is entered into a resume database. This database enables employers attending the job fair to review the resumes online before and after the job fair.

3. **Plan ahead.** Prior to attending the event, try to get a list of companies that will be attending. Research several of the

companies on the Internet. Discover what they do, who they employ, and what is particularly unique or different about them. When you go the job fair, you will have some knowledge of those employers you want to meet. Better still, you'll impress the representatives when you indicate you know something about what they do. You'll avoid asking that killer question – *"What do you do?"* Being prepared in this manner also means you will be more at ease in talking with employers, because you have some common ground knowledge for engaging in an intelligent job-oriented conversation.

4. **Be prepared to interview for the job.** Since some employers will actually interview candidates, don't assume a job fair is merely a casual "get together" to just meet employers. Prepare for a job fair in the same way you would prepare for a job interview – bring a positive attitude, be enthusiastic and energetic, anticipate questions, prepare your own questions, and observe all the verbal and nonverbal rules for interview success (see Chapter 15).

5. **Bring copies of your resume to the job fair.** Since you will be meeting many employers at the job fair as you circulate from one table or booth to another, your calling card is your resume. A good rule of thumb is to bring 25 to 50 copies of your resume to the job fair. Many job fairs also provide copying services, just in case you need to make more copies of your resume. If the employer is interested in you, they will want to see your resume. Best of all, they will give you instant feedback on your qualifications. In many cases, they will interview you on the spot, asking questions you may be unprepared to answer! So make sure you write a terrific resume as well as bring enough copies for every employer you are interested in meeting. Anticipate being asked questions that normally arise during a formal job interview.

6. **Dress appropriately.** Job fairs are places where first impressions are very important. Be sure to dress as if you were going to a formal job interview – conservative and neat. Most military job fair organizers recommend two types of attire – service dress uniform or business attire. Remember, you are meeting representatives of employers, and some encounters may turn into actual interviews in the representative's booth.

7. **Prepare a 30-second pitch.** Your 30-second pitch should tell an employer who you are and what skills and experience you have that should be of interest to the employer. Tell them why they should consider interviewing and hiring you.

8. **Expect the unexpected.** Many first-time job fair attendees are surprised and unprepared to respond to prospective employer's questions. As a result, many make mistakes that could negatively affect their employment prospects and income. For example, don't be shocked to encounter this question: *"What are your salary expectations?"* or *"What kind of salary are looking for?"* Be very careful how you respond to this killer inquiry, which is primarily designed to quickly screen you in or out of further consideration. Not prepared for this question, some attendees stammer and then blurt out a specific figure that may be too low or too high. At this stage in your job search, your answer should always be something like this: *"I'm open at this stage. Could you tell me more about the job and what it normally pays for someone with my qualifications?"* This puts the salary ball in the employer's court, which is where it should always be. Remember the old poker saying – he who reveals his hand first loses the advantage. As we will see later when we examine salary negotiations, salary is always that last thing you discuss after you have received a job offer. **Never** discuss salary at a job fair.

9. **Follow up your contacts within five days.** Job fairs are all about networking with employers. If you're interested in an employer and you've had a chance to meet a representative and get his or her name and business card, be sure to follow up with a phone call and/or e-mail within five days of your meeting. This communication will remind the individual of your continuing interest and may result in a formal job interview with other company representatives.

Network With Family, Friends, and Others

The single most effective way of getting a job is through networking. Your network consists of family, friends, commanders, service buddies, former supervisors, acquaintances, minister, people you do business with, and even strangers whom you meet and with whom you develop a relationship. These people can be of assistance in finding a job, because many

have useful information, advice, and referrals to others who know about jobs appropriate for you. You want to plug into these informal yet rich channels of job information and communications.

As we noted earlier, most jobs are not advertised. Through networking, you tap into the **hidden job market** where many of the best jobs can be found. These jobs are located through word-of-mouth. People in your network – family members, friends, and colleagues – know about such jobs, or they may know people who may know, and thus they refer you to others in the know. The more networking you do, the more likely you will find a job on the hidden job market.

However, many people are reluctant to network because it involves initiating conversations and meetings with strangers. The fear of rejection (they may say *"No, I can't help you"*) works against many job seekers. But this is a false fear that seldom materializes. Instead, people who learn to network well are surprised how supportive others are in giving them useful information, advice, and referrals. Many of these people have been in similar situations and others helped them with their job search. Most people enjoy helping others, as long as they are not put on the spot and

> *The single most effective way of getting a job is through networking in the hidden job market.*

asked to take responsibility for your employment fate! Networkers are not beggars – they are nice people who are in search of information and advice, and hopefully useful referrals to people who have the power to hire.

We devote Chapter 14 to the whole process of networking in the job search. We show you how to launch an effective networking campaign. Read it carefully and put it into practice immediately. It may well become your most important approach to landing a job that's right for you!

Part II

Develop Powerful Career Transition Skills

8

Discover the Truth About You

W E LIVE IN A SKILLS-BASED society where individuals market their skills to employers in exchange for money, position, and power. The ease by which they change jobs and careers is directly related to their ability to communicate their skills to employers and then transfer them to new work settings.

To best position yourself in the job markets of today and tomorrow, you should pay particular attention to refining your present skills as well as acquiring new and more marketable skills.

Identify Your Skills

But before you can refine your skills or acquire additional skills, you need to know what skills you presently possess. As a transitioning service member or veteran, you have many skills you acquired in the military that are transferable to civilian jobs. Unfortunately, few people can identify and talk about their skills even though they possess hundreds of skills which they use on a regular basis. This becomes a real problem when they must write a resume or go to a job interview. Since employers want to know about your specific abilities and skills, you must both identify and communicate your skills to them. You should be able to explain what it is you do well and give examples relevant to employers' needs.

What skills do you already have to offer employers? If you have just completed an educational program, the skills you have to offer are most likely related to the subject matter you studied. If you are changing jobs

153

or careers, the skills you wish to communicate to employers will be those things you already have demonstrated you can do in specific jobs.

As we noted earlier, the skills required for **finding a job** are no substitute for the skills necessary for **doing the job**. Learning new skills requires a major investment of time, money, and effort. Nonetheless, the long-term pay-off should more than justify the initial costs. Indeed, research continues to show that well selected education and training provide the best returns on individual and societal investment.

Types of Skills

Most people possess two types of skills that define their accomplishments and strengths as well as enable them to enter and advance within the job market: work-content skills and functional skills. You need to acquaint yourself with these skills at the beginning of your job search, before writing your resume and interviewing for jobs. These skills become the key language for communicating your qualifications to employers through your resumes and letters as well as in interviews. They can be expressed in the form of both verbs and nouns – an important distinction that differentiates a conventional paper resume from an electronic scannable resume.

We assume you have already acquired certain **work-content skills** necessary to function effectively in today's job market. These "hard skills" are easy to recognize since they are often identified as "qualifications" for specific jobs; they are the subject of most educational and training programs. Work-content skills tend to be technical and job-specific in nature. Examples of such skills include proficiency in designing Web pages, programming computers, teaching accounting, or operating an X-ray machine. They may require formal training, are associated with specific trades or professions, and are used only in certain job and career settings. Employers in those settings use a separate skills vocabulary, jargon, and subject matter for specifying technical qualifications of individuals entering and advancing in an occupation. While these skills do not transfer well from one occupation to another, they are critical for entering and advancing within certain occupations.

At the same time, you possess numerous **functional/transferable skills** employers readily seek along with your work-content skills. These "soft skills" are associated with numerous job settings, are mainly acquired through experience rather than formal training, and can be communicated through a general vocabulary. Functional/transferable skills are less easy to recognize since they tend to be linked to certain **personal characteristics** (energetic, intelligent, likable) and the ability to **deal**

with processes (communicating, problem-solving, motivating) rather than do things (programming a computer, building a house, repairing air-conditioners). While most people have only a few work-content skills, they may have numerous – as many as 300 – functional/transferable skills. These skills enable job seekers to more easily change jobs. But you must first be aware of your functional skills before you can relate them to the job market.

Most people view the world of work in traditional occupational job skill terms. This is a **structural view** of occupational realities. As such, occupational fields are seen as consisting of separate and distinct jobs which, in turn, require specific work-content skills. From this perspective, occupations and jobs are relatively self-contained entities. Social work, for example, is seen as being different from paralegal work; social workers, therefore, are not "qualified" to seek paralegal work.

> *Functional skills can be transferred from one job or career to another.*

On the other hand, a **functional view** of occupations and jobs emphasizes the similarity of job characteristics as well as common linkages between different occupations. Although the structure of occupations and jobs may differ, they have similar functions. They involve working with people, data, processes, and objects. If you work with people, data, processes, and objects in one occupation, you can transfer that experience to other occupations which have similar functions. Once you understand how your skills relate to the functions as well as investigate the structure of different occupations, you should be prepared to make job changes from one occupational field to another. Whether you possess the necessary work-content skills to qualify for entry into the other occupational field is another question altogether.

The skills we identify and help you organize in this chapter are the functional skills career counselors normally emphasize when advising clients to assess their **strengths**. In contrast to work-content skills, functional skills can be transferred from one job or career to another. They enable individuals to make some job and career changes without acquiring additional education and training. They constitute an important bridge for moving from one occupation to another.

Before you decide if you need more education or training, you should first assess both your functional and work-content skills to see how they can be transferred to other jobs and occupations. Once you do this, you should be better prepared to communicate your qualifications to employers with a rich skills-based vocabulary.

Translating Military Skills Into Civilian Terms

Many of the skills you acquired in the military may appear to be specific to particular military jobs. While some of the jobs may not have a civilian equivalent, most skills you use in performing those jobs can be expressed in civilian terms.

One of the best ways to identify the civilian equivalent to your military skills is to visit the TAOnline website: http://taonline.com. Under their "Transition Tools" section, you'll find something called **Mil-Skills Translator**™ which is linked to the Department of Defense's Military Occupational Title Database (MOTD) at http://www.odh.asmt.com. This database includes detailed narrative descriptions and requirements of 152 joint-service military occupations. Just enter your service branch, rank, and military occupational code and this program will give you details on the occupational skills associated with your military work. This information will be especially helpful for identifying your skills and writing the work experience section on your resume.

These two websites, operated by Military.com and HelmutstoHard hats.org, also include online programs that translate your MOS, Rate, AFSC, or designator into civilian terms:

> www.military.com/Careers/Content1/0,13587,skills_leader,,00.html
> http://employers.helmetstohardhats.org/action/codeLookup

Your Strengths

Regardless of what combination of work-content and functional skills you possess, a job search must begin with identifying your strengths. Without knowing these, your job search will lack content and focus. After all, your goal should be to find a job that is fit for you rather than one you think you might be able to fit into. Of course, you also want to find a job for which there is a demand. This particular focus requires a well-defined approach to identifying and communicating your skills to others. You can best do this by asking the right questions about your strengths and then conducting a systematic self-assessment of what you do best.

Ask the Right Questions

Knowing the right questions to ask will save you time and steer you into productive job search channels from the very beginning. Asking the wrong questions can leave you frustrated. The questions must be understood from the perspectives of both employers and applicants.

Two of the most humbling questions you will encounter in your job search are *"Why should I hire you?"* and *"What are your weaknesses?"* While employers may not directly ask these questions, they are asking them nonetheless. If you can't answer these questions in a positive manner – directly, indirectly, verbally, or nonverbally – your job search will likely founder and you will join the ranks of the unsuccessful and disillusioned job searchers who feel something is wrong with them. Individuals who have lost their jobs are particularly vulnerable to these questions since many have lowered self-esteem and self-image as a result of the job loss. Many such people focus on what is wrong rather than what is right about themselves. Such thinking creates self-fulfilling prophecies and is self-destructive in the job market. By all means avoid such negative thinking.

> *Employers want to hire your value or strengths – not your weaknesses.*

Employers want to hire your **value or strengths** – not your weaknesses. Since it is easier to identify and interpret weaknesses, employers look for indicators of your strengths by trying to identify your weaknesses. The more successful you are in communicating your strengths to employers, the better off you will be in relation to both employers and fellow applicants.

Unfortunately, many people work against their own best interests. Not knowing their strengths, they market their weaknesses by first identifying job vacancies and then trying to fit their "qualifications" into job descriptions. This approach often frustrates applicants; it presents a picture of a job market which is not interested in the applicant's strengths. This leads some people toward acquiring new skills which they hope will be marketable, even though they do not enjoy using them. Millions of individuals find themselves in such misplaced situations. Your task is to avoid joining the ranks of the misplaced and unhappy workforce by first understanding your skills and then relating them to your interests and goals. In so doing, you will be in a better position to target your job search toward jobs that should become especially rewarding and fulfilling.

Functional/Transferable Skills

We know most people stumble into jobs by accident. Some are at the right place at the right time to take advantage of opportunities. Others work hard at trying to fit into jobs posted on the Internet; listed in classified ads, employment agencies, and personnel offices; identified through friends and acquaintances; or found by knocking on doors. After 15 to 20 years in the work world, many people wish they had better

planned their careers from the very start. All of a sudden they are unhappily locked into jobs because of retirement benefits and family responsibilities of raising children and meeting monthly mortgage payments.

After 10 or 20 years of work experience, most people have a good idea of what they don't like to do. While their values are more set than when they first began working, many people are still unclear as to what they do well and how their skills fit into the job market. What other jobs, for example, might they be qualified to perform? If they have the opportunity to change jobs or careers – either voluntarily or forced through termination – and find the time to plan the change, they can move into jobs and careers that fit their skills.

The key to understanding your non-technical strengths is to identify your transferable or functional skills. Once you have done this, you will be better prepared to identify what it is you want to do. Moreover, your self-image and self-esteem will improve. Better still, you will be prepared to communicate your strengths to others through a rich skills-based vocabulary. These outcomes are critically important for writing your resume and letters as well as for conducting informational and job interviews.

Your goal should be to find a job that is fit for you rather than one you think you might be able to fit into.

Let's illustrate the concept of functional/transferable skills for educators. Many educators view their skills in strict work-content terms – knowledge of a particular subject matter such as math, history, English, physics, or music. When looking for jobs outside education, many seek employment which will use their subject matter skills. But they soon discover non-educational institutions are not a ready market for such "skills."

On the other hand, educators possess many other skills that are directly transferable to business and industry. Unaware of these skills, many educators fail to communicate their strengths to others. For example, research shows that graduate students in the humanities most frequently possess these transferable skills, in order of importance:

- critical thinking
- research techniques
- perseverance
- self-discipline
- insight
- writing

- general knowledge
- cultural perspective
- teaching ability
- self-confidence
- imagination
- leadership ability

Most functional/transferable skills can be classified into two general skill and trait categories – organizational/interpersonal skills and personality/work-style traits:

Organizational and Interpersonal Skills

___ communicating
___ problem solving
___ analyzing/assessing
___ planning
___ decision-making
___ innovating
___ thinking logically
___ evaluating
___ identifying problems
___ synthesizing
___ forecasting
___ tolerating ambiguity
___ motivating
___ leading
___ selling
___ performing
___ reviewing
___ attaining
___ team building
___ updating
___ coaching
___ supervising
___ estimating
___ negotiating
___ administering

___ trouble-shooting
___ implementing
___ self-understanding
___ understanding
___ setting goals
___ conceptualizing
___ generalizing
___ managing time
___ creating
___ judging
___ controlling
___ organizing
___ persuading
___ encouraging
___ improving
___ designing
___ consulting
___ teaching
___ cultivating
___ advising
___ training
___ interpreting
___ achieving
___ reporting
___ managing

Personality and Work-Style Traits

___ diligent
___ patient
___ innovative
___ persistent
___ tactful
___ loyal
___ successful
___ versatile
___ enthusiastic

___ honest
___ reliable
___ perceptive
___ assertive
___ sensitive
___ astute
___ risk taker
___ easygoing
___ calm

__ outgoing	__ flexible
__ expressive	__ competent
__ adaptable	__ punctual
__ democratic	__ receptive
__ resourceful	__ diplomatic
__ determinative	__ self-confident
__ creative	__ tenacious
__ open-minded	__ discrete
__ objective	__ talented
__ warm	__ empathic
__ orderly	__ tidy
__ tolerant	__ candid
__ frank	__ adventuresome
__ cooperative	__ firm
__ dynamic	__ sincere
__ self-starter	__ initiator
__ precise	__ competent
__ sophisticated	__ diplomatic
__ effective	__ efficient

These are the types of skills you need to identify and then communicate to employers in your resumes and letters as well as during interviews.

Identify Your Skills

If you have little or no civilian work experience, you probably should take a battery of vocational tests and psychological inventories to identify your interests and skills. If you have a great deal of work experience, chances are you don't need complex testing. You have experience, you have well defined values, and you know what you don't like in a job. Therefore, we outline several alternative skills identification exercises – simple to complex – assisting you at this stage. We recommend using the most complete and extensive activity – Motivated Skills Exercise – to gain a thorough understanding of your strengths.

Use the following exercises to identify both your work-content and transferable skills. These self-assessment techniques stress your positives or strengths rather than identify your negatives or weaknesses. They should generate a rich vocabulary for communicating your "qualifications" to employers. Each exercise requires different investments of your time and effort as well as varying degrees of assistance from other people.

These exercises, however, should be used with caution. There is nothing magical nor particularly profound about them. Most are based

upon a very simple and somewhat naive **deterministic theory of behavior** – your past patterns of behavior are good predictors of your future behavior. Not a bad theory for most individuals, but it is rather simplistic and disheartening for individuals who wish to, and can, break out of past patterns as they embark on a new future. Furthermore, most exercises are **historical devices**. They provide you with a clear picture of your past, which may or may not be particularly useful for charting your future. Nonetheless, these exercises do help individuals (1) organize data on themselves, (2) target their job search around clear objectives and skills, and (3) generate a rich vocabulary of skills and accomplishments for communicating strengths to potential employers.

If you feel these exercises are inadequate for your needs, by all means seek professional assistance from a testing or assessment center staffed by a licensed psychologist. These centers do in-depth testing which goes further than these self-directed skill exercises.

When using the following exercises, keep in mind that some individuals can and do change – often very dramatically – their behavior regardless of such deterministic and historical assessment devices. Much of the "motivation and success," "power of positive thinking," "thinking big," and "empowerment" literature, for example, challenges the validity of these standardized assessment tests that are used to predict or pattern future individual behavior. So be careful how you use such information for charting your career future. You **can** change your future. But at least get to know yourself before making the changes. Critiques of, as well as alternatives to, these exercises are outlined in Ron and Caryl Krannich's *I Want to Do Something Else, But I'm Not Sure What It Is* (Impact Publications, 2005).

Checklist Method

This is the simplest method for identifying your strengths. Review the different types of transferable skills outlined on pages 159-160. Place a "1" in front of the skills that **strongly** characterize you; assign a "2" to those skills that describe you to a **large extent**; put a "3" before those that describe you to **some extent**. After completing this exercise, review the lists and rank order the 10 characteristics that best describe you on each list.

Skills Map

Richard N. Bolles has produced two well-known exercises for identifying transferable skills based upon John Holland's typology of work environ-

ments. Both are historical devices structured around a deterministic theory of behavior. In his book, *The Three Boxes of Life* (Ten Speed Press), he develops a checklist of 100 transferable skills. They are organized into 12 categories or types of skills: using hands, body, words, senses, numbers, intuition, analytical thinking, creativity, helpfulness, artistic abilities, leadership, and follow-through.

Bolles's second exercise, *"The Quick Job Hunting Map,"* expands upon this first one. The *"Map"* is a checklist of 222 skills. This exercise requires you to identify seven of your most satisfying accomplishments, achievements, jobs, or roles. After writing a page about each experience, you relate each to the checklist of 222 skills. The *"Map"* should give you a comprehensive picture of what skills you (1) use most frequently and (2) enjoy using in satisfying and successful settings. While this exercise may take six hours to complete, it yields an enormous amount of data on past strengths. Furthermore, the *"Map"* generates a rich skills vocabulary for communicating your strengths to others. The *"Map"* is found in Bolles's *What Color Is Your Parachute* and *What Color Is Your Parachute Workbook* (Ten Speed Press). His books can be ordered directly from Impact Publications by completing the order form at the end of this book.

Autobiography of Accomplishments

Write a lengthy essay about your life accomplishments. This could range from 20 to 100 pages. After completing the essay, go through it page by page to identify what you most enjoyed doing (working with different kinds of information, people, and things) and what skills you used most frequently as well as enjoyed using. Finally, identify those skills you wish to continue using. After analyzing and synthesizing this data, you should have a relatively clear picture of your strongest skills.

The Magical World of Tests and Inventories

A frequent question asked of career counselors by individuals in search of greater clarity in their lives is this:

> *"Do you have a test I can take that will tell me what jobs or careers are best for me?"*

This question is responsible for a huge, lucrative, and fascinating self-assessment industry that offers hundreds of paper-and-pencil, computerized, and Internet-based tests and inventories taken by millions of individuals, especially students at all levels, each year. Asked in this form,

this question yields an answer that is both simple and complex: *"Yes, but . . ."* Sometimes this industry gives one the impression of peddling a scientific version of snake oil. You'll have to be your own judge based upon the actual results you get from taking such tests and inventories.

There's something very appealing, almost magical, about taking computerized and/or pencil-and-paper psychological, career planning, and guidance tests and inventories that are designed to simplify reality. For some people, these tests are potentially the magic bullet to discovering what they should do with the rest of their life. By looking within themselves, they believe they can find answers to important questions about their future. While no such bullet exists, nonetheless, these self-focused devises can be very useful at the initial stage of one's job search. Many who take these tests respond with a temporary *"Wow!"* or *"Aha!"* when they get the results and inter-pretations. Whether or not these tests have behavioral consequences (what you actually do with this information) is another question altogether.

> *These self-focused devises can be very useful at the initial stage of one's job search.*

Here's how most assessment tests and instruments work. You answer a series of questions about yourself (multiple-choice, true/false, Likert-type scale) and someone, usually a certified counselor, analyzes the results. If all goes well, an analysis will give you a general picture of who you really are in terms of your personality, interests, skills, abilities, aptitudes, and temperaments, as well as evidence of where you may be going in the future, especially if the results are matched to related jobs and careers. While many of these assessments have multiple applications – assess addictions, relationships, conflict, dating, parenting, educational choices, personal growth, character, motivation, management styles, leadership, and organizational effectiveness – many of these same tests are used for career counseling, especially in reference to career choices.

You will encounter hundreds of career-related tests for assessing who you are, how you relate to others, and where you best fit into the future. Many of these tests are based on the psychological "type" theories and approaches of psychologist Carl Gustav Jung and popularized through the *Myers-Briggs Type Indicator®* and a variety of related applications. Other more vocational-oriented tests attempt to relate decision-making data to specific jobs and careers identified in the databases of the U.S. Department of Labor, especially the O*NET, as well as the job search process. Some of the most widely used assessment tests administered by career professionals include the following:

Personality and Motivation

- **California Psychological Inventory Form 434 (CPI™ 434):** Designed to assess personality characteristics across three Structural Scales, 20 Folk Scales, and 13 Special Purpose Scales. Used to determine psychological personality fit for employment and differences in management style, organizational impact, and team leadership. Available through Consulting Psychologists Press (www.cpp.com).

- **Edwards Personal Preference Schedule:** Assesses individual personality in reference to 15 needs and motives, such as achievement, order, affiliation, dominance, nurturance, endurance, and aggression. Available through The Psychological Corporation (www.psychcorp.com).

- **Enneagram:** Analyzes nine distinct personality types in order to better understand individual personalities and how people relate to one another – Reformer, Helper, Achiever, Individualist, Investigator, Loyalist, Enthusiast, Challenger, and Peacemaker. Available through the Enneagram Institute (www.enneagraminstitute.com) and other sources such as www.ennea.com.

- **Keirsey Character Sorter:** This personality type approach is designed to analyze and apply the four basic "people pattern" temperaments, as developed in David Keirsey's popular book, *Please Understand Me II,* to different situations: Artisans, Guardians, Idealists, and Rationals. Available through David Mark Keirsey (http://keirsey.com).

- **Myers-Briggs Type Indicator® (MBTI®):** This is the most popular personality inventory in the world used by psychologists and career counselors. It has multiple applications for everything from marital counseling to executive development programs. Based on Carl Gustav Jung's theory of personality types, this simplified application of his complex theory attempts to measure personality dispositions and interests – the way people absorb information, decide, and communicate. It analyzes preferences to four dichotomies (extroversion/introversion, sensing/intuiting, thinking/feeling, judging/perceiving), which results in 16 personality types. The MBTI® comes in a variety of forms. Available through Consulting Psychologists Press (www.cpp.com

and www.skillsone.com) and most colleges, universities, and testing centers.

- **16-Personality Factor Questionnaire (16PF):** This 185-question inventory analyzes adult personality in reference to 16 primary and eight secondary personality factors. Used for counseling, coaching, training, and self-assessment purposes to help individuals determine which occupations are best suited for them. Available through Pearson Assessments (www.pearson assessments.com).

Values

- **Career Beliefs Inventory (CBI):** Designed to assess an individual's beliefs about himself/herself and the work world. Includes a 96-item multiple-choice test. Available through Consulting Psychologists Press (www.cpp.com).

- **Minnesota Importance Questionnaire (MIQ):** Designed to measure an individual's vocational needs and values, which are important ingredients of work personality. Measures six vocational values (and 20 vocational needs that are the basis of these values): Achievement, Altruism, Comfort, Safety, Status, and Autonomy. Available through Vocational Psychology Research of the University of Minnesota (www.psych.umn.edu).

- **Survey of Interpersonal Values (SIV):** This 30-item inventory is designed to assess six interpersonal values as they relate to relationships with others as well as employment: support, conformity, recognition, independence, benevolence, and leadership. Available through NCS Pearson Reid London House (www.reidlondonhouse.com).

- **Temperament and Values Inventory:** This device is designed to identify how individuals react to different activities and situations. In helping to determine job fit, this test measures what aspects of a job are most motivating to the individual.

- **O*NET Career Values Inventory:** Analyzes work values in reference to the major jobs outlined in the O*NET database of the U.S. Department of Labor. Available through JIST Publishing (http://jist.com).

Interests and Attitudes

- **Career Assessment Inventory™ – Enhanced Version (CAI-E):** Assesses the career interests of individuals re-entering the job market or making a career change. Includes a 370-item test using a 5-point Likert-type scale. Available through NCS Pearson (www.pearsonassessments.com).

- **Career Exploration Inventory:** Helps users assess their work, leisure, and learning interests in reference to 120 activity statements related to codes in the _Guide to Occupational Exploration._ Available through JIST Publishing (http://jist.com).

- **Career IQ and Interest Test (CIQIT):** Designed to help individuals identify jobs they do well and enjoy doing. Available through PRO-ED, Inc. (www.proedinc.com).

- **Guide to Occupational Exploration Interest Inventory:** Uses a multiple-choice and true/false testing format to explore career, education, and lifestyle options. Available through JIST Publishing (http://jist.com).

- **Harrington-O'Shea Career Decision-Making System:** Based on Holland's theory of vocational development, this device helps individuals to better understand their values and abilities for making career choices. Available through American Guidance Service (www.ags.com).

- **Jackson Vocational Interest Survey (JVIS):** Designed to assist counselors in evaluating the career interests of students and adults in transition. Available through Sigma Assessment Systems (http://jvis.com).

- **Job Search Attitude Inventory (JSAI):** Helps users better understand their motivation for conducting a job search. Available through JIST Publishing (http://jist.com).

- **Kuder Occupational Interest Survey:** This interest inventory is similar to the _Strong Interest Inventory®_ and the six themes central to Holland's _Self-Directed Search._ It relates an individual's test results to six career clusters: Outdoor/Mechanical, Science/Technical, Arts/Communication, Social/Personal Ser-

vices, Sales/Management, and Business Operations. It's especially useful in predicting job dissatisfaction. Available through National Career Assessment Services (www.kuder.com) and CareerLab (www.careerlab.com).

- **Leisure to Occupational Connection Search (LOCS):** Measures the relationship between vocational interests and leisure activities by examining 100 leisure activities to information on 250 jobs. Available through JIST Publishing (http://jist.com).

- **Leisure/Work Search Inventory:** Users respond to 96 leisure activity statements to assess how their leisure interests relate to employment opportunities. Available through JIST Publishing (http://jist.com).

- **Ohio Vocational Interest Survey:** This 253-item test assesses occupational and vocational interests in reference to three orientations – data, people, and things. Available through Harcourt Brace Educational Measurement (www.harcourt.com).

- **Self-Directed Search® (SDS):** One of the most widely used and adapted interest inventories in career counseling. Designed to assist individuals in making career choices based on an analysis of different orientations toward people, data, and things. It matches interests with six types (realistic, investigative, artistic, social, enterprising, and conventional) that are, in turn, related to different types of occupations that match these types. Used in helping determine how one's interests fit with various occupations. Influential in developing the assessment approach found in Richard Nelson Bolles's *What Color Is Your Parachute?* and *What Color Is Your Parachute Workbook.* Also available in other versions, such as *Self-Directed Search® Career Explorer (SDS® CE)* and *Self-Directed Search® Form R (SDS® Form R).* Available through Psychological Assessment Resources (www.parinc.com).

- **Strong Interest Inventory®:** Next to the *Myers-Briggs Type Indicator®* and the *Self-Directed Search®*, this remains one of the most popular assessment devices used by career counselors. Individuals respond to 317 multiple-choice items to determine their occupational interests according to six occupational

themes, 25 interest scales, occupational scales, and personal style scales. Used extensively for career guidance, occupational decisions, employment placement, educational choices, and vocational rehabilitation programs. Available through Consulting Psychologists Press (www.cpp.com) and most schools, colleges, universities, and testing centers.

- **Vocational Interest Inventory:** Assists individuals with learning and other disabilities in making vocational decisions. Available through JIST Publishing (http://jist.com).

Skills, Behaviors, Aptitudes

- **Barriers to Employment Success Inventory:** Designed to assist the unemployed in identifying barriers to conducting a successful job search, this instrument includes 50 multiple-choice, short-answer, and true/false items. Available through JIST Publishing (http://jist.com).

- **BRIGANCE® Diagnostic Employability Skills Inventory:** Helps identify basic employability skills and training needs. Available through Curriculum Associates, Inc. (www.curriculum associates.com).

- **Career Decision Scale:** Assists counselors in assessing a client's barriers to career decision-making. Available through Psychological Assessment Resources, Inc. (www.parinc.com).

- **FIRO-B®:** Used to assess individuals' interpersonal needs and how their behavior relates to the workplace. Measures "expressed" and "wanted" behaviors to help them better manage their behavior and increase productivity in the workplace. Available through Consulting Psychologists Press (www.cpp.com).

Multiple Indicators

- **APTICOM:** A popular vocational guidance and counseling instrument for assessing interests, aptitudes, and work-related math and language skills. Available through Vocational Research Institute (www.vri.org).

- **Armed Services Vocational Battery (ASVAB):** A 334-item test used to measure vocational interests and aptitudes related to military service. Available through the U.S. Department of Defense.

- **Assessment of Career Decision Making (ACDM):** Assists individuals in selecting a career compatible with their interests and abilities. Includes 96 true/false items. Available through Western Psychological Services (www.wpspublish.com).

- **The Birkman Method:** Used in many companies to both measure and enhance personal, team, and organizational effectiveness. Available online through Birkman International (www.birkman.com) and CareerLab (www.careerlab.com).

- **CAM Computerized One-Stop:** Designed to assess interests, aptitudes, attitudes, temperament, and learning styles of job applicants. Available through PESCO International (www.pesco.org).

- **Campbell™ Interest and Skill Survey (CISS®):** One of the most popular assessments devised for measuring interests and skills. Includes 320 items divided into 200 interest and 120 skill categories. Available through NCS Pearson (www.pearsonassessments.com).

- **Career Scope:** Includes 141 items that measure 12 interest and aptitude areas. Available through Vocational Research Institute (www.vri.org).

- **Key Educational Vocational Assessment System (KEVAS):** This device is designed to measure vocational interests and aptitudes. It matches aptitudes with specific jobs. Available through Key Education, Inc.

- **Vocational Interest, Temperament, and Aptitude System (VITAS):** A vocational guidance instrument used for assessing aptitudes, vocational interests, and work-related temperaments of the special needs population. Available through Vocational Research Institute (www.vri.org).

For a quick review of these and many other assessment tests, see the following references:

Career Tests, Louis Janda (Avon, MA: Adams Media)

The ETS Test Collection Catalog (New York: Oryx Press)

Mental Measures Yearbook (Lincoln, NE: University of Nebraska Press)

Tests, Taddy Maddox, ed. (Austin, TX: Pro-Ed)

What Type Am I?, Renee Baron (New York: Penguin Books)

Computerized Assessment Programs

While some of the various inventories outlined above are available in computer programs, others are strictly computerized career guidance programs available for Windows and the Internet. Most are expensive licensed programs that can be found at career centers in high schools, colleges, one-stop career centers, libraries, and community-based organizations. Two of the most popular and comprehensive such programs are:

- **SIGI Plus** (System of Interactive Guidance and Information): Designed to help individuals make better education and career decisions. Helps clarify work values and then relates those values to specific occupations which also relate to the user's interests and work skills. Assists students in identifying education and training paths appropriate for their particular mix of values, interests, and skills. Available through Educational Testing Services (www.ets.org/sigi).

- **Discover:** Available in both Windows and Internet versions, this program also helps individuals make better educational and career choices through an analysis of their values, interests, and abilities. Users identify their strengths and needs and then relate them to specific occupational and educational alternatives. Includes a comprehensive database of occupations, college majors, schools and training institutions, financial aid/scholarships, and military options. Available through ACT (www.act.org).

These programs require users to answer a series of questions, which are analyzed and then related to different occupations that best match the individual's interests, skills, and values profile. Other popular computerized assessment programs include:

- *Career Navigator*
- *Choices*
- *Guidance Information System* (GIS)
- *Self-Directed Search (SDS) Form R*

Most of these comprehensive career planning programs do much more than just assess skills. They also integrate other key components in the career planning process – interests, goals, related jobs, college majors, education and training programs, and job search plans. These programs are widely available in schools, colleges, and libraries across the country. You might check with the career or counseling center at your local community college to see what computerized career assessment systems are available for your use. Relatively easy to use, they generate a great deal of useful career planning information. Many will print out an analysis of how your interests and skills are related to specific jobs and careers.

Online Assessments

Within the past few years, several companies have developed online assessment devices which you can quickly access via the Internet 24 hours a day in the comfort of your home or office. Some tests are self-scoring and free of charge while others require interacting with a fee-based certified career counselor or testing expert. SkillsOne (www.skillsone.com), for example, is operated by the producers of the *Myers-Briggs Type Indicator®* and *Strong Interest Inventory®* – Consulting Psychologists Press. CareerLab (www.careerlab.com) offers one of the largest batteries of well respected assessment tools: *Campbell Interest and Skills Survey, Strong Interest Inventory®, Myers-Briggs Type Indicator®, 16-Personality Factors Profile, FIRO-B®, California Psychological Inventory (CPI), The Birkman Method,* and *Campbell Leadership Index.* The following seven websites are well worth exploring for both free and fee-based online assessments tools:

- **SkillsOne** (Consulting www.skillsone.com
 (Psychologists Press) www.cpp-db.com
- **CareerLab.com** www.careerlab.com

- Self-Directed Search® www.self-directed-search.com
- Personality Online www.personalityonline.com
- Keirsey Character Sorter www.keirsey.com
- MAPP™ www.assessment.com
- PersonalityType www.personalitytype.com

These 16 additional sites also include a wealth of related assessment devices that you can access online:

- Analyze My Career www.analyzemycareer.com
- Birkman Method www.birkman.com
- Career Key www.careerkey.org/english
- CareerLeader™ www.careerleader.com
- CareerPlanner.com www.careerplanner.com
- CareerPerfect.com www.careerperfect.com
- Careers By Design® www.careers-by-design.com
- CollegeBoard.com www.myroad.com
- Enneagram www.ennea.com
- Humanmetrics www.humanmetrics.com
- Jackson Vocational
 Interest Inventory www.jvis.com
- My Future www.myfuture.com
- People Management
 International www.sima-pmi.com
- Profiler www.profiler.com
- QueenDom.com www.queendom.com
- Tests on the Web www.2h.com

9

Identify Your
Interests and Values

K
NOWING WHAT YOU DO well – your skills, abilities, and aptitudes – is essential for understanding your strengths and for linking your capabilities to specific jobs that require those strengths. Usually referred to as one's "qualifications," your skills, abilities, and aptitudes also are important for targeting your job search and communicating your strengths to employers. However, just knowing your abilities and skills will not give your job search the direction it needs for finding a job that's right for you – one you both do well and enjoy doing. You also need to know your **work values and interests**. These are the basic building blocks for setting goals and targeting your abilities toward certain jobs and careers.

Take, for example, individuals who type 120 words a minute, design Web pages, or repair computers. While they possess highly marketable skills, if they don't regularly enjoy using these skills and are more interested in working outdoors or with people, these abilities will not become **motivated skills**. These individuals will most likely not pursue jobs relating to word processing, the Internet, or computers, or they may be unhappy in jobs that use such skills. In the end, your interests and values will determine whether or not certain skills should play a central role in your job search.

Work, Leisure, and Home-Based Interests

We all have interests. Most change over time. Many of your interests may center on your present job whereas others relate to activities that define

your hobbies and leisure activities. Other interests may relate to your dreams.

While many of the self-assessment tests and inventories discussed in Chapter 8 focus on identifying and analyzing interests, the exercises included in this chapter are more open-ended and require self analysis rather than the involvement of a career professional. A good place to start identifying your interests is by examining the information and exercises found in both *The Guide for Occupational Exploration* and *The Enhanced Guide for Occupational Exploration*. Widely used by students and others first entering the job market, these are also relevant to individuals who already have work experience. These books classify all jobs in the United States into 12 interest areas. Examine the following list of interest areas. In the first column check the work areas that appeal to you. In the second column rank order those areas you checked in the first column. Start with "1" to indicate the most interesting:

Your Work Interests

Yes/No (x)	Ranking (1-12)	Interest Area
___	___	**Artistic:** An interest in creative expression of feelings or ideas.
___	___	**Scientific:** An interest in discovering, collecting, and analyzing information about the natural world, and in applying scientific research findings to problems in medicine, the life sciences, and the nature sciences.
___	___	**Plants and animals:** An interest in working with plants and animals, usually outdoors.
___	___	**Protective:** An interest in using authority to protect people and property.
___	___	**Mechanical:** An interest in applying mechanical principles to practical situations by using machines or hand tools.

___ ___ **Industrial:** An interest in repetitive, concrete, organized activities done in a factory setting.

___ ___ **Business detail:** An interest in organized, clearly defined activities requiring accuracy and attention to details (office settings).

___ ___ **Selling:** An interest in bringing others to a particular point of view by personal persuasion, using sales and promotion techniques.

___ ___ **Accommodating:** An interest in catering to the wishes and needs of others, usually on a one-to-one basis.

___ ___ **Humanitarian:** An interest in helping others with their mental, spiritual, social, physical, or vocational needs.

___ ___ **Leading and influencing:** An interest in leading and influencing others by using high-level verbal or numerical abilities.

___ ___ **Physical performing:** An interest in physical activities performed before an audience.

The Guide for Occupational Exploration also includes other checklists relating to home-based and leisure activities that may or may not relate to your work interests. If you are unclear about your work interests, you might want to consult several other interest exercises. You may discover that some of your home-based and leisure activity interests should become your work interests. Examples of such interests include:

Leisure and Home-Based Interests

___ Acting in a play or amateur variety show.

___ Advising family members on their personal problems.

___ Announcing or emceeing a program.

___ Applying first aid in emergencies as a volunteer.

___ Building model airplanes, automobiles, or boats.

___ Building or repairing radio or television sets.

___ Buying large quantities of food or other products for an organization.

___ Campaigning for political candidates or issues.

___ Canning and preserving food.

___ Carving small wooden objects.

___ Coaching children or youth in sports activities.

___ Collecting experiments involving plants.

___ Conducting house-to-house or telephone surveys for a PTA or other organization.

___ Creating or styling hairdos for friends.

___ Designing your own greeting cards and writing original verses.

___ Developing film/printing pictures.

___ Doing impersonations.

___ Doing public speaking or debating.

___ Entertaining at parties or other events.

___ Helping conduct physical exercises for disabled people.

___ Making ceramic objects.

___ Modeling clothes for a fashion show.

___ Mounting and framing pictures.

___ Nursing sick pets.

___ Painting the interior or exterior of a home.

___ Playing a musical instrument.

___ Refinishing or re-upholstering furniture.

___ Repairing electrical household appliances.

___ Repairing the family car.

___ Repairing or assembling bicycles.

___ Repairing indoor plumbing.

___ Speaking on radio or appearing on television.

___ Taking photographs.

___ Teaching in Sunday School.

___ Tutoring pupils in school subjects.

___ Weaving rugs or making quilts.

___ Writing articles, stories, or plays.

___ Writing songs for club socials or amateur plays.

Indeed, many people turn hobbies or home activities into full-time jobs after deciding that such "work" is what they really enjoy doing.

Other popular exercises designed to identify your work interests include John Holland's *"The Self-Directed Search,"* which is found in his book, *Making Vocational Choices: A Theory of Careers.* It is also published as a separate testing instrument, *The Self-Directed Search – A Guide to Educational and Vocational Planning.* Developed from Holland's Vocational Preference Inventory, this popular self-administered, self-scored, and self-interpreted inventory helps individuals quickly identify what type of work environment they are motivated to seek – realistic, investigative, artistic, social, enterprising, or conventional – and aligns these work environments with lists of common occupational titles. An easy exercise to use, it gives you a quick overview of your orientation toward different types of work settings that interest you. Holland's *"The Self-Directed Search"* is also the basic framework used in developing Bolles's *"The Quick Job Hunting Map"* (see discussion on page 162).

For more sophisticated treatments of work interests, which are also validated through testing procedures, contact career counselors, women's centers, testing and assessment centers, or the appropriate publishers for information on these tests:

- *Career Assessment Inventory*
- *Career Exploration Inventory*
- *Jackson Vocational Interest Survey*
- *Kuder Occupational Interest Survey*
- *Leisure/Work Search Inventory*
- *Ohio Vocational Interest Survey*
- *Strong Interest Inventory*®
- *Vocational Interest Inventory*

Numerous other job and career interest inventories are also available. For further information, contact a career counselor or consult Educational

Testing Service, which compiles such tests. *The ETS Test Collection Catalog* (New York: Oryx Press) and *Tests* (Austin, TX: Pro-Ed), which are available in many library reference sections, list most of these tests. The *Mental Measurements Yearbook* (Lincoln, NE: University of Nebraska Press) also surveys many of the major testing and assessment instruments.

Keep in mind that not all testing and assessment instruments used by career counselors are equally valid for career planning purposes. Indeed, many are over-used and of questionable validity. While the *Strong Interest Inventory®* appears to be the most relevant for career decision-making, the *Myers-Briggs Type Indicator®* has become an extremely popular instrument in recent years. It's used extensively by psychologists and career counselors for identifying 16 personality types. Widely used in pastoral counseling, student personnel, and business and religious organizations, it is more useful for classifying individual personality and decision-making styles than for identifying job fit and predicting career choices. For more information on this test, including online versions, contact Consulting Psychologists Press, Inc. (Tel. 800-624-1765; websites: www.cpp.com and www.skillsone.com). Many career counselors who work with students in exploring careers find Holland's *The Self-Directed Search®* an excellent self-directed alternative to these professionally administered and interpreted tests. Our advice is to use several instruments, as well as our self-directed exercises, rather than rely on any one or two such devices. The more extensive tests, such as the Minnesota Importance Questionnaire (page 165), may prove most useful.

Key Work Values

Work values are those things you like to do. They give you pleasure and enjoyment. Most jobs involve a combination of likes and dislikes. By identifying what you both like and dislike about jobs, you should be able to better identify jobs that involve tasks you will most enjoy doing.

Several exercises can help you identify your work values. First, identify what most satisfies you about work by completing the following exercise:

My Work Values

I prefer employment which enables me to:

___ contribute to society	___ be creative
___ have contact with people	___ supervise others
___ work alone	___ work with details

____ work with a team	____ gain recognition
____ compete with others	____ acquire security
____ make decisions	____ make money
____ work under pressure	____ help others
____ use power and authority	____ solve problems
____ acquire new knowledge	____ take risks
____ be a recognized expert	____ work at own pace

Select four work values from the above list which are the most important to you and list them in the space below. List any other work values (desired satisfactions) which were not listed above but are nonetheless important to you:

1. _____

2. _____

3. _____

4. _____

Another approach to identifying work values is outlined in *The Guide for Occupational Exploration.* If you feel you need to go beyond the above exercises, try this one. In the first column check those values that are most important to you. In the second column rank order the five most important values:

Ranking Work Values

Yes/No (x)	Ranking (1-5)	Work Values
____	____	**Adventure:** Working in a job that requires taking risks.
____	____	**Authority:** Working in a job in which you use your position to control others.
____	____	**Competition:** Working in a job in which you compete with others.

____ ____ **Creativity and self-expression:** Working in a job in which you use your imagination to find new ways to do or say something.

____ ____ **Flexible work schedule:** Working in a job in which you choose your hours to work.

____ ____ **Helping others:** Working in a job in which you provide direct services to persons with problems.

____ ____ **High salary:** Working in a job where many workers earn a large amount of money.

____ ____ **Independence:** Working in a job in which you decide for yourself what to do and how to do it.

____ ____ **Influencing others:** Working in a job in which you influence the opinions of others or decisions of others.

____ ____ **Intellectual stimulation:** Working in a job that requires a great amount of thought and reasoning.

____ ____ **Leadership:** Working in a job in which you direct, manage, or supervise the activities of other people.

____ ____ **Outside work:** Working out-of-doors.

____ ____ **Persuading:** Working in a job in which you personally convince others to take certain actions.

____ ____ **Physical work:** Working in a job that requires substantial physical activity.

____ ____ **Prestige:** Working in a job that gives you status and respect in the community.

____ ____ **Public attention:** Working in a job in which you attract immediate notice because of appearance or activity.

____ ____ **Public contact:** Working in a job in which you daily deal with the public.

____ ____ **Recognition:** Working in a job in which you gain public notice.

____ ____ **Research work:** Working in a job in which you search for and discover new facts and develop ways to apply them.

____ ____ **Routine work:** Working in a job in which you follow established procedures requiring little change.

____ ____ **Seasonal work:** Working in a job in which you are employed only at certain times of the year.

____ ____ **Travel:** Working in a job in which you take frequent trips.

____ ____ **Variety:** Working in a job in which your duties change frequently.

____ ____ **Work with children:** Working in a job in which you teach or care for children.

____ ____ **Work with hands:** Working in a job in which you use your hands or hand tools.

____ ____ **Work with machines or equipment:** Working in a job where you use machines or equipment.

____ ____ **Work with numbers:** Working in a job in which you use mathematics or statistics.

Second, develop a comprehensive list of your past and present **job frustrations and dissatisfactions**. This should help you identify negative factors you should avoid in future jobs.

My Job Frustrations and Dissatisfactions

List as well as rank order as many past and present things that frustrate or make you dissatisfied and unhappy in job situations:

 Rank

1. _____ _____

2. _____ _____

3. _____ _____

4. _____ _____

5. _____ _____

6. _____ _____

7. _____ _____

8. _____ _____

9. _____ _____

10. _____ _____

Third, brainstorm a list of "Ten or More Things I Love to Do." Identify which ones could be incorporated into what kinds of work environments:

Ten or More Things I Love To Do

	Item	Related Work Environment
1.	_____	_____
2.	_____	_____
3.	_____	_____
4.	_____	_____
5.	_____	_____
6.	_____	_____

7. _____ _____

8. _____ _____

9. _____ _____

10. _____ _____

Fourth, list at least 10 things you most enjoy about work and rank each item accordingly:

Ten Things I Enjoy the Most About Work

Rank

1. _____ _____

2. _____ _____

3. _____ _____

4. _____ _____

5. _____ _____

6. _____ _____

7. _____ _____

8. _____ _____

9. _____ _____

10. _____ _____

Fifth, you should also identify the types of interpersonal environments you prefer working in. Do this by specifying the types of people you like and dislike associating with:

Interpersonal Environments

Characteristics of people I like working with:	Characteristics of people I dislike working with:
_____	_____
_____	_____
_____	_____
_____	_____
_____	_____
_____	_____
_____	_____
_____	_____

Alternative Programs and Services

Several computerized self-assessment programs and online assessment services identified in Chapter 8 largely focus on career interests and values. Again, you may be able to get access to several of these programs through your local community college, one-stop career center, or library. Many of the testing and assessment websites identified on pages 171-172 include instruments for measuring interests and values.

As we stress throughout this book, no one test, instrument, or exercise will give you complete assessment information. Profit from redundancy by using a variety of approaches to answer your self-assessment questions in the process of identifying what you really want to do.

Project Your Values Into the Future

All of these exercises are designed to explore your past and present work-related values. At the same time, you need to project your values into the future. What, for example, do you want to do over the next 10 to 20 years? We'll return to this type of value question in Chapter 11 when we

address the critical objective-setting stage of the career planning and job search process. Once you formulate your objective, you'll be prepared to take action that should lead to your dream job. Highly motivated and focused, you should be able to organize an effective job search that focuses laser-like on what you do well and enjoy doing.

10

Analyze Your Motivated Abilities and Skills (MAS)

JOE LEFT THE ARMY IN 1998 after 20 years of service. He now has a pattern of civilian employment. Extremely talented, he has held three jobs with three different defense contractors over the past seven years. At a recent military transition job fair, he was seen walking the aisles with three different versions of his resume in the hope of finding an employer who would be interested in what he thought were his many stellar qualifications.

Don't Become Another Joe

Joe has all the signs of the classic job-hopper – he can do many things, but he's not sure what he really wants to do. Once he lands a job, he soon becomes bored and starts looking for another job, just in case the grass may be greener with another company. Joe spends lots of time posting his resume and browsing job postings on several Internet employment sites as well as attending job fairs.

Feeling he is very well qualified to do several different things, but never sure what he really wants to do (he also avoids putting an objective on his resume), Joe communicates an image of uncertainty and instability. Employers increasingly "read between the lines" when analyzing Joe's resume – three employers in seven years raises a red flag about Joe's focus and motivation. Just how long will he stay with his next employer?

Joe will find another job, but he probably won't be happy with it. Chances are Joe won't stay with his next employer for more than two

years. When you hire Joe, you inherit his pattern of employment behavior, which will be costly to any company that invests training dollars in its employees. Who wants to train Joe for his next employer? If Joe had a better idea of his motivated pattern, he would approach the job market from a very different perspective and find a job he really loved. Whatever you do, don't become another Joe!

Recognize Your Pattern

Once you know what you really do well and enjoy doing, your next task should be to analyze those interests, values, abilities, skills, and temperaments that form a **recurring motivated pattern**. This **pattern** is the single most important piece of information you need to know about yourself in the whole self-assessment process. Knowing your skills and abilities alone without understanding how they relate to your interests, values, and temperament will not give you the necessary direction for finding the job you want. You simply **must** know your pattern. Once you do, your career planning and job search activities may take on a whole new direction that will produce amazing results. You'll be able to state a clear objective that will guide you toward achieving your goals. So let's discover your pattern.

> *Your **pattern** is the single most important piece of information you need to know about yourself.*

What's Your MAS?

The concept of motivated abilities and skills (MAS) enables us to relate your interests and values to your skills and abilities. But how do we identify your MAS beyond the questions and exercises outlined thus far?

Your pattern of motivated abilities and skills becomes evident once you analyze your **achievements or accomplishments**. For it is your achievements that tell us what you both do well and enjoy doing. If we analyze and synthesize many of your achievements, we are likely to identify a **recurring pattern** that probably goes back to your childhood and which will continue to characterize your achievements in the future.

An equally useful exercise is to identify your **weaknesses** by analyzing your failures. These, too, would fall into recurring patterns. Understanding what your weaknesses are might help you avoid jobs and work situations that bring out the worst rather than the best in you. Indeed, you may learn more about yourself by analyzing your failures than by

focusing solely on your accomplishments.

Another interesting approach is to examine how you have dealt with some of life's most **challenging situations,** such as an illness, accident, divorce, financial difficulties, starting a business, or a death in the family. Many of these difficult situations required character, drive, persistence, and problem-solving strategies beyond the ordinary. They may have drawn on inner strengths or a reservoir of skills you never knew you had but which occasionally came to the forefront when you were under extreme pressure. Moreover, your handling of these difficult situations might have led to life-altering consequences for you and those around you.

For now, let's focus on your **positives** rather than identify your negatives or how you coped with difficult situations. After you complete the strength exercises in this chapter, you may want to reverse the procedures to identify your weaknesses and challenges.

> *Once you uncover your pattern, get prepared to acknowledge it and live with it in the future.*

Numerous self-directed exercises can assist you in identifying your pattern of motivated abilities and skills. The basic requirements for making these exercises work for you are **time and analytical ability.** You must spend a great deal of time detailing your achievements by examining your history of accomplishments. Once you complete the historical reconstruction task, you must comb through your "stories" to identify recurring themes and patterns. This requires a high level of analytical ability which you may or may not possess. If analysis and synthesis are not two of your strong skills, you may want to seek assistance from a friend or professional who is good at analyzing and synthesizing information presented in narrative form. Career management firms such as BH Careers International (www.bhcareers.com) and People Management, Inc. (www.sima-pmi.com) are known for their use of this type of motivated pattern approach. Their versions of this assessment technique are presented in *Haldane's Best Resumes for Professionals* (Impact Publications) and *The Truth About You* (Ten Speed Press – currently out of print) as well as many career counselors and coaches who use Success Factor Analysis and the SIMA Technique for identifying, analyzing, and directing motivated abilities and skills.

Several paper-and-pencil exercises are designed to help identify your pattern of motivated abilities and skills. We outline some of the most popular and thorough such exercises that have proved useful to thousands of people.

Behavioral Versus Personality Approaches

Keep in mind that, like most self-assessment devices, there is nothing magical about Success Factor Analysis, the SIMA Technique, our MAS approach, or other related approaches which we will shortly discuss (Bolles's *Map* and the Autobiography of Accomplishments). The basic organizing principles of these approaches are both simple and similar. Like other exercises designed to uncover your pattern of motivated abilities and skills, these are based on a theory of historical determinism and probability. In other words, once you uncover your pattern, get prepared to acknowledge it and live with it in the future. There's a high probability that you will repeat your past patterns of behavior, especially if you focus on your achievements. While some people manage to transform their behavior (the subject of many "change your life" motivational gurus and coaches who help people stop smoking, lose weight, raise their self-esteem, or become more assertive), the truth is that most people tend to repeat their past patterns of behavior after the gurus and coaches go home!

> *The truth is that most people tend to repeat their past patterns of behavior after the gurus and coaches go home!*

We much prefer this type of assessment, because it focuses on an analysis of **positive behaviors** in contrast to many other assessment devices, including the popular *Myers-Briggs Type Indicator®*, that primarily focus on personality types. While inherently interesting for people fascinated with psychology, many such personality approaches raise more questions than they answer, especially when one tries to relate personality characteristics to actual occupational choices, job satisfaction, workplace compatibility, and career direction. We believe you will get much more accurate information about yourself for making smart career choices by using our self-directed MAS approach.

The Skills Map

Richard Nelson Bolles's *"Quick Job Hunting Map"* has become a standard self-assessment tool for thousands of job seekers and career changers who are willing to spend the time and effort necessary for discovering their pattern of motivated abilities and skills. Offering a checklist of over 200 skills organized around John Holland's concept of *"The Self-Directed Search"* for defining work environments (realistic, investigative, artistic, social, enterprising, and conventional), the *Map* requires you to identify

seven of your most satisfying accomplishments, achievements, jobs, or roles. After describing each achievement, you analyze the details of each in relation to the checklist of skills. Once you do this for all seven achievements, you should have a comprehensive picture of what skills you (1) use most frequently and (2) enjoy using in satisfying and successful settings. This exercise not only yields an enormous amount of information on your interests, values, skills, and abilities, it also assists you in the process of analyzing the data. If done properly, the *Map* should also generate a rich "skills" vocabulary which you should use in your resumes and letters as well as in interviews. For information on this instrument, see our *Map* discussion on pages 161-162. The latest version of the *Map* can be found in Richard Nelson Bolles's *What Color Is Your Parachute Workbook* (Ten Speed Press, 2006), which is available in libraries, bookstores, or through Impact Publications's online bookstore: www.impactpublications.com.

We highly recommend using the *Map* because of the ease in which it can be used. If you will spend the six to 20 hours necessary to complete it properly, the *Map* will give you some important information about yourself. Unfortunately, many people become overwhelmed by the exercise and either decide not to complete it, or they try to save time by not doing it according to the directions. You simply must follow the directions and spend the time and effort necessary if you want the maximum benefits from this very inexpensive exercise.

Autobiography of Accomplishments

Less structured than the *Map* device, this exercise requires you to write a lengthy essay about your life accomplishments. Your essay may run anywhere from 20 to 200 pages. After completing it, go through it page by page to identify what you most enjoyed doing (working with different kinds of data, people, processes, and objects) and what skills you used most frequently as well as enjoyed using. Finally, identify those skills you wish to continue using. After analyzing and synthesizing this data, you should have a relatively clear picture of your strongest skills.

This exercise requires a great deal of self-discipline and analytic skill (content analysis). To do it properly, you must write as much as possible, and in as much detail as possible, about your accomplishments. The richer the detail, the better will be your analysis. If you have difficulty analyzing your story, find someone who can assist you in distilling your accomplishments into a distinct set of behavioral patterns.

Motivated Skills Exercise

Our final exercise is one of the most complex and time-consuming self-assessment exercises. However, it yields some of the best data on motivated abilities and skills, and it is especially useful for those who feel they need a more thorough analysis of their past achievements. It's our preferred device which is used by many career counselors. Initially developed by Dr. Bernard Haldane, the father of modern career counseling, this exercise is variously referred to as *"Success Factor Analysis," "System to Identify Motivated Skills,"* or *"Intensive Skills Identification."*

This technique helps you identify which skills you **enjoy** using. While you can use this technique on your own, it is best to work with someone else. Since you will need six to eight hours to properly complete this exercise, divide your time into two or three work sessions.

The exercise consists of six steps. The steps follow the basic pattern of generating raw data, identifying patterns, analyzing the data through reduction techniques, and synthesizing the patterns into a transferable skills vocabulary. You need strong analytical skills to complete this exercise on your own. The six steps include:

1. **Identify 15-20 achievements:** While ideally you should inventory over 100-150 achievements, let's start by focusing on a minimum of 15-20 achievements. These consist of things you enjoyed doing, believe you did well, and felt a sense of satisfaction, pride, or accomplishment in doing. You can see yourself performing at your best and enjoying your experiences when you analyze your achievements. This information reveals your motivations since it deals entirely with your voluntary behavior. In addition, it identifies what is right with you by focusing on your positives and strengths. Identify achievements throughout your life, beginning with your childhood. Your achievements should relate to specific experiences – not general ones – and may be drawn from work, leisure, education, military, or home life. Put each achievement at the top of a separate sheet of paper on which you will further elaborate. For example, your achievements might appear as follows:

Sample Achievement Statements

"When I was 10 years old, I started a small paper route and built it up to the largest in my district."

"I started playing chess in ninth grade and earned the right to play first board on my high school chess team in my junior year."

———————

"Learned to play the piano and often played for church services while in high school."

———————

"Designed, constructed, and displayed a dress for a 4-H demonstration project."

———————

"Played a major role in developing my high school website, which resulted in starting a small but very successful web design business at age 16 that helped finance my way through college."

———————

"Although I was small compared to other guys, I made the first string on my high school football team."

———————

"I graduated from high school with honors even though I was very active in school clubs and had to work part-time."

———————

"I was the first in my family to go to college and one of the few from my high school. Worked part-time and summers. A real struggle, but I made it."

———————

"Completed flight school training, which was the toughest and proudest moment of my life!"

———————

"Earned my bachelor's degree in psychology from Old Dominion University while serving in the Navy in Norfolk, Virginia. Completed most degree requirements by attending evening courses while working full-time."

———————

"Became a SEAL after completing the most physically and mentally challenging training of my life!"

"Although I was the smallest soldier in my unit, I won the intramural wrestling title for my weight group three consecutive years."

———————————

"Designed our house and had it constructed in time and under budget."

———————————

"Taught myself advanced digital photo methods that resulted in winning first place in a prestigious photo contest of amateur photographers."

———————————

"Raised two wonderful daughters who are studying to become medical doctors."

———————————

2. Prioritize your seven most significant achievements.

Your Most Significant Achievements

1. _____

2. _____

3. _____

4. _____

5. _____

6. _____

7. _____

3. Write a full page on each of your prioritized achievements. You should describe:

- How you initially became involved.
- The details of **what you did** and **how you did it**.
- What was especially enjoyable or satisfying to you.

Use copies of the "Detailing Your Achievements" form on page 194 to outline your achievements.

Detailing Your Achievements

ACHIEVEMENT # ___: _____

1. How did I initially become involved? _____

2. What did I do? _____

3. How did I do it? _____

4. What was especially enjoyable about doing it?

4. **Elaborate on your achievements:** Have one or two other people interview you. For each achievement have them note on a separate sheet of paper any terms used to reveal your skills, abilities, and personal qualities. To elaborate details, the interviewer(s) may ask:

- What was involved in the achievement?
- What was your part?
- What did you actually do?
- How did you go about that?

Clarify any vague areas by providing an example or illustration of what you actually did. Probe with the following questions:

- Would you elaborate on one example of what you mean?
- Could you give me an illustration?
- What were you good at doing?

This interview should clarify the details of your activities by asking only "what" and "how" questions. It should take 45 to 90 minutes to complete. Make copies of the "Strength Identification Interview" form on page 196 to guide you through this interview.

5. **Identify patterns by examining the interviewer's notes:** Together, identify the recurring skills, abilities, and personal qualities **demonstrated** in your achievements. Search for patterns. Your skills pattern should be clear at this point; you should feel comfortable with it. If you have questions, review the data. If you disagree with a conclusion, disregard it. The results must accurately and honestly reflect how you operate.

6. **Synthesize the information by clustering similar skills into categories:** For example, your skills might be grouped according to the cluster at the top of page 197.

Strength Identification Interview

Interviewee _____ Interviewer _____

INSTRUCTIONS: For each achievement experience, identify the **skills** and **abilities** the achiever actually demonstrated. Obtain details of the experience by asking **what** was involved with the achievement and **how** the individual made the achievement happen. Avoid "why" questions which tend to mislead. Ask for examples or illustrations of what and how.

Achievement #1:

Achievement #2:

Achievement #3:

Recurring abilities and skills:

Synthesized Skill Clusters

Investigate/Survey/Read	Teach/Train/Drill
Inquire/Probe/Question	Perform/Show/Demonstrate
Learn/Memorize/Practice	Construct/Assemble/Put together
Evaluate/Appraise/Assess	
Compare	Organize/Structure/Provide
	definition/Plan/Chart course
Influence/Involve/Get	Strategize/Coordinate
participation/Publicize	
Promote	Create/Design/Adapt/Modify

This exercise yields a relatively comprehensive inventory of your skills. The information will better enable you to use a **skills vocabulary** when identifying your objective, writing your resume and letters, and interviewing. If you are like many others who have successfully completed this exercise, your self-confidence and self-esteem should increase accordingly.

Other Alternatives

Several other techniques also can help you identify your motivated abilities and skills:

1. List all of your hobbies and analyze what you do in each, which ones you like the most, what skills you use, and your accomplishments.

2. Conduct a job analysis by writing about your past jobs and identifying which skills you used in each job. Cluster the skills into related categories and prioritize them according to your preferences.

3. Acquire a copy of Arthur F. Miller and Ralph T. Mattson's *The Truth About You* (now out of print) and work through the exercises found in the Appendix. While its overt religious message, extreme deterministic approach, and laborious exercises may turn off some users, you may find this book useful nonetheless. This is an abbreviated version of the authors' SIMA (System for Identifying Motivated Abilities) technique used by their career counseling firm, People Management, Inc. (www.sima-pmi.com). If you need professional assistance, contact this firm directly. They can provide you with several alter-

native services consistent with the career planning philosophy and approach outlined in this chapter.

4. Complete John Holland's *"The Self-Directed Search (SDS®)."* You'll find it in his book, *Making Vocational Choices: A Theory of Vocational Personalities and Work Environments* or in a separate publication entitled *The Self-Directed Search – A Guide to Educational and Vocational Planning.* Also, check out the publisher's (Psychological Assessment Resources) website for an online version of the SDS®: www.self-directed-search.com.

Benefit From Redundancy

The self-directed MAS exercises generate similar information. They identify interests, values, abilities, and skills you already possess. While the many paper-and-pencil and computerized tests outlined in Chapter 4 (pages 164-171) may yield similar information, the self-directed exercises have three major advantages over the standardized tests: less expensive, self-monitored and evaluated, and measure motivation **and** ability.

Employers rightfully believe that past performance is the best predictor of future performance. You need to clearly communicate your "pattern of performance" to employers.

Each exercise demands a different investment of time. Writing your life history and completing the Motivated Skills Exercise and Bolles's *Map* are the most time consuming. On the other hand, Holland's *"Self-Directed Search"* can be completed in a few minutes. But the more time you invest with each technique, the more useful information you will generate.

We recommend creating redundancy by using at least two or three different techniques, such as the professionally administered *Myers-Briggs Type Indicator®* and *Strong Interest Inventory®*. This will help reinforce and confirm the validity of your observations and interpretations. If you have a great deal of work experience, we recommend using the more thorough exercises. The more you put into these techniques and exercises, the greater the benefit to other stages of your job search. You will be well prepared to target your job search toward specific jobs that fit your MAS as well as clearly communicate your qualifications to employers. A carefully planned career or career change should not do less than this.

Bridging Your Past and Future

Many people want to effortlessly know about their future. If you expect the self-assessment techniques in Chapters 8, 9, and 10 to spell out your future, you will be disappointed. Fortune tellers, horoscopes, positive thinking, spiritual advisors, and various forms of mysticism that look **outside** the individual may be what you need.

These are historical and deterministic devices that look **inside** the individual for answers to the future. They integrate past achievements, abilities, and motivations into a coherent framework for projecting future performance. They clarify past strengths and recurring motivations for targeting future jobs. Abilities and motivations are the **qualifications** employers expect for particular jobs. Qualifications consist of your past experience **and** your motivated abilities and skills.

The assessment techniques provide a bridge between your past and future. They treat your future preferences and performance as functions of your past experiences and demonstrated abilities. This common sense notion – **past performance is the best predictor of future performance** – is shared by employers, especially among those who increasingly conduct situational and behavior-based interviews that are designed to uncover such patterns.

Yet, employers hire a person's **future** rather than their past. And herein lies an important problem you can help employers overcome. Getting the job that is right for you entails communicating to prospective employers that you have the necessary qualifications. Indeed, employers will look for signs of your future productivity **for them**. Since you are an unknown and risky quantity for prospective employers, you must communicate evidence of your past productivity so they can better predict your future performance. This evidence is revealed clearly in your past achievements as outlined in our assessment techniques.

The overall value of using these assessment techniques is that they should enhance your occupational mobility over the long run. The major thrust of all these techniques is to identify abilities and skills which are **transferable** to different work environments. This is particularly important if you are making a career change. You must overcome employers' negative expectations and objections toward career changers by clearly communicating your transferable abilities and skills in the most positive terms possible. These assessment techniques are designed to do precisely that.

11

Specify Your Objective

O NCE YOU HAVE IDENTIFIED YOUR motivated abilities and skills (MAS), you should be well prepared to develop a clear and purposeful objective for targeting your job search toward specific jobs, organizations, and employers. With a renewed sense of direction and versed in an appropriate language, you should be able to clearly communicate to prospective employers, using many interesting examples and stories of success, that you are a talented and purposeful individual who **achieves results**. Your objective must tell employers what you will **do for them** rather than what you want from them. It targets your pattern of accomplishments around employers' needs. In other words, your objective should be employer-centered rather than self-centered.

Mission Statements, Goals, and Objectives

Your objective is not the same as a mission statement, which is usually associated with the kind of person you would like to become. A mission statement is more closely associated with your purpose or significance in life and it might be identified through an obituary exercise – a statement of how you would like to be remembered after death.

Goals and objectives are statements of what you want to do in the future. When combined with an assessment of your interests, values,

abilities, and skills, and related to specific jobs, they give your job search needed direction and meaning for the purpose of targeting specific employers. Without them, your job search may founder as you present an image of uncertainty and confusion to potential employers. Employers want to hire talented, enthusiastic, and purposeful individuals.

When you identify your strengths, you also create the necessary database and vocabulary for developing your job objective. Using this vocabulary, which is really the language of employers, you should be able to communicate your strengths to prospective employers.

If you fail to do the preliminary self-assessment work necessary for developing a clear objective, you will probably wander aimlessly in a highly decentralized, fragmented, and chaotic job market looking for interesting jobs you might fit into. Your goal, instead, should be to find a job or career that is compatible with your interests, motivations, skills, and talents as well as related to a vision of your future. In other words, try to find a job fit for you and your future rather than try to fit into a job that happens to be advertised and for which you think you can qualify. Remember, your ultimate goal should be to find a job and career you really love.

> *Your objective should be employer- or work-centered rather than self-centered. It should reflect your honesty and integrity; it should not be "hyped."*

Your MAS and Vision of the Future

Depending on how you approach your job search, your goals can be largely a restatement of your past MAS patterns (Chapter 8) or a vision of your future. If you base your job search on an analysis of your motivated abilities and skills, you may prefer restating your past patterns as your present and future goals. On the other hand, you may want to establish a vision of your future and set goals that motivate you to achieve that vision through a process of self-transformation.

The type of goals you choose to establish will involve different processes. However, the strongest goals will be those that combine your motivated abilities and skills with a realistic vision of your future.

A Work- and Employer-Centered Focus

Your objective should be a concise statement of what you want to do and what you have to offer to an employer. The position you seek is "what

you want to do"; your qualifications are "what you have to offer." Your objective should state your strongest qualifications for meeting employers' needs. It should communicate what you have to offer an employer without emphasizing what you expect the employer to do for you. In other words, your objective should be **work-centered**, not self-centered; it should not contain trite terms which emphasize what you want, such as give me a(n) "opportunity for advancement," "position working with people," "progressive company," or "creative position." Such terms are viewed as "canned" job search language which say little of value about you. Above all, your objective should reflect your honesty and integrity; it should not be "hyped."

Identifying what it is you want to do can be one of the most difficult job search tasks. Indeed, most job hunters lack clear objectives. Many engage in a random and somewhat mindless search for jobs by identifying available job opportunities and then adjusting their skills and objectives to fit specific job openings. While you can get a job using this approach, you may be misplaced and unhappy with what you find. You will fit into a job rather than find a job that is fit for you.

> *The strongest goals will be those that combine your motivated abilities and skills with a realistic vision of your future.*

Knowing what you want to do can have numerous benefits. First, you define the job market rather than let it define you. The inherent fragmentation and chaos of the job market should be advantageous for you, because it enables you to systematically organize job opportunities around your specific objectives and skills. Second, you will communicate professionalism to prospective employers. They will receive a precise indication of your interests, qualifications, and purposes, which places you ahead of most other applicants. Third, being purposeful means being able to communicate to employers what you really want to do. Employers are not interested in hiring indecisive and confused individuals who will probably have difficulty taking initiative because they really don't know what they should be doing in the first place. Employers want to know what it is you can and will do **for them**. With a clear objective – based upon a thorough understanding of your motivated skills and interests – you can take control of the situation as you demonstrate your value to employers.

Finally, few employers really know what they want in a candidate. Like most job seekers, employers often lack clear employment objectives and knowledge about how the job market operates. If you know what you want and can help the employer define his or her "needs" as your

objective, you will have achieved a tremendously advantageous position in the job market.

A Realistic Objective

Your objective should communicate that you are a **purposeful individual who achieves results**. It can be stated over different time periods as well as at various levels of abstraction and specificity. You can identify short, intermediate, and long-range objectives and very general to very specific objectives. Whatever the case, it is best to know your prospective audience before deciding on the type of objective. Your objective should reflect your career interests as well as employers' needs.

Objectives also should be **realistic**. You may want to become president of the United States or solve all the world's problems. However, these objectives are probably unrealistic. While they may represent your ideals and fantasies, you need to be more realistic in terms of what you can personally accomplish in the immediate future given your particular skills, pattern of accomplishments, level of experience, and familiarity with the job market. What, for example, are you prepared to deliver to prospective employers over the next few months? While it is good to set challenging objectives, you can overdo it. Refine your objective by thinking about the next major step or two you would like to make in your career advancement. Develop a realistic action plan that focuses on the details of progressing your career one step at a time. By all means avoid making a grandiose leap outside reality!

Incorporate Your Dreams

Even after identifying your abilities and skills, specifying an **objective** can be the most difficult and tedious step in the job search process; it can stall the resume writing process indefinitely. This simple one-sentence, 25-word statement can take days or weeks to formulate and clearly define. Yet, it must be specified prior to writing the resume and engaging in other job search steps. An objective gives meaning and direction to all other activities.

Your objective should be viewed as a function of several influences. Since you want to build upon your strengths and you want to be realistic, your abilities and skills will play a central role in formulating your work objective. At the same time, you do not want your objective to become a function solely of your past accomplishments and skills. You may be very skilled in certain areas, but you may not want to use these skills in the future. As a result, your values and interests filter which skills you will or

will not incorporate into your work objective.

Overcoming the problem of historical determinism – your future merely reflecting your past – requires incorporating additional components into defining your objective. One of the most important is your ideals, fantasies, or dreams. Everyone engages in these, and sometimes they come true. Your ideals, fantasies, or dreams may include making $1,000,000 by age 40; owning a Mercedes-Benz and a Porsche; taking trips to Rio, Hong Kong, and Rome; owning your own business; developing financial independence; writing a best-selling novel; solving major social problems; or winning the Nobel Peace Prize. If your fantasies require more money than you are now making, you will need to incorporate monetary considerations into your work objective. For example, if you have these fantasies, but your sense of realism tells you that your objective is to move from a $40,000 a year position to a $42,000 a year position, you will be going nowhere – unless you can fast-track in your new position. Therefore, you will need to set a higher objective to satisfy your fantasies.

You can develop realistic objectives many different ways. We don't claim to have a new or magical formula, only one which has worked for many individuals. We assume you are capable of making intelligent career decisions if given sufficient data. Using redundancy once again, our approach is designed to provide you with sufficient corroborating data from several sources and perspectives so that you can make preliminary decisions. If you follow our steps in setting a realistic objective, you should be able to give your job search clear direction.

Four major steps are involved in developing a work objective. Each step can be implemented in a variety of ways:

STEP 1: Develop or obtain basic data on your functional/transferable skills, which we discussed in Chapter 6.

STEP 2: Acquire corroborating data about yourself from other people, tests, and yourself. Several resources are available for this purpose:

A. From other people: Ask three to five individuals whom you know well to evaluate you according to the questions in the "Strength Evaluation" form on page 205. Explain to them that you believe their candid appraisal will help you gain a better understanding of your strengths and weaknesses from the perspectives of others. Make copies of this form and ask your

Strength Evaluation

TO: _____

FROM: _____

I am going through a career assessment process and thought you would be an appropriate person to ask for assistance. Would you please candidly respond to the questions below? Your comments will be given to me by the individual designed below; s/he will not reveal your name. Your comments will be used for advising purposes only. Thank you.

What are my strengths?

What weak areas might I need to improve?

In your opinion, what do I need in a job or career to make me satisfied?

Please return to: _____

evaluators to complete and return it to a designated third party who will share the information – but not the respondent's name – with you.

B. **From vocational tests:** Although we prefer self-generated data, vocationally oriented tests can help clarify, confirm, and translate your understanding of yourself into occupational directions. If you decide to use vocational tests, contact a professional career counselor who can administer and interpret the tests. We suggest several of the following tests:

- *Myers-Briggs Type Indicator®*
- *Strong Interest Inventory®*
- *Self-Directed Search (SDS)®*
- *Campbell Interest and Skill Survey*
- *Keirsey Character Sorter*
- *Birkman Method*
- *Enneagram*
- *FIRO-B®*
- *California Psychological Inventory (CPI)*
- *16 Personality Factors Profile*
- *Edwards Personal Preference Schedule*
- *Kuder Occupational Interest Survey*
- *APTICOM*
- *Jackson Vocational Interest Survey*
- *Vocational Interest Inventory*
- *Career Assessment Inventory*
- *Temperament and Values Inventory*

C. **From yourself:** Numerous alternatives are available for you to practice redundancy. Refer to the exercises in Chapter 7 that assist you in identifying your work values, job frustrations and dissatisfactions, things you love to do, things you enjoy most about work, and your preferred interpersonal environments.

STEP 3: Project your values and preferences into the future by completing simulation and creative thinking exercises:

A. **Ten Million Dollar Exercise:** First, assume that you are given a $10,000,000 gift; now you don't have to work. Since the gift is restricted to your use only, you cannot give any

part of it away. What will you do with your time? At first? Later on? Second, assume that you are given another $10,000,000, but this time you are required to give it all away. What kinds of causes, organizations, charities, etc. would you support? Complete the following form in which you answer these questions:

What Will I Do With Two $10,000,000 Gifts?

First gift is restricted to my use only:

Second gift must be given away:

B. **Obituary Exercise:** Make a list of the most important things you would like to do or accomplish before you die. Two alternatives are available for doing this. First, make a list in response to this lead-in statement: *"Before I die, I want to..."*

Before I Die, I Want to . . .

1. _____

2. _____

3. _____

4. _____

5. _____

6. _____

7. _____

8. _____

9. _____

10. _____

Second, write a newspaper article which is actually your obituary for 10 years from now. Stress your accomplishments over the coming 10-year period.

My Obituary

Obituary for Mr./Ms. _____ to appear in the _____ Newspaper in 20____.

C. My Ideal Work Week: Starting with Monday, place each day of the week as the headings on seven sheets of paper. Develop a daily calendar with 30-minute intervals, beginning at 7am and ending at midnight. Your calendar should consist of a 118-hour week. Next, beginning at 7am on Monday (sheet one), identify the **ideal activities** you would enjoy doing, or need to do, for each 30-minute segment during the day. Assume you are capable of doing anything; you have no constraints except those you impose on yourself. Furthermore, assume that your work schedule consists of 40 hours per week. How will you fill your time? Be specific.

My Ideal Work Week

Monday

am		pm	
7:00	_____	4:00	_____
7:30	_____	4:30	_____
8:00	_____	5:00	_____
8:30	_____	5:30	_____
9:00	_____	6:00	_____
9:30	_____	6:30	_____
10:00	_____	7:00	_____
10:30	_____	7:30	_____

11:00 _____	8:00 _____
11:30 _____	8:30 _____
Noon _____	9:00 _____
12:30 _____	9:30 _____
pm	10:00 _____
1:00 _____	10:30 _____
1:30 _____	11:00 _____
2:00 _____	11:30 _____
2:30 _____	12:00 _____
3:00 _____	Continue for Tuesday, Wednesday, Thursday,
3:30 _____	and Friday

D. **My Ideal Job Description:** Develop your ideal future job. Be sure you include:

- Specific interests you want to build into your job
- Work responsibilities
- Working conditions
- Earnings and benefits
- Interpersonal environment
- Working circumstances, opportunities, and goals

Description of My Ideal Job

Use "My Ideal Job Specifications" on page 212 to outline your ideal job. After completing this exercise, synthesize the job and write a detailed paragraph which describes the kind of job you would most enjoy.

STEP 4: Test your objective against reality. Evaluate and refine it by conducting market research, a force field analysis, library research, and informational interviews.

A. **Market Research:** This type of research involves four key steps:

1. **Products or services:** Based upon all other assessment activities, make a list of what you **do** or **make**:

Products/Services I Do or Make

1. _____

2. _____

3. _____

My Ideal Job Specifications

Job Interests	Work Responsibilities	Working Conditions	Earnings /Benefits	Circumstances / Opportunities / Goals

4. _____

5. _____

6. _____

7. _____

8. _____

9. _____

10. _____

2. Market: Identify who needs, wants, or buys what you do or make. Be very specific. Include individuals, groups, and organizations. Then, identify **what** specific **needs** your products or services fill. Next, assess the **results** you achieve with your products or services.

The Market for My Products/Services

Individuals, groups, and organizations needing me:

1. _____

2. _____

3. _____

4. _____

5. _____

Needs I fulfill:

1. _____

2. _____

3. _____

4. _____

5. _____

Results/outcomes/impacts of my products/services:

1. _____

2. _____

3. _____

4. _____

5. _____

3. **New Markets:** Brainstorm a list of **who else** needs your products or services. Think about ways of expanding your market. Next, list any new needs your current or new market has which you might be able to fill:

Developing New Needs

Who else needs my products/services?

1. _____

2. _____

3. _____

4. _____

5. _____

New ways to expand my market:

1. _____

2. _____

3. _____

4. _____

5. _____

New needs I should fulfill:

1. _____

2. _____

3. _____

4. _____

5. _____

4. **New products and/or services:** List any new products or services you can offer and any new needs you can satisfy:

New Products/Services I Can Offer

1. _____
2. _____
3. _____
4. _____
5. _____

New Needs I Can Meet

1. _____
2. _____
3. _____
4. _____
5. _____

B. **Force Field Analysis:** Once you develop a tentative or firm objective, force field analysis can help you understand the various internal and external forces affecting the achievement of your objective. Force field analysis follows this sequence of activities:

- **Clearly state your objective or course of action.** Make sure it's based upon your MAS and is employer-oriented rather than self-centered.

- **List the positive and negative forces affecting your objective.** Specify the internal and external forces working **for** and **against** you in terms of who, what, where, when, and how much. Estimate the impact of each on your objective.

- **Analyze the forces.** Assess the importance of each force upon your objective and its probable effect upon you. Some forces may be irrelevant to your goal. You may need additional information to make a thorough analysis.

- **Maximize positive forces and minimize negative ones.** Identify actions you can take to strengthen positive forces and to neutralize, overcome, or reverse negative forces. Focus on real, important, and probable key forces.

- **Assess the feasibility of attaining your objective** and, if necessary, modifying it in light of new information.

C. **Conduct Online and Library Research:** This research should strengthen and clarify your objective. Consult various reference materials on alternative jobs and careers. Most of these resources are available in print form at your local library or bookstore. Some are available in electronic versions online. If you explore the numerous company profiles and career sites available on the Internet, you should be able to tap into a wealth of information on alternative jobs and careers. Two good resources for initiating online research are Margaret Riley Dikel's *The Guide to Internet Job Search* (McGraw-Hill) and Pam Dixon's *Job Searching Online for Dummies* (IDG Books). For directories to key employment websites, see Ron and Caryl Krannich, *America's Top Internet Job Sites* and *The Directory of Websites for International Jobs* (Impact Publications); Bernard Haldane Associates, *Haldane's Best Employment Websites for Professionals* (Impact Publications); and Gerry Crispin and Mark Mehler, *CareerXroads* (MMC Group). Many of the resources traditionally found in libraries are available online. The following websites function as excellent gateway sites, online databases, and research tools:

■ CEO Express	www.ceoexpress.com
■ Hoover's Online	www.hoovers.com
■ Dun and Bradstreet's Million Dollar Databases	www.dnbmdd.com/mddi
■ Corporate Information	www.corporateinformation.com
■ BizTech Network	www.brint.com

- AllBusiness www.allbusiness.com
- BizWeb www.bizweb.com
- Business.com www.business.com
- America's CareerInfoNet www.acinet.org
- Newspapers USA www.newspapers.com
- Salary.com www.salary.com
- Annual Report Service www.annualreportservice.com
- Bloomberg www.bloomberg.com
- Chamber of Commerce www.chamberofcommerce.com
- CNN Money http//money.cnn.com
- Daily Stocks www.dailystocks.com
- The Corporate Library www.thecorporatelibrary.com
- Forbes Lists www.forbes.com/lists
- Fortune 500 www.fortune.com
- Harris InfoSource www.harrisinfo.com
- Inc. 500 www.inc.com/500
- Moodys www.moodys.com
- Motley Fool www.fool.com
- NASDAQ www.nasdaq.com
- One Source Corp Tech www.onesource.com
- Standard & Poors www.standardandpoors.com
- The Street www.thestreet.com
- Thomas Regional www.thomasregional.com
- Thomas Register www.thomasregister.com

Career and Job Alternatives

- *25 Jobs That Have It All*
- *50 Best Jobs for Your Personality*
- *50 Cutting Edge Jobs*
- *300 Best Jobs Without a Four-Year Degree*
- *Almanac of American Employers*
- *Almanac of American Employers Mid-Size Firms*
- *America's Top Jobs for People Re-Entering the Workforce*
- *America's Top 100 Jobs for People Without a Four-Year Degree*
- *Enhanced Guide for Occupational Exploration*
- *Guide to Occupational Exploration*
- *Quick Prep Careers*
- *Occupational Outlook Handbook*
- *Occupational Outlook Quarterly*
- *O*NET Dictionary of Occupational Titles*

Industrial Directories

- *Dun and Bradstreet's Middle Market Directory*
- *Dun and Bradstreet's Million Dollar Directory*
- *Encyclopedia of Business Information Sources*
- *Geography Index*
- *Poor's Register of Corporations, Directors, and Executives*
- *Standard Directory of Advertisers*
- *The Standard Periodical Directory*
- *Standard and Poor's Industrial Index*
- *Standard Rate & Data Business Publications Directory*
- *Thomas' Register of American Manufacturers*

Associations

- *Associations USA*
- *Encyclopedia of Associations*
- *National Trade and Professional Associations*
- Access thousands of associations online through: www.ipl.org/ref/AON and www.asaenet.org.

Government Sources

- *The Book of the States*
- *Congressional Directory*
- *Congressional Staff Directory*
- *Congressional Yellow Book*
- *Federal Directory*
- *Federal Yellow Book*
- *Municipal Yearbook*
- *Taylor's Encyclopedia of Government Officials*
- *United Nations Yearbook*
- *United States Government Manual*
- *Washington Information Directory*

Newspapers

- Major city newspapers and trade newspapers. Many are available online through these gateway sites: www.ipl.org/reading/news, http://newsdirectory.com, www.newspaperlinks.com, and www.newspapers.com.
- Your targeted city newspaper – the Sunday edition.

Business Publications

- *Business 2.0, Business Week, Economist, Fast Company, Inc., Forbes, Fortune, Harvard Business Review, Newsweek, Smart Money, Time, U.S. News and World Report, Wired.* Many of these and other business-oriented publications can be viewed online through this terrific website: www.CEOExpress.com.

- Annual issues of publications surveying the best jobs and employers for the year: *Money, Fortune, Forbes,* and *U.S. News and World Report.* Several of these reports and publications are available online: www.money.com, www.fortune.com, and www.forbes.com/lists.

Other Library Resources

- Trade journals
- Publications of Chambers of Commerce; state manufacturing associations; and federal, state, and local government agencies
- Telephone books – The Yellow Pages
- Books on "how to get a job" (visit the publisher's online bookstore: www.impactpublications.com)

D. **Conduct Informational Interviews:** This may be the most useful way to clarify and refine your objective. See Chapter 14 for details on how to conduct such interviews.

After completing these steps, you will have identified what it is you **can** do (abilities and skills), enlarged your thinking to include what it is you would **like** to do (aspirations), and probed the realities of implementing your objective. Thus, setting a realistic work objective is a function of the diverse considerations outlined on page 220.

Your work objective is a function of both subjective and objective information as well as combines idealism with realism. We believe the strongest emphasis should be placed on your competencies and should include a broad database. Your work objective is realistic in that it is tempered by your past experiences, accomplishments, skills, and current research. An objective formulated in this manner permits you to think beyond your past experiences.

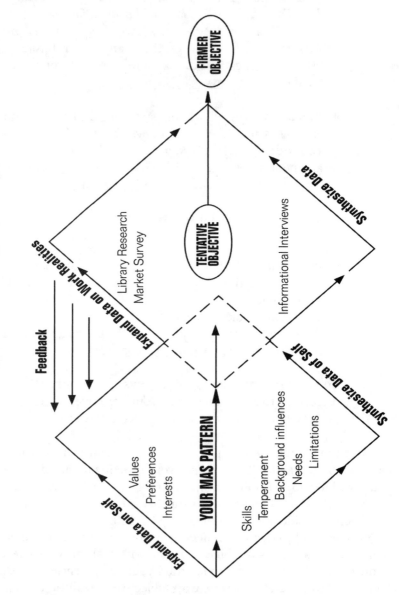

Objective Setting Process

FIRMER OBJECTIVE

TENTATIVE OBJECTIVE

Synthesize Data

Library Research
Market Survey

Informational Interviews

Expand Data on Work Realities

Feedback

Synthesize Data of Self

Values
Preferences
Interests

YOUR MAS PATTERN

Skills
Temperament
Background influences
Needs
Limitations

Expand Data on Self

State a Functional Objective

Your job objective should be oriented toward skills and results or outcomes. You can begin by stating a functional job objective at two different levels: a general objective and a specific one for communicating your qualifications to employers both on resumes and in interviews. Thus, this objective-setting process sets the stage for other key job search activities. For the general objective, begin with the statement:

Stating Your General Objective

I would like a job where I can use my ability to _____, which will result in _____.

The objective in this statement is both a **skill** and an **outcome**. For example, you might state:

Skills-Based and Results-Oriented Objective

I would like a job where my experience in program development, supported by innovative decision-making and systems engineering abilities, will result in an expanded clientele and a more profitable organization.

At a second level you may wish to re-write this objective in order to target it at various consulting firms. For example, on your resume it becomes:

Job-Targeted Objective

An increasingly responsible research position in consulting, where proven decision-making and systems engineering abilities will be used for improving organizational productivity.

The following are examples of weak and strong objective statements. Various styles are also presented.

Weak Objectives

Management position which will use business administration degree and will provide opportunities for rapid advancement.

A position in social services which will allow me to work with people in a helping capacity.

———————

A position in Human Resources with a progressive firm.

———————

Sales Representative with opportunity for advancement.

———————

Stronger Objectives

*To use computer science training in **software development** for designing and implementing operating systems.*

———————

A public relations position which will maximize opportunities to develop and implement programs, to organize people and events, and to communicate positive ideas and images. Effective in public speaking and in managing a publicity/promotional campaign.

———————

A position as a General Sales Representative with a pharmaceutical house which will use chemistry background and ability to work on a self-directed basis in managing a marketing territory.

———————

A position in data analysis where skills in mathematics, computer programming, and deductive reasoning will contribute to new systems development.

———————

Retail Management position which will use sales/customer service experience and creative abilities for product display and merchandising. Long term goal: Progression to merchandise manager with corporate-wide responsibilities for product line.

———————

Responsible position in investment research and analysis. Interests and skills include securities analysis, financial planning, and portfolio management. Long range goal: to become a Chartered Financial Analyst.

It is important to relate your objective to your audience. While you definitely want a good job that pays well, your audience wants to know what you can do for them in exchange for a good paying job. Remember, your objective should be work-centered, not self-centered.

Your objective will become the key to organizing all other elements in your job search. It should become the central organizing element on your resume. It gives meaning and direction to your job search. Your objective says something very important about how you want to conduct your life with the employer. It gives them an important indicator of the value you will bring to this job. Most important of all, it tells them who you really are

> *Your objective will become the key to organizing all other elements in your job search.*

in terms of your key values and accomplishments – a short answer to the big question of *"Why should I hire you?"*

12

Write Powerful Applications, Resumes, and Letters

NOW THAT YOU KNOW (1) what you do well, (2) what you enjoy doing, and (3) what you want to do in the future – based on your assessment and objective-setting work in the previous four chapters – you have the basic information necessary for communicating your key qualifications to employers. But what will you do with this information? What messages do you want to send to employers about yourself? How will you convey these messages – by telephone, letter, e-mail, fax, or in face-to-face meetings? What's the best way to the next step in your job search?

Communicating Positive Images

At every stage in the job search you must communicate a positive image to potential employers. The initial impression you make on an employer through applications, resumes, letters, telephone calls, or informational interviews will determine whether the employer is interested in interviewing you and offering you a position.

Developing and managing effective job search communication should play a central role in everything you do related to finding employment. While this communication will take several verbal and nonverbal forms, your first communication with employers will most likely be by application, letter, e-mail, fax, or telephone. Applications and job search letters

often include your calling card – the resume. Since they are essentially nonverbal forms of communication, applications, resumes, and letters should be written and distributed with impact.

Completing Applications

Certain types of positions may necessitate just a formal application. Many blue-collar, minimum wage, and entry-level positions, for example, only require job seekers to complete an application that asks standard questions about an individual's educational level, previous work experience, salary history, and references. If, for example, you go into a grocery store or retail business (Costco, Wal-Mart, Home Depot, Best Buy, Comp USA, Circuit City, Radio Shack, Macy's, Nordstrom, UPS, FedEx), you may be asked to go to a computer screen, or kiosk, to complete an online application, or you will be given a two- to four-page application form to be completed by hand. Many companies routinely give anyone interested in a job a chance to fill out an application. Such applications help employers standardize the application process and quickly screen candidates in or out for positions.

Applications are increasingly used for all types of positions, including many white-collar and professional positions that pay well. Employers increasingly require applicants to visit the company website to submit their credentials; this usually involves completing an online resume or "profile" which, in effect, is a formatted online application.

The following tips should help you complete a job application to the expectations of employers and improve your chances of getting a job interview:

1. **Dress neatly.** Assume that you will be observed when you complete the application. The person taking your application may make a note about your appearance and communication skills. Since you may end up being interviewed on the spot, dress as if you were going to a job interview and observe all the rules for positive verbal and nonverbal behavior (see Chapter 15). First impressions are always important, be it on an application, over the telephone, or in person.

2. **Take two copies of the application form.** If you are picking up an application form to take with you, get two copies. Use the one copy to draft your answers and the other copy to submit as a neat, clean, and error-free application.

3. **Read the instructions carefully and follow them completely.** An application is your first screening test in more ways than you may think. Start by reading through the whole application to see exactly what information is required for completion. If you lack sufficient information, don't complete the application since you will be submitting an incomplete application, which is a negative. Return later with the missing information. Follow the instructions. If it says print, then you print. If it says last name first, then write accordingly. If it asks for a phone number, provide one. If it asks for your supervisor's name, reason for leaving each job, and pay rates, supply this information. If it says provide three references, then give the details on three references. Failure to complete an application according to instructions communicates a terrible message – you simply can't follow instructions, or you have something to hide! No one wants to hire such people. You've just wasted your time filling out an incomplete application.

4. **Use a black ink pen when writing.** Avoid using a pencil or an ink color other than black. In fact, many applications will ask you to use a black pen. An application completed in pencil looks unprofessional, and non-black ink may not copy well if the application is run through a copy machine.

5. **Answer each question.** It's important to respond to each question – no blanks left that could raise questions in the mind of the reviewer about your willingness to disclose or whether you have something to hide. For example, if you don't have a permanent address or telephone number, use the address and number of a friend or relative who has agreed to serve as your contact location. If a question does not relate to your situation, type or write "N/A," which means "Not Applicable."

6. **Try to write as neatly as possible.** The neatness and style of your handwriting may be interpreted by the reader as an indication of your personality and work habits. If it looks sloppy, with letters or words crossed out, the reader may think you are unfocused, careless, or sloppy in your work habits.

7. **Be prepared to complete each section of the application.** If you know you will be applying for a job, take to the application center all information you may need to complete the

application in full. You may want to fill out beforehand a mock or draft application form, which you keep with you, that contains most information you are likely to be asked on an application. This would include a list of previous employers, addresses, telephone numbers, employment dates, information about your work, and documents (Social Security number and driver's license). You also want to have with you details on your educational background and references. Trying to recall this information by memory may lead to inaccurate statements or an incomplete application; you'll be demonstrating two negatives to the employer even before the job interview – you are unprepared and you're not serious about employment.

8. **Include all previous employers.** Reveal all of your previous employers, even if you were fired. Many people get fired and it's not held against them by other employers. You can always explain the situation, but you will have greater difficulty trying to explain a major employment gap. No one wants to hire someone who is deceptive. If you can't be trusted with the truth at the application stage, why would anyone want to trust you on the job?

9. **Try to explain your military occupation and skills in civilian terms.** When describing your work experience, avoid military jargon that may not be understood by civilians. Your goal should be to show employers that you acquired important skills in the military that are directly transferable to civilian jobs. Try to use comparable civilian work terms, which you should have identified when you translated your military specialty (MOS, Ratings, or AFSCS) into civilian skills and occupations (see Chapter 8).

10. **Appear educated, even if you lack formal credentials.** If you only have a high school diploma, try to expand on this educational milestone by including information about your military training experience. While educational credentials are important, and especially with government and contracting firms that work with government, most employers are looking for demonstrated work experience and skills as well as the ability of individuals to learn new skills. If you've completed training programs or acquired specialized skills, include them on your application under Education. Make sure you appear educated and thoughtful – no misspelling,

poor grammar, or stupid statements – in each section of your application.

11. **Handle sensitive questions with tact.** An application is not a place to confess all your sins, reveal red flags, or prematurely show your hand. Like a resume, an application becomes your calling card to be invited to the interview. Take, for example, an individual who has a criminal record. In this case, the most sensitive question will be *"Have you ever been convicted of a crime? If yes, please explain."* Most applicants believe they have three choices in responding to this question: lie, tell the truth, or leave it blank. All three choices may have negative consequences for getting the job interview or keeping the job. In addition, the law may require you to disclose your criminal record to employers, and you must sign the applications, indicating your answers are truthful. However, there is a fourth choice in answering this question which leaves the door open: simply write *"Please discuss with me"* or *"Will discuss at the interview."* These statements indicate you have a conviction, you're not hiding it, and you are prepared to discuss it at the appropriate time. This question is best dealt with in a face-to-face meeting where you will have a chance to explain and demonstrate six things: (1) you made a serious mistake, (2) you took respon- sibility, (3) you've done several things to change your life, (4) you're not a risk, (5) you want a chance to prove yourself, and (6) you are positive, enthusiastic, energetic, and ready to perform beyond the employer's expectations. A similar response should be given to another sensitive question: *"Have you ever been fired?"* Respond by writing *"Please see me"* or *"Will discuss at the interview."*

12. **Avoid abbreviations.** Not all readers share the same knowledge of abbreviations. You can abbreviate the obvious, such as Street (St.), Avenue (Ave.), or Boulevard (Blvd.), but spell out the not-so-obvious. If, for example, you lived or worked in Los Angeles, your application should say Los Angeles rather than L.A.

13. **Avoid vague statements.** If you state that you can operate a computer, indicate at what level and the programs you are familiar with. If you are a driver, indicate what type of

vehicle or equipment you work with. The more details you give, the more impressive your application will be.

14. **Avoid revealing salary information.** If the application asks for your salary expectations (pay or salary desired), state *"Open"* or *"Will discuss at the interview."* Always try to keep this question to the very end of the interview – **after** you have been offered the job. The old poker saying that *"He who reveals his hand is at a disadvantage"* is very true in the job search. Get the employer to first reveal his hand before you talk about your salary expectations. We'll have more to say on this subject in Chapter 16.

15. **Include interests and hobbies relevant to the job.** If asked about any interests and hobbies, try to select examples relevant to the job. If, for example, you are applying for an outdoor job that requires physical stamina, outdoor sports interests would be supportive of such a job.

16. **Include additional comments if appropriate.** Some applications will have a section for additional comments. This is where you want to indicate your goals, state your interests, and make a pitch for the job. Get yourself set up for the job interview by stating something to this effect:

 "I'm especially interested in this job, because I love working with inventory management software and stream- lining operations that save companies both time and money. I would appreciate an opportunity to discuss how my experience can best meet your needs."

17. **Remember to sign the application.** The very last thing you need to do is sign and date your application. Failure to do so may invalidate your application and raise questions about your ability to follow instructions.

18. **Read and re-read your answers.** Make sure you proof- read your application for any errors, omissions, or misspell- ings. Like the perfect resume, you want an error-proof application.

19. **Attach your resume to the application form.** At least for employers, applications are a necessary evil in the screening and hiring processes. Most applications follow a similar and rather dull format that yields little information about who you really are and what you have done, can do, and will do in the future. Few applications allow the flexibility to state your goals, skills, and accomplishments. If you write an achievement-oriented resume, as we will shortly discuss, submit it with your application. A resume lets you structure the reader's thinking around your major strengths rather than allow the reader to control information about you, which is exactly what an application does for the employer. With a well written resume, you may quickly grab the attention of the employer, who will want to invite you to a job interview. Your resume, not your application, becomes the central focus of the job interview.

20. **Be sure to follow up.** When you submit the application, ask when you might expect to hear from the employer on the status of your application. If they say within two weeks, be sure to call and ask about your candidacy in two weeks. In some cases, the follow-up telephone call will result in a job interview. After all, the employer may still be reviewing applications, and your call may force him or her to take a second look at your application (and attached resume). Most important of all, your call indicates that you are still interested in the job.

Writing Resumes

Resumes used to be required for most white-collar or professional positions. They were seen as necessary documents for well educated and skilled individuals. However, today many employers expect to see a resume for more and more blue-collar and entry-level positions.

There are two basic reasons you need to write a resume rather than just rely on completing applications:

1. **Employers want to see you on paper in the form of a resume.** More and more employers require resumes as part of the pre-employment screening process. They expect candidates to present their qualifications in this form. Many employers include employment sections on their websites

which require prospective candidates to complete an online application or questionnaire, submit an electronic resume, or complete a "profile," which is essentially a mini-resume.

2. **You need to organize yourself around a resume.** As you will quickly discover, a resume is a powerful device for organizing you and your job search. A relatively simple one-page resume requires you to develop an objective, identify your key skills and accomplishments, and document your education and work history. Most important of all, it gives you and others a snapshot of who you really are in terms of your goals and accomplishments. Many job seekers find that a well-crafted resume showcasing their major strengths significantly improves their self-esteem (*"Wow . . . this is who I really am!"*) as well as transforms the way they see and approach the world of work.

Resumes are important tools for communicating your purpose and capabilities to employers. While many jobs only require a completed application form, you definitely should prepare a resume for influencing the hiring process. Application forms do not substitute for resumes.

Many myths surround resumes and letters. Some people still believe a resume should summarize one's history. Others believe it will get them a job. And still others believe a resume should be mailed or e-mailed in response to classified ads, job listings, or resume databases. The reality is closer to this: A resume advertises your qualifications to prospective employers. It is your calling card for getting interviews that lead to job offers. It should be used at any time to enhance your employability.

Ineffective Resumes

Most people write ineffective resumes. Misunderstanding the purpose of resumes, they make numerous mistakes commonly associated with weak resumes and poor advertising copy. Their resumes often lack an objective, include unrelated categories of information, are too long, and appear unattractive. Other common pitfalls identified by employers include:

- Poor layout
- Misspellings and punctuation errors
- Poor grammar
- Unclear purpose
- Too much jargon

- Irrelevant data
- Negative comments about employers
- Poorly typed and reproduced
- Unexplained time gaps
- Too boastful
- Deceptive or dishonest
- Difficult to understand or interpret

Your resume, instead, should incorporate the characteristics of strong and effective resumes. It should:

- Clearly communicate your purpose and competencies in relation to employers' needs.
- Be concise and easy to read.
- Outline a pattern of success highlighted with examples of key accomplishments.
- Motivate the reader to read it in-depth.
- Tell employers that you are a responsible and purposeful individual – a doer who can solve their problems.

Keep in mind that most employers are busy people who normally glance at a resume for only 20 to 30 seconds. Your resume, therefore, must sufficiently catch their attention to pass the 20- to 30-second evaluation test. Above all, it must motivate the reader to take action. When writing your resume, ask yourself the same question asked by employers: *"Why should I read this or contact this person for an interview?"*

Your answer should result in an attractive, interesting, unique, and skills-based resume.

Common Resume Errors

From the perspective of job seekers, a resume is an **advertisement** for a job. Within the space of one or two pages, it should give just enough information to persuade the reader to interview the writer. As such, the resume becomes a calling card for a job interview.

Unfortunately, many job seekers produce poorly designed resumes that neither grab the attention of employers nor satisfy their need to know what the candidate has done, can do, and will do in the future. Many misunderstand the purpose of resumes and lose focus on what it is the resume should do – convince the reader to take action. Worst of all, many resumes are "dead upon arrival," because the writer makes numerous

writing, production, and distribution mistakes that quickly turn off employers. Whatever you do, make sure your resume does not include these **writing errors**:

1. Unrelated to the position in question.
2. Too long or too short.
3. Unattractive with a poorly designed format, small type style, and crowded copy.
4. Misspellings, poor grammar, wordiness, and repetition.
5. Punctuation errors.
6. Lengthy phrases, long sentences, and awkward paragraphs.
7. Slick, amateurish, or "gimmicky" – appears over-produced.
8. Boastful, egocentric, and aggressive.
9. Dishonest, untrustworthy, or suspicious information.
10. Missing critical categories, such as experience, skills, and education.
11. Difficult to interpret because of poor organization and lack of focus – uncertain what the person has done or can do.
12. Unexplained time gaps between jobs.
13. Too many jobs in a short period of time – a job hopper with little evidence of career advancement.
14. No evidence of past accomplishments or a pattern of performance from which to predict future performance; primarily focuses on formal duties and responsibilities that came with previous jobs.
15. Lacks credibility and content – includes much fluff and "canned" resume language.
16. States a strange, unclear, or vague objective.
17. Appears over-qualified or under-qualified for the position.
18. Includes distracting personal information that does not enhance the resume nor the candidate.
19. Fails to include critical contact information (telephone number and e-mail address) and uses an anonymous address (P.O. Box number).
20. Uses jargon and abbreviations unfamiliar to the reader.
21. Embellishes name with formal titles, middle names, and nicknames which make him or her appear odd or strange.
22. Repeatedly refers to "I" and appears self-centered.
23. Includes obvious self-serving references that raise credibility questions.
24. Sloppy, with handwritten corrections – crosses out "married" and writes "single"!

25. Includes red flag information such as being incarcerated, fired, lawsuits or claims, health or performance problems, or stating salary figures, including salary requirements, that may be too high or too low.

Employers also report encountering several of these **production, distribution, and follow-up errors**:

1. Poorly typed and reproduced – hard to read.
2. Produced on odd-sized paper.
3. Printed on poor quality paper or on extremely thin or thick paper.
4. Soiled with coffee stains, fingerprints, or ink marks.
5. Sent to the wrong person or department.
6. Mailed, faxed, or e-mailed to "To Whom It May Concern" or "Dear Sir."
7. E-mailed as an attachment which could have a virus if opened.
8. Enclosed in a tiny envelope that requires the resume to be unfolded and flattened several times.
9. Arrived without proper postage – the employer gets to pay the extra!
10. Sent the resume and letter by the slowest postage rate possible.
11. Envelope double-sealed with tape and is indestructible – nearly impossible to open by conventional means!
12. Back of envelope includes a handwritten note stating that something is missing on the resume, such as a telephone number, e-mail address, or new mailing address.
13. Resume taped to the inside of the envelope, an old European habit practiced by paranoid letter writers. Need to destroy the envelope and perhaps also the resume to get it out of the envelope.
14. Accompanied by extraneous or inappropriate enclosures which were not requested, such as copies of self-serving letters or recommendations, transcripts, or samples of work.
15. Arrived too late for consideration.
16. Came without a cover letter.
17. Cover letter repeated what was on the resume – did not command attention nor move the reader to action.
18. Sent the same or different versions of the resume to the same person as a seemingly clever follow-up method.

19. Follow-up call made too soon – before the resume and letter arrived!
20. Follow-up call was too aggressive or the candidate appeared too "hungry" for the position – appeared needy or greedy.

Since the resume is vitally important to getting a job interview, make sure your resume is error-free. Spend sufficient time crafting a resume that shouts loud and clear that you are someone who should be interviewed for a position.

Types of Resumes

You have four basic types of resumes to choose from: chronological, functional, combination, or resume letter. Each form has various advantages and disadvantages, depending on your background and purpose. For example, someone first entering the job market or making a major career change should use a functional resume. On the other hand, a person who wants to target a particular job may choose to use a powerful resume letter that may also function as a "T" letter or "Focus Piece." Examples of these different types of resumes are included at the end of this chapter. Further assistance in developing each section of your resume can be found in three comprehensive resume development books by Ron and Caryl Krannich, *High Impact Resumes and Letters*, *Nail the Resume!*, and *The Savvy Resume Writer* (Impact Publications).

The **chronological resume** is the standard resume used by most applicants who are not very job-search savvy. It often comes in two formats: traditional and improved. The **traditional chronological resume** is also known as the "obituary resume," because it both "kills" your chances of getting a job and is a good source for writing your obituary. Summarizing your work history, this resume lists dates and names first and duties and responsibilities second; it includes extraneous information such as height, weight, age, marital status, gender, and hobbies. While relatively easy to write, this is the most ineffective resume you can produce. Its purpose at best is to inform people of what you have done in the past as well as where, when, and with whom. It tells employers little or nothing about what you want to do, can do, and will do for them.

The **improved chronological resume** better communicates to employers your purpose, past achievements, and probable future performance. This resume format works best for individuals who have extensive experience directly related to a position. This resume should include a clear work objective. The work experience section should include the names and locations of former employers followed by a brief description

of relevant accomplishments, skills, and responsibilities; inclusive employment dates should appear at the end. It should stress **accomplishments** and **skills** rather than formal duties and responsibilities – that you are a productive and responsible person who gets things done, a doer. While this resume performs better than the traditional chronological resume, it still has major limitations because of its chronological format. It simply doesn't highlight well major accomplishments and a pattern of success.

Functional resumes should be used by individuals making a significant career change, first entering the workforce, or re-entering the job market after a lengthy absence. This resume should stress your accomplishments and transferable skills regardless of previous work settings and job titles. This could include accomplishments as a housewife, volunteer worker, or Sunday school teacher. Names of employers and dates of employment should not appear on this resume.

Functional resumes have certain weaknesses. While they are important bridges for the inexperienced and for those making a career change, many employers dislike these resumes. Since they still look for names, dates, and direct job experience, this resume does not meet their expectations. You should use a functional resume only if you have limited work experience or your past experience doesn't support your objective when making a career change.

Combination resumes, also known as hybrid resumes, combine the best features of both chronological and functional resumes. Having more advantages than disadvantages, this resume best communicates accomplishments to employers. It's an ideal resume for experienced professionals who are advancing in their careers or making a career change.

Combination resumes have the potential to both **meet** and **raise** the expectations of employers. You should stress your accomplishments and skills as well as include your work history. Your work history should appear as a separate section immediately following your presentation of accomplishments and skills in the "Areas of Effectiveness," "Experience," or "Achievements" section. It is not necessary to include dates unless they enhance your resume. This is the perfect resume for someone with work experience who wishes to change to a job in a related career field.

Resume letters are substitutes for resumes. Appearing as a job inquiry or application letter, resume letters highlight various sections of your resume, such as work history, experience, areas of effectiveness, objective, or education, in relation to employers' needs. These letters are used when you prefer not sending your more general resume. Resume letters have one major weakness: they give employers insufficient information and thus may prematurely eliminate you from consideration.

Structuring Resume Content

After choosing an appropriate resume format, you should generate the necessary information for structuring each category of your resume. You developed much of this information when you identified your motivated abilities and skills and specified your objective in Chapters 8 through 11. Include the following information on separate sheets of paper:

Contact Information: Name, street address, and telephone/fax numbers, e-mail address.

Work Objective: Refer to your data in Chapter 11 on writing an objective.

Education: Degrees, schools, dates, highlights, special training.

Work Experience: Paid, unpaid, civilian, military, and part-time employment. Include job titles, employers, locations, dates, skills, accomplishments, duties, and responsibilities. Use the functional language outlined in Chapters 8 and 9.

Achievements: Things you did that provided **benefits** to others, especially initiatives that resulted in outcomes for previous employers.

Other Experience: Volunteer, civic, and professional memberships. Include your contributions, demonstrated skills, offices held, names, and dates.

Special Skills or Licenses/ Certificates: Computer, Internet, foreign languages, teaching, paramedical, etc., relevant to your work objective.

Other Information: References, expected salary, willingness to relocate/travel, availability dates, and other information supporting your work objective.

Producing Drafts

Once you generate the basic data for constructing your resume, your next task is to synthesize this data into draft resumes. If, for example, you write a combination resume, the internal organization of the resume should be as follows:

- Contact information
- Work objective
- Qualifications/experience/achievements
- Work history or employment
- Education

Be careful in including any extraneous or negative information on your resume. You should only include information designed to strengthen your work objective.

While your first draft may run more than two pages, try to get everything into one or two pages for the final draft. Most employers lose interest after reading the first page. If you produce a two-page resume, one of the best formats is to attach a supplemental page to a self-contained one-page resume.

Your final draft should conform to the following rules for creating an excellent resume:

Rules for Effective Resumes

RESUME "DON'TS"

- **Don't** use abbreviations except for your middle name.
- **Don't** create a cramped and crowded look.
- **Don't** make statements you can't document.
- **Don't** use the passive voice.
- **Don't** change tense of verbs.
- **Don't** use lengthy sentences and descriptions.
- **Don't** refer to yourself as "I."
- **Don't** include negative information.
- **Don't** include extraneous information.

RESUME "DO'S"

- **Do** include an employer-centered objective.
- **Do** focus on your major accomplishments as they relate to the needs of the employer.

- **Do** use action verbs and the active voice.
- **Do** include nouns so your resume can be scanned for keywords.
- **Do** be direct, succinct, and expressive with your language.
- **Do** produce a neat, well organized, and professional looking document.
- **Do** use ample spacing and highlights (all caps, underlining, bulleting) for different emphases (except if it's an electronic resume).
- **Do** maintain an eye-pleasing balance.
- **Do** check carefully your spelling, grammar, and punctuation.
- **Do** clearly communicate your purpose and value to employers.
- **Do** communicate your strongest points first.

Final Production

Your final resume can be typed, word-processed, or typeset. If you produce it the old fashioned way – on a typewriter – make the final product look as professional as possible. But being old technology, a typewriter doesn't yield a top-notch professional look. Furthermore, producing a resume in this manner communicates that you are probably a generation behind with your communication skills – still using a typewriter rather than a computer. Typeset resumes are largely a waste of time and money since you can achieve the same print quality using a computer and printer.

It's best to word-process your resume and print it on a laser printer (600 dpi or higher preferred). Dot matrix and near letter quality printers make your resume look both unprofessional and mass produced. Word-processed resumes give you the greatest flexibility to customize your resume for individual employers. If you lack good word-processing skills, take your resume to a quick copy center, such as FedEx Kinko's, which should be able to give you a first-class product for under $50.00.

Be sure to proofread the final copy. Don't spend good money on production only to later find errors. Better still, have someone else proofread your resume. You may be too close to your subject to catch all errors.

When reproducing the resume, you must consider the quality and color of paper as well as the number of copies you need. By all means use good quality paper. You should use 20-pound or heavier bond paper. Costing 3¢ to 7¢ per sheet, this paper can be purchased through stationery stores and printers. It is important not to cut corners at this point by purchasing cheap paper or using copy machine paper. You may save $5 on 100 copies, but you also will communicate an unprofessional image to employers.

Use one of the following paper colors: white, cream, light tan, light gray, or light blue. Avoid blue, yellow, green, pink, orange, red, or any other bright or pastel colors. Conservative, light, neutral colors are the best. Any of these colors can be complemented with black ink. In the case of light gray – our first choice – a navy blue ink looks best. Dark brown ink is especially attractive on light tan paper. However, be very careful in using any co lor o ther than white since mo re and more employers electronically scan resumes. Resumes printed on colored paper do not scan well.

Your choices of paper quality and color say something about your personality and professional style. They communicate nonverbally your potential strengths and weaknesses. Employers will use these as indicators for screening you in or out of an interview. At the same time, these choices may make your resume stand out from the crowd of standard black-on-white resumes.

Whatever your choices, do not try to cut costs when it comes to producing your resume. It simply is not worth it. Remember, your resume is your calling card – it should represent your best professional image. Put your best foot forward at this stage. Go in style; spend a few dollars on producing a first-class resume.

Produce Both a Paper and Electronic Resume

Since more and more employers want you to e-mail your resume, which can be scanned into a resume database, you are well advised to complete both a traditional paper resume and an electronic resume. Electronic resumes follow different rules, such as using keywords and electronic formatting. In fact, in today's job market you will encounter several different types of electronic resumes that are more or less accepted by employers, depending on their particular requirements:

1. ASCII or plain-text resumes
2. Formatted resumes
3. PDF resumes
4. HTML or web page resumes
5. Online portfolios
6. Posted resumes

For more information on electronic resumes, see Joyce Lain Kennedy's *Resumes for Dummies* (John Wiley & Sons) and Susan Britton Whitcomb's and Pat Kendall's *e-Resumes* (McGraw-Hill).

For innovative alternatives to the traditional resume, see Wendy S.

Enelow's and Louise M. Kursmark's *Executive Job Search for $100,000 to $1 Million+ Jobs* (Impact Publications). This is the first book to examine career portfolios, leadership profiles, executive branding statements, achievement summaries, and other paper and Web-based marketing documents for executive-level candidates.

Prepare to Mail, Fax, and E-mail Your Resume

Since more and more employers want candidates to e-mail them their resume, you need to be able to send a first-class e-mailed resume. Do not send your resume as an attachment, unless an employer asks you to do so. Because attachments these days may contain viruses, many people routinely delete e-mail messages sent to them by strangers or refuse to open attachments from strangers. If you send an ASCII, plain-text, or PDF resume, make sure you know what it looks like at the recipient's end by either e-mailing it to yourself or to a friend first.

Many employers still ask for mailed and faxed resumes, although fewer and fewer do so. If you fax your resume, be sure to include a cover sheet as well as a cover letter. Mailed resumes are best sent flat in a 9 x 12" envelope.

Evaluate the Final Product

You should subject your resume drafts to two types of evaluations. An **internal evaluation** consists of reviewing our lists of "do's" and "don'ts" to make sure your resume conforms to these rules. An **external evaluation** should be conducted by circulating your resume to three or more individuals whom you believe will give you frank, objective, and useful feedback. Avoid people who tend to flatter you. The best evaluator would be someone in a hiring position similar to one you will encounter in the actual interview. Ask these people to critique your draft resume and suggest improvements in both form and content. This will be your most important evaluation. After all, the only evaluation that counts is the one that helps get you an interview. Asking someone to critique your resume is one way to spread the word that you are job hunting. As we will see in Chapter 14, this is one method for getting invited to an interview!

Conduct an Internal Evaluation

An internal resume evaluation identifies the strengths and weaknesses of your resume in reference to numerous principles of effective resume writing. Be sure to follow each weak rating with a note to yourself on

improving your resume. This activity enables you to evaluate **and** follow through in revising the resume. Refer to the following evaluation criteria as you conduct your internal evaluation.

INSTRUCTIONS: Examine your resume writing skills in reference to the following evaluation criteria. Respond to each statement by circling the appropriate number to the right that most accurately describes your resume:

1 = Strongly agree	4 = Disagree
2 = Agree	5 = Strongly disagree
3 = So-so (neutral)	

1. Wrote the resume myself – no creative
 plagiarizing from others' resume examples. 1 2 3 4 5

2. Conducted a thorough self-assessment which
 became the basis for writing each resume
 section. 1 2 3 4 5

3. Have a plan of action that relates my resume
 to other job search activities. 1 2 3 4 5

4. Selected an appropriate resume format that
 best presents my interests, skills, and
 experience. 1 2 3 4 5

5. Included all essential information
 categories in the proper order. 1 2 3 4 5

6. Eliminated all extraneous information
 unrelated to my objective and employers'
 needs (date, picture, race, religion, political
 affiliation, age, sex, height, weight, marital
 status, health, hobbies) or better saved for
 discussion in the interview (salary history
 and references). 1 2 3 4 5

7. Put the most important information first. 1 2 3 4 5

8. Resume is oriented to the future rather
 than to the past. 1 2 3 4 5

9. Contact information is complete – name,
 address, phone and fax numbers, e-mail.
 No P.O. Box numbers or nicknames. 1 2 3 4 5

10. Limited abbreviations to accepted words. 1 2 3 4 5

11. Contact information attractively
 formatted to introduce the resume. 1 2 3 4 5

12. Included a thoughtful employer-oriented
 "Objective" that incorporates both skills
 and benefits/outcomes. 1 2 3 4 5

13. "Objective" clearly communicates to
 employers what I want to do, can do,
 and will do for them. 1 2 3 4 5

14. "Objective" is neither too general nor too
 specific. 1 2 3 4 5

15. "Objective" serves as the central organizing
 element for all other sections of the resume. 1 2 3 4 5

16. Included a powerful "Summary of
 Qualifications" or "Professional Profile"
 section immediately following the
 "Objective." 1 2 3 4 5

17. Elaborated work experience in detail,
 emphasizing my skills, abilities, and
 achievements. 1 2 3 4 5

18. Each "Experience" section is short and to
 the point. 1 2 3 4 5

19. Consistently used action verbs and active
 voice. 1 2 3 4 5

20. Did not refer to myself as "I." 1 2 3 4 5

21. Used specifics – numbers and percentages –
 to highlight my performance. 1 2 3 4 5

22. Included positive quotations about my
 performance from previous employers. 1 2 3 4 5

23. Eliminated any negative references,
 including reasons for leaving. 1 2 3 4 5

24. Does not include names of supervisors or
 others involved with my professional or
 personal life. 1 2 3 4 5

25. Summarized my most recent job and then
 included other jobs in reverse chronological
 order. 1 2 3 4 5

26. Descriptions of "Experience" are consistent. 1 2 3 4 5

27. Put the most important skills information
 first when summarizing "Experience." 1 2 3 4 5

28. No time gaps nor "job hopping" apparent
 to reader. 1 2 3 4 5

29. Documented "other experience" that might
 strengthen my Objective and decided to
 either include or exclude it on the resume. 1 2 3 4 5

30. Included complete information on my
 educational background, including
 important highlights. 1 2 3 4 5

31. If a recent graduate with little relevant
 work experience, emphasized educational
 background more than work experience. 1 2 3 4 5

32. Put education in reverse chronological
 order and eliminated high school if a
 college graduate. 1 2 3 4 5

33. Included special education and training
 relevant to my major interests and skills. 1 2 3 4 5

34. Included professional affiliations and
 membership relevant to my objective and
 skills; highlighted any major contributions. 1 2 3 4 5

35. Documented any special skills not included
 elsewhere on resume and included those
 that appear relevant to employers' needs. 1 2 3 4 5

36. Included awards or special recognition
 that further document my skills and
 achievements. 1 2 3 4 5

37. Weighed pros and cons of including a personal statement on my resume. 1 2 3 4 5

38. Did not mention salary history or expectations. 1 2 3 4 5

39. Did not include names, addresses, and phone number of references. 1 2 3 4 5

40. Included additional information to enhance the interest of employers. 1 2 3 4 5

41. Used language appropriate for the employer, including terms that associate me with the industry. 1 2 3 4 5

42. My language is crisp, succinct, expressive, and direct. 1 2 3 4 5

43. Used highlighting and emphasizing techniques to make the resume most readable. 1 2 3 4 5

44. Resume has an inviting, uncluttered look, incorporating sufficient white space and using a standard type style and size. 1 2 3 4 5

45. Kept the design basic and conservative. 1 2 3 4 5

46. Kept sentences short and succinct. 1 2 3 4 5

47. Resume runs one or two pages. 1 2 3 4 5

TOTAL []

Add the numbers you circled to the right of each statement to get a cumulative score. If your score is higher than 85, you need to work on improving various aspects of your resume.

Conduct an External Evaluation

You should conduct an **external resume evaluation** by circulating your resume to three or more individuals. For guidelines, give your evaluators the form on page 246. But most important of all, choose people whose

External Evaluation

INSTRUCTIONS: Circle the number that best characterizes various aspects of my resume. Please include any recommendations on how I could best improve the resume:

1 = Excellent 2 = Okay 3 = Weak

Recommendations for Improvement

1. Overall appearance 1 2 3 _____

2. Layout 1 2 3 _____

3. Clarity 1 2 3 _____

4. Consistency 1 2 3 _____

5. Readability 1 2 3 _____

6. Language 1 2 3 _____

7. Organization 1 2 3 _____

8. Content/completeness 1 2 3 _____

9. Length 1 2 3 _____

10. Contact information/
 header 1 2 3 _____

11. Objective 1 2 3 _____

12. Experience 1 2 3 _____

13. Skills 1 2 3 _____

14. Achievements 1 2 3 _____

15. Education 1 2 3 _____

16. Other information 1 2 3 _____

opinions are objective, frank, and thoughtful. Do not select friends and relatives who usually flatter you with positive comments. Professional acquaintances or people you don't know personally but whom you admire may be good evaluators. An ideal evaluator has experience in hiring people in your area of job interest. In addition to sharing their experience with you, they may refer you to other individuals who would be interested in your qualifications. If you choose such individuals to critique your resume, ask them for their frank reaction – not what they would politely say to a candidate presenting such a resume. You want the people to role play with you – a potential candidate for an interview. Ask your evaluators:

> *"If you don't mind, would you look over my resume? Perhaps you could comment on its clarity or make suggestions for improving it."*

> *"How would you react to this resume if you received it from a candidate? Would it grab your attention and interest you enough to invite the person to an interview?"*

> *"If you were writing this resume, what changes would you make? Any additions, deletions, modifications?"*

Such an evaluation should especially take place in the process of networking and conducting informational interviews (Chapter 14).

You will normally receive good cooperation and advice by approaching people in this manner. In addition, you will probably get valuable unsolicited advice on other job search matters, such as job leads, job market information, and employment strategies.

In contrast to the closed and deductive nature of the internal evaluation, the external evaluation should be open-ended and inductive. Avoid preconceived evaluation categories; let the evaluator react to you and your resume as if you were in a job interview situation.

Taken together, the internal and external evaluations should complement each other by providing you with maximum information for revising your draft resume.

Post Your Resume Online

The Internet has quickly become the best friend of both employers and headhunters who can recruit personnel much faster and cheaper than through more traditional recruitment channels. Even small companies,

with fewer than 10 employees, now use the Internet to advertise jobs and search resume databases for qualified candidates. At the same time, the Internet offers job seekers an important tool to add to their job search arsenal. Make sure you include the Internet in your job search by posting your resume on numerous sites, conducting research, and networking for information, advice, and referrals. While you may not get your next job through the Internet, at least you will acquire lots of useful information over the Internet for enhancing your overall job search.

Over 25,000 websites in the United States deal with employment. Yes, there's a jungle out there in cyberspace as many job seekers face a daunting task of deciding which sites to visit and possibly use. A good starting point for making such decisions is the AIRS gateway site to job boards:

<u>www.airsdirectory.com/directories/job_boards</u>

This site includes over 6,500 job boards which are classified by industry, function, occupations, and other useful categories. In the end, however, you'll probably want to concentrate on several of the most popular employment websites and then select a few sites from the AIRS directory that specialize in your occupational field:

- Monster.com — www.monster.com
- Direct Employers — www.directemployers.com
- America's Job Bank — www.ajb.dni.us
- CareerBuilder — www.careerbuilder.com
- NationJob — www.nationjob.com
- Hot Jobs Yahoo — http://hotjobs.yahoo.com
- Jobs.com — www.jobs.com
- JobSearch — http://jobsearch.monster.com
- CareerJournal — www.careerjournal.com
- CareerFlex — www.careerflex.com
- Employment911.com — www.employment911.com
- EmploymentSpot — www.employmentspot.com
- WorkTree — www.worktree.com
- Job Sniper — www.jobsniper.com
- Vault.com — www.vault.com
- WetFeet.com — www.wetfeet.com
- PlanetRecruit — www.planetrecruit.com
- BestJobsUSA — www.bestjobsusa.com
- BrilliantPeople.com — www.brilliantpeople.com
- Career Shop — www.careershop.com

- CareerSite www.careersite.com
- MonsterTrak.com www.monstertrak.monster.com
- ClearChannel www.jobopps.net
- Brass Ring www.brassring.com
- Career.com www.career.com
- JobBank USA www.jobbankusa.com
- Net-Temps www.net-temps.com
- CareerTV.net www.careertv.net
- CareerSite www.employmentwizard.com
- Jumbo Classified Careers www.jumboclassifieds.com
- American Preferred Jobs www.preferredjobs.com
- ProHire www.prohire.com
- CareerExchange www.careerexchange.com
- Career Magazine www.careermag.com
- Employers Online www.employersonline.com
- EmployMax www.employmax.com
- EmploymentGuide www.employmentguide.com
- WantedJobs www.wantedjobs.com
- RecruitUSA www.recruitusa.com
- Recruiters Online Network www.recruitersonline.com
- kForce.com www.kforce.com
- Dice.com www.dice.com
- Washington Post www.washingtonjobs.com/wl/jobs

While you should visit the large employment websites, don't put much hope in locating a job or employer through them. Large employment websites such as Monster.com, HotJobs.Yahoo.com, and CareerBuilder.com offer a wealth of information and services to both employers and job seekers. However, these sites are primarily run for the benefit of the paying customers – employers. Job seekers can post their resumes online, browse job postings, and apply for jobs through these sites, but few ever get jobs this way. The most valuable aspects of these sites for job seekers are the peripheral services which are designed to keep you coming back again and again (in this online business, you're known as "traffic" when sites set their advertising rates for employers):

- Job Search Tips
- Featured Articles
- Career Experts or Advisors
- Career Tool Kit
- Career Assessment Tests
- Community Forums
- Discussion or Chat Groups
- Message Boards
- Job Alert ("Push") E-mails
- Company Research Centers
- Networking Forums
- Salary Calculators/Wizards

- Resume Management Center
- Resume and Cover Letter Advice
- Multimedia Resume Software
- Job Interview Practice
- Relocation Information
- Reference Check Checkers
- Employment or Career News
- Free E-mail for Privacy
- Success Stories
- Career Newsletter
- Career Events
- Online Job Fairs

- Affiliate Sites
- Career Resources
- Featured Employers
- Polls and Surveys
- Contests
- Online Education and Training
- International Employment
- Talent Auction Centers
- Company Ads (buttons and banners)
- Sponsored Links
- Special Channels for Students, Executives, Free-lancers, Military, and others

Huge mega employment sites such as Monster.com include over 80 percent of these add-on services. That site alone is well worth visiting again and again for tips and advice. Most sites, however, only include job postings and resume databases and maybe a newsletter designed to capture e-mail addresses of job seekers, who must register in order to receive the newsletter. Again, don't expect too much from these sites in terms of connecting with employers who will invite you to interviews. They have hundreds of thousands of resumes in their databases. Your chances of getting a job interview based on your presence in such databases are not very good. However, you may get lucky given your particular mix of skills and experience. Our advice is to post your resume on many such websites and see what happens. Make sure your resume includes lots of keywords descriptive of your skills and accomplishments, since employers will scan resume databases based upon a keyword search.

You are well advised to focus on smaller specialty websites relevant to your occupation and industry. Many users of Internet employment websites focus most of their attention on a few huge employment sites, such as Monster.com and HotJobs.Yahoo.com. However, they would be better using employment websites that specialize in their industry. For example, if you are an IT professional, your chances of connecting with an employer are much greater on Dice.com and ItCareers.com than on the top 10 mega employment sites. Employers interested in hiring IT professionals are more likely to use these specialty sites than the more general mega employment sites.

Using the Internet in your job search is relatively easy once you have some basic guidance on where to go and what to do. The following books

provide details on using the Internet for finding a job. Several of these resources go through the whole process of using the Internet for conducting employment research, posting resumes, and communicating by e-mail. Others primarily annotate the best sites on the Internet:

> *100 Top Internet Job Sites* (Kristina M. Ackley)
> *Adams Internet Job Search Almanac* (Michelle Roy Kelly, ed.)
> *America's Top Internet Job Sites* (Ron and Caryl Krannich)
> *Career Exploration on the Internet* (Ferguson Publishing)
> *The Directory of Websites for International Jobs* (Ron and Caryl Krannich)
> *The Everything Online Job Search Book* (Stephen Graber)
> *The Guide to Internet Job Searching* (Margaret Riley Dikel)
> *Haldane's Best Employment Websites for Professionals* (Bernard Haldane Associates)
> *The Job Hunter's Online Goldmine* (Janet E. Wall)
> *Job-Hunting on the Internet* (Richard Nelson Bolles)
> *Weddle's Job-Seeker's Guide to Employment Web Sites* (Peter D. Weddle)

Also, be sure to examine these Internet resources on writing electronic and Internet resumes:

> *Cyberspace Resume Kit* (Fred Jandt and Mary Nemnich)
> *Electronic Resumes and Online Networking* (Rebecca Smith)
> *e-Resumes* (Pat Criscito)
> *e-Resumes* (Susan Britton Whitcomb and Pat Kendall)
> *Internet Resumes* (Peter D. Weddle)

Job Search Letters

Regardless of how you send your resume, it should be accompanied by a cover letter. Indeed, certain types of cover letters – especially powerful "T" letters and "Focus Pieces" – are often more important than resumes. After interviewing for information or a position, you should send a thank you letter. Other occasions will arise when it is both proper and necessary for you to write different types of job search letters. Numerous examples of job search letters are presented in our *High Impact Resumes and Letters, Nail the Cover Letter!*, and *201 Dynamite Job Search Letters*. For a unique set of powerful "T" letters and Focus Pieces, see *Haldane's Best Cover Letters for Professionals*. All of these resources are published by Impact Publications.

Your letter writing should follow the principles of good resume and business writing. Job hunting letters are like resumes – they advertise you for interviews. Like good advertisements, these letters should follow four basic principles for effectiveness:

1. Catch the reader's attention.
2. Persuade the reader of your benefits or value.
3. Convince the reader with evidence.
4. Move the reader to acquire the product – you!

In addition, the content of your letters should be the basis for conducting screening interviews as well as a face-to-face interviews.

Basic Preparation Rules

Before you begin writing a job search letter, ask yourself several questions to clarify the content of your letter:

- What is the **purpose** of the letter?
- What are the **needs** of my audience?
- What **benefits** will my audience gain from hiring me?
- What is a good opening sentence or paragraph for grabbing the **attention** of my audience?
- How can I maintain the **interest** of my audience?
- How can I best end the letter so that the audience will be **persuaded** to contact me?
- If accompanied by a resume, how can my letter best **advertise the resume?**
- Have I spent enough time **revising** and **proofreading** the letter?
- Does the letter represent my **best professional effort?**

Since your letters are a form of business communication, they should conform to the rules of good business correspondence:

Principles of Good Business Communication

- Organize what you will say by outlining the content of your letter.
- Know your purpose, and structure your letter accordingly.
- Communicate your message in a logical, sequential manner.

- State your purpose immediately in the first sentence and paragraph; main ideas always go first.
- End by stating what your reader can expect next from you.
- Use short paragraphs and sentences; avoid complex sentences.
- Punctuate properly and use correct grammar and spelling.
- Use simple and straightforward language; avoid jargon.
- Communicate your message as directly and briefly as possible.

The rules stress how to both **organize and communicate** your message with impact. At the same time, you should always have a specific purpose in mind as well as know the needs of your audience.

Types of Letters

Cover letters provide cover for your resume. You should avoid overwhelming a one-page resume with a two-page letter or repeating the contents of the resume in the letter. A short and succinct one-page letter that highlights one or two points in your resume is sufficient. Three paragraphs will suffice. The first paragraph should state your interest in the employer and purpose for writing. The second paragraph should highlight your possible value to the employer. The third paragraph should state that you will call the individual at a particular time to schedule an interview.

However, do not expect great results from cover letters. Many professional job search firms use computers and mailing lists to flood the job market with thousands of unsolicited resumes and cover letters each day. Other job seekers use "canned" job search letters produced by computer software programs, such as *WinWay Resumes*, designed to generate model job search letters. As a result, employers are increasingly suspicious of the authenticity of such letters. To cope with the sheer volume of communications, many employers use resume management software to scan, store, and retrieve such communications – or they throw away most of the unsolicited resumes and letters they receive.

Approach letters are written for the purpose of developing job contacts, leads, or information as well as for organizing networks and getting interviews – the subjects of Chapter 14. Your primary purposes should be to get employers to engage in the 5R's of informational interviewing:

- **Reveal** useful information and advice.
- **Refer** you to others.
- **Read** your resume.

- **Revise** your resume.
- **Remember** you for future reference.

These letters help you gain access to the hidden job market by making important networking contacts that lead to those all-important informational interviews.

Approach letters can be sent out en masse to uncover job leads, or they can target particular individuals or organizations. It is better to target these letters since they have maximum impact when personalized in reference to a position.

The structure of approach letters is similar to other letters. The first paragraph states your purpose. In so doing, you may want to use a personal statement for openers, such as *"Mary Tillis recommended that I write to you..."* or *"I am familiar with your..."* State your purpose, but do not suggest that you are asking for a job – only career advice or information. In your final paragraph, request a meeting and indicate you will call to schedule such a meeting at a mutually convenient time.

Thank you letters may well become your most effective job search letters. They especially communicate your thoughtfulness. These letters come in different forms and are written for various occasions. The most common thank you letter is written after receiving assistance, such as job search information and advice or a critique of your resume. Other occasions include:

- **Immediately following an interview:** Thank the interviewer for the opportunity to interview for the position. Repeat your interest in the position.

- **Receive a job offer:** Thank the employer for his or her faith in you and express your appreciation.

- **Rejected for a job:** Thank the employer for the "opportunity" to interview for the job. Ask to be remembered for future reference.

- **Terminate employment:** Thank the employer for the experience and ask to be remembered for future reference.

- **Begin a new job:** Thank the employer for giving you this new opportunity and express your confidence in producing the value he or she is expecting from you.

Examples of these letters are found on pages 295-298.

Several of these thank you letters are unusual, but they all have the same goal – to be remembered by potential employers in a positive light. In a job search, being remembered by employers is the closest thing to being invited to an interview and offered a job.

Distribution and Management

The only good resumes are the ones that get read, remembered, referred, and result in a job interview. Therefore, after completing a first-rate resume, you must decide what to do with it. Are you planning to only respond to classified ads with a standard mailing piece consisting of your conventional or electronic resume and a formal cover letter? Do you prefer posting your resume online with resume databases or e-mailing it to potential employers? But wait a minute; classified ads and resume databases only represent one portion of the job market. What other creative distribution methods might you use, such as sending it to friends, relatives, and former employers; mailing it in a shoe box with a note (*"Now that I've got my foot in the door, how about an interview?"*); gift wrapping it; or having it delivered by a singing messenger? What's the best way to proceed?

Responding to Classified Ads

Most of your writing activities should focus on the hidden job market where jobs are neither announced nor listed. At the same time, you should respond to job listings in newspapers, magazines, human resources offices, and on websites, as well as get your resume into online resume databases. While this is largely a numbers game, you can increase your odds by the way you respond to the listings.

You should be selective in your responses. Since you know what you want to do, you will be looking for only certain types of positions. Once you identify them, your response entails little expenditure of time and effort – a quick e-mail, fax, or a paper envelope, stamp, letter, and resume. You have little to lose. While you have the potential to gain by sending a letter and resume in response to an ad, remember the odds are usually against you.

It is difficult to interpret job listings, regardless of whether they are in print or electronic format. Some employers place blind ads with P.O. Box numbers and e-mail addresses in order to collect resumes for future reference. Others wish to avoid aggressive applicants who telephone or "drop in" for interviews. Many employers work through professional recruiters

who place these ads or they post job listings on electronic bulletin boards. While you may try to second guess the rationale behind such ads, it's always best to respond to them as you would to ads with an employer's name, address, or telephone number. Assume there is a real job behind each ad.

Most ads request a copy of your resume. Employers increasingly ask that it be sent by e-mail or fax. You should respond with a cover letter and resume as soon as you see the ad. Depending on how much information about the position is revealed in the ad, your letter should be tailored to emphasize your qualifications vis-a-vis the ad. Examine the ad carefully. Underline any words or phrases that relate to your qualifications. In your cover letter, you should use similar terminology in emphasizing your qualifications. The most powerful cover letter you can send is the classic "T" letter, which literally matches your skills and accomplishments with each of the employer's requirements. Keep the letter brief and to the point. A "T" letter example appears on page 288.

If the ad asks you to give your salary history or salary requirements, state "negotiable" or "open." Alternatively, you can include a figure by citing a salary range 20 percent above your present salary base or include a total compensation figure. For example, if you are making $40,000 a year, you can say *"My current salary is in the $40,000 to $45,000 range"* or *"My current compensation package is worth $63,000 a year."*

Use your own judgment in addressing the salary question. There is no hard and fast rule on stating a figure or range. We recommend that you **be honest but not stupid**. A figure helps the employer screen out individuals with too high a salary expectation. However, most people prefer to keep salary considerations to the end of the final interview – after they have demonstrated their value and have more information about the position. This may occur during the initial interview but more likely during the second, third, or even fourth interview.

You may be able to increase your odds by sending a second copy of your letter and resume two or three weeks after your initial response. Most applicants normally reply to an ad during the seven-day period immediately after it appears in print. Since employers often are swamped with responses, your letter and resume may get lost in the crowd. If you send a second copy of your resume two or three weeks later, the employer will have more time to give you special attention. By then, he or she also will have a better basis on which to compare you to the others. However, if the employer electronically scans resumes, sending a second copy of your resume and letter will not affect the outcome.

Keep in mind that your cover letter and resume may be screened among 400 other resumes and letters. Thus, you want your cover letter

to be eye-catching and easy to read. Keep it brief and concise and highlight your qualifications as stated in the employer's ad. If you know your resume will be electronically scanned, make sure it includes lots of keywords and is formatted properly for scanners. Don't spend a great deal of time responding to an ad or waiting anxiously at your mailbox, telephone, or computer for a reply. Keep moving on to other job search activities.

Self-Initiated Distribution Methods

Your letters and resumes can be distributed and managed in various ways. Many people broadcast or "shotgun" hundreds of cover letters and resumes to prospective employers. This is a form of gambling where the odds are always against you. For every 100 people you contact in this manner, expect one or two who might be interested in you. After all, successful direct-mail experts at best expect only a 2-percent return on their mass mailings!

If you choose to use the broadcast method, you can increase your odds by using the **telephone**. Call the prospective employer within a week after he or she receives your letter. This technique will probably increase your effectiveness rate from 1 to 5 percent.

However, many people are broadcasting their resumes today, and more and more employers are using automated resume management systems. As more resumes and letters descend on employers, the effectiveness rates may be even lower. This also can be an expensive marketing method. You would be much better off posting an electronic version of your resume on various online employment sites where your exposure rate will be much higher and more targeted to the needs of specific employers. Start by surveying job listings and posting your resume on these top Internet sites:

- www.directemployers.com
- www.monster.com
- www.careerbuilder.com
- www.careerjournal.com
- www.4work.com
- http://hotjobs.yahoo.com
- www.nationjob.com
- www.careerflex.com
- www.employment911.com

This electronic form of broadcasting is also the cheapest way to go – it's usually free to job seekers.

Your best distribution strategy will be your own modification of the following procedure:

1. Selectively identify with whom you are interested in working.
2. Send an approach letter.
3. Follow up with a telephone call requesting an informational interview.

In more than 50 percent of the cases, you will get an interview. It is better not to include a copy of your resume with the approach letter. If you include a resume, you communicate the wrong message – you want a job rather than information and advice. Keep your resume for the very end of the interview. Chapter 14 outlines how to conduct this interview.

Recordkeeping

Once you begin distributing letters and resumes, you also will need to keep good records for managing your job search writing campaign. You can do this the old fashioned way by purchasing file folders for your correspondence and notes. Be sure to make copies of all letters you write, since you may need to refer to them over the telephone or before interviews. Record your activities with each employer – letters, resumes, telephone calls, interviews – on a 4x6 card and file it according to the name of the organization or individual. These files will help you quickly access information and evaluate your job search progress.

If you're computer savvy, you may want to electronically organize your recordkeeping activities using a database program. Check your current software programs for a contact manager, calendar, or tracking/follow-up program. Several software programs are now available for networking and tracking activities. Some, such as *WinWay Resume*, *ResumeMaker*, and *Custom Resume Creator*, are designed specifically for tracking job leads and following up specific job search activities. Many of the large employment websites, such as www.monster.com, allow you to manage your resume and track applications online.

Resume and Letter Examples

The resume and letter examples on pages 262 through 298 incorporate the many principles we've outlined thus far for conducting an effective job search. Most of these examples are drawn from other three resume and cover letter books by Ron and Caryl Krannich and Carl Savino: *Military Resumes and Cover Letters*, *Nail the Resume!*, and *Nail the Cover Letter!* (Impact Publications). Use these examples for ideas in crafting your own resume. Pay particular attention to the format, categories, and language.

For additional examples of military transition resumes and letters, we recommend the following books:

Military Resumes and Cover Letters (Impact Publications)
Expert Resumes for Military-to-Civilian Transitions (JIST Publishing)
Job Search: Marketing Your Military Experience (Stackpole Books)
Resumes for Former Military Personnel (McGraw-Hill)
Resumes and Cover Letters That Have Worked for Military Professionals (Prep Publishing Co.)

When It's Time to Use a Professional

While many job seekers can write their own resumes and letters by following our advice and examples, others find this exercise to be extremely difficult. They have difficulty being objective about themselves, putting all the elements together, and writing in the language of employers. After all, many of them were taught from childhood not to brag about themselves! At some point, you may want to consider contacting a professional resume writer for assistance. These are talented professionals who work with hundreds of job seekers, including many who assist military in transition. In addition to writing resumes, many of these individuals also craft letters, provide job search advice, and serve as career coaches.

While we prefer that you write your own resume because it will more accurately reflect your interests, skills, abilities, and goals, we recognize that professional help is sometimes needed at critical stages of one's job search. If writing a resume is something you have difficulty doing, by all means seek professional help. Paying a professional to put together a winning resume will more than pay for itself if it results in job interviews and offers. A professional resume writer may charge from $100 to $600 to produce a first-class resume.

If you are interested in contacting a professional resume writer, you are well advised to explore the resources on these professional resume writing websites:

- **Career Masters Institute** www.cminstitute.com

- **Professional Association of Resume Writers and Career Coaches** www.parw.com

- Professional Resume Writing
 and Research Association www.prwra.com

- National Resume Writers'
 Association www.nrwaweb.com

Check out some of these websites which are sponsored by professional resume writers. Most of them will give you a free resume critique prior to using their fee-based services:

▪ A and A Resume	www.aandaresume.com
▪ A-Advanced Resume Service	www.topsecretresumes.com
▪ Advanced Career Systems	www.resumesystems.com
▪ Advanced Resume Services	www.resumeservices.com
▪ The Advantage	www.advantageresume.com
▪ Cambridge Resume Service	www.cambridgeresume.com
▪ Career Resumes	www.career-resumes.com
▪ CertifiedResumeWriters	http://certifiedresume writers.com
▪ eResumes (Rebecca Smith's)	www.eresumes.com
▪ e-resume.net	www.e-resume.net
▪ Executiveagent.com	www.executiveagent.com
▪ Free-Resume-Tips	www.free-resume-tips.com
▪ Impact Resumes	www.impactresumes.com
▪ Leading Edge Resumes	www.leadingedgeresumes.com
▪ Resume Agent	www.resumeagent.com
▪ Resume.com	www.resume.com
▪ ResumeMaker	www.resumemaker.com
▪ Resume Writer	www.resumewriter.com
▪ WSACORP.com	www.wsacorp.com

The following professional resume writers are experienced in working with transitioning military personnel. Examples of their work are showcased on their websites and/or in Wendy S. Enelow's and Louise M. Kursmark's *Expert Resumes for Military-to-Civilian Transition* (JIST Publishing):

▪ A First Impression Resume	www.resumewriter.com
▪ About Jobs	www.gotthejob.com
▪ Advanced Employment Concepts	www.aresumewriter.net

- Appelbaum's Resume Professionals — www.appelbaumresumes.com
- Arnold-Smith Associates — www.ResumeSOS.com
- BBCS Counseling Services — www.baskincareer.com
- Best Impression Career Services — www.yourbestimpression.com
- Career Directions, LLC — www.resumeimpact.com
- Career Marketing Techniques — www.polishedresumes.com
- Career Success Coach — www.careerdesigns.biz
- Corbel Communications — www.corbelonline.com
- Evans Resumes — www.EvansResumes.com
- Executive Correspondents — www.WorkingToLive.com
- Gatehouse Business Services — www.bestjobever.com
- Grafix Services — www.GrafixServices.com
- Florida Executrak — www.executrak.net
- Job Training Center — www.job.trainincenter.org
- Keystrokes by Kerry — www.keystrokesbykerry.com
- Mil-Roy Consultants — www.milroyconsultants.com
- Northwest Resumes — www.nwresumes.com
- Printed Pages — www.printedpages.com
- Resume Suite — www.resumesuite.com
- ResumeGuru.com — www.ResumeGuru.com
- Resumes "R" Us — www.powerresumesandcoaching.com
- Sterling Career Concepts — www.sterlingcareerconcepts.com
- To the Point Resumes — www.ResumeSOS.com
- Write Away Resume and Career Coaching — www.writeawayresume.com

You Are What You Write

Always remember the purpose of resumes and letters – **advertise you for job interviews**. They do not get jobs. Since employers know nothing about you and your accomplishments – you're a stranger at their door – **you must effectively communicate your value in writing prior to meeting them in person for the critical job interview**. While you should not overestimate the importance of this written communication, neither should you underestimate it. After all, in the eyes of most employers, you essentially are what you write.

Account Executive *Available: September 20__*

ANTHONY BROWN
123 Americana Lane
Aiken, SC 12345
H: (222) 111-8888 / W: (222) 123-4567
BrownA@aol.com

OBJECTIVE: An account executive position where sales ability and knowledge of the aviation industry will result in increased revenue for a firm specializing in aviation-related equipment.

QUALIFICATIONS SUMMARY: Extensive experience in purchasing and managing aviation materiel for large organizations. Excellent phone and sales presentation skills. Results-driven, detail-oriented professional who understands the importance of fulfilling customer demands in a timely manner. Know how to "close the deal."

EXPERIENCE: **Aviation Logistics Operations Director**, Oceana Naval Air Station, Virginia Beach, VA, 2003-present.
- Managed a 145-person aviation supply depot with $105 million in assets. Saved $360,000 annually by streamlining maintenance procedures.
- Surpassed aircraft readiness goals by 15% in the management of over 34,000 line items, from aircraft engines to flight clothing.

Repairable Materiel Acquisition and Control Manager, Pearl Harbor, HI, 1999-2002
- Led 30-person team in aviation logistics operations. Exceeded supply effectiveness goals by 7%.
- Managed all facets of a $20 million repairable aviation materiel account with 1,700 line items. Improved purchasing, storage, and issuance procedures. Streamlined maintenance repair activities.

Squadron Supply Officer, Twentynine Palms, CA, 1995-1998
- Supervised 9-person team in squadron supply activities. Exceeded inventory accuracy goals for a $225,000 inventory by 18%.
- Surpassed timeliness standards for requisition processing in support of all equipment in air traffic control squadron.

Human Resources Manager, Camp Lejune, NC, 1992-1994
- Developed integrated training, retention, and promotion plans for 165,000 people in 330 occupational specialties.
- Used computer planning models to identify and eliminate logistics acquisition inefficiencies, resulting in a savings of $12 million.

EDUCATION: **MBA**, University of Hawaii, Honolulu, HI, 2000
B.S., **Business Administration**, University of South Carolina, 1992

Airline Pilot *Available: April 20___*

CHARLES SCHUSTER
9851 Kennedy Lane, Apt. #123
Travis Air Force Base, CA 32542
W: 904-232-1832 / H: 904-763-1321
SchusterC@aol.com

OBJECTIVE

Position as a pilot for a well-established commercial airline where extensive flight experience will positively impact the carrier's safety and on-time performance record.

SUMMARY OF QUALIFICATIONS

Air Force pilot with 20 years of single- and multi-engine aircraft experience in domestic and international environments. Technically proficient leader with over 6,000 flight hours in a variety of high-performance jet aircraft, including the C-130 and B-1. Polished communicator who inspires and motivates subordinates to excel in all assigned tasks. Consistently accomplished difficult missions while minimizing the associated risks to assigned crews. Caring leader who sets and enforces high standards of personal and professional conduct. Active DoD Secret clearance.

EDUCATION

M.S. Aeronautical Engineering, Air Force Institute of Technology, 1996
B.S. Aeronautical Engineering, U.S. Air Force Academy, 1986

PROFESSIONAL EXPERIENCE

Squadron Commander, Eglin Air Force Base, FL, 2003-Present
 Responsible for successful performance of a B-2 squadron supporting operations in Haiti. Plan, organize, and lead the activities of 25 pilots. Maintain combat readiness through efficient execution of training sorties. As the senior safety officer, ensure pilots and their crews adhere to flight procedures and policies. Strictly enforce rules of engagement for assigned aircraft. Effectively guide and advise pilots in all aspects of flight operations.

Operations Officer, Eglin Air Force Base, FL, 2000-2002
 As second in command of a B-1 bomber squadron, ensured the combat readiness of all pilots assigned to the squadron. Performed numerous flight evaluations of B-1 pilots to verify their flying skills. Performed safety checks of squadron pilots, assessing crew's knowledge of safety procedures, and ensured combat readiness of aircraft. High quality program resulted in perfect safety record.

Staff Officer, Operations and Plans, Office of the Air Force Deputy Chief of Staff, Operations, Pentagon, Washington DC, 1996-1999
Served as a principal advisor to the Deputy Chief of Staff for Operations and Plans. Developed plans and policies affecting the worldwide operation of Air Force aircraft. Wrote decision papers and prepared briefings for senior management. Interfaced effectively with members of the House and Senate Armed Services Committees on national security issues.

Instructor Pilot, C-130, Kelly Air Force Base, TX, 1992-1995
Instructed over 60 student pilots through C-130 jet training in all phases of flight, including aerobatics, formation, instrument, and navigation. Enhanced the existing training program by integrating new, innovative training techniques that reduced the training period by a week, thereby saving the government $50,000 per student. Maximized the use of simulator training. Trained new instructors on the use of simulators. Voted top instructor by 3 consecutive classes.

Aircraft Commander, Travis Air Force Base, CA, 1990-1991
Supervised 4-member crew in all phases of C-130 flight operations. As the lead pilot, flew 2200 hours both domestically and internationally under all weather conditions. Managed, supervised, and evaluated the performance of aircrew personnel. Instructed crew members on all aspects of flight operations, aircraft maintenance, and safety procedures. Developed a strong team atmosphere to accomplish assigned missions.

Pilot, U.S. Air Force, 1986-1989
Gained extensive flying experience in both day and night environments, both domestically and internationally. Overseas flight experience in South and Central America, Europe, Canada, Southeast Asia, and the Pacific Rim. Consistently rated as one of the best pilots in the squadron.

TRAINING

Air Command and Staff College, 1998
Instructor Pilot Training, Air Training Command (Distinguished Graduate), 1993
Instrument Flight Course, Strategic Air Command, 1986
Squadron Officer School, 1983

Attorney *Available: August 20__*

STEVEN MARSH

2001 West James Court Home: 501-789-4321
Seattle, WA 98322 Work: 501-789-5539
 smarsh@aol.com

OBJECTIVE

A position in aviation law where proven management, organization, and supervisory skills and an exceptional record of success in investigating, adjudicating, settling, defending, and prosecuting cases will be used in settling cases to the benefit of employer and clients.

EXPERIENCE

<u>**Chief Circuit Defense Counsel, Davis AFB, Ogden, UT, 2004-Present**</u>
Personally defended all Flying Evaluation Boards, winning every one. Successfully defended felony trials covering offenses of drug use, distribution, assault, DUI, and perjury. Supervised, trained, and directed 22 attorneys and 17 paralegals responsible for total defense services across 16 Air Force installations located in 12 states. Included oversight of over 500 trials with every offense up to and including premeditated murder.

<u>**Chief, Aviation Settlement Branch, U.S. Air Force, Washington, DC, 2002-2003**</u>
Directed the investigation, adjudication, and either settlement or litigation of all aviation, environmental, medical malpractice, and other tort claims filed against the Air Force. In 1993, this topped a $40 billion dollar exposure with the percentage of payout to claimed amount the lowest in over a decade. Supervised staff of 13 attorneys and 5 paralegals. Re-formulated U.S. Air Force policy on tort claim and litigation matters in conjunction with the Department of Justice, leading to a better concept and application of paying the losers and spending time and resources to win the winners.

<u>**Chief, Tort Section, U.S. Air Force, Washington, DC, 1999-2001**</u>
Supervised the investigation and recommended adjudication or litigation of all aviation tort claims against the Air Force, including the last of the Agent Orange cases and the KAL 007 Korean airliner shoot-down by the Soviet Union. Supervised staff of 3 attorneys and 1 paralegal. Recommended U.S. Air Force policy change on aviation tort claims that directly resulted in greater Agency latitude for meritorious claims independent of the previously required GAO Office requirements.

<u>**Staff Judge Advocate, Stevens Air Force Base, Miami, FL, 1997-1998**</u>
Advised top management of all legal issues to include the convening of Aircraft Accident Boards and Flying Evaluation Boards. Directed tort, labor, environmental, procurement, and criminal law procedures. During this period,

defended two state environmental Notice of Violations successfully, and over 40 criminal cases were prosecuted without a single acquittal. Served as management's Chief Labor Resolution Negotiator securing settlements at 60 percent of the previously approved maximums. Supervised staff of 4 attorneys and 5 paralegals.

Assistant Staff Judge Advocate, Lowry Air Force Base, CO, 1993-1996
Served as government prosecutor for over 35 trials with no acquittals. Served as government representative in over 20 administrative hearings with no losses. Counseled clients on rights/duties under state and federal law.

Area Defense Counsel, Marshall Air Force Base, Austin, TX, 1989-1992
Defended over 300 clients in criminal trials, administrative hearings, or minor disciplinary concerns.

EDUCATION

J.D., Boston University College of Law, Boston, MA, 1983
B.A. (Political Science), University of North Carolina, Chapel Hill, NC, 1980

TRAINING

Air War College, USAF, Seminar Program, 2001
Armed Forces Staff College, Joint Service Program, Residence, 1998
Air Command and Staff College, USAF, Seminar Program, 1997

AWARDS

Stuart Reichart Award, Senior Attorney, HQ USAF, 2000
Ramirez Award, Outstanding Attorney Tactical Air Command, 1996
Outstanding Attorney, U.S. Air Forces Colorado, 1993

OTHER EXPERIENCE

U.S. Parole Board Hearing Member, USAF, 1998
Joint Services Consolidation Committee, 1996-1997

BAR MEMBERSHIPS

U.S. Supreme Court, 2000
U.S. Court of Appeals, 4th Circuit, 1996
U.S. Court of Military Appeals, 1993
Supreme Court of Texas, 1989

Construction Supervisor *Available: June 20__*

MICHAEL RAMIREZ
313 Bradley Drive
Bremerton, WA 90972
W: (206) 222-3333 / H: (206) 888-3321
RamirezM@aol.com

OBJECTIVE A foreman position where skills and experience as
 a construction supervisor will benefit a firm
 seeking to its scope of operations.

QUALIFICATIONS SUMMARY

MANAGEMENT
- Supervised construction crew of 25 personnel involved in building new homes and offices.
- Trained numerous junior operators on the proper use and maintenance of construction equipment.
- Attained a 100% safety record through strict adherence to standard operating procedures.

CONSTRUCTION
OPERATIONS
- Operated bulldozers, roadgraders, and other heavy equipment in building over 25 miles of runway in record time, under combat conditions.
- Used scrapers and other heavy machinery to remove ice and snow from runways.
- Operated winches, cranes, and hoists in constructing over 200 new homes.

INTERNATIONAL
- Fluent in Spanish.

WORK HISTORY

Construction Supervisor, 23rd Engineer Battalion, McChord AFB, WA, 2003-Present
Construction Equipment Operator, 110th Construction Battalion, Keesler AFB, MO, 1999-2002

EDUCATION & TRAINING

A.A., Construction, Washington Community College, Seattle, WA, 2003
Air Force certified apprenticeship program in Heavy Construction, 1999
Diploma, Homer High School, Homer, NY, 1998

Electronic Maintenance Supervisor *Available: 20__*

THOMAS JONES
2121 Main Street
Norfolk, VA 22211
H: (757) 333-4444 / W: (757) 112-2345
E-mail: ThomasJ@aol.com

OBJECTIVE

Electronics Maintenance Supervisor position where electronics expertise and management know-how can be used by an aerospace firm to significantly improve its maintenance operations.

SUMMARY OF QUALIFICATIONS

- Results-oriented professional with significant management and hands-on electronic and mechanical maintenance experience.
- Skilled technician with expertise in an array of electro-mechanical disciplines.
- Articulate communicator who conveys technical concepts in clear terms.
- Adept problem solver who easily transfers knowledge to teammates.

PROFESSIONAL EXPERIENCE

MANAGEMENT

- Supervised over 45 electronics technicians in 5 shops performing a wide range of electrical and mechanical repair on over 20 aircraft.
- Coordinated and implemented technical training and reassignment of technicians in a manner that mitigated the impact of manpower shortages.
- Maintained 100% accountability of over 2,000 component parts, electronic test equipment, and materials with inventory values in excess of $3 million.
- Ensured strict adherence to quality control in repair cycle by conducting receiving, in-process, and final inspections of electronic systems and associated components.

ELECTRONIC REPAIR

- Repaired 10 different, high-tech electrical and electronic aircraft systems and components using industry-standard equipment, such as oscilloscopes, signal generators, voltmeters, ammeters, and time domain reflectometers.
- Employed standard troubleshooting methods using technical manuals, wiring schematics, block diagrams, and drawings to rapidly isolate malfunctions in system wiring, sub assemblies, and other components.
- Skilled at wire, cable bundle, coaxial, and connector repair.

TRAINING & EDUCATION

Total Quality Management Training, 2001
Advanced Electrical/Electronic Technical Training, 1999
Miniature Electronics Repair QA/Supervisor Course, 1997
Diploma, Martin Luther King High School, Biloxi, MI, 1996

Emergency Medical Technician *Available: 20__*

KATHLEEN SMITH
8841 Greensboro Drive
Boston, MA 01755
W: 617-632-1343 / H: 617-232-3212

OBJECTIVE

Position as an Emergency Medical Technician where my military-refined health care skills and experience will benefit a private health care facility seeking to improve its patient care quality.

SUMMARY OF QUALIFICATIONS

- Over 10 years experience in the health care profession as a Navy corpsman.
- Trained to provide emergency medical care in response to accidents, fire, natural disasters, etc.
- Proficient in a variety of first-line tasks, including: recording of vital signs, reading and updating of patients' medical records, and taking of blood for laboratory analysis.
- Communicated effectively with patients and administrators.
- Demonstrated ability to work well under stressful conditions.

WORK HISTORY

Emergency Medical Technician, U.S.S. Mercy, 2003-Present

Provide first-line emergency medical care to sailors and Marines onboard ship. Take patients' vital signs, including temperature, pulse, and blood pressure. Prepare patients for follow-up treatment by registered nurses or medical doctors. Update patients' medical records.

Medical Service Technician, Bethesda Naval Hospital, MD, 1999-2002

Responsible for ensuring 500 patients' records were properly filed. Responded to record requests by nurses and doctors. Performed quality assurance checks of medical records. Identified missing documents and persevered until records were properly completed. Recommended an innovative color-coding scheme that reduced confusion and saved health care professionals' time.

Medical Service Technician, Tripler Army Hospital, Honolulu, HI, 1996-1998

Drew patients' blood for analysis by laboratory technicians. Resuscitated those patients who fainted during the procedure. Explained the importance of wellness programs that emphasize proper diet and exercise.

EDUCATION AND TRAINING

Emergency Medical Training, Bethesda Naval Hospital, MD, 1999
St. Elizabeth Seton High School, Rockville, MD, 1995

Financial Management　　　　　　　　*Available: June 20__*

JEFFREY SIMMONS
2913 West Broad St.
Fairfax, VA 22313
(703) 888-3333
SimmonsJ@erols.com

OBJECTIVE　　Financial management position where extensive finance and accounting background can be used to improve a startup company's financial operations.

QUALIFICATIONS SUMMARY

ACCOUNTING
AND FINANCE
- Experience in general ledger, financial analysis, budgets, projections, cash management, and supervision of accounting staff.
- Project manager for conversion to new computerized accounting system, which saved $1 million annually through reductions in personnel expenses.
- Senior accountant for a $10 million organization involved in national defense.

PLANNING
- Accurately forecasted organizations' expenditures over a 5 year period.
- Projected shortfalls and modified plans to mitigate the impact.
- Developed financial plans for organizations ranging in size from 300 to 10,000.

MANAGEMENT
- Supervised groups of 5-37 personnel involved in all facets of finance and accounting operations.
- Trained and mentored staff in both individual and team-based settings.
- Evaluated employee performance and provided suggestions for improvement.

EMPLOYMENT HISTORY

Senior Finance Director, Defense Information Systems Agency, Arlington, VA, 2005-Present
Finance Manager, Fort Hood, TX, 2000-2002
Staff Finance Officer, Fort Carson, CO, 1997-1999

EDUCATION & TRAINING

M.B.A., Finance, American University, 2004
B.S., Accounting, University of Colorado, 1997
Planning, Programming, and Budgeting Course, Fort Harrison, IN, 1999

Healthcare Administration *Available: September 20___*

TRACY LAKELAND
2913 West Broad St.
Fairfax, VA 22313
H: (703) 888-3333
LakelandT@erols.com

OBJECTIVE Healthcare administrator position where extensive financial management experience can be used to improve the profitability of a multi-specialty ambulatory care clinic.

QUALIFICATIONS SUMMARY

HEALTHCARE
ADMINISTRATION
- Ten years experience in Healthcare Administration in positions of increasing responsibility within the U.S. Navy.
- Managed health service activities, including plans and operations, human resources, logistics, patient administration, and finance.
- Directed the hospital accreditation program, which was successfully completed two months ahead of schedule.

FINANCIAL
MANAGEMENT
- Managed departments from 25-600 personnel, responsible for direct supervision of up to 10 second line supervisors.
- Established and administered a $15 million budget.
- Increased third party collections by 45% while reducing expenditures by $3 million through aggressive follow-up communication.
- Developed automated financial plan, which was adopted and implemented, saving the hospital approximately $39,000 annually.

CERTIFICATION
- Certified Healthcare Executive
- Member, ACHE's Regents Advisory Council for the Army Regent

EMPLOYMENT HISTORY

Director, Healthcare Services, Walter Reed Army Medical Hospital, 2004-Present
Senior Healthcare Service Administrator, Walter Reed Army Medical Hospital, 1999-2003
Healthcare Service Administrator, Eisenhower Army Medical Center, Fort Gordon, GA, 1995-1998
Developmental Medical Service Corps positions, U.S. Army, 1986-1994

EDUCATION & TRAINING

MBA, Finance, University of Maryland, 2002
B.S.N., Penn State University, 1986

Homeland Security Manager *Available: March 1, 20__*

<div align="center">

DAVID BROWN
3211 Guadalcanal Way
San Diego, CA 92111
(619) 222-3333 / BrownD@hotmail.com

</div>

OBJECTIVE: A senior-level management position where my skills and experience can be used to enhance the nation's security.

SUMMARY OF QUALIFICATIONS:

As a senior-level Marine Corps officer, have been responsible for a wide range of security and anti-terrorism related activities. In this capacity, have designed and implemented a comprehensive protection scheme that to ensure key Government leaders can continue to perform their responsibilities, even under the highest threat levels. Demonstrated ability to complete complex and dangerous missions while remaining sensitive to the morale and well being of those under my charge. Possess a current Top Secret clearance with full life-style polygraph.

CORE COMPETENCIES:

■ Management	■ Leadership	■ Strategic Planning
■ Team Building	■ Problem Solving	■ Financial Management

ACCOMPLISHMENTS:

Management/Leadership:

Over 20 years of experience training, managing, supervising, and leading diverse organizations to meet warfighting and readiness requirements. Established and led the Fleet-Antiterrorism Security Team Company, the first Marine Corps anti-terrorism unit on the West Coast. *Results:* High-level awards for the organization's outstanding performance.

Team Building/Problem Solving:

Developed and orchestrated the reorganization of a 5,000-person organization to more effectively accomplish its mission. *Results:* Reorganization was completed 90 days in advance of timeline with minimum personnel turbulence and frustration.

Commanded Marine Corps infantry units at every level up to Brigade. Gained combat experience as a team leader and squad leader in Vietnam. *Results:* Awarded Navy Achievement Medal with Combat "v" for valor.

Financial Management:

Developed and supervised the programming, budgeting, and execution of a $150 million operational budget, while achieving cost avoidance of over $10 million in the Marine Corps Recruiting Command. Over 20 years of fiscal management in key leadership billets. Budgets have ranged from $3 million to $150 million.

Strategic Planning:

Developed, reviewed, and assessed major operational plans for Bosnia and Kosovo while serving on the Joint Staff.

As Chief of Staff for the Marine Corps Recruiting Command, developed and orchestrated a strategic plan that resulted in major fiscal and personnel efficiencies, including an annual savings of over $67,000.

WORK HISTORY

Chief of Staff, Marine Corps Recruiting Command, Quantico, VA, 2004-Present

Orchestrate the development of all aspects of policy, marketing, advertising, sales, facilities, fiscal and personnel management, safety and training of a 5000-person, civilian and military, organization. *Results:* Annually recruited 41,000 high quality new men and women, nationwide, with the most successful year in history in FY02. Annual operating budget is $150 million.

Commanding Officer, 3d Marine Regiment, 3d Marine Division, Hawaii, 2002-2004

Led a 4000-person crisis force focused on assessing requirements and developing anti-terrorism programs for the Asia-Pacific Region. Maintained a 6-hour crisis response element 365 days per year. Developed major operational plans for strategic events with other countries in the Region. Served as the Marine Corps' Regional Force Commander, overseeing complex planning and execution of maritime forces prepared to respond to security threats throughout the world.

Head, Bosnia Desk, Central Eastern European Division, Joint Staff, 2000-2002

Developed strategy, policy and plans for Bosnia security, anti-terrorism operations incident to interactions with senior executive members of the White House, State Department, CIA, NATO, Office of Secretary of Defense, and key European, Russian, and Japanese representatives.

Commanding Officer, 1st Battalion, 3d Marines, Hawaii, 1997-1998

Led a 1000-person crisis force focused on security, anti-terrorism requirements in the Asia-Pacific Region. Developed anti-terrorism programs. Established training, unit cohesiveness, sound fiscal and personnel management of a short notice reaction force.

AWARDS AND RECOGNITIONS

Joint Staff Badge - 1991
Defense Superior Service Medal - 2002
Legion of Merit (2 awards) - 2004/2005
Meritorious Service Medal (2 awards) - 1997 and 1999

Industrial Engineer *Available: December 20__*

TERRY HARPER
139 Georgia Avenue
Denver, CO 80808
499-217-3219 (H) / 499-217-9123 (W)
HarperT@earthlink.net

OBJECTIVE: Industrial Engineering position with a broad-based manufacturing firm in the Northeast where leadership experience and technical skills will enhance operations.

EXPERIENCE: <u>Operations Research Analyst</u>, U.S. Total Army Personnel Command, Alexandria, VA, 2003 to present
Direct a four-person analytical team developing, evaluating, and recommending personnel reduction policies mandated by Congress.
- Applied SAS programming expertise to develop computer models that optimized employees' opportunities to advance based on performance and organizational needs.
- Created and implemented a system acceptance testing plan for a $3 million out-sourced optimization model. Resulted in four critical design enhancements and an 8.2% reporting accuracy increase.

<u>Personnel Officer</u>. US Army, 3rd Support Command, Germany, 2000-2002
Managed human resource matters for a 750-employee organization including finance, education, legal support, performance appraisals, reassignments, and personnel strength.
- Standardized office on the Microsoft suite, reducing administrative processing time by 35%.
- Achieved marked improvements in personnel action processing time through enhanced training and motivational techniques.

<u>General Manager</u>. US Army, 32d Air Defense Command, Germany, 1997-1999
Supervised 180 employees with 34 different specialty skills performing maintenance and supply operations. Managed a 24-hour repair and warehouse facility servicing 13 retail customers' vehicles, missile, and communications equipment valued at $2.1 million.
- Reduced annual operating expenses from $1.5 million to $1.3 million in first year of operation while increasing customer support levels by 7.2%.
- Decreased maintenance backlog by 62.4% in three months through production control policy changes.
- Relocated $20.3 million supply stockage increasing on-hand inventory accountability by 7.8%.

EDUCATION: **Louisiana State University**, Baton Rouge, LA.
B.S. in Industrial Engineering, 1995, Dean's List;
3.6 GPA in major

Intelligence Analyst *Available: February 20__*

CHRIS SIMPSON

2312 Columbus Ave W: (222) 231-1232
Fort Meade, MD 99902 H: (222) 231-5423

OBJECTIVE Intelligence Analyst position where imagery interpretation and data analysis will benefit a company seeking to expand its intelligence support services.

QUALIFICATIONS SUMMARY

IMAGERY
INTERPRETATION
- Over 10 years of specialized imagery experience with the Army
- Keen ability to translate and interpret imagery data.
- Applied imagery interpretation skills to identify equipment location, troop movement, and other intelligence information.

SUPERVISION
- As a manager, applied technical imagery interpretation knowledge and skills to expertly guide and advise staff in all facets of imagery interpretation.
- Briefed senior management on imagery interpretation findings.
- Maintained files on imagery interpretation data and findings.

PROJECT
MANAGEMENT
- As project leader for a new imagery system, provided technical guidance and direction that ensured the system met all requirements.
- Participated in all phases of system development. Evaluated operational effectiveness of imagery interpretation equipment. Suggested cost reduction measures that, when implemented, resulted in savings of $1.5 million.

TRAINING
- Trained classes of 35 students on imagery activities, including imagery interpretation methods, computer renditions, and pattern recognition.
- Developed innovative curriculum that blended classroom training with hands-on field exercises requiring demonstrated proficiency. Evaluated student understanding of imagery interpretation theory through oral and written exams.
- Ensured students mastered the use of sophisticated imagery equipment.

EMPLOYMENT HISTORY

Intelligence Project Specialist, Fort Meade, MD, 2004-Present
Intelligence Manager, 23rd Military Intelligence Detachment, Fort Drum, NY, 2000-2003
Intelligence Specialist, 22nd Military Intelligence Battalion, Baumholder, Germany, 1997-1999
Intelligence Specialist, 12th Military Intelligence Battalion, Fort Polk, IA, 1994-1996

EDUCATION & TRAINING

B.S., Geology, University of Maryland, College Park, MD, 2002
Military Intelligence Warrant Officer Technical Certification Course, 1995
Army Basic and Individualized Training, 1989

PERSONAL

Top Secret security clearance with recent Special Background Investigation.

Law Enforcement *Available: February 20___*

JOSEPH A. MARTINEZ
95 Colgate Drive, Apt. 131
Killeen, TX 45886
H: (333) 222-1256 / W: (333) 111-5667

OBJECTIVE

Law enforcement position where leadership skills and military police experience will benefit a large metropolitan police force seeking dedicated, community-sensitive law enforcement professionals.

SUMMARY OF QUALIFICATIONS

- Over 10 years experience as a military policeman.
- Extensive training in traditional law enforcement operations.
- Hand-picked for clandestine counter-drug operations.
- Developed innovative and highly effective approaches to crime solving.
- Qualified expert in 9 mm hand gun.

PROFESSIONAL EXPERIENCE

Counter-Drug Specialist, 109th Military Intelligence Company, Fort Bliss, TX, 2003-Present

> Infiltrate drug operations in an effort to curtail the import of illegal drugs. Employ specialized police training techniques to identify and eradicate illegal substances in foreign countries. Train foreign security forces in counter-drug techniques.

Operations Manager, 35th Military Intelligence Detachment, Fort Polk, LA, 2000-2002

> Assigned tasks daily to 15 military police professionals responsible for maintaining law and order in a community of 25,000. Interacted with colleagues on a daily basis to ensure complete understanding of assigned tasks. Assisted in the training and evaluation of 9 junior military police specialists. Counseled and mentored assigned staff.

Supervisor, 12th Military Police Company, Fort Lewis, WA, 1997-1999

> Supervised activities of 8 military personnel responsible for maintaining law and order. Trained and led personnel in all facets of daily police operations. Motivated staff to attain high levels of weapons proficiency. Ensured team members acted professionally and courteously at all times.

Military Policeman, 53rd Military Police Company, Fort Bragg, NC, 1994-1996

> Served with distinction as a member of the 82nd Airborne Division's Military Police company. Skillfully applied military police training. Handled infractions with minimal confrontation. Received Commendation Medal for excellence.

EDUCATION

High School diploma, Martin Luther King High School, Atlanta, GA, 1993

Logistics Supervisor

Available: June 20___

EDWARD DANIELS
2813 Lincoln Lane
Tacoma, WA 98031
W: (206) 918-7623 / H: (206) 231-8710

OBJECTIVE Logistics Supervisor position for an international distribution company where leadership skills and supervisory ability will enhance operational effectiveness and increase profitability.

QUALIFICATIONS SUMMARY

LOGISTICS

- Assisted in directing logistics support operations of 9 Federal Aviation Administration sites and 4 Air National Guard units.
- Executed the redistribution of 2,500 items of supply from deactivating sites.
- Optimized maintenance cycles, thereby decreasing time on aircraft repairable from 72 to 12 hours and costs by 28%.
- Provided subject matter expertise to the development of the Air National Guard's Mission Critical Logistics Reporting System, which enhanced the effectiveness of air operations management.

DISTRIBUTION

- Directed the requisitioning and control of aircraft parts to support a fleet of 54 aircraft and 680 vehicles. Cited by senior leaders as a major contributor to improved efficiency of warehouse operations.
- Developed the first Air National Guard inspection checklist for warehouse operations, thereby reducing customer complaints by 55% in the first year.

SUPERVISORY

- Led and guided four inspectors in performing quality control evaluations of 24 line personnel. Achieved 23% increase in proficiency without deviating from standards.
- Coordinated technical training for approximately 300 personnel over 24 month period.
- Prevented the loss of $109,000 in equipment assets by developing and enforcing strict accounting and control procedures.

INTERNATIONAL

- Extensive experience in Europe.
- Fluent in Italian.

EMPLOYMENT HISTORY: U.S. Army, 1986-Present

Warehouse Supervisor, McChord Air Force Base, WA, 2003-Present
Distribution Manager, Travis Air Force Base, CA, 1999-2002
Quality Assurance Manager, Aviano AB, Italy, 1996-1998
Training Supervisor, Andrews Air Force Base, MD, 1990-1992
Developmental Logistics Assignments, U.S. Air Force, 1983-1989

EDUCATION & TRAINING

A.A., Business Administration, San Francisco State University, CA, 1997
Relevant Training: Total Quality Management Course (1991); NCO Academy (1990), Airman Leadership Course (1986)

Network Specialist *Available: December 20__*

DAVID P. JONES
2311 Park Avenue
Langley AFB, VA 22312
Work: 540-123-4567 / Home: 540-123-1234
JonesD@aol.com

OBJECTIVE

Position as a Network Specialist for a small-to-medium size telecommunications firm where proven communication skills and self-motivation will help the organization obtain increased market share.

SUMMARY OF QUALIFICATIONS

Technically adept technician with over seven years experience providing telecommunications support to executives at the highest levels of the U.S. Government. Significant experience installing and maintaining cellular, VHF, UHF satellite, wireline, and line of sight voice and data systems. Articulate, motivated professional with strong desire to excel. Possess a Top Secret security clearance with SCI and Presidential Access Clearance.

PROFESSIONAL EXPERIENCE

Senior Radio Technician, White House Communications Agency, 2001-Present
Supervised five to eight person teams deployed worldwide to provide uninterrupted communications support for Presidential-level officials. Managed $80 million worth of communications equipment with no loss or damage. Received Army medal for outstanding communications support provided to the President and his staff.

Mobile Communication System Technician, White House Communications Agency, 1997-2000
Designed and implemented a mobile communications system that provided secure/nonsecure voice, data, and facsimile service via cellular, VHF, UHF satellite, and HF mediums. Ensured high level government officials had uninterrupted communications regardless of their itinerary. Maintained 98% readiness rate on fleet of 25 mobile communication vehicles.

Radio Operator, 101st Airmobile Division, Fort Cambell, KY, 1994-1997
Operated radio communication systems in support of unit operations. Set up and tuned radio equipment to pre-established frequencies. Transmitted, received, and logged radio messages according to military procedures. Maintained equipment in operational condition.

EDUCATION AND TRAINING

A.S., Computer Technology, Northern Virginia Community College, 2000
Tactical Satellite/Microwave Communications, Fort Gordon, GA, 1994

Project Management *Available: August 20__*

LYNN JONES
1229 East York Ave.
New Livery, CT 09558
(Home) 913-558-9877 / (Work) 913-487-8993

OBJECTIVE: A product management position in a fast growing cellular communication company where organization, leadership, and communication experience will be used for improving product quality and innovation.

EDUCATION ■ B.S., Electrical Engineering, Brigham Young University,
& TRAINING: Salt Lake City, UT, 1997
 ■ Information Management Course, Fort Gordon, GA, 2002
 ■ U.S. Army Signal Officer Advanced Course, Fort Gordon, GA, 2000
 ■ U.S. Army Signal Officer Basic Course, Fort Gordon, GA, 1997

EXPERIENCE: 1995-Present, U.S. Army, Captain, Signal Corps

Organization Designed and coordinated communications for Pacific Command Joint Training Exercises. Organized and chaired engineering conferences. Presented decision briefings and prepared staff action papers for a variety of communication-related issues of considerable importance to the command. Served as Watch Officer during field exercises.

Leadership Installed, operated, and maintained satellite, switching, cable, and message communications in support of numerous U.S. Army units distributed throughout central Germany. Led 110 soldiers in performing all assigned communications missions. Total responsibility for the the soldiers under my command.

Communication Planned and supervised installation of telecommunication systems of V Corps exercises. Maintained and accounted for vehicle and communications equipment valued at approximately $1.5 million. Planned and conducted individual and collective training in technical skills and general military subjects. Supervised, trained, and led 23 personnel.

WORK *Communication Staff Officer*, 12th Signal Brigade,
HISTORY: Fort Lewis, Washington, 2000-Present

 Communications Company Commander, C Company, 430th Signal Battalion, Mainz, Germany, 2000-2002

 Platoon Leader, B Company, 17th Signal Battalion, Hoechst, Germany, 1997-1999.

Security *Available: January 20__*

FRANCIS MITCHELL
1100 Main Street
Dugway, UT 84000
Home: (801) 890-1234 / Work: (801) 123-4567
MitchellF@earthlink.net

PROFESSIONAL PROFILE

Over 15 years experience in Security and Intelligence Operations worldwide. Combines strong planning, analysis, organizational and communications skills with excellent qualifications in the development of security operations. Skilled personnel manager and budget administrator. Expertise includes:

- Scientific & Technical Intelligence
- Tactical Assessment/Planning
- Document Security/Control
- Security Training & Team Leadership
- Operations & Personnel Security
- Counter-Terrorism
- Counter-Espionage
- Reporting/Analysis

Excellent knowledge of the Freedom of Information Act and security policies of U.S. and foreign governments. Familiar with general security practices followed by major industries and corporations nationwide. Held highest level U.S. Government security clearance and positions of trust.

PROFESSIONAL EXPERIENCE

Intelligence & Security Officer, U.S. Army 1991 to Present
Logistics Officer, U.S. Army 1985-1990

Fast-track promotion throughout career. Advanced through a series of increasingly responsible security and intelligence positions with organizations operating worldwide. Won numerous honors and commendations for capabilities in threat analysis, intelligence collection/analysis, security operations planning and personnel training. Career highlights include:

Security Operations Planning & Management

- Authored several major documents impacting security and intelligence operations worldwide. Provided the strategy, organizational structure and processes for security operations development, management and expansion in response to changing demands of worldwide operations.

- Hosted two intelligence planning committees of multi-disciplinary intelligence and operating management personnel challenged to enhance security and operations planning worldwide.

- Provided high-level security and intelligence support to technologically advanced systems and engineering projects.

Intelligence Collection & Analysis

- Directed large-scale intelligence research, collection, analysis and dissemination operations to provide top management with critical information regarding potential threats and breeches to security.

- Initiated processes to overcome shortcomings in intelligence collection and analysis vital for the success of major projects.

- Authored reports, led executive-level presentations and coordinated information flow between various public and private organizations.

Personnel Training, Supervision & Development

- Designed and led training programs in security and intelligence for operative personnel, management and executives worldwide. Created customized presentations to meet specific operating requirements.

- Trained, scheduled, supervised and evaluated work performance of up to 85 personnel.

Budgeting & Financial Management

- Participated in the long-term administration of a $7 million annual budget. Provided timely and accurate input to high-level reports and discussions addressing operations planning and budget requirements.

Achievements & Project Highlights

- Developed processes to maintain control of more than 70,000 sensitive security documents.

- Managed systems development and implementation project to computerize a large technical scientific library and integrate advanced optical data technology for long-term document retention.

- Built cooperative working relationships with government agencies worldwide to facilitate the timely exchange of information critical to intelligence and security operations.

- Extensive technical knowledge of chemical, biological, and radiological security threats, electronic surveillance technology, electronic counter-measures and munitions technologies.

EDUCATION

Bachelor of General Studies, Kent State University, 1985

Completed 350+ hours of continuing professional training in Security and Intelligence. Program included scientific and technical intelligence collection/analysis, leadership, and supervisory skills.

Senior Program Administrator *Available: June 20__*

SAMUAL MATTISON
10 Parkwood Lane
Groton, CT 06300
(860) 412-3456 / MattisonS@aol.com

OBJECTIVE

A Senior Program Administrator position where knowledge and technical expertise in facilities management will improve the efficiency of a firm's manufacturing operations.

PROFESSIONAL EXPERIENCE

UNITED STATES NAVY, 1980-Present

Project/Program Manager

- Managed a $200 million budget in an increasingly constrained and technically complex environment. *Saved $6 million in maintenance resources through skillful fixed-price negotiations.*
- Monitored General Electric operations of four Nuclear Propulsion Prototypes ensuring compliance with Naval Reactors, OSHA and EPA procedures for training and test requirements. Graded satisfactory on annual audits.
- Directed multiple industrial activities: job scoping and sequencing; quality control procedures; and personnel training. Ensured best product, least cost, shortest time.

 Special recognition: *"The success of the NR-1 $80 million Refueling Overhaul is due to LCDR Mattison's superior management and attention to detail."* – J. P. Smith, Vice Admiral, Navy Commendation Medal

Supervisor/Trainer

- Directed and supervised 40 technical writers in preparation of detailed, step-by-step, user friendly preventive and corrective maintenance procedures (3M) for a 1000-man production work force.
- Assessed department needs and problems, identified and recommended solution, developed realistic and achievable goals, and designed on-the-job training programs to eliminate discrepancies, increased productivity and enhanced skills of employees (e.g., revised the Basic Nuclear Electrician's Rate curriculum). *Reduced attrition by 23%*
- Evaluated personnel semiannually: focused on contributions, character and accomplishments; counseled on ways to increase skills and advance in career. *Achieved a 95% success rate for electricians' advancement to E-5. Eighteen students were selected for officer commissioning programs.*

- Administered and implemented preventive and corrective maintenance program (3M), assigned and scheduled technicians based on skill and experience, inspected work ensuring compliance with regulations and technical specifications, and verified accurate documentation into records.

Technical

- Researched, compiled and evaluated data and statistics to write reports and make formal presentations, with decision points to department heads and Chief Executive Officers. *Saved $2 million by identifying and eliminating an outdated time phased hydraulic control valve maintenance program.*
- Planned, scheduled and directed attack submarine employment, resulting in on-time departure and electronic suite certification.
- As quality assurance officer, continuously inspected Naval equipment to ensure operational readiness in a safe manner.

Quality Control

- Implemented radiological controls, nuclear work practices, radiographic operations and quality control procedures. Identified and developed solutions to resolve work practices discrepancies, before they impact production.
- Sent weekly letters to the Director, Naval Nuclear Propulsion Program, on mechanical and fluid systems compliance, with recommended solutions. *One recommendation to a nuclear valve was incorporated locally and fleet-wide, saving an estimated $1 million in corrective maintenance.*

EDUCATION & TRAINING

B.S., Nuclear Engineering Technology, Thomas Edison State College, Trenton, NJ, 1999

PROFESSIONAL AFFILIATIONS

American Nuclear Society
American Society of Mechanical Engineers

HONORS/AWARDS

Numerous awards and citations for leadership, supervision, and project management.

"Singled out by Squadron Four Commanding Officers and the Force Commander for timely and expert preparation of four SSN's for deployment." – A. W. Adams, Commodore, Navy Commendation Medal

"Conceived and implemented a harbor tug overhaul plan with a cost savings of $750,000. The success of this project was due to his thorough planning and resourceful initiatives by obtaining a harbor tug from Naval Station Rota, Spain." – M. D. Frank, Commodore

Telecommunications Specialist *Available: July 20__*

CHRIS R. KELLY
112 Oleander Road
Quantico, VA 21221
(777) 795-1467 / KellyC@hotmail.com

OBJECTIVE
Local Area Network administrator position where LAN skills and knowledge will improve the range of services offered by a small to mid-sized telecommunications firm located in the East.

HIGHLIGHT OF QUALIFICATIONS
- Telecommunications professional with over 12 years experience in the installation, operation, and maintenance of local area networks.
- Demonstrated knowledge of telecommunication protocols, including TCP/IP and IPX.
- Designed and installed LANs of various configurations and topologies.
- Microsoft Certified Systems Engineer (MCSE).

AREAS OF EXPERTISE
Network Administration: Installed and administered Banyan Vines LANs that interconnected 100 microcomputer users in an MS Windows environment. Expertly employed network management software to optimize network performance. Upgraded communications equipment and operating system software in a manner that minimized disturbances in LAN operations. Maintained accurate list of authorized users. Controlled passwords for direct and remote access to the LAN. Hands-on experience with many communication protocols.

Communications Training: Provided classroom and 1-on-1 telecommunications training for the organization's 200+ computer users. Instructed staff on the use of various applications, including electronic mail (cc:Mail), Internet/World Wide Web, and office automation software (Microsoft Office). Developed curriculum and taught specialized courses. Received top performance - awards.

Computer Operations: Maintained large tape and disk library for 300-staff organization in an IBM mainframe environment. Coordinated activities and briefed senior operations managers on important issues. Interfaced with the organization's staff members to answer computer-related questions. Facilitated mainframe connection by installing Etherlink card in personal computers. Maintained accurate inventory of computer and peripheral equipment valued at $1.5 million.

EMPLOYMENT HISTORY
Computer Operations Supervisor, Henderson Hall, VA, 2004-Present
Network Supervisor, Cherry Point, NC, 2000-2003
Computer Network Specialist, San Diego, CA, 1997-1999

EDUCATION
B.S. (Candidate, 2007), Information Systems, George Mason University, Fairfax, VA
A.A., Computer Technology, North Carolina State University, 2003

Warehouse Supervisor *Available: February 20__*

DANA PHILLIPS
2813 Lincoln Lane
Madison, CT 02521
(206) 918-7623 / PhillipsD@aol.com

OBJECTIVE

Position in inventory management for a large department store where skills
and experience in warehouse operations can be used to improve efficiency
and profitability.

QUALIFICATIONS SUMMARY

- Skilled inventory stocking specialist with over 6 years experience.
- Disciplined, dedicated supply professional trained in proper procedures
 for shipping, receiving, storing, and issuing stock.
- Extensive experience handling medicine, food, and other perishable
 supplies.
- Knowledgeable about stock control and accounting procedures.
- Effective in team or individual-based settings.

EMPLOYMENT HISTORY

Stock Control Specialist, 9th District, Cleveland, OH, 2003-Present
 Locate and catalog supply items in a timely manner using a computer-
 based tracking system. Improved stock verification procedures, resulting in
 no discrepancies found over a two-year period. Load, unload, and move
 stock using forklifts and hand trucks. Maintain accurate records on
 incoming and outgoing stock, which comprises over 1,000 line items.

Stock Control Clerk, Support Center, Elizabeth City, NJ, 1999-2002
 Designed innovative system to better organize storage space for incoming
 stock of 5,500 line items. Closely followed established procedures for
 shipping, receiving, storing, and issuing stock. Verified quantity and
 description of stock received against bills of lading, ensuring 100%
 accuracy. Maintained accurate records of quantities on hand. Received
 commendation medal for results achieved.

EDUCATION & TRAINING

A.A., Business Administration, Ohio State, 2004
Materials Management Course, Fort Lee, VA, 2000
Army Basic Training, Fort Lee, VA, 1999

Resume Letter

4921 Tyler Drive
Washington, D.C. 20011
March 15, 20 ____

Doris Stevens
STR Corporation
179 South Trail
Rockville, Maryland 21101

Dear Ms. Stevens:

STR Corporation is one of the most dynamic computer companies in the nation. In addition to being a leader in the field of small business computers, STR has a progressive employee training and development program which could very well become a model for other organizations. This is the type of organization I am interested in joining.

I am seeking a training position with a computer firm which would utilize my administrative, communication, and planning abilities to develop effective training and counseling programs. My experience includes:

Administration: Supervised instructors and counselors. Coordinated job vacancy and training information for businesses, industries, and schools.

Communication: Conducted over 100 workshops on interpersonal skills, stress management, and career planning. Frequent guest speaker to various agencies and private firms. Experienced writer of training manuals and public relations materials.

Planning: Planned and developed counseling programs for 5,000 employees. Reorganized interviewing and screening processes for public employment agency. Developed program of individualized and group counseling for community school.

In addition, I am completing my Ph.D. in industrial psychology with emphasis on developing training and counseling programs for technical personnel.

Could we meet to discuss your program as well as how my experience might relate to your needs? I will call your office on Tuesday morning, March 23, to arrange a convenient time to meet with you.

I especially want to show you a model employee counseling and career development program I recently developed. Perhaps you may find it useful for your work with STR.

Sincerely yours,

James C. Astor

James C. Astor
astorc@mymail.com

Cover Letter

2842 South Plaza
Chicago, Illinois 60228
March 12, 20 ____

David C. Johnson
Director of Personnel
Bank of Chicago
490 Michigan Avenue
Chicago, Illinois 60222

Dear Mr. Johnson:

The accompanying resume is in response to your listing in the Chicago Tribune for a loan officer.

I am especially interested in this position because my experience with the Small Business Administration has prepared me for understanding the financial needs and problems of the business community from the perspectives of both lenders and borrowers. I wish to use this experience with a growing and community-conscious bank such as yours.

I would appreciate an opportunity to meet with you to discuss how my experience will best meet your needs. My ideas on how to improve small business financing may be of particular interest to you. Therefore, I will call your office on the morning of March 17 to inquire if a meeting can be scheduled at a convenient time.

I look forward to meeting you.

Sincerely yours,

Joyce Pitman

Joyce Pitman
pitmanj@mymail.com

"T" Letter: Responding to Classified Ad

16 Bella Vista Place
Cincinnati, OH 45206
April 16, 20___

Ms. Cecily Dorfmann
Vice President, Human Resources
Nair Industries
257 Vine Street
Cincinnati, OH 45202

Re: Sales Manager, Cincinnati Enquirer, April 12

Dear Ms. Dorfmann:

As a Sales Manager, I have planned and scheduled direct sales programs and trade shows with consistently profitable results. Here is a list of my qualifications as they relate to your requirements for the position of Sales Manager:

Your Requirements	My Qualifications
2 years Direct Sales Management (Self-contained sales region)	Over 7 years aggressive direct sales management experience as proven by opening 8 area offices which escalated regional sales average to #1 position among 200 offices.
Individual Sales Experience	Dynamic individual sales success proved by exceeding all sales goals for 18 months and reaching "Top ½%" among 250.
Excellent Verbal and Written	Exceptional Communicator as demonstrated by over 40 major group presentations, writing "direct sales" promotional materials and column (reaching 11,000) and 3-day demonstrations at 22 national trade shows.
Problem Solving and Strategic Planning Skills	Excellent Problem Solver and Strategic Planner indicated by structuring daily control meetings for staff of 25 resolving problem of "peak time" business loss (increased 35%)
Marketing and Corporate Office	Strong Marketing Experience (4 years) at corporate office level, proven skills in creating innovative team format and realigning 35 inside-outside sales/support staff to generate 15% sales increase to $3.5MM.

Enclosed is a resume that lists other accomplishments that may be of interest to you.

I look forward to meeting with you to explore the use of my talents to support the growth of your company. I will call on Wednesday, April 21, to schedule an interview at your convenience.

Sincerely,

Susan Ariani

Susan Ariani
Enclosure

Cover Letter for a Focus Piece
(Also functions as a thank you letter for a referral interview)

21 East State Street
Hartford, CT 03455

August 21, 20___

Mr. John Marston
Vice President, Operations
ABC, Inc.
2441 Uptown Drive
Hartford, CT 03450

Dear Mr. Marston:

I wanted to thank you again for our meeting last Wednesday. I also wanted to express my appreciation to you for taking the additional time to define some of the areas where you feel my skills might have some impact.

It is of great value to me to be as clear as possible on what seemed to be most important to you. I also want to be confident in my own mind that my background, skills, and abilities, will meet those types of challenges, so I've taken the liberty of developing a focus piece for your review.

I clearly understand that there are no immediate openings in your organization, but I also understand the inevitability of change. As such, should there be an opportunity in the future where you might need help in these areas, I would like to know if you see me as a resource for this type of position.

To that end, I would very much appreciate your feedback, and will call you on Tuesday, May 6, to see what you think.

Thank you again for your help!

Sincerely,

Jonathan Edwards

Jonathan Edwards

enclosure

Focus Piece

Why Jonathan Edwards Would Be an Asset to Your Company

<u>YOUR NEEDS</u>:	<u>MY ABILITIES</u>:
GROW BUSINESS FOCUSING ON QUALITY AND BEING THE BEST. NOT NECESSARILY THE BIGGEST	"Volume growth of 37% doesn't happen without a lot of effort on your part. You are certainly aware of the importance of this project towards future growth with Roberts Cookies. Thanks for your efforts! It's great to see you accomplish a very tough goal. <u>Nice Job!</u>" – Jenny Aloe, Director of Marketing, Roberts Cookies

15 years in quality customer and account services marketing both intangible and tangible products based on:

Transaction successes:
- Secured competitor's accounts by accepting "Prove it" challenge resulting In exceeding competitor's 6 month's best in 6 weeks.

- Grew business 67% over previous year and secured three new accounts.

Long term relationship successes:
- Expanded product exposure by developing and implementing an advocacy program based on categorical research and customer trend studies. **Result:** Increased dollar volume 124% and additional item exposure by 145%

- Selected to create and manage two test market programs simultaneously by developing marketing campaign strategy including sales plans and staff training. **Result:** Revitalized 3 year sales slump and increased market share from a 5th place position to a 2nd place position.

"QUALITY CUSTOMER SERVICE" — "<u>Great follow-up</u>. It's really a pleasure to have a pro like you on the team." – Mark Burkett, Sales Manager, Star Bars

Developed a proven record of exemplary client retention and satisfaction through perceptive needs assessment, highly responsive services, and consistent follow through.

Provided clients with a more "user friendly" process by revamping support materials and documentation procedures resulting in 41% faster turn around.

VERBAL/VERSATILE
COMMUNICATOR

"...Handled his duties with outstanding professionalism." – William West, Manager, Rising Sun Grocery

Built a reputation for diplomatic, tactful, and need based business relationships.

Presented marketing plans on a regular basis to district, regional, and national management.

Facilitated numerous training sessions, both as seminars and workshops.

Turned around the company's #1 customer by <u>listening</u> to specific concerns. **Result:** improved relations and an additional 2.3% growth in sales.

Consistent, progressive recognition for strong, interpersonal skills through evaluations, awards, and reviews.

As an INTJ/Amiable Expressive, I am:

- Natural decision maker
- Builder of systems and applier of theoretical models
- No idea to too far fetched to be entertained
- National brainstormer, open to and seeking new concepts
- Keen eye for the consequences of the application of new ideas or positions
- Have a drive to completion, always with an eye to long-term consequences
- Difficulties are highly stimulating and love to respond to a challenge that requires creativity
- Communicates values and trust
- Natural tendency to be helpful to others
- Open, cooperative, and supportive
- Accepting, with a high priority to get along with others
- Achieves goals while establishing strong personal ties.

"OWNERSHIP" OF COMPANY
MISSION

"Jonathan's maturity, thoughtfulness, and good judgment for him, engendering the respect of his reports, as well as other managers..." – Bernard T. Slaney, Future4 Was

Ownership to company mission recognized by a promotions in 7 years.

REFINED, EDUCATIONAL, "NON-AGGRESSIVE" APPROACH

"Jonathan, great job!! You're making a large contribution very fast!! Thanks for a great job!" – Ezra June, Regional Sales Manager, Star Bars

Extensive training in "Non-Threatening" techniques through:

- Murray Associates (Sandler System – Teaches how to help the client find out what they need).

- Wilson Learning (14 month course work including Needs Assessment, Social Styles, Creative Selling, Communications, and many others).

FAMILIARITY WITH BUSINESS CLIMATE AND KEY DECISION MAKERS IN HARTFORD

"...Well organized, thorough, dedicated." – Larry Cochran, National Sales Manager, Windjammer Communications

Numerous contacts in the market, but what is more important, trained in and educated others in how to get in front of people by using referrals, cold contacts, etc.

Have made over 5,040 market calls in the last seven years, of which over 40% were cold calls.

Ability to get referrals from clients, co-workers, etc.

Willingness and desire to network at chamber events, trade shows, etc.

Read *Business First, Small Business News, Columbus CEO, National Employment News, Columbus Employment News,* and many others.

ABLE TO WORK INDEPENDENTLY/ SELF MOTIVATED

"Jonathan has many strengths, including being a motivated self starter along with the ability to complete projects thoroughly and accurately. He is always willing to take on additional responsibilities... and is very well organized, trustworthy, conscientious, and punctual." – Larry Cochran, National Sales Manager, Windjammer Communications.

SUCCESS

"I know of no other individual in my 10 years of management who has so consistently striven for and achieved success on a regular basis." – W. Arlin Gossamer, President, Albatross Confections

Approach Letter
Referral

821 Stevens Point
Boston, MA 01990
April 14, 20 ____

Terri Fulton
Director of Personnel
TRS Corporation
6311 W. Dover
Boston, MA 01991

Dear Ms. Fulton:

Alice O'Brien suggested that I contact you about my interest in personnel management. She said you are one of the best people to talk to in regard to careers in personnel.

I am leaving government after seven years of increasingly responsible experience in personnel. I am especially interested in working with a large private firm. However, before I venture further into the job market, I want to benefit from the experience and knowledge of others in the field who might advise me on opportunities for someone with my qualifications.

Perhaps we could meet briefly sometime during the next two weeks to discuss my career plans. I have several questions which I believe you could help clarify. I will call your office on Tuesday, April 22, to schedule a meeting time.

I look forward to discussing my plans with you.

Sincerely yours,

Katherine Kelly

Katherine Kelly
kellyk@mymail.com

Approach Letter
Cold Turkey

2189 West Church Street
New York, NY 10011
May 3, 20 ____

Patricia Dotson, Director
Northeast Association for
 the Elderly
9930 Jefferson Street
New York, NY 10013

Dear Ms. Dotson:

I have been impressed with your work with the elderly. Your organization takes a community perspective in trying to integrate the concerns of the elderly with those of other community groups. Perhaps other organizations will soon follow your lead.

I am anxious to meet you and learn more about your work. My background with the city Volunteer Services Program involved frequent contacts with elderly volunteers. From this experience I decided I preferred working primarily with the elderly.

However, before I pursue my interest further, I need to talk to people with experience in gerontology. In particular, I would like to know more about careers with the elderly as well as how my background might best be used in the field of gerontology.

I am hoping you can assist me in this matter. I would like to meet with you briefly to discuss several of my concerns. I will call next week to see if your schedule permits such a meeting.

I look forward to meeting you.

Sincerely,

Carol Timms

Carol Timms
timmsc@mymail.com

Thank You Letter
Post-Informational Interview

9910 Thompson Drive
Cleveland, Ohio 43382
June 21, 20 ____

Jane Evans, Director
Evans Finance Corporation
2122 Forman Street
Cleveland, Ohio 43380

Dear Ms. Evans:

Your advice was most helpful in clarifying my questions on careers in finance. I am now reworking my resume and have included many of your thoughtful suggestions. I will send you a copy next week.

Thanks so much for taking time from your busy schedule to see me. I will keep in contact and follow through on your suggestion to see Sarah Cook about opportunities with the Cleveland-Akron Finance Company.

Sincerely,

Daryl Haines

Daryl Haines
hainesd@mymail.com

Thank You Letter
Post-Job Interview

2962 Forrest Drive
Denver, Colorado 82171
May 28, 20 ____

Thomas F. Harris
Director, Personnel Department
Coastal Products Incorporated
7229 Lakewood Drive
Denver, Colorado 82170

Dear Mr. Harris:

Thank you again for the opportunity to interview for the marketing position. I appreciated your hospitality and enjoyed meeting you and members of your staff.

The interview convinced me of how compatible my background, interest, and skills are with the goals of Coastal Products Incorporated. My prior marketing experience with the Department of Commerce has prepared me to take a major role in developing both domestic and international marketing strategies. I am confident my work for you will result in increased profits within the first two years.

For more information on the new product promotion program I mentioned, call David Garrett at the Department of Commerce; his number is 202/726-0132. I talked to Dave this morning and mentioned your interest in this program.

I look forward to meeting you again.

Sincerely,

Tim Potter

Tim Potter
pottert@mymail.com

Thank You Letter
Job Rejection

564 Court Street
St. Louis, MO 53167
April 29, 20 ___

Ralph Ullman, President
S.T. Ayer Corporation
6921 Southern Blvd.
St. Louis, MO 53163

Dear Mr. Ullman:

I appreciated your consideration for the Research Associate position. While I am disappointed in not being selected, I learned a great deal about your corporation, and I enjoyed meeting with you and your staff. I felt particularly good about the professional manner in which you conducted the interview.

Please keep me in mind for future consideration. I have a strong interest in your company. I believe we would work well together. I will be closely following the progress of your company over the coming months. Perhaps we will be in touch with each other at some later date.

Best wishes.

Sincerely,

Martin Tollins

Martin Tollins
tollinsm@mymail.com

Thank You Letter
Job Offer Acceptance

7694 James Court
San Francisco, CA 94826
June 7, 20 ____

Judith Greene
Vice President
West Coast Airlines
2400 Van Ness
San Francisco, CA 94829

Dear Ms. Greene:

I am pleased to accept your offer, and I am looking forward to joining you and your staff next month.

The customer relations position is ideally suited to my background and interests. I assure you I will give you my best effort in making this an effective position within your company.

I understand I will begin work on July. If, in the meantime, I need to complete any paper work or take care of any other matters, please contact me.

I enjoyed meeting with you and your staff and appreciated the professional manner in which the hiring was conducted.

Sincerely,

Joan Kitner

Joan Kitner
kitnerj@mymail.com

13

Research Alternative Jobs, Employers, and Communities

T HE OLD ADAGE THAT "knowledge is power" is especially true when conducting a job search. Your job search is only as good as the knowledge you acquire and use for finding the job you want. You should avoid making critical job-related decisions based upon limited information. You want to cast as large an information net as possible in order to make smart decisions about your future.

Gathering, processing, and using information is the lifeblood of any job search. Research integrates the individual job search activities and provides feedback for adapting strategies to the realities of the job market. Given the numerous individuals and organizations involved in your job search, you must develop an information gathering strategy that will help you gain knowledge about, as well as access to, those individuals and organizations that will play the most important role in your job search.

Research Purposes

Research is the key to gathering, processing, and using information in your job search. It is a skill that will help you minimize job search frustrations and maximize your successes. Be sure to make research one of your top priorities. It should be something you do every day of your job search.

However, most people are reluctant to initiate a research campaign, which involves using libraries and computers, telephoning, and meeting

new people. Such reluctance is due in part to the lack of knowledge about how to conduct research and where to find resources, and in part to a certain cultural shyness which inhibits individuals from initiating contacts with strangers. But research is not a difficult process. After all, most people conduct research daily as they read and converse with others about problems. This daily research process needs to be specifically tailored to and focused on your job search campaign.

Research serves several purposes when adapted to your job search. First, knowing the who, what, when, and where of organizations and individuals is essential for targeting your resume and conducting informational and job interviews.

Second, the research component should broaden your perspective on the job market in relation to your motivated abilities and skills and job objective. Since there are over 1,100 different job titles as well as thousands and thousands of job markets, even a full-time research campaign will uncover only a small segment of the job market relevant to your interests and skills.

A third purpose of research is to better understand how to relate your motivated abilities and skills (Chapter 10) to specific jobs and work environments. Once you research and understand the critical requirements of a given job in a specific work environment, you can assess the appropriateness of that job for you vis-a-vis your pattern of motivated abilities and skills (MAS).

Fourth, researching organizations and individuals should result in systematically uncovering a set of contacts for developing your job search network. One of your major research goals should be to compile names, addresses, and telephone numbers of individuals who may become important resources in your new network of job contacts.

A fifth purpose of research is to learn the **languages** (jargon) of alternative civilian jobs and careers. You can learn to better converse in these languages by reading trade journals, annual reports, pamphlets, and other organizational literature as well as talking with people in various occupational fields. Knowing these languages – especially asking and answering intelligent questions in the language of the employer – is important for conducting successful referral and job interviews (Chapters 14 and 15) as well as using the right keywords on your resume.

Finally, research should result in bringing some degree of structure, coherence, and understanding to the inherently decentralized, fragmented, and chaotic job market. Without research, you place yourself at the mercy of chance and luck; thus, you become a subject of your environment. Research enables you to take control of your situation, and empowers you to change your life.

Your research activities should focus on four major targets: occupational alternatives, organizations, individuals, and communities. If you give equal time to each, you will be well on your way to getting job interviews and offers.

Investigate Alternative Jobs and Careers

Your initial research should help familiarize you with **job and career alternatives**. For example, the U.S. Department of Labor now identifies over 1,100 job titles (condensed from over 13,000 job titles a few years ago). Most individuals are occupationally illiterate; they are unaware of the vast array of available jobs and careers. Therefore, it is essential to investigate occupational alternatives in order to broaden your perspective on the job market.

You should start your research by examining several key directories that provide information on alternative jobs and careers:

- *Occupational Outlook Handbook*
- *Encyclopedia of Careers and Vocational Guidance*
- *Enhanced Guide for Occupational Exploration*
- *Guide for Occupational Exploration*
- *O*NET Dictionary of Occupational Titles*

The latest version of the *Occupational Outlook Handbook*, most data related to the *O*NET*, and other useful career exploration information are now available online by visiting these three websites operated by the U.S. Department of Labor:

- *OOH* www.bls.gov/oco
- *O*NET* www.onetcenter.org
- America's CareerInfoNet www.acinet.org

You will also find several books that focus on alternative jobs and careers. McGraw-Hill, for example, produces one of the most comprehensive series of books on alternative jobs and careers. Their books address 85 different job and career fields. Representative titles in their *Opportunities in...* series include:

- *Opportunities in Acting*
- *Opportunities in Aerospace*
- *Opportunities in Banking*
- *Opportunities in Business Management*

- *Opportunities in Cable Television*
- *Opportunities in Computer Systems*
- *Opportunities in Electronics Careers*
- *Opportunities in Eye Care Careers*
- *Opportunities in Health and Medical Careers*
- *Opportunities in Interior Design and Decorating*
- *Opportunities in Laser Technology*
- *Opportunities in Medical Imaging*
- *Opportunities in Occupational Therapy*
- *Opportunities in Pharmacy Careers*
- *Opportunities in Public Relations*
- *Opportunities in Teaching*
- *Opportunities in Visual Arts*

This company also publishes two other useful sets of books: the *Careers in...* and *Careers for You* series. Titles in the *Careers in...* series include:

- *Accounting*
- *Advertising*
- *Business*
- *Child Care*
- *Communications*
- *Computers*
- *Education*
- *Engineering*
- *Environment*
- *Finance*
- *Government*
- *Health Care*
- *High Tech*
- *Horticulture and Botany*
- *International Business*
- *Journalism*
- *Law*
- *Marketing*
- *Medicine*
- *Nursing*
- *Science*
- *Social and Rehabilitation Services*
- *Travel, Tourism, and Hospitality*

Over 50 books in the *Careers for You* series include such titles as:

- *Animal Lovers*
- *Bookworms*
- *Car Buffs*
- *Caring People*
- *Computer Buffs*
- *Class Clowns & Other Engaging Types*
- *Color Connoisseurs & Other Visual Types*
- *Computer Buffs & Other Technological Types*
- *Courageous People*
- *Crafty People*
- *Culture Lovers and Other Artsy Types*

- *Cybersurfers*
- *Environmental Types*
- *Fashion Plates*
- *Film Buffs*
- *Financial Mavens & Other Money Movers*
- *Foreign Language Aficionados*
- *Good Samaritans*
- *Gourmets*
- *Health Nuts*
- *High Energy People*
- *History Buffs*
- *Introverts & Other Solitary Types*
- *Kids at Heart*
- *Legal Eagles*
- *Music Lovers*
- *Mystery Lovers*
- *Nature Lovers*
- *Night Owls*
- *Number Crunchers*
- *Perfectionists & Other Meticulous Types*
- *Plant Lovers*
- *Self Starters*
- *Shutterbugs*
- *Sports Nuts*
- *Talkative Types*
- *Travel Buffs*
- *Writers*

Facts on File publishes 20 volumes on alternative jobs and careers in various industries, including such titles as *Career Opportunities in...*

- *Advertising and Public Relations*
- *Aviation and the Aerospace Industry*
- *Computers and Cyberspace*
- *Food and Beverage Industry*
- *Health Care*
- *Music Industry*
- *Politics, Government, and Activism*
- *Theater and Performing Arts*
- *Travel and Tourism*

Impact Publications publishes several volumes on international, public service, nonprofit, and alternative careers as well as a nontraditional career series for girls:

- *America's Top 100 Jobs for People Without a Four-Year Degree*
- *America's Top Jobs for People Re-Entering the Workforce*
- *Best Jobs for the 21st Century*
- *Directory of Federal Jobs and Employers*
- *Directory of Websites for International Jobs*
- *Complete Guide to International Jobs and Careers*
- *Complete Guide to Public Employment*
- *Cool Careers for Girls as Crime Solvers*
- *Cool Careers for Girls as Environmentalists*
- *Cool Careers for Girls in Air and Space*
- *Cool Careers for Girls in Computers*
- *Cool Careers for Girls in Construction*
- *Cool Careers for Girls in Cybersecurity and National Safety*
- *Cool Careers for Girls in Engineering*
- *Cool Careers for Girls in Food*
- *Cool Careers for Girls in Health*
- *Cool Careers for Girls in Law*
- *Cool Careers for Girls in Performing Arts*
- *Cool Careers for Girls in Sports*
- *Cool Careers for Girls in Travel and Hospitality*
- *Cool Careers for Girls With Animals*
- *Federal Applications That Get Results*
- *Federal Jobs in Law Enforcement*
- *International Jobs Directory*
- *Jobs and Careers With Nonprofit Organizations*
- *Jobs for Travel Lovers*
- *Jobs in Russia and the Newly Independent States*

Many other books examine a wide range of jobs and careers. Some are annual or biannual reviews of today's most popular jobs. You should find several of these books particularly helpful:

- *50 Coolest Jobs in Sports*, David Fischer (Arco)
- *100 Best Careers For the 21st Century*, Shelly Fields (Arco)
- *101 Careers*, Michael Markavy (Wiley & Sons)
- *Adams Jobs Almanac* (Adams Media)
- *American Almanac of Jobs and Salaries*, John W. Wright (Avon)
- *Careers Encyclopedia*, Craig T. Norback, ed. (McGraw-Hill)
- *Cool Careers for Dummies*, Nemko and Edwards (IDG)
- *High-Tech Careers for Low-Tech People*, William Schaffer (Ten Speed)
- *Jobs Rated Almanac*, Les Krantz (St. Martin)

If you are unable to find these books in your local library or bookstore, they can be ordered directly from Impact Publications (www.impactpubli cations.com).

Target Organizations

After completing research on occupational alternatives, you should identify specific organizations which you are interested in learning more about. Next, compile lists of names, addresses, and telephone numbers of important individuals in each organization. Also, explore the home pages of various companies on the World Wide Web and write or telephone them for information, such as an annual report and recruiting literature.

The most important information you should be gathering concerns the organizations' goals, structures, functions, problems, and projected future opportunities and development. Since you invest part of your life in such organizations, treat them as you would a stock market investment. Compare and evaluate different organizations.

Several directories will assist you in researching organizations. Most are available in the reference sections of libraries:

- *Almanac of American Employers*
- *Directory of American Firms Operating in Foreign Countries*
- *The Directory of Corporate Affiliations: Who Owns Whom*
- *Dun & Bradstreet's Middle Market Directory*
- *Dun & Bradstreet's Million Dollar Directory*
- *Dun & Bradstreet's Reference Book of Corporate Managements*
- *Encyclopedia of Business Information Sources*
- *Fitch's Corporation Reports*
- *MacRae's Blue Book*
- *Moody's Manuals*
- *The Multinational Marketing and Employment Directory*
- *Plunkett's Companion to the Almanac of American Employers: Mid-Size Firms*
- *Standard & Poor's Industrial Index*
- *Standard Rate and Data Business Publications Directory*
- *Thomas' Register of American Manufacturers*

Many of the business research websites we identified on pages 216-217 are "must surfing" sites for job seekers. If you have only time to visit a few of these sites, make sure they include our top six:

- CEO Express www.ceoexpress.com
- Hoover's Online www.hoovers.com
- Dun & Bradstreet's
 Million Dollar Database www.dnbmdd.com/mddi
- Corporate Information www.corporateinformation.com
- BizTech Network www.brint.com
- Plunkett Research www.plunkettresearch.com

If you are interested in jobs with a particular organization, you should visit their website for employment information and/or contact the human resources office for information on the types of jobs offered within the organization. Many companies include an extensive and relatively sophisticated employment section on their home page that allows individuals to enter their resumes into a company database or apply online for specific positions. Indeed, companies are increasingly recruiting online for all types of positions, from entry level to top management. Good examples include Cisco Systems (www.cisco.com), Motorola (www.motorola.com), Microsoft (www.microsoft.com), and the Boston Consulting Group (www.bcg.com). You may be able to examine vacancy announcements which describe the duties and responsibilities of specific jobs as well as survey the profiles of key company personnel. Some companies even include information about the company culture and tips on conducting an effective job search with the company! Most of the top companies we identify in the next few sections include employment information on their websites.

If you are interested in working for federal, state, or local governments, each agency will have a personnel office which can supply you with descriptions of their jobs. To gain quick Internet access to **federal government** agencies, including vacancy announcements, go to the following websites:

- FedWorld www.fedworld.gov
- USA Jobs www.usajobs.opm.gov
- FederalJobsCentral www.fedjobs.com
- Federal Jobs Digest www.jobfed.com

If you wish to work in **law enforcement**, visit these websites:

- Law Enforcement Jobs www.lawenforcementjobs.com
- Cop Career.com www.copcareer.com
- Job Cop www.jobcop.com

Individuals oriented toward working in the **nonprofit sector** should visit these useful gateway websites:

- GuideStar www.guidestar.org
- Action Without Borders www.idealist.org
- Foundation Center www.fdncenter.org
- Independent Sector www.independentsector.org
- Internet Nonprofit Center www.nonprofits.org

Identify Today's Top Employers

Each year several organizations conduct surveys to identify who are reputed to be today's top employers. We prefer the *Fortune* magazine annual surveys. You can access their most recent surveys by going to the home page of their website: www.fortune.com. They identified the following 100 employers as the best ones to work for in 2005, which appeared in the January 24, 2005, issue of *Fortune*:

Large Companies (10,000 - 200,000 employees)

1.	Wegmans Food Markets	www.wegmans.com
2.	Starbucks	www.starbucks.com
3.	Valero Energy	www.valero.com
4.	Cisco Systems	www.cisco.com
5.	Whole Foods Market	www.wholefoodsmarket.com
6.	Baptist Health So. Florida	www.baptisthealth.net
7.	Amgen	www.amgen.com
8.	Goldman Sachs	www.gs.com
9.	American Express	www.americanexpress.com
10.	Synovus	www.synovus.com
11.	Four Seasons Hotels	www.fourseasons.com
12.	Station Casinos	www.stationcasinos.com
13.	A.G. Edwards	www.agedwards.com
14.	Microsoft	www.microsoft.com
15.	General Mills	www.generalmills.com
16.	Principal Financial Group	www.principal.com
17.	Marriott International	www.marriott.com
18.	Procter & Gamble	www.pg.com
19.	First Horizon National	www.firsthorizon.com
20.	Medtronic	www.medtronic.com
21.	Vanguard Group	www.vanguard.com
22.	Eli Lilly	www.lilly.com
23.	Booz Allen Hamilton	www.boozallen.com

24.	Pfizer	www.pfizer.com
25.	Ernst & Young	www.ey.com
26.	Mayo Clinic	www.mayoclinic.org
27.	PricewaterhouseCoopers	www.pwc.com
28.	Popular	www.bancopopular.com
29.	Texas Instruments	www.ti.com
30.	CarMax	www.carmax.com
31.	Nordstrom	www.nordstrom.com
32.	MBNA	www.mbna.com
33.	Deloitte & Touche	www.deloitte.com
34.	Publix Super Markets	www.publix.com
35.	FedEx	www.fedex.com
36.	Bright Horizons	www.brighthorizons.com
37.	Sherwin-Williams	www.sherwin-williams.com

Midsized Companies (2,500 - 9,000 employees)

1.	W.L. Gore	www.gore.com
2.	Genentech	www.gene.com
3.	J.M. Smucker	www.smuckers.com
4.	S.C. Johnson & Son	www.scjohnson.com
5.	CDW	www.cdw.com
6.	SAS Institute	www.sas.com
7.	Qualcomm	www.qualcomm.com
8.	QuikTrip	www.quiktrip.com
9.	JM Family Enterprises	www.jmfamily.com
10.	American Cast Iron Pipe	www.acipco.com
11.	Bronson Healthcare Group	www.bronsonhealth.com
12.	Pella	www.pella.com
13.	Alcon Laboratories	www.alconlabs.com
14.	Symantec	www.symantec.om
15.	SRA International	www.sra.com
16.	Recreational Equip. (REI)	www.REI.com
17.	Memorial Health	www.memorialhealth.com
18.	Guidant	www.guidant.com
19.	MITRE	www.mitre.org
20.	Hot Topic	www.hottopic.com
21.	IKEA North America	www.ikea-usa.com
22.	Intuit	www.intuit.com
23.	Aflac	www.aflac.com
24.	Discovery Communications	www.discovery.com
25.	St. Luke's Episcopal Hlth.	www.stlukestexas.com
26.	Emmis Communications	www.emmis.com
27.	Wm. Wrigley Jr.	www.wrigley.com

28. Granite Construction	www.graniteconstruction.com
29. Monsanto	www.monsanto.com
30. Men's Warehouse	www.menswearhouse.com
31. Harley-Davidson	www.harley-davidson.com
32. Simmons	www.simmons.com
33. Roche	www.roche.us

Small Companies (1,000 - 2,400 employees)

1. Republic Bancorp.	www.republicbancorp.com
2. Xilinx	www.xilinx.com
3. Griffin Hospital	www.griffinhealth.org
4. Alston & Bird	www.alston.com
5. Vision Service Plan	www.vsp.com
6. Quicken Loans	www.quickenloans.com
7. Adobe Systems	www.adobe.com
8. Container Store	www.containerstore.com
9. Robert W. Baird	www.rwbaird.com
10. HomeBanc Mortgage	www.homebanc.com
11. David Weekley Homes	www.davidweekleyhomes.com
12. TDIndustries	www.tdindustries.com
13. Network Appliance	www.netapp.com
14. American Century Invest.	www.americancentury.com
15. Stew Leonard's	www.steleonards.com
16. Arnold & Porter	www.arnoldporter.com
17. American Fidelity Assur.	www.afadvantage.com
18. Timberland	www.timberland.com
19. National Instruments	www.ni.com
20. Plante & Moran	www.plantemoran.com
21. Kimley-Horn & Assoc.	www.kimley-horn.com
22. Perkins Coie	www.perkinscoie.com
23. Sterling Bank	www.banksterling.com
24. Arbitron	www.arbitron.com
25. SEI Investments	www.seic.com
26. Bingham McCutchen	www.bingham.com
27. Morrison & Foerster	www.mofo.com
28. John Wiley & Sons	www.wiley.com
29. Valassis	www.valassis.com

Fortune's most recent annual survey (published in September 5, 2005) also identified the following 100 employers as the **hottest (fastest growing)** ones for 2005:

1.	Yahoo	Sunnyvale, CA
2.	Compucredit	Atlanta, GA
3.	Ceradyne	Costa Mesa, CA
4.	Vineyard National Bancorp	Rancho Cucamonga, CA
5.	Laserscope	San Jose, CA
6.	Kos Pharmaceuticals	Canbury, NY
7.	ASV	Grand Rapids, MI
8.	Sandisk	Sunnyvale, CA
9.	Imergent	Orem, UT
10.	Clinical Data	Newton, MA
11.	J2 Global Communications	Los Angeles, CA
12.	Omnivision Technologies	Sunnyvale, CA
13.	Eresearchtechnology	Philadelphia, PA
14.	Sonic Solutions	Novato, CA
15.	Deckers Outdoor	Goleta, CA
16.	Lifecell	Branchburg, NU
17.	Schnitzer Steel Industries	Portland, OR
18.	Central European Distribution	Bala Cynwyd, PA
19.	Valero Energy	San Antonio, TX
20.	Southern Peru Copper	Phoenix, AZ
21.	Cognizant Technology Solutions	Teaneck, NJ
22.	American Healthways	Nashville, TN
23.	Comtech Telecommunications	Melville, NJ
24.	Devon Energy	Oklahoma City, OK
25.	William Lyon Homes	Newport Beach, CA
26.	Maverick Tube	Chesterville, MO
27.	Friedman Billings Ramsey Group	Arlington, VA
28.	Middleby	Elgin, IL
29.	Gilead Sciences	Foster City, CA
30.	Genentech	South San Francisco, CA
31.	Stell Dynamics	Fort Wayne, TX
32.	Healthestras	Rockville, MD
33.	Silicon Laboratories	Austin, TX
34.	Euronet Worldwide	Leawood, KS
35.	eBay	San Jose, CA
36.	SFBC International	Miami, FL
37.	Hansen Natural	Corona, CA
38.	Advanced Neuromodulation Systems	Plano, TX
39.	Urban Outfitters	Philadelphia, PA
40.	Edge Petroleum	Houston, TX
41.	Conocophillips	Houston, TX
42.	Consolidate-Tomoka Land	Daytona Beach, FL
43.	Countrywide Financial	Calabasas, CA

44.	Coach	New York, NY
45.	Overseas Shipholding Group	New York, NY
46.	Chesapeake Energy	Oklahoma City, OK
47.	Armor Holdings	Jacksonville, FL
48.	Bluegreen	Boca Raton, FL
49.	Biosite	San Diego, CA
50.	Collegiate Pacific	Dallas, TX
51.	Chico's FAS	Fort Myers, FL
52.	Remington Oil and Gas	Dallas, TX
53.	Sands Regent	Reno, NV
54.	Holly	Dallas, TX
55.	Pioneer Natural Resources	Irving, TX
56.	Endo Pharamaceuticals Holdings	Chadds Ford, PA
57.	Capital Title Group	Scottsdale, AZ
58.	Headwaters	South Jordan, UT
59.	Leucadia National	New York, NY
60.	Packeteer	Cupertino, CA
61.	Pixar Animation Studios	Emeryville, CA
62.	Newmont Mining	Denver, CO
63.	Nucor	Charlotte, NC
64.	Hovnanian Enterprises	Red Bank, NJ
65.	Symantec	Cupertino, CA
66.	Stratasys	Eden Prairie, MN
67.	Constellation Energy Group	Baltimore, MD
68.	Webex Communications	Santa Clara, CA
69.	W.R. Berkley	Greenwich, CT
70.	St. Mary Land & Exploration	Denver, CO
71.	Sanders Morris Harris Group	Houston, TX
72.	Bentley Pharmaceuticals	Exeter, NH
73.	Universal American Financial	Rye Brook, NY
74.	XTO Energy	Fort Worth, TX
75.	Navigant Consulting	Chicago, IL
76.	Energy Partners	New Orleans, LA
77.	Pilgrim's Pride	Pittsburg, TX
78.	Encore Wire	McKinney, TX
79.	Wilshire Bancorp	Los Angeles, CA
80.	Career Education	Hoffman Estates, IL
81.	Websense	San Diego, CA
82.	Boston Scientific	Natick, MA
83.	TTM Technologies	Santa Ana, CA
84.	Proassurance	Birmingham, AL
85.	Penn Virginia	Radnor, PA
86.	Quality Systems	Irvine, CA
87	Carrizo Oil & Gas	Houston, TX

88.	Odyssey Re Holdings	Stamford, CT
89.	Meritage Homes	Scottsdale, AZ
90	United Panam Financial	Newport Beach, CA
91.	American Capital Strategies	Bethesda, MD
92.	Penn National Gaming	Wyomissing, PA
93.	Engineered Support Systems	St. Louis, MO
94.	Standard Pacific	Irvine, CA
95.	Talx	St. Louis, MO
96.	Cal Dive International	Houston, TX
97.	Berry Petroleum	Bakersfield, CA
98.	Encore Acquisition	Fort Worth, TX
99.	Apache	Houston, TX
100.	Commercial Metals	Irving, TX

Fortune also annually (March) identifies nearly 600 of the most respected companies as ranked by 10,000 executives, directors, and seasoned analysts and classifies them by 65 major industries. The top company in each of these industries for 2005 included:

Finance Industry	**Most Respected Company**
▪ Securities	Bear Stearns
▪ Megabanks	Bank of America
▪ Superregional Banks	Mellon Financial
▪ Consumer Credit	American Express
▪ Mortgage Services	Golden West Financial
▪ Insurance: Life, Health	Northwestern Mutual
▪ Insurance: Property, Casualty	Berkshire Hathaway

Consumer Products

▪ Food Production	Tyson Foods
▪ Beverages	Anheuser-Busch
▪ Consumer Food Products	PepsiCo
▪ Apparel	Liz Claiborne
▪ Household, Personal Products	Procter & Gamble
▪ Tobacco	Altria Group

Contracted Services

▪ Diversified Outsourcing	Cintas
▪ Temporary Help	Manpower
▪ Health Care	UnitedHealth Group

Shelter

- Furniture Herman Miller
- Real Estate Boston Properties
- Home Equipment, Furnishings Fortune Brands
- Engineering, Construction Jacobs Engineering Group
- Homebuilders Centex

Stores and Distribution

- Wholesalers: Electronic, Office CDW
- Wholesales: Diversified Hughes Supply
- Wholesalers: Food, Grocery CHS
- Wholesalers: Health Care Patterson Dental
- General Merchandisers Wal-Mart Stores
- Specialty Retailers Home Depot
- Food and Drug Stores Walgreen
- Food Services Starbucks

Computers and Communications

- Computers IBM
- Computer and Data Services Accenture
- Computer Software Intuit
- Telecommunications Verizon Communications
- Network Communications Qualcomm
- Computer Peripherals Storage Technology

Natural Resources

- Mining, Crude-Oil Production Apache
- Metals Alcoa
- Pharmaceuticals Johnson & Johnson
- Packaging, Containers Pactiv
- Chemicals BASF
- Forest and Paper Products International Paper

Power

- Petroleum Refining BP
- Electric and Gas Utilities Exelon
- Energy Constellation Energy
- Oil and Gas Equipment Svcs. FMC Technologies
- Pipelines Kinder Morgan Energy Prtnrs.

Precision

▪ Semiconductors	Texas Instruments
▪ Electronics	General Electric
▪ Precision Equipment	3M
▪ Medical Products, Equipment	Styker

Media and Entertainment

▪ Entertainment	Walt Disney
▪ Newspapers	New York Times
▪ Hotels, Casinos, Resorts	Marriott International
▪ Printing	R.R. Donnelley & Sons
▪ Advertising, Marketing	Omnicom Group

Things That Move

▪ Airlines	Southwest Airlines
▪ Motor-Vehicle Parts	Lear
▪ Industrial and Farm Equip.	Illinois Tool Works
▪ Transportation, Logistics	C.H. Robinson Worldwide
▪ Railroads	Norfolk Southern
▪ Delivery	FedEx
▪ Aerospace, Defense	United Technologies
▪ Trucking	Yellow Roadway
▪ Automotive Retailing, Svcs.	AutoNation
▪ Motor Vehicles	Toyota Motor

If you are a minority, you may be interested in researching the 50 best employers for **minorities** identified by *Fortune* magazine in 2005:

▪ **Abbot Laboratories**	www.abbott.com
▪ **Aetna**	www.aetna.com
▪ **Aflac**	www.aflac.com
▪ **Alcoa**	www.alcoa.com
▪ **Applied Materials**	www.appliedmaterials.com
▪ **Aramark**	www.aramark.com
▪ **Archstone-Smith**	www.archstonesmith.com
▪ **AT&T**	www.att.com
▪ **Avon Products**	www.avoncompany.com
▪ **BellSouth**	www.bellsouth.com
▪ **Brinker International**	www.brinker.com
▪ **Cisco Systems**	www.cisco.com
▪ **Citigroup**	www.citigroup.com
▪ **Coca-Cola**	www.cocacola.com

- DaimlerChrysler — www.daimlerchrysler.com
- Darden Restaurants — www.dardenrestaurants.com
- DTE Energy — www.dteenergy.com
- DuPont — www.dupont.com
- FedEx — www.fedex.com
- Freddie Mac — www.freddiemac.com
- General Motors — www.gm.com
- Golden West Financial — www.gdw.com
- H.J. Heinz Company — www.heinz.com
- Hilton Hotels — www.hiltonworldwide.com
- HSBN-North America — www.hsbcnorthamerica.com
- Intel — www.intel.com
- JPMorgan Chase — www.jpmorganchase.com
- Kellogg Company — www.kelloggcompany.com
- Knight-Ridder — www.kri.com
- Lucent Technologies — www.lucent.com
- Marriott International — www.marriott.com
- Nike — www.nike.com
- Nordstrom — www.nordstrom.com
- PacificCare Health Systems — www.pacificare.com
- Pepco Childings, Inc. — www.pepcoholdings.com
- PepsiCo — www.pepsico.com
- PG&E Corp. — www.pgecorp.com
- Pitney Bowes — www.pb.com
- PONM Resources Inc. — www.pnm.com
- Prudential Financial — www.prudential.com
- Safeway Inc. — www.safeway.com
- SBC Communications — www.sbc.com
- Sempra Energy — www.sempra.com
- Southern California Edison — www.sce.com
- Texas Instruments — www.ti.com
- TIAA-CREF — www.tiaa-cref.com
- Time Warner Inc. — www.timewarner.com
- Tribune Company — www.tribune.com
- United Parcel Service — www.ups.com
- Wells Fargo & Co. — www.wellsfargo.com
- Yum! Brands Inc. — www.yum.com

CollegeGrad.com (www.collegegrad.com) identified the following 33 companies and organizations as being the **top entry-level employers**, which were projected to hire from 1,000 to 7,000 new employees each in 2005:

- Enterprise Rent-A-Car 7,000
- Lockheed Martin 4,300
- Walgreen Company 4,300
- PricewaterhouseCoopers 3,200
- Federal Bureau of Investigation 3,000
- Schlumerger 3,000
- U.S. Department of Agriculture 3,000
- Ernst & Young 2,900
- Cendant Car Rental Group 2,500
- Hertz 2,500
- IBM 2,250
- Target 2,250
- U.S. Customs and Border Protection 2,250
- KPMG 2,240
- Teach for America 2,100
- Jos. A. Bank Clothiers 2,086
- Deloitte & Touche 1,800
- Wells Fargo 1,800
- Boeing 1,600
- National Security Agency 1,600
- Accenture 1,500
- Intel 1,500
- 84 Lumber 1,300
- Wal-Mart Stores 1,300
- Northrop Grumman 1,265
- Cerner 1,200
- General Electric 1,100
- Johnson & Johnson 1,100
- Finish Line 1,100
- Raytheon 1,000
- PNC Financial Services Group 1,000
- National Cancer Institute 1,000
- SBC Communications 1,000

If you or your spouse is a **working mother,** or soon to be working mother, you should research this list of the top 100 family-friendly employers, which is published annually (October) by *Working Mother* magazine. These are family-friendly companies that offer generous child-care and educational services, flexible work schedules, and attractive leave policies. For October 2005, the 100 best companies for working mothers included:

- Abbott Laboratories www.abbott.com
- Accenture www.accenture.com

- Allstate Insurance Company — www.allstate.com
- American Express Company — www.americanexpress.com
- Ameritas Acacia Companies — www.ameritasacacia.com
- Arnold & Porter — www.arnoldporter.com
- Astrazeneca — www.astrazeneca-us.com
- Avon Products — www.avon.com
- Bank of America — www.bankofamerica.com
- Baptist Health South Florida — www.baptisthealth.net
- Bayer Corporation — www.bayerus.com
- Bayfront Health System — www.bayfront.org
- Bon Secours Richmond Health System — www.bonsecours.com
- Booz Allen Hamilton — www.boozallen.com
- BP America — www.bp.com
- Bristol-Myers Squibb — www.bma.com
- Bronson Healthcare Group — www.bronsonhealth.com
- Children's Healthcare of Atlanta — www.choa.org
- Children's Memorial Hospital — www.childrensmemorial.org
- Cinergy Corporation — www.cinergy.com
- Cisco Systems — www.cisco.com
- Citigroup — www.citigroup.com
- Cleveland Clinic Foundation — www.clevelandclinic.org
- Colgate-Palmolive Company — www.colgate.com
- Credit Suisse First Boston — www.csfb.com
- Deloitte & Touche USA — www.deloitte.com
- Deutsche Bank — www.db.com
- Discovery Communications — www.discovery.com
- Dow Corning Corporation — www.dowcorning.com
- Dupont — www.dupont.com
- Eli Lilly and Company — www.lilly.com
- Ernst & Young — www.ey.com
- Fannie Mae — www.fanniemae.com
- First Horizon National Corp. — www.firsthorizon.com
- First National Bank — www.firstnational.com
- Ford Motor Company — www.ford.com
- Freddie Mac — www.freddiemac.com
- Genentech — www.gene.com
- General Electric Company — www.ge.com
- General Mills — www.generalmills.com
- General Motors — www.gm.com
- Glaxosmithkline — www.gsk.com
- Harvard University — www.harvard.edu
- Hewlett-Packard Company — www.hp.com
- HSBC-North America — www.hsbcusa.com

- IBM Corporation — www.ibm.com
- IKEA — www.ikea.com
- Inova Health System — www.inova.org
- Intel Corporation — www.intel.com
- JFK Medical Center — www.jfkmc.com
- Johnson & Johnson — www.jnj.com
- JPMorgan Chase — www.jpmorganchase.com
- King's Daughters Medical Center — www.kdmc.com
- KPMG LLP — www.us.kpmg.com
- Lego Systems — www.lego.com
- Lehman Brothers — www.lehman.com
- Lincoln Financial Group — www.lfg.com
- Marriott International — www.marriott.com
- Massachusetts Mutual Life Insurance Company — www.massmutual.com
- MBNA American Bank, N.A. — www.mbna.com
- McGraw-Hill Companies — www.mcgraw-hill.com
- Merck & Company — www.merck.com
- Metlife, Inc. — www.metlife.com
- Microsoft Corporation — www.microsoft.com
- Morgan Stanley — www.morganstanley.com
- Motorola — www.motorola.com
- Northern Trust Corporation — www.northerntrust.com
- Northwestern Memorial Healthcare — www.nmh.org
- Novartis Pharmaceuticals — www.novartis.com
- Patagonia, Inc. — www.patagonia.com
- Pearson Education — www.pearsoned.com
- Pfizer Inc. — www.pfizer.com
- Phoenix Companies — www.phoenixwm.com
- Pitt County Memorial Hospital — www.uhseast.com
- PNC Financial Services Group — www.pnc.com
- Pricewaterhousecoopers — www.pwc.com
- Principal Financial Group — www.principal.com
- Procter & Gamble Company — www.pg.com
- Providence Alaska Medical Ctr. — www.providence.org
- Prudential Financial — www.prudential.com
- Republic Bancorp — www.republicbancorp.com
- S.C. Johnson & Son — www.scjohnson.com
- St. Mary's Medical Center — www.st-marys.org
- Schering-Plough — www.schering-plough.com
- Scripps Health — www.scripps.org
- Shawnee Mission Medical Center — www.shawneemission.org
- Texas Instruments — www.ti.com
- Timberland Company — www.timberland.com

- Trihealth www.trihealth.com
- Turner Broadcasting System www.turner.com
- UBS www.ubs.com
- Union Pacific Railroad www.up.com
- USAA www.usaa.com
- Verizon Wireless www.verizonwireless.com
- Virginia Commonwealth
 University Health System www.vcuhealth.org
- Wachovia Corporation www.wachovia.com
- West Virginia University
 Hospitals www.health.wvu.edu
- Wyeth www.wyeth.com
- Yale-New Haven Hospital www.ynhh.org
- Zurich in North America www.zurichna.com

Other lists of top employers (employee-owned, employers of choice, world's most respected, for Latinas, for executive women, etc.) can be conveniently accessed from the Quintessential and JobStar websites:

> www.quintcareers.com/best_place_to_work.html
> www.jobstar.org

Survey Military-Friendly Employers

Most employers recognize the value of hiring ex-military. However, certain companies take action by disproportionately hiring transitioning military personnel.

Most transitioning military are familiar with the nine largest military contractors:

- Boeing-MacDonnell
 Douglas
- General Dynamics
- General Electric
- General Motors
- Grumman
- Lockheed
- Martin Marietta
- Raytheon
- United Technologies

However, few people are knowledgeable about smaller contractors that do work with various military-, intelligence-, and security-related agencies of the government. Many of these companies specialize in such critical technology areas as chemical and biological systems, electronics, guidance and navigation control, information warfare, marine systems, nuclear systems, sensors and lasers, signature control, space systems, and weapons effects and countermeasures. In addition, many nonmilitary-related employers, including such large retailers as Wal-Mart, Target, and Home

Research Tip: "Follow the money" is a good rule to observe when trying to locate military-friendly employers. Each week several firms receive millions of dollars in contracts from the federal government for performing a variety of services. Once awarded contracts, these firms need to "staff up" for projects. If you know which firms receive contracts, you'll know who has new hiring needs. One of the best sources for following the money is the Monday business section of *The Washington Post.* Here, under "Contracts Awarded," you'll find a list of companies that have just been awarded federal government contracts. This section identifies the name of the company, size of the award, and the nature of the project. For example, on October 3, 2005, these three contracts were listed among 41 contracts:

> **CACI International Inc.** of Arlington; **Camber Corp.** of Huntsville, Ala.; **Dynamics Research Corp.** of Andover, Mass.; **Northrop Grumman Corp.** of Los Angeles; and **Research Triangle Institute** of Research Triangle Park, N.C., will share a $97 million, five-year contract from the U.S. Army Armor Center for training and combat development for the Army's Future Combat Systems.

> **EAI Corp.** of Abingdon, Va., won a $21.5 million contract from the Marine Corps Logistics Command to support the Commercial Equipment Direct Assistance Program, a Homeland Security Department-sponsored program helping state and local agencies provide first responders with selected equipment and training for natural and man-made crises.

> **Anteon Corp.** of Fairfax won a $6.1 million contract from the Naval Surface Warfare Center for continuing surface combat system configuration management, technical, and administrative support.

A good researcher might be interested in contacting some of these companies to inquire about their current personnel needs, especially related to such projects. Once you follow the money in this manner, you'll quickly identify companies that are very military-friendly, since they work with government agencies that do military-related work. Much of this work requires the expertise of ex-military personnel who have specialized knowledge and skills acquired while working in the military.

Depot, are eager to hire ex-military because of the positive attitudes, work habits, skills, and learning and leadership abilities they bring to the job.

The following companies, most of which recruit in the Washington, DC metropolitan area, regularly seek ex-military through classified ads, websites, and job fairs. Many of these companies also have operations elsewhere in the country as well as abroad. If you are interested in working for a military-friendly employer, visit the websites of these companies for information on what they do and how to apply for positions:

- AAI Corporation www.aaicorp.com
- Advanced Resource
 Technologies Inc. www.team-arti.com
- AFLAC www.aflac.com
- Alban Caterpillar www.albancat.com
- Alion Science and Technology www.alionscience.com
- Altarum www.altarum.org
- American Casino and www.stratospherehotel.com/
 Entertainment Properties employment/
- American Systems Corporation www.2asc.com
- Anteon Corporation www.anteon.com/careers
- ARAMARK – Healthcare www.aramark.com
- Argon ST Inc. www.argonst.com
- ASM Research www.asmr.com
- Atlas Van Lines International www.atlasintl.com
- BearingPoint www.bearingpoint.com
- Bell Helicopter Textron www.bellhelicopter.textron.
 com
- Beta Analytics International www.betaanalytics.com
- Blackwater USA www.blackwaterusa.com
- Booz Allen Hamilton www.boozallen.com
- Burlington Northern
 Santa Fe Railway www.bnsf.com
- CACI www.caci.com
- CALIBRE www.calibresys.com
- Camber Corporation www.camber.com
- Carson Solutions, LLC www.carsonsolutionsllc.com
- Centennial Contractors
 Enterprises www.cce-inc.com
- COLSA Corporation www.colsa.com
- Computer Sciences Corp. http://careers.csc.com
- Comtech Mobile Datacom www.comtechmobile.com
- CVS Pharmacy www.careers-cvs.com
- DaimlerChrysler www.cap.daimlerchrysler.
 com
- Daston Corporation www.daston.com
- DCS Corporation www.dcscorp.com
- Decisive Analytics Corp. www.dac.us
- Defense Intelligence Agency www.dia.mil/employment
- DESE Research www.aag.dese.com
- Dynamics Research Corp. www.drc.com
- EAI Corporation www.eaicorp.com
- EDO Corporation www.edo-services.com
- EG&G Technical Services www.egginc.com

- Federal Aviation Administration — www.faa.gov
- First Command Financial Planning — www.firstcommand.com
- GC Services — www.gcserv.com
- General Dynamics Network Systems — www.gd-ns.com/careers
- Global Professional Solutions — www.gps.hq.com
- GMRI — www.gmri.com
- Home Depot — www.careers.homedepot.com
- Honeywell Technology Solutions — www.honeywell-tsi.com
- Inova Health System — www.inova.org/careers
- Institute for Defense Analyses — www.ida.org
- IntelliDyne — www.intellidyne-llc.com
- International and Development Resources — www.idrnet.com
- Integic Corporation — www.integic.com
- JB Management — www.jbmanagement.com
- Jiffy Lube — www.jiffylube.com
- KBR — www.kbrjobs.com
- L-3 Communications GSI — www.L-3gsi.com
- Leads Corporation — www.LeadsCorp.com
- Lockheed Martin — www.lockheedmartin.com
- Logistics Management Resources — www.lmr-inc.com
- ManTech International — www.mantech.com
- Mastec Advanced Technologies — www.mastec.com
- Miele — www.miele.com/cg
- Military Sealift Command — www.sealiftcommand.com
- MPRI — www.mpri.com
- MTC Technologies — www.mtctechnologies.com
- MTS Technologies — www.mtstech.com
- National Geospatial-Intelligence Agency — www.nga.mil
- Nortel PEC Solutions — www.nortelpec.com
- Northrop Grumman — http://careers.northropgrumman.com
- Northwest Federal Credit Union — www.northwestfcu.org
- Office of Naval Intelligence — www.nmic.navy.mil
- OMNIPLEX World Services Corp. — www.omniplex.com
- Overseas Military Sales Corp. — www.encs.com
- Pentagon Force Protection Agency — www.pfpa.mil
- Perot Systems Government Srvs. — www.perotsystems.com
- Pfizer Pharmaceuticals — www.pfizer.com
- Pragmatics — www.pragmatics.com
- PricewaterhouseCoopers — www.pwc.com

- Professional Services
 www.profserve.com/careers.php
- Prudential Financial
 www.prudential com
- Quantum Research International
 www.quantum-intl.com
- Raytheon
 www.rayjobs.com
- RDR
 www.rdr.com/careers
- Ryan's Restaurant Group
 www.ryans.com
- SAIC
 www.saic.com
- Securitas Security Services USA
 www.securitasinc.com
- Sentara Healthcare
 www.sentara.com
- Southwest Airlines
 www.southwest.com
- SRA International
 www.sra.com/career/
- Stanley Associates
 www.stanleyassociates.com
- State Farm Insurance
 www.statefarm.com
- SY Coleman Corporation
 www.sycoleman.com
- Systems Planning and Analysis
 www.spa.com
- Target Corporation
 www.target.com/careers
- Tidewater Skanska
 www.usacivil.skanska.com
- The Titan Corporation
 www.titan.com
- The Shaw Group
 www.shawgrp.com
- U.S. Army Reserve
 www.goarmy.com
- U.S. Coast Guard (civilian careers)
 www.uscg.mil/hq/cgpc/cpm/jobs
- U.S. Secret Service
 www.secretservice.gov
- United Laboratories
 www.beearthsmart.com
- University of Maryland Department of Public Safety
 www.umpd.umd.edu
- Verizon FNS
 www22.verizon.com/fns
- Vinnell Corporation
 www.vinnell.com
- Virginia Hospital Center
 www.virginiahospitalcenter.com
- Virginia Linen Service
 www.virginialinen.com
- VISTA Technology Services
 www.vistatsi.com
- Weichert, Realtors
 www.weichert.com
- Wexford Group International
 www.thewexfordgroup.com
- Zel Technologies
 www.zeltech.com/employment

Most state departments of corrections, local police departments, local governments as well as any company dealing with security issues are particularly interested in recruiting ex-military personnel. Examples of such groups that regularly recruit transitioning military include:

- Arlington (VA) County www.arlingtonva.us/
 Sheriff's Office departments/sheriff/
 Sheriffmain.aspx
- Athens-Clarke County Unified www.athensclarkecounty.
 Government com/~jobs
- California Department of
 Corrections www.cdcr.ca.gov
- County of Los Angeles http://lacounty.info
- Fort Lauderdale Police
 Department www.flpd.org
- Georgia Department of
 Corrections www.dcor.state.ga.us
- San Diego Sheriff's Department www.sdsheriff.net/jobs

The following 200+ companies recruit individuals with **military intelligence backgrounds**. Many – but not all – of the positions advertised with these firms require top secret clearances:

- AboutWeb www.aboutweb.com
- Accenture www.accenture.com
- Acclaim Technical Services www.acclaimtechnical.com
- ACS Defense Services www.acsdefense.com
- Action Technologies www.actiontech.com
- Advanced Concepts www.aci-hq.com/jobs.php
- Aegis Research Corporation www.aegisresearch.com
- Alion Science and Technology www.alionscience.com
- All World Language Consultants www.alcinc.com
- Alliant Techsystems www.atk.com
- Alphainsight Corporation www.alphainsight.com
- Analysis Group www.analysisgroup.com
- Analytic Services www.anser.org
- American Systems Corporation www.2asc.com
- Anteon Corporation www.anteon.com
- Applied Integrated Technologies www.ait-i.com
- Applied Marine Technology www.amti.net
- Applied System Technology www.astusa.com
- Applied Systems Research www.asr-reman.com
- Applied Signal Technology www.appsig.com
- Aerospace Corporation www.aero.org
- AT&T Government Solutions www.att.com/hr
- BAE Systems www.eis.na.baesystems.com
- BAE Systems, North America www.baesystems.com
- BAE Systems–Analytical Solutions www.mevatec.com
- BAE Systems–Enterprise Systems www.esi.na.baesystems.com

- Baer Group — www.baergroup.com
- Ball Aerospace & Technologies Corporation — www.ballaerospace.com
- Battelle Memorial Institute — www.battelle.org
- Beta Analytics International — www.betaanalytics.com
- Blackwater — www.blackwaterusa.com
- Boeing–Advanced Info. Systems — www.conquestnet.com
- Boeing Company — www.boeing.com
- Boeing Satellite Systems — www.boeing.com/defense-space/space/bss
- Booz, Allen, Hamilton — www.boozallen.com
- CACI, International — www.caci.com
- Celerity IT — www.celerityit.com
- CENTRA Technology — www.centrava.com
- Central Intelligence Agency (CIA) — www.cia.gov
- Chenega Technology Services Corporation — www.ctsc.net
- CherryRoad Technologies — www.cherryroad.com
- Chugach Alaska Corporation — www.chugach-ak.com
- CGI — www.cgi.com
- Collaborx — www.collaborx.com
- Command Decisions Systems and Solutions — www.cds2.com
- COMSO — www.comso.com
- Computer Sciences Corporation — http://careers.csc.com/index.shtml
- Concurrent Technologies Corp. — www.ctc.com
- Executive Placement Associates — www.executive-placement.com
- Convergent Technologies — www.gocvt.com/index2.html
- CPSI — www.cpsinet.com
- CSSS.NET — www.csss.net
- CTGi — www.ctgusa.com/interior/over.htm
- Cubic Defense Applications Group — www.cubic.com/cda1/index.html
- Dahl Morrow International — http://dahl-morrowintl.com
- DanSources Technical Services — www.dansources.com
- Data Computer Corp. of America — www.dcca.com
- Dauntless — www.dauntless.com/dauntless/resume.do
- Delex Systems — www.delex.com
- Deloitte — http://careers.deloitte.com/gateway.aspx

- Design Staffing, LLC www.designstaffing.com
- DFI Government Services www.dfi-intl.com/govt
- Digital Receiver Technology www.drti.com
- Diligent Consulting www.diligent-us.com
- Dynamics Research Corporation www.drc.com
- Dynetics www.dynetics.com
- Eagle Alliance www.eagle-alliance.com
- EAI Corporation www.eaicorp.com
- Edge Technologies www.edge-technologies.com
- EDO Corporation www.edocorp.com
- EMW www.emu.com
- ENSCO www.ensco.com
- Esenai Corporation www.esenai.com
- Essex Corporation www.essexcorp.com
- ETG www.etgtech.com
- Exceptional Software Strategies www.exceptionalsoftware.com
- Force 3 www.force3.com
- Future Technologies www.futuretechnologies.com
- General Dynamics-C4 Systems www.gdc4s.com
- General Dynamics Advanced Information Systems www.gd-ais.com
- General Dynamics Network Systems www.gd-ns.com
- Geo-Centers www.geo-centers.com
- Global Analytic Information Technology Services www.gaits.com
- GLS Associates www.gls.net
- GMRI www.gmri.com
- Gray Hawk Systems www.mantech.com/grayhawk
- Great-Circle Technologies www.great-circletech.com
- Harris Corporation www.harris.com
- Honeywell Technology Solutions www.honeywell-tsi.com
- Houston Associates www.hai.com
- Hewlett-Packard www.hp.com
- IBM www.ibm.com/planetwide/us
- iGov www.igov.com
- Impact Innovations Group www.iig1.com
- IMSI www.imsicorp.com
- Indus Corporation www.induscorp.com
- Innovative Management and Technology Approaches www.imtas.com
- Ingenium Corporation www.ingeniumcorp.com
- Integic Corporation www.integic.com

- IntelData — www.inteldata.com
- Intervise — www.intervise.com
- In-Q-Tel — www.in-q-tel.org
- Institute for Defense Analyses — www.ida.og
- IntelliDyne — www.intellidynellc.com
- Intelligent Decisions — www.intelligent.net
- ITT Industries — www.itt.com
- JIL Information Systems — www.jil.com
- Joseph Group — www.josefgroup.com
- KEI Pearson — www.keipearson.com
- Kepler Research — www.keplerresearch.com
- Kforce — www.kforce.com
- KPMG International — www.kpmg.com
- L-3 Communications Government Services — www.eer.com
- Lingual Information System Technologies — www.lingualistek.com
- Lockhead Martin Company — www.lockheedmartin.com/careers
- Lucas Group — www.lucasgroup.com
- Maden Technologies — www.madentech.com
- ManTech International Corp. — www.mantech.com
- Matrixx Group — www.matrixx-group.com
- MAXIM Systems — www.maximsys.com
- McClendon Corporation — www.mcc-cop.com
- McDonald Bradley — www.mcdonaldbradley.com
- Meridian KSI — www.meridianksi.com
- Milestone Group — www.milestonegroup.net
- Military Sealift Command — www.sealiftcommand.com
- Minerva Engineering — www.minervaengineering.com
- Mitretek Systems — www.mitretek.org
- Miltec Corporation — www.mil-tec.com
- Mitre — www.mitre.org
- Modern Technology Solutions — www.mtsi-va.com
- MTC Technologies — www.commtechinc.com
- National Security Agency — www.nsa.gov
- NCI Information Systems — www.nciinc.com
- NJVC — https://www.njvc-llc.com
- Nortel PEC Solutions — www.pec.com
- Northrop Grumman IT — www.it.northropgrumman.com
- NW Systems — www.nw-systems.com
- Oberon Associates — www.oberonassociates.com

- Observera — www.observera.com
- Oracle Corporation — www.oracle.com
- Perot Systems Government Services — www.perotsystems.com/government
- Pinnacle CSI — www.pinncsi.com
- Planned Systems International — www.plan-sys.com
- Pluribus International Corp. — www.pluribusinternational.com
- Praxis Engineering Technologies — www.PraxisEng.com
- Premier Technology Group — www.ptginc.net
- PriceWaterhouseCoopers — www.pwglobal.com
- ProObject — www.proobject.com
- PROSOFT Engineering — www.prosoft-eng.com
- Protelligent — www.protelligent.com
- Radiance Technologies — www.radiance.com
- Raytheon — www.rayjobs.com
- Red Mill Group — www.redmillgroup.com
- Riverside Research Institute — www.rri-usa.org
- RS Information Systems — www.rsis.com
- RTGX — www.rtgx.com
- SAIC — www.saic.com
- SBI Technologies Corp. — www.sbi-tech.com
- Sebenza — www.sebenzasource.com
- SI International — www.si-intl.com
- Sierra Nevada Corporation — www.sncorp.com
- Sikorsky Aircraft Corporation — www.sikorsky.com
- SM Consulting — www.smcteam.com
- SOS International — www.sosiltd.com
- Southwestern Business Resources — www.thinkingahead.com
- Sparta — www.sparta.com
- Spatial Data Analytics Corp. — www.spadac.com
- SPS Technologies — www.spstech.net
- SRA International — www.sra.com
- Stanley Associates — www.stanleyassociates.com
- Strategic Data Systems — www.sdatasystems.com
- Sun Microsystems — www.sun.com
- SyColeman Corporation — www.sycoleman.com
- Sytex Group — www.SytexGroup.com
- TechOpps — www.techopps.net
- Tenacity Solutions — www.tenacityinc.net
- Texcom — www.texcominc.com
- Thales Communications — www.thalescomminc.com
- Titan Corp. — www.titan.com

- Trinity Technology Group www.trinitytechnology group.com
- Triton Services, Inc. www.tritonsvc.com
- Triumph Technologies www.triumph-tech.com
- Trusted Computer Solutions www.tcs.sec.com
- Unisys Corporation www.unisys.com/public_ sector/index.htm
- US Investigations Services, LLC www.usis.com
- Vaxcom Services www.vaxcom.com
- Verizon–Federal Network Systems www.verizon.com/fns
- Viatech www.viatechinc.com
- Vision Systems & Technology www.vsticorp.com
- Wallach Associates www.wallach.org
- Wexford Group International www.thewexfordgroup.com
- WFI Government Services www.htshq.com
- Windermere www.windermeregroup.com
- Winter, Wyman & Co. www.winterwyman.com
- Xelas Systems Engineering www.xelas-systems.com
- Zel Technologies www.zeltech.com
- ZKD www.zkdinc.com

Many of these and other employers interested in hiring ex-military with intelligence backgrounds can be found on Corporate Gray's, Intelligence Career's, and Security Clearance Expo's websites, which also include current job postings and sponsor "Security Clearance Only" job fairs:

<div style="text-align:center">

www.corporategray.com
www.intelligencecareers.com
www.securityclearanceexpo.com

</div>

Individuals interested in starting a business or acquiring a franchise should investigate these military-friendly companies:

- Chick-fil-A www.chick-fil-a.com
- The Entrepreneur's Source www.theesource.com

Entrepreneur Magazine includes a FranchiseZone page on its website, which is a great gateway to the world of franchise opportunities. It includes the top 500 franchises as well as over 100 of the fastest growing franchises:

<div style="text-align:center">

www.entrepreneur.com/franzone/listings/fastestgrowing/0,5844,,00.html

</div>

Chapter 19 includes additional resources for veterans interested in starting a business.

Contact Individuals

While examining websites and directories and reading books on alternative jobs and careers will provide you with useful job search information, much of this material may be too general for specifying the right job for you. In the end, the best information will come directly from people in specific jobs in specific organizations. To get this information you must interview people. You especially want to learn more about the people who make the hiring decisions.

You might begin your investigations by contacting various professional and trade associations for detailed information on jobs and careers relevant to their members. Since most of these organizations have home pages on the Internet, you should be able to locate their websites by using one of the standard search engines, such as www.google.com and www.yahoo.com, or by visiting these two gateway websites to trade and professional associations:

- Associations on the Net www.ipl.org/ref/AON
- AssociationCentral www.associationcentral.com

For names, addresses, telephone numbers, websites, e-mails, and publications of such associations, consult the following key directories, which are available in most libraries:

- *Associations USA* (Omnigraphics)
- *The Encyclopedia of Associations* (Thomson/Gale)
- *National Trade and Professional Associations* (Columbia Books)

Your most productive research activity will be talking to people or networking for information, advice, and referrals. Given your military experience, you should know many former service buddies or officers who have successfully transitioned to jobs in the civilian world. Now is the time to renew your contacts and talk with them about their jobs as well as ask for information, advice, and referrals (See Chapter 14 for details on this important networking and communication process). In some cases, their employers may actually give them a new employee referral bonus if they hire someone recommended by them. (Such networking recruitment substantially cuts the cost of recruiting employers by other means.)

Informal, word-of-mouth communication is still the most effective channel of job search information. In contrast to books or surfing the Internet, **people** have more current, detailed, and accurate information. Ask them about:

- Occupational fields
- Job requirements and training
- Interpersonal environment
- Performance expectations
- Their problems
- Salaries
- Advancement opportunities
- Future growth potential of the organization
- How to acquire more information and contacts in a particular field

You may be surprised how willingly friends, acquaintances, and strangers will give you useful information. But before you talk to people, do your research so that you will be able to ask thoughtful and relevant questions.

Ask the Right Questions

The quality of your research will only be as good as the questions you ask as you begin. Therefore, you should focus on a few key questions that will yield useful information for guiding your job search. Answers to these questions will help you make important job search decisions pursuant to informational and job interviews.

Who Has the Power to Hire?

Finding out who has the power to hire may take some research effort on your part. Keep in mind that human resources offices normally do not have the power to hire. Instead, they handle much of the paperwork involved in announcing vacancies, taking applications, testing candidates, screening credentials, and placing new employees on the payroll. In other words, personnel offices tend to perform auxiliary support functions for those who do the actual hiring – usually individuals in operating units.

If you want to learn who really has the power to hire, you need to conduct research on the particular organization that interests you. You should ask specific questions concerning who normally is responsible for various parts of the hiring process:

- Who describes the positions?
- Who announces vacancies?
- Who receives applications?
- Who administers tests?
- Who selects eligible candidates?
- Who chooses whom to interview?
- Who conducts the interview?
- Who offers the jobs?

If you ask these questions about a specific position, you will quickly identify who has what powers to hire. Chances are the power to hire is **shared** between the human resources office and the operating unit. You should not neglect the personnel office, and in some cases it will play a powerful role in all aspects of the hiring. Your research will reveal to what degree the hiring function is centralized, decentralized, or fragmented within a particular organization.

How Does Organization X Operate?

It's best to know as much as possible about the internal operations of an organization before joining it. Your research may uncover information that would convince you that a particular organization is not one in which you wish to invest your time and effort. You may learn, for example, that Company X has a history of terminating employees before they become vested in the company retirement system. Or Company Y may be experiencing serious financial problems and morale may be extremely low. They may lie to their employees or engage in unethical behavior. Or advancement within Company Z may be very political, and company politics are vicious and debilitating.

You can get financial information about most companies by examining their annual reports as well as by talking to individuals who know the organization well. Information on the internal operations, especially company politics and power, must come from individuals who work within the organization. Ask them: *"Is this a good organization to work for?"* and let them expand on specific areas you wish to probe –advancement opportunities, working conditions, relationships among co-workers and supervisors, growth patterns, internal politics, management style, work values, opportunities for taking initiative.

What Do I Need to Do to Get a
Job With Organization X?

The best way to find how to get a job in a particular organization is to follow the advice in the next chapter on prospecting, networking, and informational interviewing. This question can only be answered by talking to people who know both the formal and informal hiring practices.

You can get information on the formal hiring system by visiting the company's website or contacting the human resources office. A telephone call should be sufficient for this information.

But you must go beyond the formal system and human resources office in order to learn how best to conduct your job search. This means contacting people who know how one really gets hired in the organization, which may or may not follow the formal procedures. The best sources of information will be individuals who play a major role in the hiring process.

Identify the Right Community

Your final research target is central to all other research targets and it may occur at any stage in your research. Identifying the geographical area where you would like to work will be one of your most important decisions. Once you make this decision, other job search decisions and activities become easier. For example, if you are from a small town, you may not want to return there because of limited job and career opportunities. If you are a member of a two-career family, opportunities for both you and your spouse will be greater in a growing metropolitan area. When you decide to move to another community, you will need to develop a long-distance job search campaign which has different characteristics from a local campaign. It involves visiting community websites, writing letters, sending e-mail, making long-distance phone calls, and visiting a community for strategic one- to two-week periods during your vacation.

Deciding where you want to live involves researching various communities and comparing advantages and disadvantages of each. In addition to identifying specific job alternatives, organizations, and individuals in the community, you need to do research on other aspects of the community. After all, you will live in the community, buy or rent a residence, perhaps send children to school, and participate in community organizations and events. Often these environmental factors are just as important to your happiness and well-being as the particular job you accept. For example, as a veteran you may be leaving a $45,000 a year job for a position in your favorite community – San Francisco. But you may

quickly find you are worse off with your new $60,000 a year job, because you must pay $700,000 for a home in San Francisco that is nearly identical to the $300,000 home in your small town community. Consequently, it would be foolish for you to take a new job without first researching several facets of the community other than job opportunities.

Research on different communities can be initiated in libraries and over the Internet. While most of this research will be historical in nature, several resources will provide you with a current profile of various communities. Statistical overviews and comparisons of states and cities are found in the *U.S. Census Data, The Book for the States,* and the *Municipal Yearbook.* Many libraries have a reference section of telephone books on various cities. If this section is weak or absent in your local library, contact your local telephone company. They have a relatively comprehensive library of telephone books. In addition to giving you names, addresses, and telephone numbers, the Yellow Pages are invaluable sources of information on the specialized structures of the public and private sectors of individual communities. The library may also have state and community directories as well as subscriptions to some state and community magazines and city newspapers. Research magazine, journal, and newspaper articles on different communities by consulting several print and online references available through your local library.

The Internet has a wealth of information on the best places to live and work. For data and perspectives on the best places to live, visit these websites:

- **Find Your Spot** — www.findyourspot.com
- **Kid Friendly Cities** — www.kidfriendlycities.org
- **Money Magazine** — www.money.cnn.com/ real_estate/index.html
- **Real Estate Journal** — www.homes.wsj.com/toolkit_res/ bestplaces.html
- **Sperling's Best Places** — www.bestplaces.net
- **School Report** — theschoolreport.com

For the best places to work, check out these websites:

- **BestJobsUSA** — www.bestjobsusa.com/sections/ CAN-bestplaces2003/index.asp
- **College Grad** — www.collegegrad.com/top employers
- **EmploymentSpot** — www.employmentspot.com/lists
- **Forbes Magazine** — www.forbes.com/lists
- **Fortune Magazine** — www.fortune.com

- Great Place to Work http://greatplacetowork.com
- Quintessential Careers www.quintcareers.com/best_
 places_to_work.html
- Working Mother www.workingmother.com

If you want to explore various communities, you should examine several of these gateway community sites:

- AOL CityGuide http://digitalcity.com
- Boulevards http://boulevards.com
- Cities.com www.cities.com
- City Guide Lycos www.cityguide.lycos.com/
 destinations
- CityGuides.Yahoo www.cityguides.local.yahoo.com
- CitySearch www.citysearch.com
- City Travel Guide http://citytravelguide.com
- Insiders' Guides http://insiders.com
- USA City Link usacitylink.com
- Yahoo www.list.realestate.yahoo.com/
 re/neighborhood/main.html

Several relocation websites also provide a wealth of information on communities. Check these sites out for linkages to major communities:

- Homestore.com http://homestore.com
- Monster.com www.monstermoving.monster.com
- Relocation Central http://relocationcentral.com

Most major communities and newspapers have websites. If you have access to the Internet, you'll find a wealth of community-based information and linkages on such home pages, from newspapers and housing information to local employers, schools, recreation, and community services. If you don't have Internet access, check with your local library. Most libraries have computers connected to the Internet for use by their patrons. Several employment sites include relocation information and salary calculators which provide information on the cost of living in, as well as the cost of moving to, different communities. These five websites provide linkages to thousands of newspapers:

- Internet Public Library www.ipl.org/div/news
- NewsDirectory.com http://newsdirectory.com
- Newslink www.newslink.org
- Newspapers.com www.newspapers.com
- Online Newspapers www.onlinenewspapers.com

If you are trying to determine the best place to live, you should start with the latest edition of Bert Sperling's and Peter Sander's *Cities Ranked and Rated* and David Savageau's *Places Rated Almanac* (John Wiley & Sons). These books rank cities by various indicators. Both *Money* magazine and *U.S. News & World Report* publish annual surveys of the best places to live in the U.S.

Andrea Kay's *Greener Pastures: How to Find a Job in Another Place* (St. Martin's) outlines useful strategies for conducting a long-distance job search campaign, including the emotional and financial challenges.

You should also consult several city job banks that will give you contact information on specific employers in major metropolitan communities. Adams Media regularly publishes *The National JobBank* and 20 annual city guides:

- *Atlanta JobBank*
- *Austin/San Antonio JobBank*
- *Boston JobBank*
- *Carolina JobBank*
- *Chicago JobBank*
- *Colorado JobBank*
- *Connecticut JobBank*
- *Dallas/Fort Worth JobBank*
- *Florida JobBank*
- *Houston JobBank*
- *Los Angeles JobBank*
- *Metropolitan New York JobBank*
- *New Jersey JobBank*
- *Ohio JobBank*
- *Philadelphia JobBank*
- *Phoenix JobBank*
- *San Francisco JobBank*
- *Seattle JobBank*
- *Virginia JobBank*
- *Washington DC JobBank*

After narrowing the number of communities that interest you, research them in greater depth. Start by exploring community home pages on the Internet (search by community name). Then kick off community-based research based on the community network concept outlined at the end of Chapter 18. Ask your relatives, friends, and acquaintances for contacts in the particular community; they may know people whom you can write,

telephone, or e-mail for information and referrals. Once you have decided to focus on one community, visit it in order to establish personal contacts with key reference points, such as the local Chamber of Commerce, real estate firms, schools, libraries, churches, 40-Plus Club (if appropriate), government agencies, and business firms and associations. Begin developing personal networks utilizing upon the research and referral strategies in the next chapter. Subscribe to the local newspaper and to any community magazines which help profile the community. Follow the help-wanted, society, financial, and real estate sections of the newspaper – especially the Sunday edition. Keep a list of names of individuals who appear to hold influential community positions; you may want to contact them for referrals. Write letters to set up informational interviews with key people; give yourself two months of lead time to complete your letter writing campaign. Your overall research should focus on developing personal contacts which may assist you in both your job search and your move to the community.

Know What's Really Important

Reviewing online and print resources can be extremely time-consuming, if taken to the extreme. While you should examine several such resources, do not spend an inordinate amount of time reading, clicking, taking notes, and responding with e-mail. Embrace the Internet, but don't fall in love with it! Like working the classified ads in newspapers, the Internet tends to be a passive medium that can give you a false sense of making prog-

> *Embrace the Internet, but don't fall in love with it!*

ress with your job search – because you're keeping yourself busy entering your resume into several online resume databases and periodically reviewing job listings, message boards, and chat groups. There are too many other important proactive job search actions, such as interpersonal networking, that you need to focus your effort on. Your time will be best spent in gathering information through meetings and conversations with key people. Your primary goals in conducting research should be identifying people to contact, making appointments, and asking the right questions that lead to more information and contacts. If you engage in these activities you will know what is important when conducting research.

As you get further into your job search, networking for information, advice, and referrals will become an important element in your overall job search strategy. At that time you will come into closer contact with potential employers who can provide you with detailed information on

their organizations and specific jobs. If you have a well defined MAS, specific job objectives, and a clearly focused resume, you should be in a good position to make networking pay off with useful information, advice, and referrals. You will quickly discover that the process of linking your MAS and objectives to specific jobs is an on-going one involving several steps in your job search.

14

Network Your Way Through the Hidden Job Market

OW THAT YOU HAVE identified your skills, specified your objective, written your resume, and conducted research on alternative jobs, employers, and communities, what should you do next? At this point let's examine where you are going so you don't get preoccupied with the trees and thus lose sight of the larger forest. Let's identify the most effective methods for linking your previous job search activities to job interviews and offers. In so doing, you should be well positioned to land the critical job interview.

Focus on Getting Interviews

Everything you do up to this point in your job search should be aimed at **getting a job interview**. The skills you identified, the goals you set, the resume you wrote, and the information you gathered are carefully related to one another so you can clearly communicate your best qualifications to employers who, in turn, will decide to invite you to a job interview.

But there are secrets to getting a job interview you should know before continuing further with your job search. The most important secret is the **informational interview** – a type of interview which yields useful job search information and may lead to job interviews and offers. Based on prospecting and networking techniques, these interviews minimize rejections and competition as well as quickly open the doors to organiza-

339

tions and employers you would not normally know about. If you want a job interview, you first need to understand the informational interview and how to initiate and use it for maximum impact. In so doing, you'll be exploring the **hidden job market** of unadvertised vacancies. You'll begin locating opportunities that are best suited for your particular motivated abilities and skills (MAS).

Prospecting and Networking

What do you do after you complete your resume? Most people send cover letters and resumes in response to job listings; they then wait to be called for a job interview. Viewing the job search as basically a direct-mail operation, many are disappointed in discovering the realities of direct mail – a 2-percent response rate is considered successful!

> *The most effective means of communication are face-to-face and word-of-mouth.*

Successful job seekers break out of this relatively passive job search role by orienting themselves toward face-to-face action. Being proactive, they develop interpersonal strategies in which the resume plays a **supportive** rather than a central role in the job search. They first present themselves to employers; the resume appears only at the end of a face-to-face conversation.

Throughout the job search you will acquire useful names and addresses as well as meet people who will assist you in contacting potential employers. Such information and contacts become key building blocks for generating job interviews and offers.

Since the best and most numerous jobs are found on the hidden job market, you must use methods appropriate for this job market. Indeed, research and experience clearly show the most effective means of communication are face-to-face and word-of-mouth. The informal, interpersonal system of communication is the central nervous system of the hidden job market. Your goal should be to penetrate this job market with proven methods for success. Appropriate methods for making important job contacts are **prospecting and networking**. Useful methods for getting these contacts to provide you with useful job information are **informational and referral interviews**.

Clearly Communicate Your Qualifications

Taken together, these interpersonal methods help you clearly **communicate your qualifications to employers**. Although many job seekers may

be reluctant to use this informal communication system, they greatly limit their potential for success if they do not.

Put yourself in the position of the employer for a moment, especially one who is not fully staffed nor automated to handle hundreds of resumes and phone, fax, and e-mail inquiries. You have a job vacancy to fill. Even under the best of circumstances, hiring is a challenging process filled with all types of potential problems. Not only is it time-consuming, the outcome is often uncertain. Worst of all, you may spend a great deal of time and money and still hire the wrong person for the position! You know if you advertise the position, you may be bombarded with hundreds of resumes, applications, phone calls, faxes, e-mails, and walk-ins. While you do want to hire the best qualified individual for the job, you simply don't have time nor patience to review scores of applications. Even if you use a P.O. Box number, the paper-work may quickly overwhelm you. Furthermore, with limited information from application forms, cover letters, and resumes, you find it hard to identify the best qualified individuals to invite for an interview; many look the same on paper.

> *There's nothing like a personal reference from someone whose professional judgment you trust.*

So what do you do? You might hire a professional search firm or use the services of a temporary employment agency to take on this additional work. Or you may decide to recruit on the Internet by doing keyword searches of various online resume databases or post a job announcement on your home page. You may even try your luck by spending a few hundred dollars to use a few major commercial recruitment sites, such as www.monster.com or www.careerbuilder.com.

On the other hand, you may want to better control the hiring process, especially since it appears to be filled with uncertainty and headaches. You want to minimize your risks and time so you can get back to what you do best – accomplishing the external goals of the organization. So you decide to "put the word out" by doing a little word-of-mouth recruiting. Like many other employers, you begin by calling your friends, acquaintances, and other business associates and ask if they or someone else might know of any good candidates for the position. If they can't help, you ask them to give you a call should they learn of anyone qualified for your vacancy. You, in effect, create your own hidden job market – an informal information network for locating desirable candidates. Best of all, your trusted contacts initially **screen** the candidates in the process of **referring** them to you. This both saves you a great deal of time and minimizes your risks in hiring a stranger. Individuals in your network begin sending you

names of individuals they feel would be ideal for your position. After all, they have either worked with these individuals or know well their ability to work with others and do the job. There's nothing like a personal reference from someone whose professional judgment you trust.

Even if you are fully staffed and technically capable to handle the recruitment process, you still may use an informal, interpersonal, and parallel recruitment approach to minimize your risks. Indeed, many large companies encourage **employee referrals** for recruiting personnel. While they may post a vacancy on their website or use a commercial recruitment site to find candidates, they also encourage and reward their employees to refer candidates. The reward may be a $1,500 to $2,500 bonus to anyone whose referral results in a new hire. These employee referral systems encourage networking within the hidden job market.

Let's shift perspectives – from the employer to the job seeker. Based on this understanding of the employer's perspective, what should you, the job seeker, do to best improve your chances of getting an interview and job offer? Networking for information, advice, and referrals should play a central role in your overall job search. Remember, employers need to solve personnel problems. By conducting **informational interviews and networking,** you help employers identify their needs, limit their alternatives, and thus make decisions and save money. Especially for career changers, such interviews and networking activities help relieve employers' anxiety about hiring such risky individuals.

At the same time, you gain several advantages by conducting these interviews:

1. You are less likely to encounter rejections since you are not asking for a job – only information, advice, referrals, and to be remembered.

2. You go after high-level positions.

3. You encounter little competition.

4. You go directly to the people who have the power to hire.

5. You are likely to be invited to job interviews based upon the referrals you receive.

Most employers want more information on candidates to supplement the "paper qualifications" represented in application forms, resumes, and letters. Studies show that employers in general seek candidates who have

these skills: communication, problem solving, analytical, assessment, and planning. Surprising to many job seekers, technical expertise ranks third or fourth on employers' lists of most desired skills. These findings support a frequent observation made by employers: the major problems with employees relate to communication, problem solving, and analysis; most individuals get fired because of political and interpersonal conflicts rather than for technical incompetence.

Employers seek individuals they **like** both personally and professionally. Therefore, communicating your qualifications to employers entails more than just informing them of your technical competence. You must communicate that you have the requisite personal **and** professional skills for performing the job. Prospecting, networking, and informational interviewing activities are the best methods for communicating such "qualifications" to employers.

Develop Networks

Networking is the process of purposefully developing relations with others. Networking in the job search involves connecting and interacting with other individuals who can possibly help you. Your network consists of you interacting with these other individuals. The more you develop, maintain, and expand your networks, the more successful should be your job search.

Your network is your interpersonal environment. While you know and interact with hundreds of people, on a day-to-day basis you may encounter no more than 20 people. You frequently encounter these people in face-to-face situations. Some people are more **important** to you than others. You **like** some more than others. And some will be more **helpful** to you in your job search than others. Your basic network may encompass the following individuals and groups: friends, acquaintances, immediate family, distant relatives, professional colleagues, spouse, supervisor, fellow workers, close friends and colleagues, and local businessmen and professionals, such as your banker, lawyer, doctor, minister, and insurance agent. You should contact many of these individuals for advice relating to your job search.

You need to **identify everyone in your network** who might help you with your job search. You first need to expand your basic network to include individuals you know and have interacted with over the past ten or more years. Make a list of at least 200 people you know. Include friends and relatives from your Christmas card list, past and present neighbors, former classmates and military buddies, politicians, business persons, previous employers, professional associates, ministers, insurance

agents, lawyers, bankers, doctors, dentists, accountants, and social acquaintances – even your postal carrier and UPS driver.

After identifying your extended network, you should try to **link your network to others' networks**. The figure on page 345 illustrates this linkage principle. Individuals in these other networks also have job information and contacts. Ask people in your basic network for referrals to individuals in their networks. This approach should greatly enlarge your basic job search network.

What do you do if individuals in your immediate and extended network cannot provide you with certain job information and contacts? While it is much easier and more effective to meet new people through personal contacts, on occasion you may need to **approach strangers without prior contacts**. In this situation, try the "cold turkey" approach. Write a letter to someone you feel may be useful to your job search. Research this individual so you are acquainted with their background and accomplishments. In the letter, refer to their accomplishments, mention your need for job information, and specify a date and time you will call to schedule a meeting. Another approach is to introduce yourself to someone by telephone and request a meeting and/or job information. While you may experience rejections in using these approaches, you also will experience successes. And those successes should lead to further expansion of your job search network.

Develop a Prospecting Campaign for Information

The key to successful networking is an active and routine **prospecting campaign**. Salespersons in insurance, real estate, Amway, Shaklee, and other direct-sales and pyramid businesses understand the importance of prospecting; indeed, many have turned the art of prospecting into a science as well as billion-dollar global businesses! The basic operating principle is **probability**: the number of sales you make is a direct function of the amount of effort you put into developing new contacts and following through. Expect no more than a 10-percent acceptance rate: for every 10-people you meet, nine will reject you and one will accept you. Therefore, the more people you contact, the more acceptances you will receive. If you want to be successful, you must collect many more "nos" than "yeses." In a 10 percent probability situation, you need to contact 100 people for 10 successes.

These prospecting principles are extremely useful for conducting a job search or making a career change. Like sales situations, the job search is a highly ego-involved activity often characterized by numerous rejections accompanied by a few acceptances. While no one wants to be rejected,

Linking Your Networks to Others

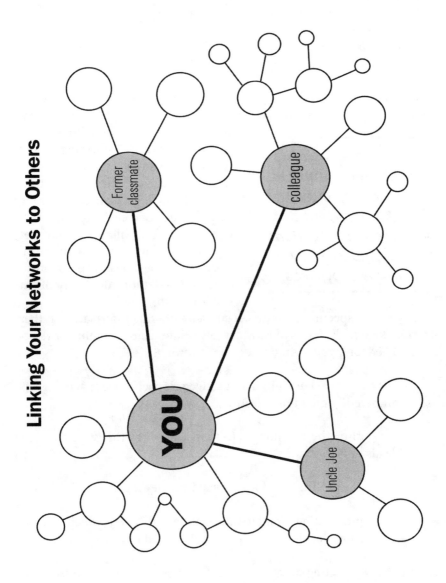

few people are willing and able to handle more than a few rejections. They take a "no" as a sign of personal failure – and quit prematurely. In fact, the typical job search looks something like this:

No, No, No, No, No, No, Maybe, No, No, No, Yes, No, No, No, No, No, No, No, Maybe, No, Maybe, Yes, No, No, No, No, Yes

If you get disillusioned and quit after receiving four rejections, you will prematurely fail. While it may be initially hard to do, you need to continue making calls and writing letters in the process of "collecting" more rejections in order to get an acceptance. In fact, we often recommend that individuals get up in the morning with the idea of collecting at least 20 rejections! You will eventually get acceptances, but you must first deal with many rejections on the road to success. **Persistence does pay off in the long run.**

> *The job search is a highly ego-involved activity often characterized by numerous rejections accompanied by a few acceptances.*

If your prospecting activities focus on gathering information rather than making sales, you will considerably minimize the number of rejections. Therefore, you should to do the following:

- Develop a well organized and active prospecting campaign for uncovering quality job leads.

- Be positive by accepting rejections as part of the game that leads to acceptances.

- Link prospecting to informational interviewing.

- Keep prospecting for more information and "yeses" which will eventually translate into job interviews and offers.

A good prospecting pace as you start your search is to make two new contacts each day. Start by contacting people in your immediate network. Let them know you are conducting a job search, but emphasize that you are only doing research. Ask for a few moments of their time to talk about what you are doing. You are only seeking **information and advice** at this time – not a job.

It should take you about 20 minutes to make a contact by letter or telephone. If you make two contacts each day, by the end of the first week you will have 10 new contacts for a total investment of less than seven hours. By the second week you may want to increase your prospecting pace to four new contacts each day or 20 each week. The more contacts you make, the more useful information, advice, and job leads you will receive. If your job search bogs down, you probably need to increase your prospecting activities.

Expect each contact to refer you to two or three others who will in turn refer you to others. Consequently, your contacts should multiply considerably within only a few weeks.

Handle and Minimize Rejections

These prospecting and networking methods are effective, and they can have a major impact on your job search and your life. While they are responsible for building, maintaining, and expanding multi-million dollar businesses, they work extremely well for job hunters. But they only work for those who have a positive attitude and who are patient and persist. **The key to networking success is to focus on gathering information while also learning to handle rejections.** Learn from rejections, forget them, and go on to more productive networking activities. The major reason direct-sales people fail is because they don't persist. The reason they don't persist is because they either can't take, or they get tired of taking, rejections. This should not happen to you. Always welcome rejections: they will eventually lead to acceptances.

Rejections are no fun, especially in such an ego-involved activity as a job search. But you will encounter rejections as you travel on the road toward job search success. This road is strewn with individuals who quit prematurely because they were rejected four or five times. Don't be one of them!

Our prospecting and networking techniques differ from sales approaches in one major respect: we have special techniques for minimizing the number of rejections. If handled properly, at least 50 percent – maybe as many as 90 percent – of your prospects will turn into "yeses" rather than "no's." The reason for this unusually high acceptance rate is how you introduce and handle yourself before your prospects. Many insurance agents and direct distributors expect a 90 percent rejection rate, because they are trying to sell specific products potential clients may or may not need. Most people don't like to be put on the spot – especially when it is in their own home or office – to make a decision to buy a product.

Be Honest and Sincere

The principles of selling yourself in the job market are similar. People don't want to be put on the spot. They feel uncomfortable if they think you expect them to give you a job. Thus, you should never introduce yourself to a prospect by asking them for a job or a job lead. You should do just the opposite: relieve their anxiety by mentioning that you are not looking for a job from them – only job information and advice. You must be honest and sincere in communicating these intentions to your contact. The biggest turn-off for individuals targeted for informational interviews is insincere job seekers who try to use this as a mechanism to get a job.

Your approach to prospects must be subtle, honest, and professional. You are seeking **information, advice, and referrals** relating to several subjects: job opportunities, your job search approach, your resume, and contacts who may have similar information, advice, and referrals. Most people gladly volunteer such information. They generally like to talk about themselves, their careers, and others. Similar to advice columnists, they like to give advice. This approach flatters individuals by placing them in the role of the expert-advisor. Who doesn't want to be recognized as an expert-advisor, especially on such a critical topic as one's employment?

This approach should yield a great deal of information, advice, and referrals from your prospects. One other important outcome should result from using this approach: people will **remember** you as the person who made them feel at ease and who received their valuable advice. If they hear of job opportunities for someone with your qualifications, chances are they will contact you with the information. After contacting 100 prospects, you will have created 100 sets of eyes and ears to help you in your job search!

Practice the 5R's of Informational Interviewing

The guiding principle behind prospecting, networking, and informational interviews is this: **The best way to get a job is to ask for job information, advice, and referrals; never ask for a job.** Remember, you want your prospects to engage in the 5R's of informational interviewing:

- **Reveal** useful information and advice.
- **Refer** you to others.
- **Read** your resume.
- **Revise** your resume.
- **Remember** you for future reference.

If you network according to this principle, you should join the ranks of thousands of successful job seekers who have experienced the 5R's of informational interviewing. Largely avoiding the advertised job market, you may find your perfect job through such powerful networking activities.

Approach Key People

Whom should you contact within an organization for an informational interview? Contact people who are busy, who have the power to hire, and who are knowledgeable about the organization. The least likely candidate will be someone in the human resources department. Most often the heads of operating units are the most busy, powerful, and knowledgeable individuals in the organization. However, getting access to such individuals may be difficult. Some people at the top may appear to be informed and powerful, but they may lack information on the day-to-day personnel changes or their influence is limited in the hiring process. It is difficult to give one best answer to this question.

The best way to get a job is to ask for job information, advice, and referrals; never ask for a job.

Therefore, we recommend contacting several types of people. Aim for the busy, powerful, and informed, but be prepared to settle for less. Secretaries, receptionists, and the person you want to meet may refer you to others. From a practical standpoint, you may have to take whomever you can schedule an appointment with. Sometimes people who are less powerful can be helpful. Talk to a secretary or receptionist sometime about their boss or working in the organization. You may be surprised by what you learn!

Nonetheless, you will conduct informational interviews with different types of people. Some will be friends, relatives, or acquaintances. Others will be referrals or new contacts. You will gain the easiest access to people you already know. This can usually be done informally by telephone. You might meet at their home or office or at a restaurant.

You should use a more formal approach to gain access to referrals and new contacts. The best way to initiate a contact with a prospective employer is to **send an approach letter** and follow it up with a phone call. Examples of approach letters are found at the end of Chapter 12. This letter should include the following elements:

OPENERS If you have a referral, tell the individual you are considering a career in _____. His or her name was given to you by _____ who suggested he or she might be a good person to give you useful information about careers in _____ _____. Should you lack a referral to the individual and thus must use a "cold turkey" approach to making this contact, you might begin your letter by stating that you are aware he or she has been at the forefront of _____ business – or whatever is both truthful and appropriate for the situation. Try to make a personal connection to this person. A subtle form of flattery will be helpful at this stage.

REQUEST Demonstrate your thoughtfulness and courtesy rather than aggressiveness by mentioning that you know he or she is busy. You hope to schedule a mutually convenient time for a brief meeting to discuss your questions and career plans. Most people will be flattered by such a request and happy to talk with you about their work – if they have time and are interested in you.

CLOSINGS In closing the letter, mention that you will call the person to see if an appointment can be arranged. Be specific by stating the time and day you will call – for example, Thursday at 2pm. You must take initiative to follow up the letter with a definite contact time. If you don't, you cannot expect to hear from the person. It is **your** responsibility to make the telephone call to schedule a meeting.

ENCLOSURE Do **not** enclose your resume with this approach letter. Take your resume to the interview and present it as a topic of discussion near the end of your meeting. If you send it with the approach letter, you communicate a mixed and contradictory message. Remember your purpose for this interview: to gather information and advice. You are not – and never should be – asking for a job. A resume accompanying a letter appears to be an application or a job request.

Many people will meet with you, assuming you are sincere in your approach. On the other hand, many people also are very busy and simply don't have the time to meet with you. If the person puts you off when you telephone for an appointment, clearly state your purpose and emphasize that you are not looking for a job with this person – only information and advice. If the person insists on putting you off, make the best of the situation: try to conduct the informational interview over the telephone. Alternatively, write a nice thank you letter in which you again state your intended purpose; mention your disappointment in not being able to learn from the person's experience; and ask to be remembered for future reference. Enclose your resume with this letter.

While you are ostensibly seeking information and advice, treat this meeting as an important preliminary interview. You need to communicate your qualifications – that you are competent, intelligent, honest, and likable. These are the same qualities you should communicate in a formal job interview. Hence, follow the same advice given for conducting a formal interview and dressing appropriately for a face-to-face meeting (Chapter 15).

Conduct the Interview Well

An informational interview will be relatively unstructured compared to a formal job interview. Since you want the interviewer to advise you, you reverse roles by asking questions which should give you useful information. You, in effect, become the interviewer. You should structure this interview with a particular sequence of questions. Most questions should be open-ended, requiring the individual to give specific answers based upon his or her experience.

The structure and dialogue for the informational interview might go something like this. You plan to take no more than 45 minutes for this interview. The first three to five minutes will be devoted to small talk – the weather, traffic, the office, mutual acquaintances, or an interesting or humorous observation. Since these are the most critical moments in the interview, be especially careful how you communicate nonverbally. Begin your interview by stating your appreciation for the individual's time:

> *"I want to thank you again for scheduling this meeting with me. I know you're busy. I appreciate the special arrangements you made to see me on a subject which is very important to my future."*

Your next comment should be a statement reiterating your purpose as stated in your letter:

> *"As you know, I am exploring job and career alternatives. I know what I do well and what I want to do. But before I commit myself to a new job, I need to know more about various career options. I thought you would be able to provide me with some insights into career opportunities, job requirements, and possible problems or promising directions in the field of _____."*

This statement normally will get a positive reaction from the individual, who may want to know more about what it is you want to do. Be sure to clearly communicate your job objective. If you can't, you may give the impression that you are lost, indecisive, or uncertain about yourself, and the person may feel you are wasting his or her time.

Your next line of questioning should focus on "how" and "what" questions centering on (1) specific jobs and (2) the job search process. Begin by asking about various aspects of specific jobs:

- Duties and responsibilities
- Knowledge, skills, and abilities required
- Work environment relating to employees, work, deadlines, stress
- Advantages and disadvantages
- Advancement opportunities and outlook
- Salary ranges

Your informer will probably take a great deal of time talking about his or her experience in each area. Be a good listener, but make sure you move along with the questions.

Your next line of questioning should focus on your job search activities. You need as much information as possible on how to:

- Acquire the necessary skills
- Best find a job in this field
- Overcome any objections employers may have to you
- Uncover job vacancies which may be unadvertised
- Develop job leads
- Approach prospective employers

Your final line of questioning should be about your resume. Do not show your resume until you focus on a final set of questions. The

purposes of these questions are to: (1) get the individual to read your resume in depth, (2) acquire useful advice on how to strengthen it, (3) refer you to prospective employers, and (4) be remembered. With the resume in front of you and your interviewee, ask the following questions:

- Is this an appropriate type of resume for the jobs I have outlined?

- If an employer received this resume in the mail, how do you think he or she would react to it?

- What do you see as possible weaknesses or areas that need to be improved?

- What about the length, paper quality and color, layout, and type style/size? Are they appropriate?

- What should I do with this resume? Broadcast it to hundreds of employers with a cover letter? Use a "T" letter instead?

- How might I improve the form and content of the resume?

- Who might be most interested in receiving this resume?

You should obtain useful advice on how to strengthen both the content and use of your resume. Most important, these questions force the individual to **read** your resume, which, in turn, may be **remembered** for future reference.

Your last question is especially important in this interview. You want to be both **remembered** and **referred**. Some variation of the following question should help:

> _"I really appreciate all this advice. It is very helpful and it should improve my job search considerably. Could I ask you one more favor? Do you know two or three other people who could help me with my job search? I want to conduct as much research as possible, and their advice might be helpful also."_

Before you leave, mention one more important item:

> _"During the next few months, should you hear of any job opportunities for someone with my interests and qualifications,_

I would appreciate being kept in mind. And please feel free to pass my name on to others."

Send a nice thank you letter – preferably by mail (e-mail may not get opened) – within 48 hours of this informational interview. Express your genuine gratitude for the individual's time and advice. Reiterate your interests, and ask to be remembered and referred.

Be sure to follow up on any useful advice you receive, particularly referrals. Approach referrals in the same manner you approached the person who gave you the referral. Write a letter requesting a meeting. Begin the letter by saying:

"Mr./Ms. _____ suggested that I contact you concerning my research on careers in _____."

If you continue prospecting, networking, and conducting informational interviews, soon you will be busy conducting interviews and receiving job offers. While 100 informational interviews over a two-month period should lead to several formal job interviews and offers, the pay-offs are uncertain because job vacancies are unpredictable. We know cases where the first referral turned into a formal interview and job offer. More typical cases require constant prospecting, networking, and informational interviewing activities. The telephone call or letter inviting you to a job interview can come at any time. While the timing may be unpredictable, your persistent job search activities will be largely responsible for the final outcome – a job offer.

Telephone for Job Leads

Telephone communication should play an important role in prospecting, networking, and informational interviews. However, controversy centers around how and when to use the telephone for generating job leads and scheduling interviews. Some people recommend writing a letter and waiting for a written or telephone reply. Others suggest writing a letter and following it with a telephone call. Still others argue you should use the telephone exclusively rather than write letters.

How you use the telephone will indicate what type of job search you are conducting. Exclusive reliance on the telephone is a technique used by highly formalized job clubs which operate phone banks for generating job leads. Using the Yellow Pages or Internet phone directories as the guide to employers, a job club member may call as many as 50 employers a day to schedule job interviews. A rather aggressive yet typical telephone

dialogue goes something like this:

> *"Hello, my name is Jim Morgan. I would like to speak to the head of the training department. By the way, what is the name of the training director?"*
>
> *"You want to talk to Ms. Stevens. Her number is 743-723-8191, or I can connect you directly."*
>
> *"Hello, Ms. Stevens. My name is Jim Morgan. I have several years of training experience as both a trainer and developer of training materials. I'd like to meet with you to discuss possible openings in your department for someone with my qualifications. Would it be possible to see you on Friday at 2pm?"*

Not surprisingly, this telephone approach generates many "nos." If you have a hard time handling rejections, this telephone approach will help you confront your anxieties. The principle behind this approach is **probability**: for every 25 telephone "nos" you receive, you will probably get one or two "yeses." Success is just 25 telephone calls away! If you start calling prospective employers at 9am and finish your 25 calls by 12 noon, you should generate at least one or two interviews. That's not bad for three hours of job search work. It beats a direct-mail approach.

While the telephone is more efficient than writing letters, its effectiveness is questionable. When you use the telephone in this manner, you are basically pitching for a job. You are asking the employer: *"Do you have a job for me?"* There is nothing subtle or particularly professional about this approach. It is effective in uncovering particular types of job leads for particular types of individuals. If you need a job – any job – in a hurry, this is one of the most efficient ways of finding employment. It sure beats standing in line at the state employment office! However, if you are more concerned with finding a job that is right for you – a job you do well and enjoy doing, one that is fit for you – this telephone approach is inappropriate.

You must use your own judgment in determining when and how to use the telephone in your job search. There are appropriate times and methods for using the telephone, and these should relate to your job search goals and needs. We prefer the more conventional approach of writing a letter requesting an informational interview and following it up with a telephone call. While you take the initiative in scheduling an appointment, you do not put the individual on the spot by asking for a job. You are only **seeking information and advice**. This low-keyed

approach results in numerous acceptances and has a higher probability of paying off with interviews than the aggressive telephone request. You should be trying to uncover jobs that are right for you rather than any job that happens to pop up from a telephoning blitz.

Networking Resources

For more information on networking, refer to our earlier discussion on pages 124-130. There we identify one of the most comprehensive collections of networking resources, from job clubs, support groups, and association to online networks, people finders, and networking advice.

15

Interview Like a Pro

AKE NO MISTAKE – the job interview is **the** most important step in the job search process. All previous job search activities lead to this one. Put simply, no interview, no job offer; no job offer, no negotiations, no salary, and no job. Your previous job search activities have assisted you in getting this far, but the interview itself will determine whether you will be invited to additional interviews and offered a position. How you approach the interview will make a difference in the outcome of the interview. Therefore, you need to know what best to do and not to do in order to make a good impression on your prospective employer.

New Behavioral and Internet Trends

Within the past few years, the job interview – as well as the whole hiring process – has changed in several important ways. These changes require both interviewees and interviewers to better prepare for the job interview. Most changes reflect the need of employers to better define their hiring needs and then make more intelligent and cost-effective hiring decisions. While employers used to hire fast and fire slow, more and more employers see the wisdom of doing just the opposite – hire slow and fire fast. This means more extensive screening of candidates and focusing on **patterns of accomplishments** in order to best **predict** employee behavior. Employers want a perfect "fit." This also means conducting a different style of interviewing. Rather than call a candidate in for two interviews, an employer may interview a single candidate four to seven times before making a job offer. So, how do you handle your fifth

interview? Not surprisingly, many candidates have difficulty remaining buoyant after the third interview! For those who have mistakenly prepared canned answers to interview questions, they have difficulty staying on message after responding to dozens of questions that require them to demonstrate their personality, likability, competence, and ability to make thoughtful decisions.

At the same time, employers are taking more time to screen candidates with everything from drug, skills, and psychological testing to in-depth background checks. Within the interview itself, more and more employers are asking **behavior-based questions** to ascertain a candidate's ability to make decisions and solve problems relevant to their organization. Consequently, candidates who prepare for interviews with memorized or canned answers to anticipated interview questions do not do well in such interviews; they appear coached, lack originality and spontaneity, and thus lack authenticity. Going beyond behavior-based questions, many employers also seek better indicators of a candidate's decision-making style and pattern of performance by conducting **situational interviews**. Giving interviewees hypothetical or real-work problems to solve, interviewers want to see how candidates actually behave, rather than what they say, within the context of the company or organization. Accordingly, employers want to know more about your motivated skills and abilities (Chapter 10) and whether or not your MAS is a good fit for their organization by actually observing you in action.

> *While employers used to hire fast and fire slow, many see the wisdom of doing just the opposite – hire slow and fire fast.*

Within the very near future, the Internet will play a key role in screening candidates, from doing background checks and administering skills and psychological tests to conducting interviews via a video link. Indeed, the Internet is proving to be the perfect medium for facilitating both the job search and the hiring processes. For employers, new Internet-based hiring software will enable them to eliminate many of the costly face-to-face steps currently involved in interviewing candidates. In so doing, interviews will be more employer-centered, with greater emphasis placed on **what you can do for the employer**.

The overall trend is simple: no more hiring surprises due to poor hiring skills! Employers want to better predict individual performance within their organizations. They can no longer make costly hiring mistakes that are often attributed to their own lack of good screening and interview skills. They simply want to take the guesswork out of hiring. They want the perfect skills set for the perfect fit.

Prepare for Stressful Interviews

Nearly 95 percent of all organizations require job interviews prior to hiring employees. In fact, employers consider an effective interview to be the most important hiring criteria – outranking grade point average, educational level, related work experience, resumes, letters, and recommendations.

While the job interview is the most important job search activity, it also is the most stressful job search experience. Your application, resume, and letters may get you to the interview, but you must perform well in person in order to get a job offer. Knowing the stakes are high, most people face interviews with dry throats and sweaty palms; it is a time of great stress. You will be on stage, and you are expected to put on a good performance.

How do you prepare for the interview? First, you need to understand the nature and purpose of the interview. Second, you must prepare to respond to different interview situations and interviewers. Make sure whoever assists you in preparing for the interview evaluates your performance. Practice the whole interviewing scenario, from the time you enter the door until you leave. You should sharpen your nonverbal communication skills and be prepared to give positive answers to questions as well as ask intelligent questions of your own. The more you practice, the better prepared you will be for the real job interview.

A Special Communication Focus

An interview is a two-way communication exchange between an interviewer and interviewee. It involves both verbal and nonverbal communication. While we tend to concentrate on the content of what we say, research shows that approximately 65 percent of all communication is nonverbal. Furthermore, we tend to give more credibility to nonverbal than to verbal messages. Regardless of what you say, how you dress, sit, stand, use your hands, move your head and eyes, and listen communicates both positive and negative messages.

Job interviews can occur in many different settings and under various circumstances. You may write job interview letters, schedule interviews by telephone, be interviewed over the phone, and encounter one-on-one as well as panel, group, series, behavioral, and situational interviews. Each situation requires a different set of communication behaviors. For example, while telephone communication is efficient, it may be ineffective for interview purposes. Only certain types of information can be effectively communicated over the telephone because this medium is only

verbal. Honesty, intelligence, and likability – three of the most important values you want to communicate to employers – are primarily communicated nonverbally. Therefore, you should be very careful of telephone interviews – whether giving or receiving them.

Job interviews have different purposes and can be negative in many ways. From your perspective, the purpose of an initial job interview is to get a second interview, and the purpose of the second interview is to get subsequent interviews as well as a job offer. However, for many employers, the purpose of the interview is to eliminate you from additional interviews or job offer. The interviewer wants to know why he or she should **not** hire you. The interviewer tries to do this by identifying your weaknesses. These differing purposes can create an adversarial relationship and contribute to the overall interviewing stress experienced by both the applicant and the interviewer.

Since the interviewer has certain expectations about required personalities and performance in candidates, he or she wants to **identify your weaknesses**. You must counter by **communicating your strengths** to lessen the interviewer's fears of hiring you. Recognizing that you are an unknown quantity to the employer, you must raise the interviewer's expectations of you.

> *You should prepare for the interview as if it were a $1,000,000+ prize.*

Answer Questions

Hopefully your prospecting, networking, informational interviewing, and resume and letter writing activities result in several invitations to interview for jobs appropriate to your objective. Once you receive an invitation to interview, you should prepare for the interview as if it were a $1,000,000+ prize. After all, that may be what you earn during your employment.

The invitation to interview will most likely come by telephone. In some cases, a preliminary interview will be conducted by telephone. The employer may want to shorten the list of eligible candidates from ten to three. By calling each individual, the employer can quickly eliminate marginal candidates as well as update the job status of each individual. When you get such a telephone call, you have no time to prepare. You may be dripping wet as you step from the shower or you may have a splitting headache as you pick up the phone. Telephone interviews always seem to occur at bad times. Whatever your situation, put your best foot forward based upon your thorough preparation for an interview. You may

want to keep a list of questions near the telephone just in case you receive such a call.

Telephone interviews often result in a face-to-face interview at the employer's office. Once you confirm an interview time and place, you should do as much research on the organization and employer as possible, as well as learn to lessen your anxiety and stress levels by practicing the interview situation. **Preparation and practice** are the keys to doing your best.

During the interview, you want to impress upon the interviewer your knowledge of the organization by asking insightful questions and giving intelligent answers. Your library and networking research should yield useful information on the organization and employer. Be sure you know something about the organization. Interviewers are normally impressed by interviewees who demonstrate knowledge and interest in their organization.

You should practice the actual interview by mentally addressing several questions interviewers ask. Most of these questions will relate to your educational background, work experience, career goals, personality, and related concerns. Frequently asked questions include:

Education

- Describe your educational background.
- Why did you attend _____ University (College or School)?
- Why did you major in _____?
- What was your grade point average?
- What subjects did you enjoy the most? The least? Why?
- What leadership positions did you hold?
- How did you finance your education?
- If you could, what would you change about your education?
- Why were your grades so low? So high?
- Did you do the best you could in school? If not, why not?
- What type of specialized training have you received?
- How do you manage to keep up in your field?

Work Experience

- What were your major achievements in each of your past jobs?
- Why did you change jobs before?
- What is your typical workday like?
- What functions do you enjoy doing the most?
- What did you like about your boss? Dislike?
- Which job did you enjoy the most? Why? Which job did you enjoy the least? Why?

- Have you ever been fired? Why?
- What did you especially like about your last job?

Career Goals

- Why do you want to join our organization?
- Why do you think you are qualified for this position?
- Why are you looking for another job?
- Why do you want to make a career change?
- What ideally would you like to do?
- Why should we hire you?
- How would you improve our operations?
- What do you want to be doing five years from now?
- How much do you want to be making five years from now?
- What are your short-range and long-range career goals?
- If you were free to choose your job and employer, where would you go?
- What other types of jobs are you considering? Companies?
- When will you be ready to begin work?
- How do you feel about relocating, traveling, working overtime, and spending weekends in the office?
- What attracted you to our organization?

Personality and Other Concerns

- Tell me about yourself.
- What are your major weaknesses? Your major strengths?
- What causes you to lose your temper?
- What do you do in your spare time? Any hobbies?
- What types of books do you read?
- What role does your family play in your career?
- How well do you work under pressure? In meeting deadlines?
- Tell me about your management philosophy.
- How much initiative do you take?
- What types of people do you prefer working with?
- How _____ (creative, analytical, tactful, etc.) are you?
- If you could change your life, what would you do differently?

Handle Objections and Negatives With Ease

Interviewers must have a healthy skepticism of job candidates. They expect people to exaggerate their competencies and overstate what they

will do for the employer. They sometimes encounter dishonest applicants, and some people they hire fail to meet their expectations. Being realists who have made poor hiring decisions before, they want to know why they should **not** hire you. Although they do not always ask you these questions, they think about them nonetheless:

- Why should I hire you?
- What do you really want?
- What can you really do for me?
- What are your weaknesses?
- What problems will I have with you?

Underlying these questions are specific employers' objections to hiring you:

- You're not as good as you say you are; you probably hyped your resume or lied about yourself.
- All you want is a job and security.
- You have weaknesses like the rest of us. Is it alcohol, sex, drugs, finances, shiftlessness, petty politics?
- You'll probably want my job in another five months.
- You won't stay long with us. Ambitious people like you join the competition or **become** the competition.

Employers raise such suspicions and objections because it is difficult to trust strangers in the employment game and some of them may have been "burned" before. Indeed, there is an alarming rise in the number of individuals lying on their resumes or falsifying their credentials.

How can you best handle employers' objections? You must first recognize their biases and stereotypes and then **raise** their expectations. You do this by stressing your strengths and avoiding your weaknesses. You must be impeccably honest in doing so.

Your answers to employers' questions should be positive and emphasize your **strengths**. Remember, the interviewer wants to know what's wrong with you – your **weaknesses**. When you are answering questions, both the **substance** and **form** of your answers should be positive. For example, such words as "couldn't," "can't," "won't," and "don't" may create a negative tone and distract from the positive and enthusiastic image you are language. While you cannot eliminate all negative words, at least recognize that the type of words you use makes a difference; try to better manage your word choice. Assuming you are a veteran who is changing jobs, compare your reactions to the following interview answers:

QUESTION: Why do you want to leave your present job?

ANSWER 1: *After working there three years, I don't feel I'm going anywhere. Morale isn't good, and management doesn't reward us according to our productivity. I really don't like working there anymore.*

ANSWER 2: *After working there three years, I have learned a great deal about managing people and developing new markets. But it is time for me to move on to a larger and more progressive organization where I can use my marketing experience in several different areas. I am ready to take on more responsibilities. This change will be a positive step in my professional growth.*

Which one has the greater impact in terms of projecting positives and strengths? The first answer communicates too many negatives. The second answer is positive and upbeat in its orientation toward skills, accomplishments, and the future.

In addition to choosing positive words, select **content information** which is positive and **adds** to the interviewer's knowledge about you. Avoid simplistic "yes/no" answers; they say nothing about you. Instead, provide information which explains your reasons and motivations behind specific events or activities. For example, how do you react to these two factual answers?

QUESTION: I see from your resume that you've been working with Company X for five years. Are you one of the employees being affected by the recent budget cuts?

ANSWER 1: *Yes, that's correct.*

ANSWER 2: *Yes. Like many others, I've been affected by the recent cutbacks. However, instead of looking at my situation as a crisis, I'm approaching it as an opportunity to explore several other strong interests of mine. I know my talents can be useful in any number of settings, and I'm particularly interested in the work your department does.*

Let's try another question reflecting possible objections to hiring you:

QUESTION: Your background bothers me somewhat. You've been with this organization for 10 years. You know, it's different working in our organization. Why should I hire you?

ANSWER 1: _I can understand that._

ANSWER 2: _I understand your hesitation in hiring someone with my background. I would, too, if I were you. Yes, many people don't do well in different occupational settings. But I don't believe I have that problem. I'm used to working with people. I work until the job gets done, which often means long hours and on weekends. I'm very concerned with achieving results. But most important, I've done a great deal of thinking about my goals. I've researched your organization as well as many others. From what I have learned, this is exactly what I want to do, and your organization is the one I'm most interested in joining. I know I will do a good job, as I have always done in the past._

The first answer is incomplete. It misses an important opportunity to give evidence that you have resolved this issue in a positive manner which is clearly reflected in the second response.

The most difficult challenge to your positive strategy comes when the interviewer asks you to describe your negatives or weaknesses. Be careful how you answer this sensitive question:

QUESTION: We all have our negatives and weaknesses. What are some of yours?

You can handle this question in any of five different ways, yet still give positive information on yourself:

1. **Discuss a negative which is not related to the job being considered:**

 I don't enjoy accounting. I know it's important, but I find it boring. Even at home my wife takes care of our books.

Marketing is what I really like to do. I'm glad this job doesn't involve any accounting!

2. **Discuss a negative which the interviewer already knows:**

I spent a great deal of time working on advanced degrees, as indicated in my resume, and thus I lack extensive work experience. However, I believe my education has prepared me well for this job. My leadership experience in college taught me how to work with people, organize, and solve problems. I write well and quickly. My research experience helped me analyze, synthesize, and develop strategies.

3. **Discuss a negative which you have improved upon:**

I used to get over-committed and miss important deadlines. But then I read a book on time management and learned what I was doing wrong. Within three weeks I reorganized my use of time and found I could meet my deadlines with little difficulty. The quality of my work also improved. Now I have time to work out at the gym each day. I'm doing more and feeling better at the same time.

4. **Discuss a "negative" which can also be a positive:**

I'm somewhat of a workaholic. I love my work, but I sometimes neglect my family because of it. I've been going into the office seven days a week, and I often put in 12-hour days. I'm now learning to better manage my time.

5. **Discuss a negative outside yourself:**

I don't feel that there is anything seriously wrong with me. Like most people, I have my ups and downs. But overall I have a positive outlook and feel good about myself and what I've accomplished so far in my life. However, I am somewhat concerned how you might view my wanting to change occupations. I want to assure you that I'm not making this change on a whim. I've taken my time in thinking through the issues and taking a hard look at what I do well and enjoy doing. Like a lot of young people, I guess I didn't have much life experience when I started my career 10 years ago, and I

> _got into sales because I enjoyed that kind of environment._
> _However, as I got more experience and had opportunities to_
> _become involved in different areas, my interest in manage-_
> _ment training developed. I found that I not only enjoyed_
> _those activities, but that I had some natural talent for them._
> _While I've enjoyed my years in sales, I am committed to_
> _finding work more in line with my interests and abilities._

All of these examples stress the basic point about effective interviewing. Your single best strategy for managing the interview is to **emphasize your strengths and positives**. Questions come in several forms. Anticipate these questions, especially the negative ones, and practice positive responses in order to project your best self in an interview situation.

Encounter Behavior-Based Questions

More and more employers are conducting a different type of interview than they did five or 10 years ago. Known as "behavior-based interviews," these interviews are filled with behavior-based questions designed to elicit clear **patterns of behavior**, which are primarily sets of accomplishments, relevant to the employer's situation. They are specific and challenge interviewees to provide concrete examples of their achievements in different types of situations. Such interviews are based on the simple belief that how a job candidate has responded to certain types of situations in the past is a good predictor of how that person will behave in a similar future situation. Their behavioral "stories" provide clues on how they will solve future problems. Behavior-based questions are likely to begin with some variation of:

- _Give me an example of a time when you . . ._
- _Give me an example of how you . . ._
- _Tell me about how you . . ._

This is an opportunity for you to sell your positives with an example or two. Briefly describe the situation, enthusiastically explain what you did (adding information as to why, if you think this would not be evident), and indicate the outcome.

For example, if the interviewer asks,

> _"Tell me about a time when you saved an account for your company."_

The applicant might respond,

> *"Just last month I was observing a one-day training session con-*
> *ducted by one of our instructors I supervise. His class evaluations*
> *were lower than what we expect of our trainers, and my boss told*
> *me the client was not happy with the way the training sessions were*
> *going. He was afraid we might lose the account.*
>
> *As I observed the session, it was apparent the instructor knew*
> *the material but was having trouble moving the participants*
> *through the material in the time allotted. They often broke into*
> *small groups to complete an activity, but it was taking a long time*
> *as some groups had to wait for others to finish. At the end of the*
> *day, Joe and I met with the client, who indicated his dissatisfaction*
> *and gave us an ultimatum: if future training couldn't be completed*
> *in a day and to his satisfaction, he would get another contractor.*
>
> *I solved the problem by having Joe develop copies of the end*
> *product the participants should have formulated at the end of each*
> *activity. At the next training session he was able to pass these out*
> *at the end of the allotted time for each phase of the activity.*
>
> *The seminar participants understood the information and gave*
> *the instructor excellent course evaluations, and the client was*
> *pleased. We not only saved this contract, but got an additional*
> *contract from the client as well. My boss and I were both pleased*
> *with the outcome."*

Obviously you want to select examples that promote your skills and
have a positive outcome. Even if the interviewer asks about a time when
something negative happened, try to select an example where you were
able to turn the situation around and something positive came out of it.
For example, if asked, *"Tell me about a time you made a bad decision,"*
try to identify an occasion where:

- Even though it wasn't the best decision, you were able to pull
 something positive out of the situation.

- Though it was a poor decision, you learned from it, and in the
 next similar situation you made a good decision or know how
 you will handle it differently the next time a similar situation
 arises.

- It was bad decision, but the negative outcome had only minor
 impact.

In other words, try to pull something positive – either that you did or that you learned – out of even a negative experience you are asked to relate. As you prepare for your interview, consider situations where you:

- demonstrated leadership
- solved a problem
- increased company profits
- made a good decision/made a poor decision
- handled change (not money, but changing events)
- handled criticism
- met a deadline/missed a deadline
- worked as part of a team

Add to this list other behavioral questions you think of that pertain to the job for which you are applying. For example, if the job includes making presentations, expect questions about a speech where you achieved your goal or conversely about a time when your speech failed miserably.

Ask others who have interviewed with the company, if possible, to find out the types of questions to expect. You may encounter hypothetical questions in which you are asked not what you did, but what you would do if something occurred. With hypothetical questions, the interviewer is less interested in your actual answer – often there is no correct or incorrect response – than in your thought process. They want to know how you would solve a problem or respond to a situation.

Develop Strong Storytelling Skills

Individuals who do well in behavior-based interviews are those who have a rich background of accomplishments as well as are good storytellers. Indeed, **storytelling** is one of the key communication skills involved in conducting effective interviews. If you want to do well in this type of interview, be sure to **anticipate questions** you might be asked so you can prepare a well thought-out response – a set of revealing stories about your performance – prior to the interview. It is far easier to formulate positive responses to questions in the relaxed setting of your living room than in the stressful and time-constrained setting of the job interview.

Face Situational Interviews

More and more employers also are conducting situational interviews, which enable them to observe the actual behavior of candidates in particular situations. While candidates can prepare for behavioral interviews

by focusing on their accomplishments and telling stories about their past performance that communicate a clear pattern of behavior, such interviews are still primarily verbal exchanges. Employers analyze answers to open-ended questions for clues of future performance.

Situational interviews rely less on analyzing verbal cues and more on analyzing both verbal and nonverbal behavior. Employers especially like conducting these interviews because they know candidates can't prepare well for the situations in which they may be asked to perform. These interviews give employers a chance to observe a candidate's decision-making skills in the process of solving work-related problems. Many of these interviews involve mock scenarios in which a candidate is asked to role play. For example, someone who is interviewing for a customer service position may be asked to play the role of a customer service representative by handling telephone calls from an irate customer. In this scenario the interviewer has a chance to observe how the candidate actually handles such a customer. Does he or she talk down to the customer, get angry, or resolve the problem to the satisfaction of the customer, who hopefully will become a repeat customer? The behavior of a competent customer service representative can be readily observed in such a role-playing scenario. Other examples of situational interviews may involve mock negotiation sessions, selling a product, counseling a client, teaching a course, constructing something, or repairing a product.

> *Employers like to conduct situational interviews because they know candidates can't prepare well for the situations in which they may be asked to perform.*

Face Illegal Questions

Many questions are illegal, but some employers ask them nonetheless. Consider how you would respond to these questions:

- Are you married, divorced, separated, or single?
- How old are you?
- Do you go to church regularly?
- Do you have many debts?
- Do you own or rent your home?
- What social and political organizations do you belong to?
- What does your spouse think about your career?
- Are you living with anyone?

- How much insurance do you have?
- How much do you weigh?
- How tall are you?

Don't get upset and say *"That's an illegal question...I refuse to answer it!"* While you may be perfectly right in saying so, this response lacks tact, which may be what the employer is looking for. For example, if you are divorced and the interviewer asks about your divorce, you might respond with *"Does a divorce have a direct bearing on the responsibilities of this position?"* Some employers may ask such questions just to see how you answer or react under stress. Others may do so out of ignorance of the law. Whatever the case, be prepared to handle these questions with tact.

Dress Appropriately

Appearance is the first thing you communicate to interviewers. Before you have a chance to speak, they notice how you are dressed and accordingly draw certain conclusions about your personality and competence. Indeed, research shows that appearance makes the greatest difference when an evaluator has little information about the other person. This is precisely the situation you find yourself in at the start of an interview.

Many people object to having their capabilities evaluated on the basis of their appearance and manner of dress. *"But that is not fair,"* they argue. *"People should be hired on the basis of their ability to do the job – not on how they look."* But debating the lack of merit or complaining about the unfairness of such behavior does not alter reality. Like it or not, people do make initial judgments about others based on their appearance. Since you cannot alter this fact and bemoaning it will get you nowhere, it is best to learn to use it to your advantage. If you effectively manage your image, you can convey marvelous messages regarding your authority, credibility, and competence.

Some estimates indicate that as much as 65 percent of the hiring decision may be based on the nonverbal aspects of the interview! Employers sometimes refer to this phenomenon in such terms as "chemistry," "body warmth," or that "gut feeling" the individual is right for the job. This correlates with findings of communication studies that approximately 65 percent of a message is communicated nonverbally.

Rules of the Game

Knowing how to dress appropriately for the interview requires knowing important rules of the game. Like it or not, employers play by these rules.

Once you know the rules, you at least can make a conscious choice whether or not you want to play. If you decide to play, you will stand a better chance of winning by using the often unwritten rules to your advantage.

The degree to which employers adhere to these rules, however, will depend on particular individuals and situations. Your job is to know when, where, and to what extent the rules apply to you. When in doubt, follow our general advice on looking professional.

Knowing and playing by the rules does not imply incompetent people get jobs simply by dressing the part. Rather, it means qualified and competent job applicants can gain an extra edge over a field of other qualified, competent individuals by dressing to convey positive professional images.

Winning the Game

Much advice has been written about how to dress for success – some of it excellent. However, there is a major flaw in most of the advice you encounter. Researchers on the subject have looked at how people in positions of power view certain colors for professional attire. Few have gone beyond this to note that colors do different things on different people. Various shades or clarities of a color or combinations of contrast between light and dark colors when worn together may be unenhancing to some individuals and actually diminish that person's "power look."

If you combine the results of research done by John Molloy in *New Women's Dress for Success* and *John Molloy's New Dress for Success* (Warner Books) on how colors relate to one's power look and that done by JoAnne Nicholson in *Dressing Smart for Men* and *Dressing Smart for Women* (Impact Publications) on how colors relate to people as unique individuals, you can achieve a win-win situation. You can retain your individuality and look your best while, at the same time, achieving a look of success, power, and competence.

Your Winning Appearance

The key to effective dressing is to know how to relate the clothing you put on your body to your own natural coloring. Into which category does your coloring fit? Let's find out where you belong in terms of color type:

- **Contrast coloring:** If you are a contrast color type, you have a definite dark-light appearance. You have very dark brown or black hair and light to medium ivory or olive toned skin. Black

men and women in this category will have clear light to dark skin tones and dark hair.

- **Light-bright coloring**: If you are of this color type, you have golden tones in your skin and golden tones in your blond or light to medium brown hair. Most of you had blond or light brown hair as children. Black men and women in this category will have clear golden skin in their face and dark hair.

- **Muted coloring**: If you are a muted-color type, you have a definite brown-on-brown or red-on-brown appearance. Your skin tone is an ivory-beige, brown-beige, or golden-beige tone – that is, you have a beige skin with a golden-brown cast. Your hair could be red or light to dark brown with camel, bronze, or red highlights. Black men and women in this category will have golden or brown skin tones and dark hair.

- **Gentle coloring**: If you are of this color type, you have a soft, gentle appearance. Your skin tone is a light ivory or pink-beige tone and your hair is ash blond or ash brown. You probably had blond or ash brown hair as a child. Black men and women in this category will have pink tones in their skin and dark hair.

There are also some individuals who may be a combination of two color types. If your skin tone falls in one category and your hair color in another, you are a combination color type.

However, if you are not certain which hair or skin tone is yours and thus cannot decide which color type category you belong to, you may wish to contact Color 1 Associates: 1-800-523-8496 (www.dressingsmart. com). They can refer you to the Color 1 consultant nearest you.

A Color 1 associate can provide you with an individualized color chart that allows you to wear every color in the spectrum, but in your best *shade* and **clarity**, as well as written material telling you how you can combine your colors for the best amounts of contrast for your natural coloring (color type).

The color chart is an excellent one-time investment considering the costs of buying the wrong colored suit, shirt, or blouse. It will more than pay for itself if it contributes to an effective interview as you wear your suit in your best shade and put your clothing together to work with, rather than against, your natural coloring. It can help you convey positive images during those crucial initial minutes of the interview – as well as over a lifetime.

Images of Success

John Molloy has conducted extensive research on how individuals can dress effectively. Aimed at individuals already working in professional positions who want to communicate an image of power and success, his advice is just as relevant for someone interviewing for a job.

Basic attire for men or women interviewing for a position is a suit. Let's look at appropriate suits in terms of color, fabric, and style. The suit color can make a difference in creating an image of authority and competence. The suit colors that make the strongest positive statements for you are **your shade** of gray in a medium to charcoal, or **your shade** of blue in a medium to navy. However, you may choose a less authoritative look for some interview settings. Camel or beige are also considered proper colors for men's suits, and women have an even greater color range. Generally even women should select fairly conservative colors for a job interview unless they are interviewing for a job in a field where nonconformity is considered a plus.

When selecting your suit, choose a shade that appears enhancing to you. Should you wear a blue-gray, a taupe-gray, or a shade in between? Do you look better in a bright navy or a more toned-down navy; a blue navy or a black navy; a navy with a purple or a yellow base to it?

In general, most people will look better in grays with a blue undertone than in grays that are closer to the taupe side of the spectrum. Most people will be enhanced by a navy that is not too bright or contain so much black that it is difficult to distinguish whether the color is navy or black. When selecting a beige or a camel, choose a tone that complements your skin color. If your skin has pink tones, avoid beiges and camels that contain gold hues and, instead, select pink-based beiges/camels that enhance your skin color. Similarly, those of you who have gold/olive tones to your skin should avoid the pink-based camel and beiges.

Your suit(s) should be made of a natural fiber. A good blend of a natural fiber with some synthetic is acceptable as long as it has the "look" of the natural fiber. The very best suit fabrics are wool, wool blends, or fabrics that look like them. Even for the warmer summer days, men can find summer-weight wool suits that are comfortable and look marvelous. They are your best buy. For really hot weather, a linen/silk fabric can work well. Normally linen will have to be blended with another fiber, often a synthetic, in order to retain a pressed, neat look. The major disadvantage of pure linen is that it wrinkles. Women's suits also should be made of a natural fiber or have the "look" of a natural fiber. The very best winter-weight suit fabrics are wool or wool blends. For the warmer climates or the summer months, women will find few, if any, summer-

weight wool suits made for them. Hence linen, blended with a synthetic so it will not look wrinkled, or a good silk or silk blend are good choices. Avoid 100 percent polyester fabric, or anything that looks like it – especially double-knits – like the plague! It is a definite negative for your look of competence, power, and success.

The style of your suit should be classic. It should be well-tailored and well-styled. Avoid suits that appear "trendy" unless you are applying for a job in a field such as the arts or perhaps advertising. A conservative suit that has a timeless classic styling and also looks up-to-date will serve you best not only for the interview, but it will give you several years wear once you land the job.

Men should select a shirt color that is lighter than the color of their suit. JoAnna Nicholson's *Dressing Smart for Men* and *John Molloy's New Dress for Success*, go into great detail on shirts, ties, and practically everything you might wear or carry with you. We recommend these books over others because they are based on research rather than personal opinion and promotional fads.

> *When deciding on your professional wardrobe, always buy clothes to last and buy quality.*

When deciding on your professional wardrobe, always buy clothes to last and buy quality. For women quality means buying silk blouses if you can afford them. Keep in mind not only the price of the blouse itself, but the cleaning bill. There are many polyester blouse fabrics that have the look and feel of silk – this is an exception to the "no polyester" rule. Silk or a polyester that has the look and feel of silk are the fabrics for blouses to go with your suits. Choose your blouses in your most flattering shades and clarity of color.

Give your outfit a more "finished and polished" look by accessorizing it effectively. Collect silk scarves and necklaces of semiprecious stones in your suit colors. Wear scarves and necklaces with your suits and blouses in such a way that they repeat the color of the suit. For example, a woman wearing a navy suit and a red silk blouse could accent the look by wearing a necklace of navy sodalite beads or a silk scarf that has navy as a predominant color.

Ask Questions

Interviewers expect candidates to ask intelligent questions concerning the organization and the nature of the work. In fact, many employers indicate that it's often the quality of the questions asked by the candidate that was instrumental in offering them the job. Moreover, you need information

and should indicate your interest in the employer by asking questions. Consider asking some of these questions if they haven't already been answered earlier in the interview:

- Tell me about the duties and responsibilities of this job.
- What's the most important thing I should know about this job and company?
- How does this position relate to other positions within this organization?
- How long has this position been in the organization?
- What would be the ideal type of person for this position? Skills? Personality? Working style? Background?
- Can you tell me about the people who have been in this position before? Backgrounds? Promotions? Terminations?
- Whom would I be working with in this position?
- Tell me something about these people? Their strengths? Their weaknesses? Their performance expectations?
- What would I be expected to accomplish during the first year?
- How would I be evaluated?
- Are promotions and raises tied to performance criteria?
- Tell me how this operates?
- What is the normal salary range for such a position?
- Based on your experience, what type of problems would someone new in this position likely encounter?
- I'm interested in your career with this organization. When did you start? What are your plans for the future?
- I would like to know how people get promoted and advance in this organization?
- What is particularly unique about working in this organization?
- What does the future look like for this organization?

You may want to write your questions on a 3x5 card and take them with you to the interview. While it is best to recall these questions, you may need to refer to your list when the interviewer asks you if you have any questions. You might do this by saying: *"Yes, I jotted down a few questions which I want to make sure I ask you before leaving."* Then pull out your card and refer to the questions.

Appear Likable

Remember, most people invited to a job interview have already been "screened in." They supposedly possess the basic qualifications for the

job, such as education and work experience. At this point employers will look for several qualities in the candidates, such as honesty, credibility, intelligence, competence, enthusiasm, spontaneity, friendliness, and likability. Much of the message communicating these qualities will be conveyed through the candidates' attire as well as through other nonverbal behaviors.

In the end, employers hire people they like and who will interact well on an interpersonal basis with the rest of the staff. Therefore, you should communicate that you are a likable candidate who can get along well with others. You can communicate these messages by engaging in several nonverbal behaviors. Four of the most important ones include:

1. **Sit with a very slight forward lean toward the interviewer.** It should be so slight as to be almost imperceptible. If not overdone, it communicates your interest in what the interviewer is saying.

2. **Make eye contact frequently, but don't overdo it.** Good eye contact establishes rapport with the interviewer. You will be perceived as more trustworthy if you will look at the interviewer as you ask and answer questions. To say someone has "shifty eyes" or cannot "look us in the eye" is to imply they may not be completely honest. To have a direct, though moderate eye gaze conveys interest, as well as trustworthiness.

3. **A moderate amount of smiling will also help reinforce your positive image.** You should smile enough to convey your positive attitude, but not so much that you will not be taken seriously. Some people naturally smile often and others hardly ever smile. Monitor your behavior or ask a friend to give you frank feedback.

4. **Try to convey interest and enthusiasm through your vocal inflections.** Your tone of voice can say a lot about you and how interested you are in the interviewer and organization.

Close the Interview

Be prepared to end the interview. Many people don't know when or how to close interviews. They go on and on until someone breaks an uneasy moment of silence with an indication that it is time to go.

Interviewers normally will initiate the close by standing, shaking hands, and thanking you for coming to the interview. Don't end by saying *"Goodbye and thank you."* As this stage, you should summarize the interview in terms of your interests, strengths, and goals. Briefly restate your qualifications and continuing interest in working with the employer. At this point it is proper to ask the interviewer about selection plans:

"When do you anticipate making your final decision?"

Follow this question with your final one:

"May I call you next week (or whatever is appropriate in response to your question about timing of the final decision) to inquire about my status?"

By taking the initiative in this manner, the employer will be prompted to clarify your status soon, and you will have an opportunity to talk again.

Many interviewers will ask you for a list of references. Be sure to prepare such a list **prior to** the interview. Include the names, addresses, and phone numbers of four individuals who will give you positive professional and personal recommendations. If asked for references, you will appear well prepared by presenting a list in this manner. If you fail to prepare this information ahead of time, you may appear at best disorganized and at worst lacking good references. Always anticipate being asked for specific names, addresses, and phone numbers of your references.

Remember to Follow Up

Once you have been interviewed, be sure to follow through to get nearer to the job offer. One of the best follow-up methods is the thank you letter; you will find examples of these letters at the end of Chapter 12. After talking to the employer over the telephone or in a face-to-face interview, send a thank you letter by e-mail and/or mail. If mailed, which we prefer, this letter should be typed – not handwritten – on good quality bond paper. In this letter express your gratitude for the opportunity to interview. Re-state your interest in the position and highlight any particularly noteworthy points made in your conversation or anything you wish to further clarify. Close the letter by mentioning that you will call in a few days to inquire about the employer's decision. When you do this, the employer should remember you as a thoughtful person.

If you call and the employer has not yet made a decision, follow through with another phone call in a few days. Send any additional information to the employer which may enhance your application. You might also want to ask one of your references to call the employer to further recommend you for the position. However, don't engage in overkill by making a pest of yourself. You want to tactfully communicate two things to the employer at this point: (1) you are interested in the job, and (2) you will do a good job.

For more information on developing interviewing skills, including follow-up and thank you letters, look for the Krannichs' *Interview for Success, Nail the Job Interview, Savvy Interviewing, Dynamite Tele-Search,* and *201 Dynamite Job Search Letters;* Richard Fein's *111 Dynamite Ways to Ace Your Job Interview* and *101 Dynamite Questions to Ask At Your Job Interview;* Wendy Enelow's *The $100,000+ Interview;* and Bernard Haldane Associates' *Haldane's Best Answers to Tough Interview Questions* (all published by Impact Publications and included in the order form at the end of this book). You also should check out the following websites, which include tips on interviewing. Most sites offer free interview tips and services, including Monster.com's "virtual interview." A few sites, such as InterviewCoach. com and WASPCorp.com, charge consulting fees for assisting individuals in preparing for the job interview:

- Monster.com www.interview.monster.com
- InterviewPro www.interviewpro.com
- JobInterview.net www.job-interview.net
- Interview Coach www.interviewcoach.com
- Quintessential Careers www.quintcareers.com/intvres.html
- Wetfeet.com www.wetfeet.com/advice/interviewing.asp
- Interview Coach www.interviewcoach.com
- The Riley Guide www.rileyguide.com/interview.html
- CareerJournal www.careerjournal.com
- Jobweb www.jobweb.com/Resumes_Interviews_default.htm
- Vault.com www.vault.com
- WinningTheJob www.winningthejob.com
- WSACorp.com www.WSACorp.com

16

Negotiate Salary, Benefits, and Your Future

WHEN WAS THE LAST TIME you negotiated your salary and benefits? Chances are you have little or no experience in dealing with compensation issues. Like many government workers, you get paid what you are offered based upon your rank and years in service rather than based upon your negotiation skills and ability to haggle over the details of compensation.

In fact, one of the most important concerns of transitioning military is the whole issue of compensation – how to negotiate a compensation package that truly reflects their worth. If you attend a military transition job fair or receive a screening telephone call, a prospective employer may quickly ask you, *"What are your salary expectations?"* Are you prepared to deal with this question? What mistakes might you make that could affect both your candidacy and the salary you will eventually receive?

In this chapter we address one of the most important issues facing transitioning military. Read it very carefully since it may well be worth thousands of dollars in additional income in the coming years. The techniques we outline here work well for those who follow them and recognize the importance of **timing**. Indeed, it's best to simply **surrender** yourself to these principles, because they have worked for thousands of individuals who have paid a great deal of money to learn the same strategies from career experts. Do this on your own, based upon your intuition about money, and you may be headed for serious trouble!

Are You a Savvy Salary Negotiator?

How prepared are you to negotiate a salary that truly reflects your worth? What knowledge and skills do you need to become a savvy salary negotiator?

Let's start by evaluating your knowledge and skill level for becoming an effective salary negotiator. Respond to the following statements by circling "Yes" or "No." If you are uncertain about your answer, just leave the statement alone and move on to the next statement.

1.	I know what I'm worth in comparison to others in today's job market.	Yes	No
2.	I know what others make in my company.	Yes	No
3.	I can negotiate a salary 15 percent higher than my current salary.	Yes	No
4.	I can negotiate a salary 5-10 percent higher than what the employer is prepared to offer me.	Yes	No
5.	I know where I can quickly find salary information for my particular position.	Yes	No
6.	I usually feel comfortable talking about compensation issues with others, including my boss.	Yes	No
7.	I'm familiar with how various compensation options work with most employers, such as signing bonuses, performance bonuses, cafeteria plans, reimbursement accounts, disability insurance, 401k plans, SEPs, CODAs, stock options, flex-time, tuition reimbursements, and severance pay.	Yes	No
8.	I understand the different types of stock options and equity incentives offered by employers in my field.	Yes	No
9.	I know what my current compensation package is worth when translated into dollar equivalents.	Yes	No
10.	I'm prepared to negotiate more than seven different compensation options.	Yes	No

11. I have a list of at least 50 accomplishments
 and a clear pattern of performance which
 I can communicate to prospective employers. Yes No

12. I'm prepared to tell at least five different
 one- to three-minute stories about my
 proudest achievements. Yes No

13. If asked to state my "salary requirements"
 in a cover letter or on an application, I
 know what to write. Yes No

14. I know when I should and should not
 discuss salary during an interview. Yes No

15. I know what to best say if the interviewer
 asks me, *"What are your salary expectations?"* Yes No

16. I know what questions to ask during the
 interview in order to get information about
 salaries in the interviewer's company. Yes No

17. I know when it's time to stop talking
 and start serious negotiations. Yes No

18. I know how to use the "salary range" to
 create "common ground" and strengthen
 my negotiation position. Yes No

19. I know how to use silence to strengthen
 my negotiation position. Yes No

20. If offered a position, I know what to
 say and do next. Yes No

If you responded "No" to more than three of the above statements or "Yes" to fewer than 15 of the statements, you should find the remainder of this chapter very useful as you prepare for effectively negotiating a compensation package. Like many clients who have followed our principles of salary success, you should be able to substantially increase your salaried income in the future by using the tips presented here.

21 Salary Errors to Avoid

Job seekers typically make several salary negotiation errors that often knock them out of consideration for the job, or they receive and accept a lower salary offer than what they could have received had they practiced

a few of the salary tips outlined in this chapter. Several of these errors also may leave a negative impression on an employer – that you have a bad attitude, or you are basically a self-centered job seeker who primarily focuses on salary and benefits rather than on the performance needs of the employer and organization. The most frequent errors you should avoid include:

1. **Engaging in wishful thinking – believing you are worth a lot more than you are currently being paid but having no credible evidence of what you really should be paid.**

 Few people will admit they are paid too much. Rather, they often feel they are being paid too little. They even suspect that many of their less talented co-workers may be making more for doing less work. Unless you know for certain that you are being underpaid (you've conducted research on salary comparables and know exactly what you should be paid for your level of skills and accomplishments) this type of thinking will be self-defeating as you become increasingly unhappy with your job. If you've done your research and know what you are really worth in today's job market, you are well advised to first talk with your boss about adjusting your compensation package rather than start looking for another job that may pay more, even though you still don't know what you're worth.

2. **Approaching the job search as an exercise in being clever and manipulative rather than being clear, correct, and competent in communicating your value to others.**

 Perhaps it's the lack of salary negotiation experience, a fear of failure, or a lack of data that leads some job seekers to engage in extreme gamesmanship. Whatever you do, make sure you approach your prospective employer in as professional a manner as possible. This is not the time to play games or demonstrate how clever you can be in negotiating compensation. Most savvy employers know when they are being manipulated by a clever job seeker. Playing games conveys all the wrong messages about your future behavior with the employer – that you are probably disingenuous, manipulative, and dishonest. Regardless of how good you may be in doing a job, no one wants to hire such individuals. Remember, how well you handle the interview and negotiate your salary sets the tone for developing important on-the-job relationships.

3. **Failing to research salary options and comparables and thus having few supports to justify your worth.**

 You best negotiate from strength when you have salary data that **supports** your negotiating position. You can easily get such data on the Internet, through your local library, or by talking with individuals who are willing to share such information. Indeed, it only takes a few minutes on the Internet to find useful salary information by visiting such sites as www.salary.com, www.wagweb.com, and www.salarysource.com. Our advice: never talk about salary with a potential employer before doing basic salary research on the value of the position for which you are interviewing.

4. **Failing to compile a list of specific accomplishments, including anecdotal one- to three-minute performance stories, that provide evidence of your value to employers.**

 Another way of providing supports for your negotiating position is to talk about your specific accomplishments with interesting stories and examples. If you are in sales, for example, can you talk about how you increased efficiency by 30 percent in six months or saved your unit thousands of dollars by eliminating unnecessary duplication? Can you tell a story about how you improved morale, cut costs, or increased productivity? Can you tell five stories about the most satisfying moments in your career? Can you explain what really turns you on? If not, it's time to begin putting together a portfolio of accomplishments and related stories.

5. **Revealing salary expectations on the resume or in a letter.**

 You should never reveal your expectations prior to interviewing for a job unless you want to quickly eliminate certain employers from consideration. However, this works both ways. In the process of revealing your salary expectations, you set certain limitations on your future negotiating position and may actually be knocked out of consideration. For example, if you state on your resume or in a letter that you expect a salary of $60,000 but the employer has the position budgeted at $80,000, one of two things might happen. First, you may not be considered for the position because your expected pay level makes you appear unqualified for it. Second, the employer may feel he can get a real bargain by offering you only $60,000 for a position that should cost $80,000. Either way, you put yourself at a disadvantage by stating your salary expectations.

6. **Prematurely answering the question _"What are your salary requirements?"_ before being offered the job.**

Employers often raise the salary question early in the interview. They may actually do this during a telephone screening interview. Their basic goal is to screen you into or out of consideration for the position on salary criteria. Like stating your salary expectations on a resume or in a cover letter, responding to this question with a figure early in the interview puts you at a disadvantage. The old poker saying that _"He who reveals his hand first is at a disadvantage"_ is especially true when negotiating salary. Time should work in your favor. After all, you need more information about the job and your responsibilities in order to determine the value of the position. Is the job really worth $60,000, $80,000, $100,000, or more? A job worth $100,000 a year has different levels of responsibility than one worth only $60,000 a year. If the employer raises the salary expectation questions early in the interview, it's best to respond by saying _"I really need to know more about the position and my responsibilities before I can discuss compensation. Can you tell me about . . . ?"_ This response will usually result in postponing the salary question and impress upon the employer that you are a thoughtful professional who is more employer-centered than self-centered with your interest in the position. Salary should be the very last thing you talk about – within the context of a job offer, which may be after two or three interviews. Once you have been offered the job, then talk about compensation. In other words, no offer, no salary discussion.

7. **Raising the salary question rather than waiting for the employer to do so.**

If you really want to appear self-centered and impress upon the employer that you are primarily interested in the money, go ahead and ask about the salary being offered. When you prematurely raise the salary question, you begin re-focusing the job interview on your needs – and possible greed. No employer wants to hire a self-centered individual who appears needy and greedy in the job interview. By asking this question, you raise a red flag that can knock you out of further consideration – you may not be called back for another interview. The irony of salary negotiations is that you are most likely to be offered a higher salary if you don't talk about salary, until forced to do so at the very end of the interview process, which could be 10, 20, or 30 days after your initial interview. And

when you do finally talk about salary, you should listen and pause a great deal rather than talk a lot about compensation. Your near silence may be handsomely rewarded! Again, he who reveals his hand first will most likely be at a financial disadvantage in the end.

8. Failing to ask questions about the company, job, and previous occupants of the position.

Self-centered candidates who primarily focus on salary and benefits, and frequently appear needy and greedy during the job interview, often fail to focus on the basics of employment. Many of them prepare for the job interview by developing canned answers to anticipated interview questions. Worst of all, they fail to ask questions that indicate an interest in the organization, employer, and job. By asking questions you also learn how to value the position – you discover what it's really worth compared to similar positions in other organizations. If, for example, a $75,000 position involves supervising 10 people with budgetary responsibilities of $1 million but you discover during the interview that you would be expected to supervise 50 people with budgetary responsibilities of $10 million, perhaps the value of the position should be much higher. But you won't be able to value this position unless you've done research on salary comparables as well as asked questions, including what exactly the past occupant of this position was expected to do and did or did not do according to expectations. For example, you might ask, *"Can you tell me a little bit about the last person who held this position. What exactly did she do? What changes do you envision?"* These questions can later be expanded into a salary-related question: *"From what I've heard about this position, what would someone with my qualifications expect to earn here?"* This question turns the tables and asks the employer to volunteer a salary figure or range.

9. Asking *"Is this offer negotiable?"*

Unless you are interviewing for an entry-level or government position, where salaries are relatively set, you should assume most salaries are somewhat negotiable. Most employers have some flexibility to negotiate both salary and benefits, although they may have more flexibility on the benefit side of the compensation equation. In addition, you may want to negotiate other aspects of the job which may normally not be part of a standard job offer, such as a signing bonus, incentivized pay scheme, cell phone, laptop

computer, and flexible hours. By asking this question – whether the offer is negotiable rather than assuming that aspects of it will be – you tend to immediately lose the advantage in the negotiation process.

10. Quickly accepting the first offer, believing that's what the position is really worth and that an employer might be offended if one tries to negotiate.

First offers are exactly that – initial offers. Employers may be prepared to extend second, third, fourth, and fifth offers, depending on your negotiating skills. Since most salaries are negotiable, you tend to diminish your value by not taking your time to think over a first offer and then negotiating the final terms of employment. In fact, since many employers expect candidates to negotiate, their first offer is usually their lowest offer. Employers also tend to respect candidates who come prepared to the salary negotiation session, present evidence of their value, and negotiate in a professional manner. In the process, they learn a great deal about their new employee.

11. Accepting the offer on the spot.

Timing is everything when negotiating salary. Timing can take several forms, from pausing to consider the offer to asking for 24 to 48 hours to think over the offer. Many of our associates report excellent results by pausing in silence for 30 seconds after receiving an initial offer – the pregnant pause that often makes the employer feel uneasy about what he senses may be seen as a low offer. This pause can result in an increase in several thousands of dollars in a second offer which can immediately come at the end of the 30-second pause. At the same time, it's common professional courtesy to ask for at least 24 hours to consider the offer. During that time, you can do additional research on salary comparables, check with other employers with whom you may have interviewed and, if you choose to, develop a well organized counter-offer.

12. Accepting the offer primarily because of compensation.

If you only focus on salary and benefits, you may be disappointed and unhappy with the job. Research continues to show that salary and benefits rank fourth and fifth in the order of importance when valuing jobs. The nature of the work, the culture of the organization, and people you work with are often more important than

salary and benefits. You should focus on learning as much as possible about the nature of the job and organization as well as the people you would be working with. You do this by asking lots of questions about the company and the job. Answers to these questions should indicate whether this job is a perfect fit for you. Is this something you can do well and enjoy doing? Will it allow you to pursue your passion? If the answers are "yes," chances are you'll be able to negotiate a satisfactory compensation package. After all, the employer also should know, based upon your previous accomplishments and interests, that you will be a good fit for the company. Your productivity will more than justify the compensation.

13. Trying to negotiate compensation during the first interview.

Today, many candidates go through three to seven interviews with an employer before receiving a job offer. The first interview seldom deals with the money question, although this question can arise at anytime to screen someone into or out of consideration. Again, you should never raise the salary issue, for to do so puts you at a disadvantage. Expect the salary offer, and accompanying salary negotiations, to take place during the final interview. The signal to talk seriously about money comes when you are offered the job. The offer precedes discussion of appropriate compensation. Another way of handling the *"What are your salary requirements?"* question is to respond by asking *"Are you offering me the position?"* If the response is *"No,"* then you might say, *"I really need to know more about the position and your company before I feel comfortable discussing compensation."* Alternatively, you might want to use this occasion to do research on the company's salary structure by asking *"By the way, how much are you paying at present for this position?"* Always try to get the employer to volunteer salary information from which you can formulate your response.

14. Forgetting to calculate the value of benefits and thus only focusing on the gross salary figure.

Benefits can account for 40 percent or more of a total compensation package, depending on the company. Therefore, you are well advised to calculate your current compensation package and separate your gross salary figure from the benefits. For example, is your current compensation package worth $90,000, with a $60,000 base salary? If so, you should figure at least $30,000 in benefits or one-third of your total compensation package as being in benefits.

You may discover your next employer is prepared to offer you a $70,000 base salary with $20,000 in benefits, which means the new position is equivalent to your present position.

15. Focusing on benefits, stock options, and perks rather than on the gross salary figure.

This is the logical corollary to Error #14. While benefits, stock options, and perks can add up to a significant percentage of one's total compensation, at the same time, many of these "extras" come with the job regardless of your negotiation skills. In other words, everyone at your pay level may receive the same benefits, stock options, and perks. Therefore, you need to determine what exactly comes with the job versus those things that are negotiable. Base salary is usually negotiable and thus should be your main focus for negotiation. Don't be overly impressed with the "extras" if they merely come with the job. Start by getting an overall understanding of what components make up the company's compensation package and how each of the components translates into cash. Start negotiating the base salary and then move on to other elements in the compensation package. As many dot-comers of 2000-2001 can testify, don't be overly impressed with stock options, since they may be worthless, if not costly, by the time you get ready to exercise them or during the time you hold them.

16. Trying to negotiate a specific salary figure rather than talking about a salary range.

Savvy salary negotiators always talk about "salary ranges" rather than specific salary figures. They do so because ranges give them flexibility in the negotiation process. If, for example, you get the employer to reveal his or her hand first by saying the job pays $75,000 a year, you should counter by putting the employer's figure at the bottom of your range: – *"Based on my salary research as well as my experience, I was thinking more in terms of $75,000 to $85,000 a year."*

By doing this, you establish common ground from which to negotiate the figure upwards toward the high end of your range. While the employer may not want to pay more than $75,000, he or she at least knows you are within budget. The employer most likely will respond by saying, *"Well, we might be able to go $78,000."* You, in turn, can counter by saying *"Is it possible to go $81,000?"*

As you will quickly discover in the salary negotiation business,

anything is "possible" if you handle the situation professionally – with supports and flexibility. In this situation, you might have been able to negotiate a $6,000 increase over the employer's initial offer because you established common ground with a salary range and then moved the employer toward the upper end of your range because you had supports and professional appeal.

17. Negotiating over the telephone or by e-mail.

Compensation is a serious business that requires face-to-face meetings to work out the details. When you negotiate, you are on stage presenting your best professional self. You're giving a presentation about yourself and the job, as well as providing supports, which may be in paper form, to justify your salary expectations. Only use the telephone and e-mail if you're really not serious about the position and thus don't want to waste your time in another meeting.

18. Talking too much and listening too little.

Employers report one of the major failings of job candidates is talking too much. Some candidates talk excessively due to nervousness – they talk and talk and talk as if they are trying to convey that they are honest, social, interested, and receptive to the employer. From the interviewer's perspective, however, such excessive talkers come across as self-centered, irritating, and poor listeners. If they talk this much in the interview, what will they be like on the job? Excessive talkers also tend to be poor compensation negotiators. They tend to talk about their needs rather than the needs of the employer.

19. Focusing on your needs rather than the employer's needs.

There's nothing worse you can do than to focus on your financial needs when negotiating salary, such as needing X number of dollars because you're buying a new house or car, your spouse is pregnant, your parents need medical attention, or you're sending two children to college next year. That's your problem – not the employer's. After all, the employer is not hiring you as a social experiment! Indeed, by focusing on your financial needs, you may be communicating a terrible message – that you are financially irresponsible and way over your head financially. Not only is that a very self-centered approach, it also communicates that you are probably needy and

greedy. Given your personal financial situation, you'll probably "need" a raise in no time! You should always focus your attention on the needs of the employer and what you plan to do for him or her in terms of **outcomes**. Always justify a higher salary figure in terms of your salary research and your predictable pattern of performance. If, for example, you expect to earn $100,000 a year, but the employer only offers $80,000 a year, present a plan in which you show that your work over the next year will generate $400,000 rather than $300,000 in additional revenue or that you will be saving the employer X number of dollars that more than justify your expected salary. Remember, most employers want one or two major outcomes from people they hire: (1) generate more income or (2) save money for the company. In other words, your presence should significantly make or save money for the employer.

20. Trying to play "hardball."

Playing hardball and being demanding in salary negotiations can backfire. Doing so also can be very revealing of one's motivations and capabilities. Some candidates prefer to lie about their past salary history, exaggerate their accomplishments, or claim they have alternative job offers waiting in the wings. Treating employers as a combination of adversaries and fools, such job seekers play a very chancy game of "hard to get." If this is the route you choose to go in order to "win" the salary game – rather than being honest, forthright, and professional in your dealings with an employer – chances are you will play similar unethical games once you're on the job. And chances are you are headed for trouble on your new job since you probably have a pattern of developing relationships on such self-centered grounds. In the end, when performance measures your professionalism, no one will really want you because you simply aren't what you say you are. The emperor really has no clothes. Keep your resume current since you may need to market yourself again soon!

21. Expressing a negative attitude toward the employer's offer.

Throughout the interview, and especially during the salary negotiation session, your attitude is on display. How you respond to the employer's offer is an important indicator of how you will most likely deal with the employer in the future. Never show your displeasure, shock, or anger at a lower than expected offer. Always

try to convey the impression that you are a professional – you've done your homework, presented your case with supports, and explained what it will take to attract you. You also may need to be tough – hold the line on what you want and be prepared to walk away from the negotiation table if the employer does not value you the way you value yourself and the position.

Seven Behaviors of Savvy Negotiators

Savvy salary negotiators tend to display seven key behaviors that contribute to success. These behaviors can be learned by following the many techniques outlined in the remainder of this chapter. The following behaviors are associated with savvy salary negotiators:

1. **Approach the job search as a process of finding a job that is a perfect "fit" for their motivational pattern – one they do well and enjoy doing.** While compensation is important, it is not the primary motivator for savvy salary negotiators. Many things may turn them on, but **pursuing a passion** is the primary motivator. They clearly communicate their passion and competence to employers who, in turn, recognize their value and compensate them accordingly.

2. **Conduct research on salary options and salary comparables.** Savvy salary negotiators know their market value because they conduct salary research by using the Internet and libraries and by interviewing informed individuals.

3. **Focus on the requirements of the job and the needs of the employer.** Savvy salary negotiators are employer-centered rather than self-centered. They talk the language of employers which focuses on their bottom line – accomplishments, benefits, and performance.

4. **Ask lots of questions about the company, employer, and position as well as listen carefully.** Savvy salary negotiators view the interview as an exchange of information between the candidate and the employer. They understand that both parties need to determine whether or not this will be a good "fit." Asking questions and listening carefully to the interviewer are the major communication techniques they use for acquiring critical information about the company, employer, and position.

5. **Emphasize their value throughout the interview.** Savvy salary negotiators focus on their accomplishments throughout each and every interview. They emphasize through examples, statistics, and short anecdotes that they have a clear record of accomplishments related to their motivational pattern or passion. They also send thank you letters which emphasize their social graces and likability.

6. **Use timing and silence to their advantage.** Savvy salary negotiators talk seriously about money only after receiving an offer. Knowing the importance of acquiring information about the job and stressing their value throughout the interview, they avoid prematurely discussing compensation. When offered the job and negotiating the salary figure, they know silence is golden by using the "30-second pause" to their advantage.

7. **Focus on the total compensation package rather than just the gross salary figure.** Savvy salary negotiators know there is much more to compensation than just a salary figure. They learn to talk intelligently about compensation options, including a variety of benefits, stock options, and equity incentives. They are prepared to offer creative win-win compensation options.

Taken together, these behaviors should result in negotiating a compensation package that truly reflects your value as well as cements a positive relationship with your new employer. When the employer says *"You're hired,"* you'll respond, *"This is the perfect job – great place, great job, great people, great compensation."* It doesn't get much better than that!

Most Salaries Are Negotiable

Many individuals do very well in handling all interview questions except the salary question. They are either too shy to talk about money or they believe you must take what you are offered – because salary is predetermined by employers. As a result, many applicants may be paid much less than they are worth. Over the years, they will lose thousands of dollars by having failed to properly negotiate their salaries. Indeed, many employees are probably underpaid by hundreds of dollars because they neglected to properly negotiate their salaries.

Contrary to what many job seekers believe, salary is seldom predetermined. Most employers have some flexibility to negotiate salary or benefits. While most employers do not try to exploit applicants, neither

do they want to pay applicants more than what they have to or what a candidate will accept.

Salaries are usually assigned to positions or jobs rather than to individuals. But not everyone is of equal value in performing the job; some are more productive than others. Since individual performance differs, you should attempt to establish your value in the eyes of the employer rather than accept a salary figure for the job. The art of salary negotiation will help you do this.

Today's Salary Influences Your Future Income

We all have financial needs which our salary helps to meet. But salary has other significance too. It is an indicator of our worth to others. It also influences our future income. Therefore, it should be treated as one of the most serious considerations in the job interview.

The salary you receive today will influence your future earnings. Yearly salary increments will most likely be figured as a percentage of your base salary rather than reflect your actual job performance. When changing jobs, expect employers to offer you a salary similar to the one you earned in your last job. Once they learn what you made in your previous job, they will probably offer you no more than a 10% to 15% increase, regardless of your productivity. If you hope to improve your income in the long run, then you must be willing to negotiate your salary from a position of strength.

Always Know What You're Worth

You should be well prepared to deal with the question of salary anytime during your job search but especially during the job interview. Based on your research (Chapter 13) as well as salary information gained from your networking activities (Chapters 6 and 14), you should know the approximate salary range for the position you are seeking. If you fail to gather this salary information prior to the screening or job interview, you may do yourself a disservice by accepting too low a figure or pricing yourself out of consideration. It is always best to be informed so you will be better able to negotiate salary and benefits.

Review Various Compensation Options

At the same time, you need to carefully consider various elements that may be included in compensation packages **before** you consider a job offer and negotiate salary. Base salary, while the most significant and

visible element, is only one of many compensation elements, which need to be considered when negotiating salary. Once your job interview begins focusing on compensation questions, consider whether or not many of the following compensation options are included in an offer. Assign dollar amounts to each element, and then add everything to get a total value for the compensation package. This checklist will help you identify what you most desire in a compensation package, evaluate a job offer, and compare the value of different job offers:

ELEMENT	VALUE

Basic Compensation Issues

- Base salary — $ _____
- Commissions — $ _____
- Corporate profit sharing — $ _____
- Personal performance bonuses/incentives — $ _____
- Cost of living adjustment — $ _____
- Overtime — $ _____
- Signing bonus — $ _____
- Cash in lieu of certain benefits — $ _____

Health Benefits

- Medical insurance — $ _____
- Dental insurance — $ _____
- Vision insurance — $ _____
- Prescription package — $ _____
- Life insurance — $ _____
- Accidental death and disability insurance — $ _____
- Evacuation insurance (international travel) — $ _____

Vacation and Time Issues

- Vacation time — $ _____
- Sick days — $ _____
- Personal time — $ _____
- Holidays — $ _____
- Flex-time — $ _____
- Compensatory time — $ _____
- Paternity/maternity leave — $ _____
- Family leave — $ _____

Retirement-Oriented Benefits

- Defined-benefit plan $ _____
- 401(k) plan $ _____
- Deferred compensation $ _____
- Savings plans $ _____
- Stock-purchase plans $ _____
- Stock bonus $ _____
- Stock options $ _____
- Ownership/equity $ _____

Education

- Professional continuing education $ _____
- Tuition reimbursement for you or your
 family members $ _____

Military

- Compensatory pay during active duty $ _____
- National Guard $ _____

Perquisites

- Cellular phone $ _____
- Company car or vehicle/mileage allowance $ _____
- Expense accounts $ _____
- Liberalization of business-related expenses $ _____
- Child care $ _____
- Cafeteria privileges $ _____
- Executive dining room privileges $ _____
- First-class hotels $ _____
- First-class air travel $ _____
- Upgrade business travel $ _____
- Personal use of frequent-flyer awards $ _____
- Convention participation: professionally related $ _____
- Parking $ _____
- Paid travel for spouse $ _____
- Professional association memberships $ _____
- Athletic club memberships $ _____
- Social club memberships $ _____
- Use of company-owned facilities $ _____
- Executive office $ _____
- Office with a window $ _____

- Laptop computers $ _____
- Private secretary $ _____
- Portable fax $ _____
- Employee discounts $ _____
- Incentive trips $ _____
- Sabbaticals $ _____
- Discounted buying club memberships $ _____
- Free drinks and meals $ _____

Relocation Expenses

- Direct moving expenses $ _____
- Moving costs for unusual property $ _____
- Trips to find suitable housing $ _____
- Loss on sale of present home
 or lease termination $ _____
- Company handling sale of present home $ _____
- Housing cost differential between cities $ _____
- Mortgage rate differential $ _____
- Mortgage fees and closing costs $ _____
- Temporary dual housing $ _____
- Trips home during dual residency $ _____
- Real estate fees $ _____
- Utilities hookup $ _____
- Drapes/carpets $ _____
- Appliance installation $ _____
- Auto/pet shipping $ _____
- Signing bonus for incidental expenses $ _____
- Additional meals expense account $ _____
- Bridge loan while owning two homes $ _____
- Outplacement assistance for spouse $ _____

Home Office Options

- Personal computer $ _____
- Internet access $ _____
- Copier $ _____
- Printer $ _____
- Financial planning assistance $ _____
- Separate phone line $ _____
- Separate fax line $ _____
- CPA/tax assistance $ _____
- Incidental/support office functions $ _____
- Office supplies $ _____
- Furniture and accessories $ _____

Severance Packages (Parachutes)

- Base salary $ _____
- Bonuses/incentives $ _____
- Non-compete clause $ _____
- Stock/equity $ _____
- Outplacement assistance $ _____
- Voice mail access $ _____
- Statement (letter) explaining why you left $ _____
- Vacation reimbursement $ _____
- Health benefits or COBRA reimbursements $ _____
- 401(k) contributions $ _____

TOTAL | $ |

Keep Salary Issues to the Very End

The question of salary may be raised anytime during the job search. Employers may want you to state a salary expectation figure on an application form, in a cover letter, or over the telephone. Most frequently, however, employers will talk about salary during the employment interview. If at all possible, keep the salary question **open** until the very last. Even with application forms, cover letters, and telephone screening interviews, try to delay the discussion of salary by stating "open" or "negotiable." After all, the ultimate purpose of your job search activities is to demonstrate your **value** to employers. You should not attempt to translate your value into dollar figures until you have had a chance to convince the employer of your worth. This is best done near the end of the job interview.

*Salary should be the last major item you discuss with the employer – **after** you have established your value.*

Although employers will have a salary figure or range in mind when they interview you, they still want to know your salary expectations. How much will you cost them? Will it be more or less than the job is worth? Employers prefer hiring individuals for the least amount possible.

You, on the other hand, want to be hired for as much as possible. Obviously, there is room for disagreement and unhappiness as well as negotiation, compromise, and agreement.

One easy way employers screen you in or out of consideration is to raise the salary question early in the interview. A standard question is:

"_What are your salary requirements?_" When asked, don't answer with a specific dollar figure. You should aim at establishing your value in the eyes of the employer prior to talking about a figure. If you give the employer a salary figure at this stage, you are likely to lock yourself into it, regardless of how much you impress the employer or what you find out about the duties and responsibilities of the job. Therefore, salary should be the last major item you discuss with the employer.

You should never ask about salary prior to being offered the job, even though it is one of your major concerns. Try to let the employer initiate the salary question. And when he or she does, take your time. Don't appear too anxious. While you may know approximately what the employer will offer, try to get the employer to state a figure first. If you do this, you will be in a stronger negotiating position.

Handle Salary Tactfully

When the salary question arises, assuming you do not want to put it off, your first step should be to clearly summarize the job responsibilities/ duties as you understand them. At this point you are attempting to do three things:

1. Seek clarification from the interviewer as to the actual job and all it involves.

2. Emphasize the level of skills required in the most positive way. In other words, you emphasize the value and worth of this position to the organization, and subtly this may help support the actual salary figure that the interviewer or you later provide.

3. Focus attention on your value in relation to the requirements of the position – the critical linkage for negotiating salary from a position of strength.

You might do this, for example, by saying,

> "As I understand it, I would report directly to the vice-president in charge of marketing and I would have full authority for marketing decisions that involve expenditures of up to $100,000. I would have a staff of five people – a secretary, two copywriters, and two marketing assistants."

Such a summary statement establishes for both you and the interviewer that (1) this position reports to the highest levels of authority; (2) this position is responsible for decision-making involving fairly large sums of money; and (3) this position involves supervision of staff.

Although you may not explicitly draw the connection, you are emphasizing the value of this position to the organization. This position should be worth a lot more than one in which the hiree will report to the marketing manager, be required to get approval for all expenditures over $100, and has no staff – just access to the secretarial pool! By doing this you will focus the salary question (which you have not yet responded to) around the exact work you must perform on the job in exchange for salary and benefits. You have also seized the opportunity to focus on the value of the person who will be selected to fill this vacancy.

Your conversation might go something like this. The employer poses the question:

> *"What are your salary requirements?"*

Your first response should be to summarize the responsibilities of the position. You might begin with a summary statement followed by a question:

> *"Let me see if I understand all that is involved with this position and job. I would be expected to _____. Have I covered everything or are there some other responsibilities I should know about?"*

This response focuses the salary question around the **value** of the position in relation to you. After the interviewer responds to your final question, answer the initial salary expectation question in this manner:

> *"What is the normal salary range in your company for a position such as this?"*

This question establishes the value, as well as the range, for the position or job – two important pieces of information you need before proceeding further into the salary negotiation stage. The employer normally will give you the requested salary range. Once he or she does, depending on how you feel about the figure, you can follow up with one more question.

> *"What would be the normal salary range for someone with my qualifications?"*

This question further establishes the value for the individual versus the position. This line of questioning will yield the salary expectations of the employer without revealing your desired salary figure or range. It also will indicate whether the employer distinguishes between individuals and positions when establishing salary figures.

Reach Common Ground and Agreement

After finding out what the employer is prepared to offer, you have several choices. First, you can indicate that his or her figure is acceptable to you and thus conclude your final interview. Second, you can haggle for more money in the hope of reaching an acceptable compromise. Third, you can delay final action by asking for more time to consider the figure. Finally, you can tell the employer the figure is unacceptable and leave.

The first and the last options indicate you are either too eager or playing hard-to-get. We recommend the second and third options. If you decide to reach agreement on salary in this interview, haggle in a professional manner. You can do this best by establishing a salary range from which to bargain in relation to the employer's salary range. For example, if the employer indicates that he or she is prepared to offer $50,000 to $55,000, you should establish common ground for negotiation by placing your salary range into the employer's range. Your response to the employer's stated range might be:

"Yes, that does come near what I was expecting. I was thinking more in terms of $54,000 to $59,000."

You, in effect, place the top of the employer's range into the bottom of your range. At this point you should be able to negotiate a salary of $55,000 to $57,000, depending on how much flexibility the employer has with salaries. Most employers have more flexibility than they are willing to admit.

Once you have placed your expectations at the top of the employer's salary range, you need to emphasize your value with **supports**, such as examples, illustrations, descriptions, definitions, statistics, comparisons, or testimonials. It is not enough to simply state you were "thinking" in a certain range; you must state why you believe you are worth what you want. Using statistics and comparisons as your supports, you might say, for example:

> *"The salary surveys I have read indicate that for the position of _*
> *_____ in this industry and region the salary is between $54,000*
> *and $59,000. Since, as we have discussed, I have extensive ex-*
> *perience in all the areas you outlined, I would not need training in*
> *the job duties themselves – just a brief orientation to the operating*
> *procedures you use here at _____. I'm sure I could be up*
> *and running in this job within a week or two. Taking everything*
> *into consideration – especially my skills and experience and what*
> *I see as my future contributions here – I really feel a salary of*
> *$58,000 is fair compensation. Is this possible here at _____?"*

Another option is to ask the employer for time to think about the salary offer. You want to sleep on it for a day or two. A common professional courtesy is to give you at least 48 hours to consider an offer. During this time, you may want to carefully examine the job. Is it worth what you are being offered? Can you do better? What are other employers offering for comparable positions? If one or two other employers are considering you for a job, let this employer know his or her job is not the only one under consideration. Let the employer know you may be in demand elsewhere. This should give you a better bargaining position. Contact the other employers and let them know you have a job offer and that you would like to have your application status with them clarified before you make any decisions with the other employer. Depending on how much flexibility an employer may have to accelerate a hiring decision, you may be able to go back to the first employer with another job offer. With a second job offer in hand, you should greatly enhance your bargaining position.

How you negotiate your salary will affect your future relations with the employer.

In both recommended options, you need to keep in mind that you should always negotiate from a position of knowledge and strength – not because of need or greed. Learn about salaries for your occupation, establish your value, discover what the employer is willing to pay, and negotiate in a professional manner. For how you negotiate your salary will affect your future relations with the employer. In general, applicants who negotiate well will be treated well on the job.

Carefully Examine Benefits

Many employers will try to impress candidates with the benefits offered by the company. These might include retirement, bonuses, stock options,

medical and life insurance, and cost of living adjustments. If the employer includes these benefits in the salary negotiations, do not be overly impressed. Most benefits are standard – they come with the job. When negotiating salary, it is best to talk about specific dollar figures. But don't neglect to both calculate and negotiate benefits according to the checklist on pages 395-398. Benefits can translate into a significant portion of one's compensation, especially if you are offered stock options, profit sharing, pensions, insurance, and reimbursement accounts. Indeed, many individuals in the 1990s who took stock options in lieu of high salaries with start-up high tech firms discovered the importance of benefits when their benefits far outweighed their salaries; making only $30,000 a year, some of them became instant millionaires when their companies went public! In fact, the U.S. Department of Labor estimates that benefits now constitute 43 percent of total compensation for the average worker. For example, a $60,000 offer with Company X may translate into a compensation package worth $80,000, but a $50,000 offer with Company Y may actually be worth more than $100,000 when you examine their different benefits.

If the salary offered by the employer does not meet your expectations, but you still want the job, you might try to negotiate for some benefits which are not considered standard. These might include longer paid vacations, some flex-time, and profit sharing.

Offer a Renegotiation Option

You should make sure your future salary reflects your value. One approach to doing this is to reach an agreement to renegotiate your salary at a later date, perhaps in another six to eight months. Use this technique especially when you feel the final salary offer is less than what you are worth, but you want to accept the job. Employers often will agree to this provision since they have nothing to lose and much to gain if you are as productive as you tell them.

However, be prepared to renegotiate in both directions – up and down. If the employer does not want to give you the salary figure you want, you can create good will by proposing to negotiate the higher salary figure down after six months if your performance does not meet the employer's expectations. On the other hand, you may accept this lower figure with the provision that the two of you will negotiate your salary up after six months if you exceed the employer's expectations. It is preferable to start out high and negotiate down rather than start low and negotiate up.

Renegotiation provisions stress one very important point: you want to be paid on the basis of your performance. You demonstrate your profes-

sionalism, self-confidence, and competence by negotiating in this manner. More important, you ensure that the question of your monetary value will not be closed in the future. As you negotiate the present, you also negotiate your future with this as well as other employers.

Take Time Before Accepting

You should accept an offer only after reaching a salary agreement. If you jump at an offer, you may appear needy. Take time to consider your options. Remember, you are committing your time and effort in exchange for money and status. Is this the job you really want? Take some time to think about the offer before giving the employer a definite answer. But don't play hard-to-get and thereby create ill-will with your new employer.

While considering the offer, ask yourself several of the same questions you asked at the beginning of your job search:

- What do I want to be doing five years from now?

- How will this job affect my personal life?

- Do I want to travel?

- Do I know enough about the employer and the future of this organization?

- How have previous occupants of this position fared? Why did they have problems?

- Are there other job opportunities that would better meet my goals?

Accepting a job is serious business. If you make a mistake, you could be locked into a very unhappy situation for a long time.

If you receive one job offer while considering another, you will be able to compare relative advantages and disadvantages. You also will have some external leverage for negotiating salary and benefits. While you should not play games, let the employer know you have alternative job offers. This communicates that you are in demand, others also know your value, and the employer's price is not the only one in town. Use this leverage to negotiate your salary, benefits, and job responsibilities.

If you get a job offer but you are considering other employers, let the others know you have a job offer. Telephone them to inquire about your

status as well as inform them of the job offer. Sometimes this will prompt employers to make a hiring decision sooner than anticipated. In addition you will be informing them that you are in demand; they should seriously consider you before you get away!

Some job seekers play a bluffing game by telling employers they have alternative job offers even though they don't. Some candidates do this and get away with it. We don't recommend this approach. Not only is it dishonest, it will work to your disadvantage if the employer learns that you were lying. But more important, you should be selling yourself on the basis of your strengths rather than your deceit and greed. If you can't sell yourself honestly, don't expect to get along well on the job. When you compromise your integrity, you demean your value to others and yourself.

Your job search is not over with the job offer and acceptance. You need to set the stage. Be thoughtful by sending your new employer a nice thank you letter. As outlined at the end of Chapter 10, this is one of the most effective letters to write for getting your new job off on the right foot. The employer will remember you as a considerate individual whom he looks forward to working with.

The whole point of our job search methods is to clearly communicate to employers that you are competent and worthy of being paid top dollar. If you follow our advice, you should do very well with employers in interviews and negotiating your salary as well as working on the job.

Know Your Value, Emphasize Your Productivity

One final word of advice. Many job seekers have unrealistic salary expectations and exaggerated notions of their worth to potential employers. Given the greater emphasis on productivity and performance in the workplace, many employers are reluctant to negotiate salaries upwards prior to seeing you perform in their organization. Make sure you make a case for justifying your salary expectations. Do you know, for example, what you're really worth in today's job market? Have you researched salary comparables by examining salary surveys found through your professional association, employment firms, and government studies, or revealed on several key websites, such as www.salary.com and www.job star.org? In a full employment economy, where your skills and experience are in high demand, you should be better able to negotiate compensation. Your ability to negotiate will in part be a function of such supply and demand factors in the labor market.

You will need to stress your **value** more than ever in employer-centered terms. Your value primarily comes in two forms: income and savings for the organization. For example, if you think you are worth

$50,000 a year in salary, will you be productive enough to generate $300,000 of business for the company to justify that amount? Alternatively, are you prepared to save the company $50,000 next year? If you can't translate your salary expectations into dollars and cents profits or savings for the employer, perhaps you should not be negotiating at all!

For more information on salary negotiations for both job seekers and employees, see Ron and Caryl Krannich's *Salary Negotiation Tips for Professionals, Dynamite Salary Negotiations*, and *Get a Raise in 7 Days: 10 Salary Steps to Success* (Impact Publications). These books outline various steps for calculating your worth and conducting face-to-face negotiations, including numerous sample dialogues. They are available through Impact's online bookstore: www.impactpublications.com. For other assistance with salary information and negotiations, be sure to visit these websites:

▪ Salary.com	www.salary.com
▪ Monster.com	http://salary.monster.com
▪ SalaryExpert	www.salaryexpert.com
▪ SalarySource	www.salarysource.com
▪ WageWeb	www.wageweb.com
▪ Abbott-Langer	www.abbott-langer. com
▪ BenefitsLink	www.benefitslink.com
▪ BenefitNews.com	www.benefitnews.com
▪ Bureau of Labor Statistics	www.bls.gov
▪ CareerJournal	www.careerjournal.com
▪ CompGeo Online	www.claytonwallis.com/cxgonl. html
▪ Employee Benefit Research Institute	www.ebri.org
▪ Homestore.com	www.homefair.com
▪ Quintessential Careers	www.quintcareers.com/salary_ negotiation.html
▪ Riley Guide	www.rileyguide.com/netintv. html
▪ Robert Half International	www.rhii.com
▪ SalaryMaster	www.salarymaster.com
▪ Salary Surveys for Northwest Employers	www.salarysurveys.milliman. com

Part III

Make Smart Decisions the Rest of Your Life

17

Survive and Thrive in Your Career

THE CAREER DECISIONS YOU make today will affect your career development tomorrow. Indeed, throughout this book we have tried to prepare you for making critical career choices for today and tomorrow. While we cannot predict the future, we do know you will gain greater control over your future when you use our careering and re-careering methods.

After negotiating the job offer, shaking hands, and feeling great that you have succeeded in getting a job that is right for you, what's next? How do you get started on the right foot and continue to advance your career? In this chapter we suggest how to best handle your job and career future after congratulating yourself on a job search well done.

Take More Positive Actions

If you managed your interviews and salary negotiations in a professional manner, your new employer should view you in a positive light. Once you've completed the interview, negotiated the salary, and accepted the offer, you should do two things:

1. Send your new employer a thank you letter.

Never underestimate the power of a simple thank you letter. It may be the single most important action you take. Mention your appreciation for the professional manner in which you were hired and how pleased you are to be joining the or-

ganization. Reaffirm your goals and your commitment to producing results. This letter should be well remembered. After all, employers seldom receive such thoughtful letters, and your reaffirmation helps ease the employer's fears of hiring an untested quantity.

2. **Send thank you letters to those individuals who assisted you with your job search, especially those with whom you conducted informational and referral interviews.**

 Tell them of your new position, thank them for their assistance, and offer your assistance in the future. Not only is this a nice and thoughtful thing to do, it also is a wise thing to do for your future.

In both cases, put your best professional foot forward by sending a traditional typed letter by mail. Such a letter means more to the recipient and will more likely be read than a quick and easy e-mail note.

Always remember your network. You work with people who can help you in many ways. Take good care of your network by sending a thank you letter and keeping in contact. In another few years you may be looking for another position. In addition, people in your network may later want to hire you away from your present employer. Since they know what you can do and they like you, they may want to keep you informed of new opportunities. While you will be developing new contacts and expanding your network in your new job, your former contacts should be remembered for future reference. An occasional letter, holiday card, or telephone call are thoughtful things to do.

Be Alert to Changing Job Requirements

In today's highly competitive and fast-paced work environments, the skills required for the job you have today may change tomorrow. The job you were initially hired to do will often expand into many different directions that can result in a substantial raise or promotion; be open to such changes. Always make sure your on-the-job skills are up to date and that you are doing more than what you consider to be "your job." This may mean acquiring new skills and redefining your job in reference to changing organizational requirements. Take initiative and demonstrate your entrepreneurial skills. Treat your boss as if he or she were your client by **exceeding performance expectations.** Your continuing employment depends on satisfying the needs of your client. Individuals who unexpect-

edly become victims of downsizing are often those who did a particular job well but suddenly discover they have the wrong set of skills for an organization undergoing transformation as it attempts to become more competitive. Never assume the skills and experience you have today will be sufficient for the job tomorrow. Always define what you are doing today in terms of the larger organization. Ask yourself, for example, *"Am I a continuing asset to what may be a rapidly changing organization? Will I be needed as much tomorrow as I am today?"*

Avoid the Pitfalls of Office Politics

After three months on the job, you should know who's who, who has clout, whom to avoid, and how to get things done in spite of people, their positions, and their personal agendas. In other words, you will become inducted into the informal structure of the organization. You should become aware of this structure and use it to your advantage.

> *Treat your boss as if he or she were your client by exceeding performance expectations.*

While it goes without saying that you should perform in your job, you need more than just performance. You should understand the informal organization, develop new networks, and use them to advance your career. This means conducting an internal career advancement campaign as well as an annual career check-up.

Don't expect to advance by sitting around and doing your job, however good you may be. Power is distributed in organizations, and politics is often ubiquitous. Learn the power structure as well as how to play positive politics. For sound advice on this subject, see Andres J. DuBrin's *Winning in Office Politics* (Van Nostrand Reinhold) and Marilyn Moats Kennedy's *Office Politics* (Follett).

After a while many organizations appear to be similar in terms of the quality and quantity of politics. Intensely interpersonal jobs are the most political. Indeed, people are normally fired because of politics – not gross incompetence. What do you do, for example, if you find yourself working for a tyrannical or incompetent boss, or a jealous co-worker is out to get you? Some organizational environments can be unhealthy for your professional development.

Conduct an Annual Career Check-Up

We recommend an annual career check-up. Take out your resume and review it. Ask yourself several questions:

- Am I achieving my objective?
- Has my objective changed?
- Is this job meeting my expectations?
- Am I doing what I'm good at and enjoy doing?
- Are my skills up to date for this job and organization?
- Am I able to fully use my skills as well as acquire new skills?
- Does this company fully value my contributions?
- Is this job worth keeping?
- How can I best achieve career satisfaction either on this job or in another job or career?
- What other opportunities elsewhere might be better than this job?

Individuals should increasingly ask these questions about their jobs and careers.

Perhaps changing jobs is not the best alternative for you. If you encounter difficulties with your job, you should first assess the nature of the problem. Perhaps the problem can be resolved by working with your present employer. Many employers prefer this approach. They are learning that increased job satisfaction translates into less job stress and absenteeism as well as more profits for the company. Progressive employers want happy workers because they are productive employees. They view job-keeping and job-revitalization as excellent investments in their futures.

Alternatively, you may want to enter your resume into various online resume databases where you can literally keep yourself in the job market 24 hours a day, 365 days a year. Whether you are actively looking for a job or just keeping in touch with potential opportunities, putting your resume online may be a good way to conduct a career check-up on a regular basis. Indeed, we expect more and more individuals will include their resume in such databases as they constantly keep in touch with what is an increasingly unpredictable job market. Many Internet recruitment sites offer a new approach to the job search: no longer will you need to start a job search campaign only when you lose your job or decide to change jobs. Putting your resume online with such websites as Monster. com, HotJobs.Yahoo.com, DirectEmployers.com, and Career Builder.com allows you to remain constantly active in the job market. In so doing, new and unexpected job opportunities may come your way even though you are perfectly happy with your current job. In other words, participation in such resume databases may result in employers coming to you rather than you seeking out employers by using the job search strategies and techniques outlined in this book.

The concept of an annual career check-up may be replaced with the concept of a lifetime membership in a career health or fitness club. You keep your career healthy and fit by always keeping yourself, via your electronic resume, on the job market.

Use 25 Job-Keeping and Advancement Strategies

Assuming you enjoy your work, how can you best ensure keeping your job as well as advancing your career in the future? How can you best avoid becoming a victim of cutbacks, politics, and terminations?

Most employers want their employees to perform according to certain expectations. As we noted earlier, employers want truthfulness, honesty, and value in their employees. They expect their workers to:

1. Be on time consistently.
2. Follow directions.
3. Be honest and truthful.
4. Be dependable in everything they do.
5. Get the job done quickly, starting with things they least like to do.
6. Do the job well and with a positive attitude.
7. Take initiative rather than wait to be given directions.
8. Be accurate and show competence.
9. Dress and groom appropriately, being both conservative and professional in their appearance.
10. Maintain good health and cleanliness.
11. Be professional and respectful.
12. Be enthusiastic and energetic.
13. Be a loyal employee who looks out for the company and boss.
14. Avoid doing personal business (phone calls, e-mail, Internet surfing) on company time.
15. Solve problems skillfully.
16. Be pleasant to work with and to be around.
17. Avoid conflicts and arguments with others.
18. Help out when needed, even if doing so is not part of their normal responsibilities.
19. Be unselfish and give credit to others, especially the boss (always make him/her look good), even though the credit should go to the employee.
20. Persevere in spite of unusual challenges and difficulties – never give up!
21. Take responsibility for their job and everything they do.

22. Make useful suggestions and find creative ways to solve the employer's problems.
23. Earn the respect of their fellow workers.
24. Become a good team player.

While using these 24 skills and personal qualities will not ensure job security, they will most likely enhance your security and potential for advancement. Most of them will make an employee indispensable to a company and a special asset to an employer or boss. When an employer asks himself whom he can most rely upon to do a job, do it well, and do it enthusiastically, make sure it's **you** he thinks about.

A final job-keeping skill – (#25) manage your political environment – is one employers don't like to talk about. It may well be more important than all the other job-keeping skills. Many people who get fired are victims of political assassination rather than failures at meeting the boss's job performance expectations or scoring well on the annual performance appraisal.

You must become savvy at the game of office politics in order to survive in many jobs. For example, what might happen if the boss you have a good working relationship with today is replaced tomorrow by someone you don't know or by someone you know but don't like? Through no fault of your own – except having been associated with a particular mentor or patron – you may become a victim of the new boss's housecleaning. Accordingly, you get a two-hour notice to clean out your desk and get out. Such political assassinations are common occurrences in the publishing, advertising, media, and other businesses.

Remember 10 Job Survival Strategies

The following 10 survival strategies can be used to minimize the uncertainty and instability surrounding many jobs today:

1. **Learn to read the signs of coming changes.** Know when to leave and when to stay by reading the signs of possible cutbacks, layoffs, and firings before they occur. How is employee morale? Are you communicating as well with others as you did before? Are others being terminated? Adjust to the danger signals by securing your job or by looking for another job.

2. **Document your achievements.** Keep a record of what you accomplish – problems you solve, contributions you make to

improving productivity and profits. Most employers look for two major outcomes – saving money or making money. How do you contribute to these two?

3. **Toot your horn for promotion.** Talk about your accomplishments with co-workers and supervisors – but don't boast. Keep them informed about your work; let them know you are available for promotion. If they don't know what you are accomplishing, they may think you are not contributing much to their operations.

4. **Expand your horizons.** Become more aware of other areas in the company and acquire skills for performing other jobs. The more skills you have, the more valuable you should be to the company.

5. **Prepare for your next job.** Most people will have three to five different careers and 15 or more jobs throughout their lives. The job you have today will most likely not be the job you have five or 10 years from now. Therefore, you need to plan ahead by acquiring more skills for your future jobs. Seek more training through:

 ▪ apprenticeships
 ▪ community colleges
 ▪ weekend colleges
 ▪ private, trade, or technical schools
 ▪ Internet and correspondence courses
 ▪ industrial training programs
 ▪ government training programs
 ▪ cooperative education
 ▪ four-year college or university

6. **Find a good mentor.** Attach yourself to someone in a position of influence and power whom you admire and who can help you acquire more responsibilities, skills, and advancement. Avoid currying favor.

7. **Continue networking.** Educate yourself as well as expand your interpersonal network of job contacts by regularly talking to people about their jobs and careers. Networking will be your ticket to job and career advancement.

8. **Use your motivated abilities and skills.** Success tends to attract more success. Regularly use the abilities and skills you enjoy in different everyday settings.

9. **Think like an entrepreneur.** You are responsible for your own employment fate. No one owes you a job. As in any workplace, you receive money in exchange for services rendered. Your boss is your most important client. Make sure you're offering good quality services to this client. If not, the boss may want to hire someone else to provide the necessary services.

10. **Keep a positive attitude.** Attitude is everything when it comes to getting ahead. Try to keep a positive attitude in everything you say and do. People like working with and promoting enthusiastic and positive people.

Assess and Change When Necessary

We are not proposing disloyalty to employers or regular job-hopping. Instead, we believe in the great American principle of "self-interest rightly understood"; your first obligation is to yourself. No one owes you a job, and nor should you feel you owe someone your career and life. Jobs and careers should not be life sentences. Periodically assess your career health and feel free to make changes when necessary. You owe it to yourself and others around you to be your very best self.

Since many jobs change for the worse, it may not be worth staying around for headaches and ulcers. Indeed, many people stay around too long; they fail to read signs that say it's time to go. If the organization does not meet your career expectations, use the same job search methods that got you into the organization. Be prepared to bail out for greener pastures by doing your job research and conducting informational and referral interviews. While the grass may not always be greener on the other side, many times it is; you will know by conducting another job search.

Revitalize and Transform Your Job

Assuming you know how to survive on your job, what do you do if you experience burnout and high levels of job stress, or are just plain bored with your job? A job change, rather than resolving these problems, may lead to a repetition of the same patterns elsewhere. Techniques for

changing the nature of your present job may prove to be your best option.

Most people will sometimes experience what Marilyn Moats Kennedy (*Career Knockouts*, Follett) calls the "Killer B's": blockage, boredom, and burnout. What can individuals do to make their jobs less stressful, more interesting, and more rewarding? One answer is found in techniques collectively referred to as "job revitalization."

Jobs and careers should not be life sentences. Periodically assess your career health and feel free to make changes when necessary.

Job revitalization involves changing work patterns. It requires you to take risks. Again, you need to evaluate your present situation, outline your career and life goals, and develop and implement a plan of action. A job revitalization campaign may include meeting with your boss to develop an on-the-job career development plan. Set goals with your boss and discuss with him or her how you can best meet these goals on the job. If your boss is not familiar with career development and job revitalization alternatives, suggest some of these options:

- Rotating jobs
- Redesigning your job
- Creating a new position
- Promotion
- Enlarging your job duties and responsibilities
- Part-time work
- Sabbatical or leave of absence
- Flex-time scheduling
- Job sharing
- Retraining/education program
- Internship

Perhaps your supervisor can think of other options which would be acceptable to company policy as well as productive for both you and the organization.

More and more companies recognize the value of introducing career development programs, and they encourage job revitalization among their employees. They know it is more cost-effective to retain good employees by offering them new job options for career growth within the organization than to see them go. They are especially protective of their star employees, trying to find new ways to keep them happy and productive! Such programs and policies support the productivity and profit goals of organizations. They are good management practices. As organizations in the coming decade stress greater productivity, hiring right, and retaining star performers, they will place more emphasis on career development and job revitalization. For extensive treatments of these subjects within the context of today's workplace, see:

Love 'Em or Lose 'Em: Getting Good People to Stay,
Dr. Beverly Kaye and Sharon Jordan-Evans (Barrett-Koehler)

Finding and Keeping Great Employees, Dr. Jim Harris and
Joan Brannick (AMACOM)

How to Be a Star At Work, Robert E. Kelley (Time Books)

Two other books also are well worth reading for tips on surviving and
prospering in the workplace:

*From Day One: CEO Advice to Launch an Extraordinary
Career*, William J. White (Prentice-Hall)

Shine, Larry Thompson (McGraw-Hill)

Prepare for Change

You should prepare yourself for the job realities associated with a society
that is undergoing major structural changes. This means avoiding organi-
zations, careers, and jobs that are declining as well as knowing what you
do well and enjoy doing. It also means regularly acquiring the necessary
training and retraining to function in a turbulent job market. And it
means using your career planning skills to effectively make job and career
changes in the decades ahead. If you do this, you should be well prepared
to turn turbulence into new opportunities and to acquire new jobs which
will become exciting and satisfying challenges. Above all, you will be fit
for the jobs and careers of the future.

18

Find Your Ideal Place to Live and Work

RELOCATION IS AN IMPORTANT job concern for millions of Americans. Whether you are currently in the military or a veteran, relocation will undoubtedly be an issue for you as you make future job and lifestyle decisions.

Like other service members, you have probably made several moves while serving in the military, courtesy of the Department of Defense. You and your family are used to packing up and moving to new and unfamiliar places. In fact, you've probably welcomed many of these moves as part of your military lifestyle – a new adventure in living. While you may have had some influence on your assignments, especially your last assignment, chances are you had little choice other than to accept relocation decisions made by others.

Once you leave the military, you're on your own as to where you want to live and work. You get one final move courtesy of the government. Make sure it's a good one in terms of your future. Many service members return to the place where they enlisted. Others remain in the community where they were last assigned. Places like Washington, DC, San Diego, California, and Norfolk, Virginia tend to be favorite places for many ex-military. In these large metropolitan areas ex-military have access to numerous military services as well as civilian employment opportunities. The Metropolitan Washington, DC area, which offers one of the hottest job markets in the country, is a favorite place for military personnel to end their military careers and transition to very vibrant business, government, and nonprofit job markets.

419

Decide to Relocate

When you are faced with a relocation decision after you leave the military, you encounter new job, community, and lifestyle issues that you may have never had to deal with before. In fact, most people change residences as frequently as they change jobs. One in every five families moves to a different residence each year; the average person changes addresses 11 times during his life. Each year approximately 7 million Americans move to another state. Relocation often means changing jobs and lifestyles.

Relocate for New Opportunities

Where will you be working and living next year, five years, or 10 years from now? If you had the freedom to pick up and move today, where would you love to live? Choosing where you want to live can be just as important as choosing what you want to do.

Whatever your choices, you should weigh the relative costs and benefits of relocating to a new community where job opportunities for someone with your skills may be plentiful. If you live in a declining community or one experiencing little economic growth, the job and career opportunities may be very limited. You should consider whether it would be better for you to explore job opportunities in other communities which may offer greater long-term career advancement as well as more flexibility to change jobs and careers in the future.

In recent years economic development has shifted toward the West, Southwest, and Southeast as well as to selected metropolitan areas in the East, South, Midwest, and Plains states. Millions of job seekers will continue to migrate to these areas in the decade ahead in response to growing job and lifestyle opportunities. Perhaps you, too, will look toward these areas as you change jobs and careers in the future.

In this chapter we examine how to conduct both a long-distance and a community-based job search campaign. We use the example of Washington, DC to illustrate the importance of conducting community research as well as for identifying alternative job networks. Nowhere do we recommend that you pull up stakes and take to the road in search of new opportunities. Many people did so in the 1980s as they headed for the reputed promised lands of Houston and Denver. As the booming economies in these communities went bust by the mid-1980s, many of these people experienced a new round of unemployment. This situation could arise in some of today's reputed "promised lands" in the decade ahead.

Don't take to the road until you have done your homework by researching communities, organizations, and individuals as well as created the necessary **bridges** for contacting employers in a new community. Most important, be sure you have the appropriate work-content and networking skills for finding employment in communities you are interested in.

Target Communities

Many people are attached to their communities. Friends, relatives, churches, schools, businesses, and neighborhoods provide an important sense of identity that makes it difficult to leave for a community of strangers. As ex-military, you're probably accustomed to moving to new places, acquiring new housing, and developing new relationships.

The increased mobility of society is partly due to the nature of the job market. Many people voluntarily move to where job opportunities are most plentiful. Thus, Atlanta has become a boom city with hundreds of additional cars entering its already congested freeways each week. The corporate structure of large businesses, with branches geographically spread throughout the national production and distribution system, requires the movement of key employees from one location to another.

When you begin your job search, you face two alternative community approaches. You can concentrate on a particular job, regardless of its geographic setting, or you can focus on one or two communities. The first approach, which we term follow-the-job, is widely used by military, clergy, migrant farm workers, cowboys, bank robbers, mercenaries, oil riggers, construction workers, newspaper reporters, college and university professors, and city managers. These people move to where the jobs are in their particular profession. Not surprisingly, many of these job seekers end up in boring communities which may limit their lifestyle options.

If you **follow the job**, you will need to link into a geographically mobile communication system for identifying job opportunities. You can do this by using placement services and job banks of professional associations; subscribing to specialized trade publications; maintaining contacts with fellow professionals in other communities; entering your resume into nationwide and local online job banks and engaging in electronic networking; or creatively advertising yourself to prospective employers through electronic bulletin boards, newspaper ads, or letter blitzes.

On the other hand, you may want to **target a community**. This may mean remaining in your present community or locating a community you find especially attractive because of job opportunities, climate, recreation,

or social and cultural environments. Regardless of rumored job opportunities, many people, for instance, would not move to Hawaii and North Dakota – the two states with the lowest unemployment rate in November 2005 (2.8 and 3.4%) – or to the "deep South" where the weather is relatively hot and humid and where the people display marked linguistic, social, and cultural differences. The same is true for Southerners who are not particularly interested in moving to what are reputed to be cold, dreary, and crime-ridden northern cities. At the same time, Washington (DC), Austin, Las Vegas, Atlanta, San Jose, Phoenix, Boulder, Charlottesville (VA), Seattle, Madison (WI), Raleigh-Durham, Minneapolis, Boston, Baltimore, Cincinnati, Nashville, Denver, Ft. Lauderdale, and St. Louis are reputed to be the new promised lands for many people. Seeming oases of prosperity and centers for attractive urban lifestyles, these cities are on the community target list of many job seekers.

We recommend using this second approach of targeting specific communities. The follow-the-job approach is okay if you are young, adventuresome, or desperate; you find yourself in a geographically mobile profession; your career takes precedence over all other aspects of your life; or you have a bad case of wanderlust and thus let others arrange your travel plans. By targeting a community, your job search will be more manageable. Furthermore, moving to another community can be a liberating experience which will have a positive effect on both your professional and personal lives.

Why not find a great job in a community you really love? Fortunately you live in a very large country consisting of numerous communities that offer a terrific range of career and lifestyle opportunities. Let's identify some communities that might be a good "fit" for you as well as eliminate many which you may wish to avoid.

Know the Growing States and Communities

Frictional unemployment – the geographic separation of underemployed and unemployed individuals from high labor demand regions and communities – should present new options for you. Numerous job opportunities may be available if you are willing to relocate to the right communities.

During 2005, unemployment averaged 5.0 percent for the nation as a whole. However, as noted in the following U.S. Department of Labor statistics (www.bls.gov), it was unevenly distributed among the states, with a high of 12.4 percent in Louisiana and a low of 2.8 in Hawaii:

State unemployment in 2005 was disproportionately high in both Louisiana and Mississippi, because of the devastating impact of hurricane Katrina in displacing hundreds of people from New Orleans and gulf region of Mississippi.

Unemployment rates were even more pronounced by cities. At the same time, the following metropolitan areas had the highest and lowest unemployment rates in October 2005 when the average unemployment rate for the country was 5.0 percent:

Highest and Lowest Unemployment By Metropolitan Area (October 2005)

Metropolitan Area	Percentage Unemployed
Highest Unemployment	
Gulfport-Biloxi, MS	23.5*
El Centro, CA	17.6
Pascagoula, MS	16.6*
Lake Charles, LA	16.2*
Yuma, AZ	15.7
New Orleans-Metairie-Kenner, LA	15.5*
Beaumont-Port Arthur, TX	11.3
Baton Rouge, LA	9.7*
Houma-Bayou Cane-Thibodaux, LA	9.7*
Sumter, SC	9.0
Visalia-Porterville, CA	8.9
Hanford-Corcoran, CA	8.6
Fresno, CA	8.5
Merced, CA	8.1
Yuba City, CA	8.0
Lafayette, LA	7.8*
Kokomo, IN	7.7
Napa, CA	7.6
Bakersville, CA	7.5
Wierton-Steubenville, OH	7.4
Anderson, SC	7.4
Clarksville, TN	7.0
Stockton, CA	7.0
Lowest Unemployment	
Fargo, ND	2.1
Bismarck, ND	2.2
Idaho Falls, ID	2.2
Grand Forks	2.4

Unemployment By State (November 2005)

Rank	State	Percentage
1	Hawaii	2.8
2	North Dakota	3.4
3	Vermont	3.5
3	Virginia	3.5
5	Alabama	3.6
5	Florida	3.6
7	Idaho	3.7
8	New Hampshire	3.8
9	Minnesota	3.9
9	Nebraska	3.9
12	South Dakota	4.0
12	Utah	4.0
14	Nevada	4.1
14	Oklahoma	4.1
16	Maryland	4.2
17	Montana	4.3
18	Delaware	4.4
19	New Jersey	4.6
20	Wisconsin	4.7
21	Arizona	4.8
21	Arkansas	4.8
21	Iowa	4.8
24	Maine	4.9
24	Massachusetts	4.9
24	West Virginia	4.9
27	Colorado	5.0
28	Connecticut	5.1
28	New Mexico	5.1
28	Pennsylvania	5.1
31	California	5.2
31	Kansas	5.2
31	North Carolina	5.2
31	Rhode Island	5.2
35	Illinois	5.3
35	Indiana	5.3
35	Texas	5.3
38	Georgia	5.4
38	New York	5.4
40	Missouri	5.6
40	Washington	5.6
42	Ohio	5.7
43	Oregon	5.8
43	Tennessee	5.8
45	District of Columbia	6.1
46	Kentucky	6.2
47	Michigan	6.6
48	Alaska	7.0
49	South Carolina	7.1
50	Mississippi	9.5
51	Louisiana	12.4

- Winchester, VA 2.5
- Jacksonville, FL 2.6
- Fayetteville-Springdale-Rogers, AR 2.6
- Harrisonburg, VA 2.6
- Honolulu, HI 2.7
- Deltona-Daytona Beach-Ormond Beach, FL 2.7
- Iowa City, IA 2.8
- Sarasota-Bradenton-Venice, FL 2.8
- Ithaca, NY 2.8
- Morgantown, WV 3.0
- Tallahassee, FL 3.0
- Gainesville, FL 3.0
- Pocatello, ID 3.0
- Cedar Rapids, IA 3.0
- Sioux Falls, SD 3.0
- Jefferson City, MO 3.0
- Lincoln, NE 3.0
- Washington-Arlington-Alexandria, VA 3.1
- Duluth, MN 3.1
- Minneapolis-St. Paul-Bloomington, MN 3.1
- State College, PA 3.1
- La Crosse, WI 3.1
- Roanoke, VA 3.1

* Disproportionately impacted by hurricane Katrina in 2005

Communities with the highest unemployment rates tend to be in the poorest areas of California, Arizona, and Texas which also have large numbers of seasonal, migrant, and agricultural workers. Unemployment was even higher in many troubled small communities outside these metropolitan areas, especially on impoverished Indian reservations, such as Pine Ridge, South Dakota (an incredible 80+ percent unemployment rate in 2005!). If you lived in one of these communities, your employment prospects were indeed bleak. Regardless of your job talents and job search skills, these communities simply did not generate enough jobs to go around. To get ahead, one needed to relocate to a more economically viable community, especially one with very low unemployment that had a steady demand for workers. More often than not, this meant relocating to a diversified metropolitan area where opportunities abounded.

Communities with low unemployment rates tend to have a large portion of highly educated and skilled professional workers, many in the high-tech and medical areas, and large higher-education complexes linked to a diversified network of support services. Many of these same communities ranked high on annual lists of the "best" communities to live in because of their combination of attractive economic, educational, and lifestyle opportunities. Many individuals who moved to these communi-

ties have had little difficulty finding jobs as well as developing new skills for the 21st century.

In the coming decade we expect Connecticut, Delaware, Georgia, Hawaii, Illinois, Idaho, Indiana, Iowa, Maryland, Minnesota, Nebraska, Nevada, New Hampshire, North Dakota, South Dakota, Vermont, Virginia, and Wyoming to have above-average employment rates. Numerous communities within these states, especially in the 250,000 to 500,000 population range, will offer some of the best job opportunities. However, don't overlook several excellent employment oases (rapidly developing cities and counties) within states that have above average unemployment rates, such as Plano, College Station, and Austin, Texas; Scottsdale, Arizona; and Anaheim, Santa Rosa, and Irvine, California.

Disproportionately found in the West, Southwest, and Southeast, many of the fastest growing communities should continue with medium to high growth rates in the decade ahead. Depending on the extent of another energy crisis, several communities in the energy-rich Rocky Mountain states may once again become boom towns. Communities with large concentrations of high-tech and service industries, supported by a strong higher-education infrastructure – will continue to expand both demographically and economically. Cities with large college and university complexes, such as Boston, Minneapolis-St. Paul, Omaha, Raleigh-Durham-Chapel Hill, Oklahoma City, Salt Lake City, Denver, Madison (WI), Columbia (SC), Knoxville, Atlanta, Austin (TX), College Station (PA), Columbus (OH), San Francisco, Seattle, Honolulu, Iowa City, Ann Arbor (MI), and Washington, DC, should experience steady employment growth in the decade ahead. These cities will also generate some of the best paying, high quality jobs.

We foresee continuing population and economic growth in and around several large cities: Las Vegas, Salt Lake City-Ogden, Denver, Milwaukee, Minneapolis-St. Paul, Rochester (MN), Nashville, Dallas-Ft. Worth, Houston, Austin, San Antonio, Gainesville (FL), Fort Lauderdale, Atlanta, Tampa-St. Petersburg, Raleigh-Durham, Pittsburgh, Madison, Philadelphia, Washington-Baltimore, Boston, Indianapolis, Louisville, Atlanta, and Cleveland. Even Southern California – especially the Los Angeles-San Diego corridor – will experience population and job growth in part stimulated by exports to the recovering economies of Mexico and the Pacific Rim and the booming economy of China.

Even though the overall growth predictions point to the Northwest, Far West, and Southwest, these trends should not deter you from considering older cities in the Northeast and North Central regions. After all, two to three million new jobs are created nationwide each year. New jobs will continue to develop in cities such as Chicago, Philadelphia, and

New York; these are still the best places to pursue careers in the fields of banking, publishing, and advertising. Boston is again an attractive employment center. Several communities in the Midwest – especially those with strong educational infrastructures – have transformed their local economies in the direction of high-tech and service industries. Minneapolis-St. Paul, Madison, Chicago, St. Louis, Iowa City, Kansas City, Bloomington-Normal, Indianapolis, Columbus, Cleveland, and Cincinnati in the Midwest, and Philadelphia, Pittsburgh, Baltimore, Washington, Raleigh-Durham-Chapel Hill, and Atlanta in the central to southern Atlantic coast area will remain some of the best cities for jobs and lifestyles in the decade ahead.

Consider the Best Places to Work

If you contemplate relocating to a new community, you should consider communities that are experiencing low unemployment coupled with steady job growth as well as attractive lifestyles. A *Fortune Magazine* survey in 2004 identified 25 cities as the best places for business and work. These cities are considered the top wealth creators which also offer attractive lifestyles and excellent quality of life. The first five cities are especially noted for their higher education institutions and high-tech orientation:

Fortune's Top 25 Metropolitan Areas (2004)

Rank	Metro Area	Percent Job Growth (5 years)	Population
1	Madison, WI	32	443,000
2	Raleigh-Durham, NC	52	1,268,000
3	Austin, TX	30	1,349,000
4	Washington, DC	23	5,162,000
5	Atlanta, GA	50	4,386,000
6	Provo, UT	35	388,000
7	Boise, ID	12	465,000
8	Huntsville, AL	46	354,000
9	Lexington, KY	114	490,000
10	Richmond, VA	53	1,023,000
11	Omaha, NE	65	734,000
12	Albuquerque, NM	42	737,000
13	Knoxville, TN	29	704,000
14	Des Moines, IA	90	471,000
15	Houston, TX	55	4,420,000
16	Appleton, WI	78	367,000
17	San Diego, CA	15	2,907,000
18	Albany, NY	68	885,000

19	Minneapolis-St. Paul, MN	74	3,055,000
20	Ann Arbor, MI	54	603,000
21	Little Rock, AR	82	596,000
22	Charleston, SC	33	563,000
23	Fort Worth, TX	58	1,802,000
24	Colorado Springs, CO	47	544,000
25	Reno, NV	28	362,000

Most of these cities are likely to experience solid growth in the decade ahead. The Washington (DC), Atlanta (GA), and Minneapolis/St. Paul (MN) areas are already star performers because of their extensive medical facilities and high-tech infrastructure as well as their attractive lifestyles. These three cities will probably continue to be great growth communities. They will generate a disproportionate number of high-paying jobs due to the high-quality nature of their jobs and workforces. They may well provide models of a new economy and workforce for the next few decades.

Find the Best Place to Live

Community growth and decline trends should be considered as part of your job and career options. If you live in a declining community with few opportunities for your skills and interests, seriously consider relocating to a growth community. Depressed communities simply do not generate enough jobs for their populations. Many communities with populations of 100,000 to 500,000 offer a nice variety of job and lifestyle options.

Different communities offer many life choices in addition to jobs. Economic development and job generation are only two of many important community choice concerns. Using several indicators of quality living, a 2004 study of the *American City Business Journal* identified what it considers to be the 20 best counties in the United States in terms of their incomes, education, housing, racial diversity, and short commuting times:

America's Top 20 Counties

Rank	Metro Area	Medium Income	Medium Home Value	Population
1	Los Alamos, NM	$78,993	$214,000	18,343
2	Omsted, MN	$51,316	$114,700	124,277
3	Pitkin, CO	$59,375	$497,000	14,872
4	Douglas, CO	$82,929	$237,600	175,766
5	Loudoun, VA	$80,638	$202,300	169,599

6	Washington, MN	$66,305	$156,200	201,130
7	Johnson, KS	$61,455	$149,300	451,086
8	Hamilton, IN	$71,026	$163,600	182,740
9	Howard, MD	$74,167	$198,600	247,842
10	Fairfax, VA	$81,050	$222,400	969,749
11	Juneau, AK	$62,034	$179,200	30,711
12	Nantucket, MA	$55,522	$583,500	9,520
13	Wake, NC	$54,988	$156,200	627,846
14	Dakota, MN	$61,863	$148,500	355,904
15	Summit, UT	$64,962	$281,600	29,736
16	Dupage, IL	$67,687	$187,600	904,161
17	Chesterfield, VA	$58,537	$119,300	259,903
18	Fayette, GA	$71,227	$170,200	91,263
19	Hennepin, MN	$51,711	$141,100	1,116,200
20	Stafford, VA	$66,809	$155,100	92,446

These rankings have already changed in other surveys; they will undoubtedly change in the coming decade. It is best to consult the latest surveys conducted by *Fortune Magazine* (www.fortune.com), Sperling (www.bestplaces.net), and City Rating (www.cityrating.com).

Money Magazine's annual survey of the best places to live came up with a different set of conclusions on the lifestyle side of the relocation equation. They found that when considering a community move, respondents most valued these five criteria: clean water, low crime, clean air, good public schools, and low property taxes. Best of all, this survey went beyond the very large metropolitan area focus of most other studies and instead identified "best places" in communities with populations from 100,000 to 249,999, from 250,000 to 999,999, and over 1,000,000. *Money Magazine's* most recent survey identifies 87 cities and towns as the best places to live. The top 29 include the following:

Money's Best Places to Live

Region/City	Population	Median Household income	Median home price
Eastern Region (over 100,000 population)			
1. Cary NC	104,210	$77,091	$207,000
2. Ramapo, NY	112,684	$64,954	$330,875
3. Coral Springs, FL	128,715	$62,632	$218,500
4. Alexandria, VA	131,918	$59,976	$290,000
5. Sully district, VA	152,169	$92,942	$290,000

Eastern Region (under 100,000 population)

1. Sugarland Run district, VA	29,115	$103,350	$278,250
2. Manalapan, NJ	34,018	$91,245	$410,000
3. Centreville, VA	50,347	$77,243	$250,000
4. Randolph, NJ	25,643	$104,121	$444,500
5. North Andover, MA	27,725	$79,169	$342,500

Central Region (over 100,000 population)

1. Naperville, IL	139,654	$94,687	$260,000
2. Lawerence, IN	113,967	$52,023	$160,930
3. Overland Park, KS	160,253	$66,674	$191,520
4. Olathe, KS	102,617	$65,111	$175,560

Central Region (under 100,000 population)

1. Woodbury, MN	50,701	$81,592	$219,000
2. Dublin, OH	33,480	$96,828	$355,100
3. Wildwood, MO	33,396	$100,278	$320,000
4. Libertyville, IL	52,147	$79,360	$350,000
5. Chesterfield, MO	55,768	$96,013	$333,000

Western Region (over 100,000 population)

1. Plano, TX	271,090	$82,857	$191,520
2. Anaheim, CA	343,855	$52,196	$340,000
3. Scottsdale, AZ	223,181	$59,596	$263,500
4. Santa Rosa, CA	152,450	$54,537	$349,500
5. Irvine, CA	150,450	$77,662	$430,000

Western Region (under 100,000 population)

1. Rancho Santa Margarita, CA	49,898	$84,159	$350,000
2. Flower Mound, TX	61,579	$99,516	$210,672
3. San Clemente, CA	52,969	$68,799	$555,000
4. Tustin, CA	70,551	$60,250	$391,000
5. Carlsbad, CA	86,511	$68,410	$446,000

For a complete list of *Money's* 87 cities and towns, visit the following website: http://money.cnn.com/best/bplive/cities_table/#analysis. For a complete listing of current data on the 300 largest metropolitan statistical areas, visit *Money's* website: http://money.cnn.com/bestplaces. Designed to be interactive, the site allows you to search for "your best city" by ranking nine factors – from weather and crime rate to health care and transportation.

Select a Location Properly

You and your family should take into consideration several factors and questions when deciding on which communities to target your job search. Start by asking yourself these questions:

- What's most important to me/us in making a move – environment, health care, safety, education, employment, economy, culture, taxes, recreation, climate?

- Where would I/we ideally like to live for the next five, 10, or 20 years?

- What is the relative cost of living?

- How attractive are the educational, social, recreational, and cultural opportunities?

- What are the economic and psychological costs of making a move?

- What job and career opportunities are there for me/us?

- How can I/we best conduct a job search in another community?

Many people answer these questions by remaining in their community or by targeting economically growing communities or ones offering excellent lifestyle options. The exodus from the declining industrial cities in the Northeast and North Central regions to the Sunbelt began in the 1960s, expanded in the 1970s, continued into the 1980s with the inclusion of the energy-rich Rocky Mountain states, and further expanded in the 1990s with high-tech industries in the West. Several metropolitan areas in all regions, but especially in the West, will have abundant job opportunities for skilled workers in the decade ahead. Many of these communities also offer attractive lifestyles. Targeting a job search in metropolitan San Francisco, Las Vegas, Denver, Phoenix, Dallas, St. Louis, Minneapolis, Atlanta, Raleigh-Durham, Nashville, Boston, or Washington, DC may be a wise move. While these areas may experience numerous urban problems over the next decade, their problems are ones of growth – traffic congestion, pollution, city planning, crime, and housing shortages – not ones of decline. We believe it is better to experience the

problems of growth than of decline, especially since growing economies are more likely to respond to their problems. In a situation of decline, your livelihood becomes threatened. In a situation of growth, your major problem may be fighting the traffic congestion in order to get to a job which offers a promising career.

New frontiers for renewed job and career prosperity abound throughout America if you are willing to pack your bags and move. But most such frontiers require highly skilled individuals, and there can be major financial costs in making such a move, especially if you are a homeowner. If you lack the necessary skills for industries in other communities, consider getting retrained before making a move. Unfortunately, many people making moves today do not have the necessary skills to succeed in many of today's growing communities.

Making a community move on your own involves taking risks. Many people, for example, are locked into financial obligations, such as a mortgaged house that doesn't sell well in what may be a declining housing market. If you find yourself locked in financially, you may want to consider taking an immediate financial loss in anticipation of renewed prosperity in a community that is experiencing promising growth and prosperity. You may recoup your losses within a year or two. However, you will have to pass through a transition period which can be difficult if you don't approach it in a positive, upbeat manner. The old saying, *"There is no gain without pain,"* is appropriate in many situations involving relocation from one community to another.

Consider Your Financial Costs

The financial costs of relocating will vary depending on your situation. They can be major, especially if you move to a community with high housing costs. Recent studies conducted by Runzheimer International, for example, found the average costs of relocating to be over $35,000 for homeowners and over $9,000 for non-homeowners. The major costs include:

1. Search for housing – travel, child care, and associated expenses.
2. Closing costs on both the old and new homes.
3. Increases in mortgage payments or apartment rent.
4. Temporary living expenses.
5. Cost of a bridge, equity, or swing loan.
6. Costs of maintaining two residences during the relocation period – very high if the old home does not sell immediately.
7. Shipment of household goods.

8. Final moving expenses.
9. Possible increase in cost of living – property and sales taxes, food, utilities.
10. Travel and job search costs for working spouse.
11. Expenses for marketing a home or subletting an apartment.
12. Miscellaneous costs – deposits, decorating costs, fees, dues.

For information on the latest such costs, see Runzheimer International's website: www.runzheimer.com. They offer detailed reports on hundreds of communities, which include comparative costs of living.

When considering a community move, you should be aware of the relative cost of living in various communities compared to your current cost of living. Several websites include useful cost-of-living calculators that enable users to compare their current salary with the cost of living in hundreds of other communities. You may, for example, discover your current salary of $50,000 in Atlanta will need to be $70,000 in San Francisco in order to maintain your current cost of living. Some also include lifestyle and moving calculators along with useful information on housing, schools, crime rates, taxes, recreation, and neighborhoods. Try these sites for starters:

- Homefair www.homefair.com
- MonsterMoving www.monstermoving.com
- Relocation Central www.relocationcentral.com
- Job Relocation www.jobrelocation.com
- Homescape www.homescape.com
- 123Relocation.com www.relo-usa.com
- Employee Relocation Council www.erc.org
- GMAC Relocation Services www.gmac-relocation.com
- Insiders' Guide www.insiders.com/relocation
- MoversNet www.usps.gov/moversnet
- Moving.com www.moving.com
- MovingCost.com www.movingcost.com
- Relocate-America www.relocate-america.com
- Relocation-net.com www.relocation-net.com
- The Wall Street Journal www.homes.wsj.com

A Web of Relocation Resources

The Internet includes a wealth of resources to assist you in identifying the best places to work, live, and relocate. For identifying the best places to live and work, be sure to check out the websites we identified on pages

334-335 of Chapter 13. Assuming you wish to explore various aspects of specific communities, you should include the community websites identified on page 335. For newspapers and magazines on specific communities, check out the gateway websites on page 335.

Conduct a Long-Distance Job Search

How do you target your job search on a particular area? If you decide to remain in your present community, your job search is relatively manageable on a day-to-day basis. If you target another community, you will need to conduct a long-distance job search which requires more extensive use of the mail and telephone as well as carefully planned visits to the area under consideration. In fact, you will probably use your job search time more efficiently with a long-distance campaign. In both situations, you need to conduct community research prior to initiating the major communication steps in your job search.

Most of your community research can be conducted in the library or on the Internet. You need names, addresses, and phone numbers of potential employers. Use the major directories we identified in Chapter 13, such as the *Dun & Bradstreet's Middle Market Directory* and *Who's Who in Commerce and Industry*. The annual *Headquarters USA* is an especially useful directory for anyone contemplating a long-distance job search. Many communities have home pages that include a wealth of information on housing, education, and employers. Homefair's website (www.homefair.com) is a good place to start checking out communities.

We particularly recommend starting with the latest edition of *The Sourcebook of ZIP Code Demographics* (CACI Marketing Systems). Found in the reference section of many libraries, this two-volume directory gives detailed information on population, housing, employment, education, income, and transportation in all U.S. communities. Organized by zip code, it yields a wealth of information on zip coded communities. For example, if you turn to the section on your current zip code, you will discover how your community is structured according to population, housing, employment, language, education, income, and transportation. You can compare your current community to thousands of other zip codes throughout the country. In some cities with five or more zip codes, you will see a wide fluctuation in average median family incomes, depending on the zip code. We recommend consulting this directory **before** committing yourself to relocating to another community. Also look for the latest edition of *The Moving and Relocation Directory* (Omnigraphics).

As noted on page 336, Adams Media publishers a series of 20 job bank guides which identify hundreds of employers and job search services in a variety of major cities and metropolitan areas. Each book includes descriptions of employers along with contact information.

The Yellow Pages of telephone directories are especially useful sources for identifying the business and commercial structure of communities. The larger the community, the more specialized the businesses. For example, New York City has several businesses manufacturing manhole covers! At the same time, you can contact chambers of commerce for information on the community and ask companies for annual reports and other organizational literature.

A good resource for conducting a long-distance job search is Andrea Kay's *Greener Pastures: How to Find a Job in Another Place* (St. Martin's).

Part of your research may involve narrowing the number of communities you are considering. If you identify 10 alternative communities, outline the criteria by which to evaluate them. For example, you may be particularly interested in moving to a community which has a good climate, excellent cultural facilities, unique recreational opportunities, and a sound educational infrastructure in addition to numerous job and career opportunities in your area of interest and skills. Select three communities and initiate a research campaign for more information. If at all possible, schedule a trip to the cities to get an on-site view or feel for the relative environments. Further try to narrow your choices by rank-ordering your preferences among the three communities. Concentrate most of your job search efforts on your top priority community.

Your next step is to develop a strategy for penetrating both the advertised and hidden job markets. If you are conducting a job search outside your present community, the advertised job market will be most accessible to you. However, you need to link into the hidden job market, where most of the good jobs are located. While doing this from a distance is somewhat difficult, nonetheless it can be managed.

Penetrate the Local Job Market

The advertised job market is always the easier to access. Buy a newspaper and read the classified ads. Search online employment sites for job listings. Contact an employment firm and they will eagerly assist you. Walk into a personnel office and they may permit you to fill out an application form.

If you target a community from a distance, begin with the Internet by searching community websites for information. Alternatively, subscribe

to a local newspaper; the Sunday edition will most likely meet your needs. The online versions of newspapers do not include classified ads. This newspaper also will give you other important information on the community – housing market, economics, politics, society, culture, entertainment, and recreation. Survey the help-wanted ads to get a feel for the structure of the advertised job market. Remember, these are not necessarily indicative of the true employment picture in a community – only 20 to 30 percent of the job market. Write letters to various companies and ask about job opportunities. You also may want to contact one or more professional employment agencies or job search firms – preferably fee-paid ones – for job leads. But remember our previous warnings about possible frauds and hucksters!

Efforts to penetrate the advertised job market should be geared toward uncovering the **hidden job market**. For example, in reading the Sunday newspaper, watch for names of important people in the society or living section. You may want to contact some of these people by using an approach letter as outlined in Chapters 13 and 14. The employment agencies may give some indication of the general employment situation in the community – both advertised and hidden job markets. The Chamber of Commerce might be able to give you some job leads other than those advertised. Perhaps you can develop local contacts through membership in an alumni network (see page 127), professional association, or church. Be sure to embrace the Internet: search for information on your targeted community, join news groups, and use message boards – whatever resources that will yield useful information and contacts for conducting a community-based job search.

If you are conducting a long-distance job search, we recommend following the same procedures we outlined in Chapter 14 on networking. Preparation is the key to success. Do your research on potential employers, write letters, make phone calls, and schedule informational and referral interviews. The major difference in this situation is your timing. In addition, you need to give more information to your contacts. In your letter mention that you are planning to move to their community and would appreciate their advice on job opportunities for someone with your qualifications. Mention that you plan to visit the area on such and such a date and would appreciate an opportunity to discuss your job search plan at that time. In this case, enclose your resume with the letter and request a reply to your inquiry. Most people will reply and schedule an interview or refer you to someone else.

You should set aside one or two weeks – preferably longer – to literally blitz the community with informational and referral interviews. This requires doing a considerable amount of advance work. For example, use

people in your present community to practice informational and referral interviewing. Contact those in your area who hold positions similar to the one(s) you are seeking. Many of them may give you referrals to friends and colleagues in your targeted community.

If you have limited contacts when conducting a long-distance job search, you will probably need to use the "cold turkey" approach more frequently. You should make most of your key contacts at least four weeks before you plan to visit your targeted community. Within two weeks of your visit, you should have scheduled most of your interviews.

Try to schedule at least three interviews each day. You will probably do more because each interview will yield one or two referrals to others. Five interviews a day are manageable if you don't need to spend a lot of time traveling from one site to another. Each day, plan to visit sites that are near one another. Within a two-week period, you should be able to conduct 40 to 60 interviews. Use the weekends to research the community further. Contact a realtor who will be happy to show you around the community and inform you of different housing alternatives, neighborhoods, schools, taxes, public services, shopping centers, and a wealth of other community information. You should reserve the last two days for following up on referrals. Scheduling interviews with referrals will have to be made by telephone because of the time factor.

After concluding your one- to two-week visit, follow up your interviews with thank you letters, telephone calls, and letters indicating continuing interest and requesting referrals.

If you receive an invitation to a formal job interview in another city, be sure to clarify who pays for your travel expenses. Normally if the employer has requested the interview, the company pays the expense to and from the out-of-town interview. However, if you have invited yourself to an interview by stating that you will be "in town," expect to pay your own expenses. If you are unclear about who initiated the interview, simply ask the employer, *"How should we handle the travel expenses?"* This question should clarify the matter so there will be no misunderstanding.

Identify Opportunity Structures

Each community has its own set of social, economic, political, and job market structures. Your job is to understand and use the particular job market structure in your targeted community. Therefore, we outline the case of Washington, DC for illustrative purposes. The principles for identifying and using the institutional and personal networks will remain the same for most communities even though the individuals, groups, and institutions differ for different communities.

The degree of structure differs for every community. However, one thing is relatively predictable: most communities lack a coherent structure for processing job information efficiently and effectively. But communities are made up of networks through which individuals can network for job information, advice, and referrals. Each community consists of numerous individuals, groups, organizations, and institutions – many of which constitute mutually dependent networks – that are involved in pursuing their own interests in cooperation and competition with one another.

The Yellow Pages of your telephone book as well as the membership directory of the local Chamber of Commerce outline the major community actors. Banks, mortgage companies, advertising firms, car dealers, schools, churches, industries, hospitals, law firms, governments, small businesses, and civic and voluntary groups do their "own thing" and have their own internal power structure. No one dominates except in small communities that also are company towns – paper mills, mining companies, universities, military bases, or steel mills.

At the same time, the groups overlap with each other because of economic, political, and social needs. The bank, for example, needs to loan money to the businesses and churches. The businesses, in turn, need the educational institutions. And the educational institutions need the businesses to absorb their graduates. Therefore, individuals tend to cooperate in seeing that people playing the other games also succeed. Members of school boards, medical boards, and the boardrooms of banks and corporations will overlap and give the appearance of a "power structure" even though power is structured in the loosest sense of the term. The game players compete and cooperate with each other as well as co-op one another. The structures they create are your **opportunity structures** for penetrating the hidden job market. They are **networks** for locating job opportunities.

Examine the case of Washington, DC. The opportunity structures for your job search networks are relatively well defined in this city. While government is the major institution, other institutions are clearly apparent in relation to the government. Within government, both the political and administrative institutions function as alternative opportunity structures in the Washington networks: congressional staffs, congressional committees, congressional subcommittees, congressional bureaucracy, executive staff, departments, independent executive agencies, and independent regulatory agencies. Outside, but clinging to, government are a variety of other groups and networks: interest groups, lobbyists, the media, professional associations, contractors, consultants, law firms, banks, and universities and colleges. As illustrated on page 440, these groups are linked to one another for survival and advancement. Charles

Peters (*How Washington Really Works*) calls them "survival networks" which function in the "make believe world" of Washington, DC. Ripley and Franklin (*Congress, Bureaucracy, and Public Policy*) identify the key political dynamics as "subgovernments" – the interaction of interest groups, agencies, and congressional committees.

Washington is the ultimate networking community. For many years Washington insiders have used these "survival networks" and "subgovernments" to advance their careers. A frequent career pattern would be to work in an agency for three to four years. During that time, you would make important contacts on Capitol Hill with congressional staffs and committees as well as with private consultants, contractors, and interest groups. Your specialized knowledge on the inner workings of government is marketable to these other people. Therefore, you make a relatively easy job change from a federal agency to a congressional committee or to an association or lobbying group. After a few years here, you move to another group in the network. Perhaps you work on your law degree at the same time so that in another five years you can go into the biggest growth industry in the city – law firms.

The key to making these moves is the **personal contact** – whom you know. Particular attention is given to maintaining a current federal application (OF-612) or resume, just in case an opportunity arises for you. Congressional staff members usually last no more than two years; they set their sights on consulting and contracting firms, agencies, or interest groups for their next job move.

Map Your Community

Whatever community you decide to focus your job search on, you should map it in order to identify its particular mix of opportunity structures and networks. If you are in a booming high-tech community, such as Seattle or Austin, expect to uncover networks consisting of strong linkages among universities, manufacturers, consultants, and a host of small business suppliers, recreational suppliers, and upscale retail operations, from restaurants to department stores. Focus your job search on the key players that define these networks. Do as much research as possible to identify the structure of the networks as well as the key people who can provide access to various elements in the opportunity structures. Washington is not unique in this respect, except for its heavy emphasis on government operations, lawyers, lobbyists, and media; it is just better known, and Washingtonians talk about it more because of their frequent job moves. The mix of players may be different, but the networks and opportunity structures are as ubiquitous as those found in other communities.

Washington Networks

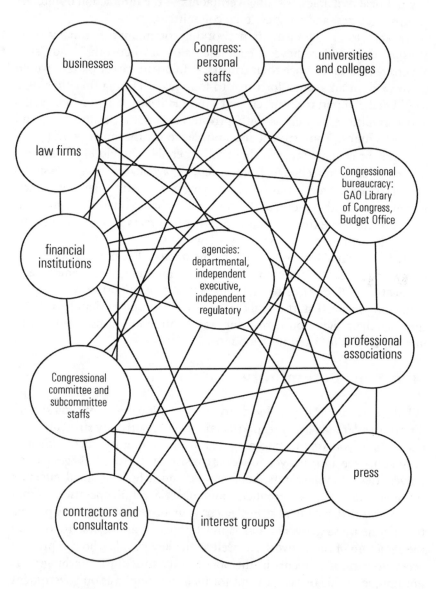

19

Start Your Own Business

Whhile the previous chapters examined strategies for finding employment in other people's organizations, you may also be interested in working for yourself. Indeed, each year nearly seven percent of Americans strike out on their own to start their own business. They do so for a variety of positive and negative reasons. If your self-assessment activities in Chapters 8, 9, and 10 indicate your motivated abilities and skills (MAS) are very entrepreneurial, you may be best suited for self-employment. You, too, may want to become your own boss as you pursue dreams of operating your own business.

The Military Entrepreneur

While many ex-military choose to work for the government, nonprofit organizations, or corporations, some decide to go into business for themselves. Many of the skills and personal qualities they acquired while in the service, such as patience, drive, perseverance, sacrifice, problem solving, and handling adversity, are well suited for becoming successful entrepreneurs.

The fact that you may have little or no business experience should not dissuade you from considering an entrepreneurial option to employment. If you have the right combination of skills, some great ideas, and the necessary drive to be an entrepreneur, you should consider working for yourself. Indeed, approximately 4.5 million veterans currently own their

441

own businesses, which represents nearly 18 percent of all businesses in the United States. Many veterans become very successful entrepreneurs.

There's both good and bad news for anyone considering the entrepreneurial life. The bad news is that the majority of business start-ups fail within the first three years. The good news is that several government and volunteer programs and services – most focusing on training, counseling, and finance – are specifically designed to assist veterans in establishing their own businesses. These programs and services can significantly reduce the failure rate and increase the probability of success among veterans who start their own businesses.

We expect the decade ahead to be another strong period for entrepreneurship in America. Millions of small businesses will develop in response to new opportunities in high-tech and service industries. True to American tradition, self-employment and start-up businesses will remain great frontiers for military-to-civilian transition in the decade ahead.

Consider Your Alternatives

Most job and career opportunities in America are found among small businesses – not large Fortune 500 corporations. In fact, between 1979 and 1993, Fortune 500 companies eliminated 4.8 million jobs; companies employing fewer than 500 people generated more than 15 million new jobs. Between 1993 and 1999, businesses with fewer than 100 employees hired at twice the rate of those with 500 or more employees.

We expect large corporations in the decade ahead to continue downsizing, outsourcing, and offshoring as they emphasize greater productivity by introducing new cost-cutting technologies, management systems, and e-commerce to improve the efficiency, effectiveness, and profitability of the workplace. In other words, they will continue to cut back on the fastest growing corporate expense – personnel. The advancement hierarchies of large companies will shorten and career opportunities narrow as these companies further automate as well as shed unwanted personnel. Many of these displaced workers will become entrepreneurs – often starting businesses in competition with their former employers.

Since nearly 90 percent of all new jobs will be created by small businesses employing fewer than 500 individuals, you may wish to target your job search toward opportunities with such businesses; companies with fewer than 100 employees will offer some of the best opportunities. Finding a job with a small business will require a great deal of research because most of these businesses are not well known among job seekers.

One other alternative is to start your own business. The trend toward entrepreneurship is stronger than ever. In 1999, for example, nearly

900,000 new businesses were started – up from 700,000 in 1991. Nearly one in 14 workers attempts to start a business each year, which represents the highest rate of entrepreneurship in the industrialized world. In the decade ahead, millions of individuals will be "pushed" or "pulled" from what were once seen as promising jobs and careers with established companies to form their own businesses. As work becomes more centralized, advancement opportunities become more limited, and starting a business becomes easier, millions of individuals will strike out on their own.

While nearly 900,000 new businesses are started each year, grim and sobering business statistics also discourage many would-be entrepreneurs: another 700,000 to 800,000 businesses fail each year; 50 percent fail within the first 38 months; and nearly 90 percent fail within 10 years. Unfortunately, starting your own business is risky; the statistical odds are against anyone becoming a successful entrepreneur.

Nonetheless, owning your business is a viable career transition alternative to working for someone else – if you approach it intelligently. Many people fail because they lack the necessary ingredients for success. In this chapter we outline the basics for getting started in owning your business and employing yourself.

Examine Risks and Motivations

You will find few challenges riskier and more time-consuming than starting your own company. It involves lots of hard work, long hours, and betting on your financial future. At the same time, you may experience your greatest professional satisfaction in running your own business, especially if you are pursuing your passions. You also may achieve considerable wealth. Indeed, small business owners disproportionately earn much more than the average employee, with incomes averaging over $100,000 a year.

Starting a business means taking risks. First, while you may have grandiose visions of becoming an overnight success, you will probably go into debt and realize little income during the first two years of building your business. You may be under-capitalized or have overhead costs higher than anticipated. It takes time to develop a regular clientele. What profits you do realize are normally plowed back into the business in order to expand operations and guarantee larger future profits. Second, business is often a trial-and-error process in which it is difficult to predict or ensure outcomes. Due to unforeseen circumstances beyond your control, you may fail even though you work hard and make intelligent decisions. Third, you could go bankrupt and lose more than just your investments

of time and money.

At the same time, however, owning your own business can be tremendously satisfying. It is the ultimate exercise of independence. Being your own boss means **you** are in control, and no one can fire you – only you and your failures. You are rewarded in direct proportion to your productivity. Your salary is not limited by a boss, nor are your accomplishments credited to others. Unless you decide otherwise, you are not wedded to a 9-to-5 work routine or a two-week vacation each year. Depending on how successful your business becomes, you may be able to retire young and pursue other interests. You can turn what you truly enjoy doing, such as a hobby, into a profitable, rewarding, and fun career.

But such self-indulgence and gratification have costs which you may or may not be willing to incur. You will probably need at least $30,000 to $50,000 of start-up capital, or perhaps as much as $350,000, depending on the type of business you start. No one will send you a paycheck every two weeks so you can regularly pay your bills. You may work 12- and 14-hour days, seven days a week, and have no vacation during the first few years. And you may become heavily indebted, experience frequent cash flow problems, and eventually have creditors descend on you. In the end, you could go bankrupt and then have to find a job working for someone else. Such risk-taking can be very stressful for both individuals and families.

> *This is the old-fashioned way of making money – hard work, long hours, and lots of hustling.*

Why, then, start your own business? If you talk to people who have worked for others and then started their own businesses, they will tell you similar stories. They got tired of drawing a salary while making someone else rich. They got bored with their work and hated coming to an office daily to engage in a 9-to-5 work routine. They wanted control over what they did. Some worked for jerks; others were victims of organizational politics; and still others had difficulty working in an environment structured by employers whom they considered less competent than they. Many simply couldn't work for others – they had to be in charge of their work. On a more positive note, many started businesses because they had a great idea or passion they wanted to pursue, or they wanted the challenge of independently accomplishing their own goals.

If you decide to go into business for yourself, be sure you know what you want to do, and be willing to take risks and work hard. Don't expect to get rich overnight or sit back and watch your business grow on its own. Starting a business is usually a very sobering experience that tests your

motivations, abilities, and skills. Success in a corporate or bureaucratic career may not transfer well to starting your own business, which initially requires a great deal of financial risk-taking and entrepreneurism. Be prepared to work long and hard hours, experience disappointments, and challenge yourself to the limits. You will quickly discover this is the old-fashioned way of making money – hard work, long hours, and lots of hustling. But at least you can choose which 18 hours a day you want to work!

There are few things that are more self-actualizing than running your own business. But you must have realistic expectations as well as a motivational pattern that is conducive to taking risks and being an entrepreneur. In Chapters 8, 9, and 10 you identified your motivational patterns and skills. If you like security, predictability, and stability, you probably are a candidate for a position where someone hands you a paycheck each week. If you read and believe in get-rich-quick books, videos, or seminars that downplay your risks and uncertainty, you probably have already been ripped off by another enterprising individual who is getting rich writing books, producing videos and audiotapes, and conducting seminars for naive people who respond well to motivational speakers!

Possess the Right Strengths for Success

How can you become self-employed and successful at the same time? No one has a magical success formula for the budding entrepreneur – only advice based on experience. We do know why many businesses fail, and we can identify some basic characteristics for success. Poor planning, management, and decision-making lie at the heart of business failures. Many people go into business without doing sufficient market research; they under-capitalize; they select a poor location; they incur extremely high and debilitating overhead costs; they lack commitment; they are unwilling to sacrifice; they can't read or count; they lack interpersonal and salesmanship skills; or they have bad luck.

On the positive side, studies continue to identify a trait called **drive** – the need to achieve or the fear of failure – as a key characteristic of successful entrepreneurs. Purpose-driven people, such individuals have a very **high energy level** – restless and hard-working individuals who pursue a passion regardless of the odds against their success. The need to **escape from insecurity** is a key motivation for many of them.

Successful business people combine certain motivations, skills, and circumstances. Contrary to popular myths, you don't need to be rich or have an MBA or business experience to get started. If you are willing to gamble

and are a self-starter, self-confident, an organizer, and you like people, you should consider this entrepreneurial alternative in your career transition plan. These characteristics, along with drive, thinking ability, communication and networking skills, technical knowledge, hard work, persistence, good luck, and a good idea to fill a need are essential ingredients for business success.

If these are among your strengths, as identified in Chapter 10, you may be a good candidate for starting your own business with a high probability of success. If you feel you have recurring weaknesses in certain areas, you may want to consider finding a business partner who has particular complementary strengths for running a business.

Know Yourself

There are many different ways to get started in business. You can buy into a franchise, which can initially cost you $20,000 to $500,000. Advertisements in the *Wall Street Journal* are a good source for hundreds of franchise opportunities from flipping hamburgers to selling animals. Several websites include comprehensive directories to franchise opportunities. One of the best directories is found in the "Franchise Zone" of the Entrepreneur.com website:

http://www.entrepreneur.com/Franchise_Zone/FZ_FrontDoor/0,4670,,00.html

Other useful online directories to franchise opportunities include:

www.franchiseopportunities.com
www.franchise.com
www.franchise.org

You can join someone else's business on a full-time or part-time basis as a partner or employee in order to get some direct business experience. You can try your hand at a direct-sales business such as Amway, Shaklee, or Avon. Hundreds of new direct-sales businesses modeled after Amway's multi-level business methods are now marketing every conceivable product – soap, computers, canoes, motor oil, and milk. You can buy someone else's business or you can start your own business from scratch.

Your decision on how to get started in business should be based upon the data you generated on your skills and goals in Chapters 8, 9, and 10. Do not go into business for negative reasons – were fired, hate your job, can't find work. Unfortunately, many people go into business with totally unrealistic expectations as well as little understanding of their own goals,

skills, and motivations. For example, while it is nice to work among racks of attractive clothes, owning a clothing shop requires handling inventory and personnel as well as paying the rent and doing bookkeeping. Getting all those lovely clothes displayed and advertised is hard work! Many people also don't understand how the business world works. It requires a great deal of interpersonal skill to develop and expand personal networks of creditors, clients, colleagues, and competitors.

Therefore, you should do two things before you decide to go into business. First, thoroughly explore your goals and motivations. The questions are familiar:

- What do you want to do?
- What do you do well?
- What do you enjoy doing?

Second, research different types of businesses in order to better understand advantages, disadvantages, procedures, processes, and possible problems. Talk to business owners about their work. Contact fellow veterans who have started their own businesses, especially those affiliated with The Veterans Corporation (www.veteranscorp.org) or found through the directory of veteran businesses located on VetFriends (www.vetfriends.com). Try to learn as much as possible

Don't be high on motivation but low on knowledge and skills, for "thinking big" is no substitute for doing the work!

about the reality before you invest your time and money. Surprisingly, few people do this. Many people leap into a business that they think will be great and then later learn it was neither right for them nor did they have realistic expectations of what was involved. This is precisely why so many businesses fail each year.

You should approach business opportunities the same way you approach the job market: do research, develop networks, and conduct informational and referral interviews. Most business people, including your competition, will share their experiences with you and assist you with advice and referrals. Such research is absolutely invaluable. If you fail to do it initially, you will pay later on by making the same mistakes that millions of others have made in starting their own businesses in the absence of adequate research. Don't be high on motivation but low on knowledge and skills, for "thinking big" is no substitute for doing the hard work involved in launching and operating the many details involved in running a successful business!

Look for New Opportunities

Most business people will tell you similar stories of the reality of running your own business. Do your market research, work long hours, plan, and be persistent. They also will give you advice on what businesses to avoid and what business routines you should be prepared to handle.

Many service and high-tech businesses will be growing in the decade ahead. Given major issues, such as energy, the environment, health care, fitness, and leisure, and the changing demographic structure – fewer young people, more elderly, the two-career family – numerous opportunities are arising for small personal-service businesses to meet the needs of the elderly and career-oriented families. Businesses relating to restaurants, home maintenance, health care, housing for the elderly, green technologies, energy, the environment, and mortuaries and cemeteries should expand considerably during the next two decades.

Opportunities are also available for inventive business people who can make more productive use of busy people's time – for example, fast food, financial planning, and mail-order Internet and catalog shopping. The information and high-tech revolutions are taking place at the same time two-career families do not have time to waste standing in lines at banks, grocery stores, and department stores. Mail-order or Internet-based home and office-based shopping should increase dramatically during the next decade.

A service business is especially attractive. It's easy to establish; many require a small initial investment; and the accounting is often simple. You may be able to operate from your home and thus keep overhead down.

Knowing these trends and opportunities is important, but they should not be the only determining factors in choosing a business. You should start with yourself by again trying to identify a business that is fit for you rather than one you think you might fit into.

Prepare the Basics

You also need to consider several other factors before starting a business. Since a business requires financing, locating, planning, developing customer relationships, and meeting legal requirements, be prepared to address these questions:

1. **How can I best finance the business?** Bootstrap with my own savings? Take out a personal or business loan with a bank? Go into a partnership in order to share the risks and costs? Get a loan from the Small Business Administration?

2. **How much financing do I need?** Many businesses fail because they are under-capitalized. Others fail because of over-spending on rent, furnishings, inventory, personnel, and advertising.

3. **Where is my market?** Just in this community, region, nation-wide, or international? Mail-order and Internet-based businesses enable you to expand your market nationwide, whereas retail and service businesses tend to be confined to particular communities and neighborhoods.

4. **Who are my suppliers?** How many must I work with? What about credit arrangements and payment terms? Are some suppliers willing to ship directly to my customers?

5. **Where is the best location for the business?** Should I open a store, operate from my home, or conduct a virtual (Internet) business? If I need a store or office, is it conveniently located for my clientele? *"Location is everything"* still best summarizes the success of many businesses, especially McDonald's and Wal-Mart, which are noted for their attention to location.

6. **How should the business be legally structured?** Sole proprietorship, partnership, or corporation? Each has certain advantages and disadvantages. For example, a corporation has several tax advantages.

7. **What licenses and permits do I need?** These consist of local business licenses and permits, federal employee identification numbers, state sales tax number, state occupational licenses, federal licenses and permits, and special state and local regulations which vary from state to state and from community to community. What type of insurance do I need? Fire, theft, liability, workers' compensation, and auto?

8. **How many employees do I need and how do I find them?** Can I do without personnel initially until my business expands? Should I use part-time and temporary help? How should I recruit? Should I use the Internet, classified ads, employment firms, headhunters, or network?

9. **What business name should I use?** If incorporated, is anyone else using the name? If a trade name, is it registered?

10. **What accounting system should I use?** Cash or accrual? Can I handle the books or do I need a part-time or full-time accountant? Who will handle the timely calculation and payment of payroll, sales, and corporate taxes as well as insurance, retirement plans, and workers compensation?

11. **What technology and communications decisions do I need to make?** What type of website should I develop? How much business should I expect to do online? What types of computer and telecommunication equipment should I acquire? Is it best to buy or lease business equipment?

12. **Do I need a lawyer?** What type of lawyer? What legal work can I do myself?

13. **How do I develop a business plan?** A business plan should include a definition of the business, a marketing strategy, operational policies, purchasing plans, financial statements, and capital-raising plans.

14. **Should I put together a board of advisors?** It's always good to include respected individuals who can contribute expertise and perspective to your operation.

Get Useful Advice

If you decide to go into business, make sure you choose the right business for your particular skills, abilities, motivation, and interests. A good starting point is the Small Business Administration's website, especially the useful section on determining whether or not you are best suited for the entrepreneurial life:

www.sba.gov/starting_business/startup/areyouready.html

You also should visit this section of their website, which includes a listing of several free online courses on starting a business:

www.sba.gov/training/courses.html

One of the most popular and useful such courses recommended by the Small Business Administration is entitled "Entrepreneurship: Starting and Managing Your Business" and presented by MyOwnBusiness.org:

www.myownbusiness.org/course_sba.html

Available in 13 sessions, it's offered as both a free or enhanced fee-based ($85.00) course. Whatever you do, make sure you take this course.

You also may want to consult Paul and Sarah Edwards's *Finding Your Perfect Work* (Putnam) and Doug Gray's *Have You Got What It Takes? The Entrepreneur's Complete Self-Assessment Guide* (Self-Counseling Press). These books provide useful exercises for assessing your suitability to becoming an entrepreneur. For a good overview of the many decisions you must make in establishing a small business, see Bernard Kamaroff's *Small-Time Operator* (Bell Springs Publishing). This book provides you with all the basic information you need for starting your own business, including ledger sheets for setting up your books. Several other books provide similar how-to advice for the neophyte entrepreneur. These titles are especially appropriate for military spouses, transitioning service members, and veterans interested in starting a business:

- *The 2-Second Commute: Join the Exploding Ranks of Freelance Virtual Assistants*
- *101 Small Business Ideas for Under $5,000*
- *199 Great Home Businesses You Can Start (and Succeed In) for Under $1,000*
- *Adams Streetwise™ Small Business Start-Up*
- *Business Plans Kit for Dummies (with CD-ROM)*
- *How to Buy, Sell, and Profit On eBay*
- *How to Start, Run, and Stay in Business*
- *Home-Based Business for Dummies*
- *Kick Start Your Dream Business*
- *McGraw-Hill Guide to Starting Your Own Business*
- *Six-Week Start-Up*
- *Small Business Kit for Dummies*
- *Small Business Marketing for Dummies*
- *The Small Business Start-Up Kit*
- *Start Your Own Business*
- *The Successful Business Plan*
- *What Business Should I Start?*
- *What No One Ever Tells You About Starting Your Own Business*

Several websites also can provide assistance in starting a business:

- **Small Business Administration** www.sba.gov/starting_business

- Startup Journal www.startupjournal.com
- BizMove.com http://bizmove.com
- Business Know-How http://businessknowhow.com
- AllBusiness www.allbusiness.com

The federal government will help you with several publications available through the Small Business Administration (SBA). Check out the "Library" section of the SBA website, which includes over 200 free publications, including e-books, as well as numerous resource links related to starting a business:

www.sba.gov/lib/library.html

The Internal Revenue Service (www.irs.gov/businesses/small/article/0,,id=99336,00.html) offers a great deal of tax and accounting information to start-up businesses. The U.S. Chamber of Commerce (www.chamberbiz.com) as well as its local chapters offer useful information. Other good online resources to help you start a business include:

- American Express http://home.americanexpress.com
 open.shtml?referrer=ushome&
 section=globalnav
- Business Owner's Toolkit http://toolkit.cch.com
- CEO Business Express www.ceoexpress.com/default.asp
- Entrepreneur.com www.entrepreneur.com
- Kaufmann eVenturing www.eventuring.org
- eWeb http://eweb.slu.edu
- Home Biz Tools http://homebiztools.com
- Inc.com www.inc.com/guides/start_biz
- Quicken Small Business www.quicken.com/smallbusiness
- SCORE www.score.org
- State Resource Centers www.itssimple.biz/resource_center
- Yahoo Small Business http://smallbusiness.yahoo.com

Acquire Veterans Assistance

Several government agencies and nonprofit organizations offer a wealth of assistance to veterans interested in starting their own business. Most of the assistance involves training, counseling, and financing. Be sure to explore the following websites and programs designed specifically for entrepreneurial veterans:

- The National Association
 of Veteran-Owned
 Businesses, Inc. www.navobi.org
- The Veterans Corporation www.veteranscorp.org
- Office of Veterans Business
 Development (SBA) www.sba.gov/vets
- Center for Veterans
 Enterprise www.vetbiz.gov
- Veterans' Business
 Outreach Center www.vboc.org
- VetFriends www.vetfriends.com
- Veterans Business Network www.veteransbusinessnetwork.com
- HireVetsFirst www.hirevetsfirst.gov/smallbizown.asp

Continue Your Success

The factors for operating a successful business are similar to the 20 principles we outlined on pages 49-52 for conducting a successful job search. Once your initial start-up problems are solved, you must organize, plan, implement, and manage in relation to your goals. Many people lack these abilities. Some people are good at initially starting a business, but they are unable to follow through in managing day-to-day routines once the business is established. And others have the ability to start, manage, and expand businesses successfully.

Be careful about business success. Many business people become obsessed with their work, put in 12- and 14-hour days continuously, and spend seven-day weeks to make the business successful. Unwilling to delegate, they try to do too much and thus become a prisoner to the business. The proverbial "tail wagging the dog" is a common phenomenon in small businesses. For some people, this lifestyle feeds their ego and makes them happy. For others, the 9-to-5 routine of working for someone else on salary may look very attractive only after a few months of self-employment. Therefore, you must be prepared to change your lifestyle when embarking on your own business. Your major limitation will be you, yourself.

So, think it over carefully, do your research, and plan, organize, implement, and manage for success. Even though running your own business is risky and involves hard work, the thrill of independence and success is hard to beat!

Index

Career Transition
Resources

IN ADDITION TO THIS BOOK, the following resources are
designed to assist service members, veterans, and their families with
career and related transition issues. Most of these books can be
found in libraries, bookstores, or through the publisher's online
bookstore: www.impactpublications.com.

Military Transition

Alternative Careers in Secret Operations, Mark I. Merritt (Impact
Publications, 1999)

Expert Resumes for Military-to-Civilian Career Transitions, Wendy
S. Enelow and Louise M. Kursmark (JIST Publishing, 2006)

Job Search: Marketing Your Military Experience, David G. Henderson
(Stackpole Books, 2004)

Jump Start Your Career: Finding the Right Job After Military Service, Jerry Crews (Thomson Custom Publishing, 2004)

Military Resumes and Cover Letters, Carl S. Savino and Ronald L.
Krannich (Impact Publications, 2004)

Military-to-Civilian Transition Guide, Janet I. Farley (JIST Publishing,
2005)

Military to Federal Career Guide, Kathryn Kraemer Troutman (The
Resume Place/JIST Publishing, 2005)

Resumes and Cover Letters That Have Worked for Military Professionals, Anne McKinney (Prep Publishing, 1997)

Resumes for Former Military Personnel (McGraw-Hill, 2006)

Military Families and Spouses

Chicken Soup for the Military Wife's Soul, Jack Canfield, Mark Victor Hansen, Charles Preston, and Cindy Pedersen (Health Communications, Inc., 2005)

Chicken Soup for the Veteran's Soul, Jack Canfield, Mark Victor Hansen, and Sidney Slagter (Health Communications, Inc., 2001)

Going Overboard: The Misadventures of a Military Wife, Sarah Smiley (NAL, 2005)

Help! I'm a Military Spouse – I Want a Life Too!, Kathie Hightower and Holly Scherer (BookSurge Publishing, 2005)

Heroes At Home: Help and Hope for Military Families, Ellie Kay (Bethany House Publishers, 2002)

Home Fires Burning: Married to the Military – for Better or Worse, Karen Houppert (Ballantine Books, 2005)

Homefront Club: The Hardheaded Woman's Guide to Raising a Military Family, Jacey Eckhart (Naval Institute Press, 2005)

In Harm's Way: Help for the Wives of Miliary Men, Police, EMTS, and Firefighters, Aphrodite Matsakis (New Harbinger Publications, 2005)

Jobs and the Military Spouse: Married, Mobile, and Motivated for Work, Janet I. Farley (Impact Publications, 2004)

Married to the Military: A Survival Guide for Military Wives, Girlfriends, and Women in Uniform, Meredith Leyva (Fireside, 2003)

Medals Above My Heart: The Rewards of Being a Military Wife, Brenda Pace and Carol Mcglothlin (Broadman & Holman Publishers, 2004)

Navy Spouse's Guide, Laura Hall Stavridis (Naval Institute Press, 2002)

New Relocating Spouse's Guide to Employment: Options and Strategies in the U.S. and Abroad, Francis Bastress (Impact Publications, 1993)

Surviving Deployment: A Guide for Military Families, Karen M. Pavlicin (Elva Resa Pub, 2003)

Today's Military Wife: Meeting the Challenges of Service Life, Lydia Sloan Cline (Stackpole Books, 2003)

Military and Veterans Benefits

The Military Advantage: A Comprehensive Guide to Your Military and Veterans Benefits, V. "Sonny Montgomery and Christopher P. Michael (Simon & Schuster, 2005)

Personal Finances

9 Steps to Financial Freedom, Suze Orman (Three Rivers Press, 2000)

Armed Forces Guide to Personal Financial Planning, David C. Trybula, et. al (Stackpole Books, 2002)

The Money Book for Young, Fabulous, and Broke, Suze Orman (Riverhead, 2005)

Smart and Simple Financial Strategies for Busy People, Jane Bryant Quinn (Simon & Schuster, 2006)

Starting a Business

The 2-Second Commute: Join the Exploding Ranks of Freelance Virtual Assistants, Christine Durst and Michael Haaren (Career Press, 2005)

101 Small Business Ideas for Under $5,000, Corey Sandler and Janice Keefe (John Wiley & Sons, 2005)

Virtual Assistant, Diana Ennen and Kelly Poelker (Another 8 Hours Publishing, 2004)

What Business Should I Start?, Rhonda Abrams (Planning Shop, 2004)

National Association of Veteran-Owned Businesses

THIS BOOK IS BROUGHT to you by members of the newly formed National Association of Veteran-Owned Businesses (NAVOBI). This organization supports the career and lifestyle goals of transitioning service members, veterans, and their families. It assists them in becoming successful entrepreneurs and strengthening their employability skills. NAVOBI's mission is to:

- Improve access to technical assistance that promotes entrepreneurship.

- Mobilize public and private resources for starting and expanding veteran-owned businesses.

- Provide employment skills training and certification.

NAVOBI will accomplish its mission by offering entrepreneurial services to veteran-owned small businesses, establishing alliances, and promoting networking opportunities among its members. It also will provide entrepreneurial education and training services through classroom instruction, seminars, and online educational programs, as well as provide professional certification of veterans in several skill and occupational areas. NAVOBI's unique Veterans' Marketplace will facilitate the marketing of veteran-owned business goods and services to government, nonprofit, and commercial sectors. NAVOBI will offer

special benefit programs such as reduced credit card and insurance rates for veterans. Its network of information and assistance centers will help veterans with the daily operation of their businesses.

Responding to the employment needs of disabled veterans and their families, NAVOBI will provide distance learning programs related to entrepreneurial and employment training.

NAVOBI also will assist veterans in finding jobs with military-friendly employers. It will sponsor the following job search and employability services:

- Employer database
- Resume database
- Online job postings
- Job fairs
- Distance learning courses
- Licensing and certification

As a new and evolving organization, NAVOBI will be undergoing numerous changes in the months and years ahead. For more information on how you can participate in the National Association of Veteran-Owned Businesses, please visit our website: www.navobi.org.